D0207064

The
AMERICAN
NORTHWEST

The
AMERICAN
NORTHWEST
A History of Oregon and Washington

Gordon B. Dodds
Portland State University

The Forum Press, Inc.
Arlington Heights, Illinois 60004

Library of Congress Cataloging-in-Publication Data

Dodds, Gordon B. (Gordon Barlow), 1932–
    The American Northwest.

    Bibliography: p.
    Includes index.
    1. Oregon—History. 2. Washington (State)—History.
3. Northwest, Pacific—History. I. Title.
F876.D57   1986   979.5   85-20727
ISBN 0-88273-238-2
ISBN 0-88273-239-0 (pbk.)

Cover illustration: Columbia River gorge. Photography by Washington State
Tourism Division.

Manufactured in the United States of America
92 91 90 89 88 MG 2 3 4 5 6 7

TO THE MEMORY OF FREDERICK MERK,
Brilliant Scholar and Inspiring Teacher,
who first interested me in the history of
the Pacific Northwest.

Contents

Preface

This short history is meant to introduce the history of Oregon and Washington to adult readers. It is the first book to do so in almost twenty years. No attempt is made to be comprehensive, but the author has tried to treat the major developments in economic, social, political, and cultural life. Although based in places on source materials, much of the content derives from secondary accounts. More would be, but the history of the region–especially for the twentieth century—is mainly unwritten. There are whole areas of life for which not one single scholarly account appears. Yet perhaps what the book lacks in depth will be compensated for by the opportunities it unveils for future study and research.

In studying and teaching the history of the Pacific Northwest for thirty years, the author has learned much from many. Men and women whose knowledge contributed with particular force and vigor to this book through their critical reading of all or part of it are: Donald G. Balmer, Herbert Beals, Edwin R. Bingham, Hugh S. Bone, Robert E. Burke, Vernon R. Carstensen, Yvonne T. Hajda, Floyd McKay, Earl Pomeroy, Kent D. Richards, Wallace Spencer, and Wayne Suttles. Assistance in other indispensable ways was given by Jennifer L. Dodds, John A. Dodds, Linda S. Dodds, Paul G. Dodds, and Ruth B. Dodds; David A. Johnson; Craig E. Wollner; and Richard P. Zenn. The staffs of the following libraries were especially helpful: Eastern Washington Historical Society, Oregon Historical Society, Portland State University, University of Oregon, University of Washington, Washington State Historical Society, and the Washington State Library. A grant from the College of Liberal Arts and Sciences of Portland State University aided in the final stages. Early versions of the manuscript were typed by Joni Marie U. Johnson and Athena Pogue. The final draft was prepared by Judy Ouchi. My comrades at Portland State, Bernard V. Burke, Philip E. Harder, Frederick M. Nunn, and John P. Rosenberg, provided intellectual stimulation beyond price and beyond belief.

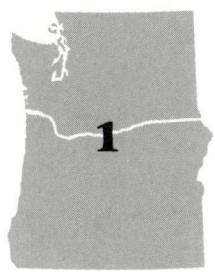

1

The First Northwesterners, c. 15,000 B.C.–1542 A.D.

The first inhabitants of the Pacific Northwest were descendants of the men and women who had crossed the land bridge from eastern Asia to North America some 12,000 to 15,000 years ago. These adventuresome, if anonymous, explorers filtered down from Alaska and western Canada to the area of Oregon and Washington both east and west of the Cascade Mountains. Their earliest site in the Northwest, 12,000 years old, is at Sequim in western Washington; the oldest sites in eastern Washington, both 9,000 to 10,000 years old, are Lind Coulee (near Warden) and Marmes Rockshelter (near Palouse Falls). In time—over many centuries—they occupied much of the lavish and diversified environment of the Pacific Northwest. For them, all of nature was of value.

The Gifts of Nature

The waters of the region gave the Indians many blessings. For the coastal groups, the Pacific Ocean, especially its bays and estuaries, furnished a rich variety of fish, shellfish, and mammals. Most important, from spring through fall, the five species of salmon returned from their ocean feeding waters to the spawning areas of the interior rivers. The ocean gave clams, mussels, seals, and whales. It was a theater for indirect trade as far north as Alaska, and for warfare as well. It was the base of the mythology of the people, their cosmology and religion.

From Puget Sound to the California line many rivers joined the ocean; their gifts were fisheries, commerce, and communication. Greatest of these was the Columbia, its enormous watershed extending 1,214 miles

Physiographic Map of the Pacific Northwest

from source to mouth. Other lesser streams from the rushing waters of Washington to the rugged Rogue were also significant. Bays and estuaries provided harbors and also the habitat of a myriad of wild fowl that the Indians took for food, clothing, and decorative and religious art.

The soils of the Pacific Northwest were fertile in several regions. In the west, the best areas for wild plants were the Willamette, Rogue, and Cowlitz valleys and the level lands of Puget Sound. Here there were prairies with adjacent forests dotted among them, becoming more frequent and dense as the flat country changed to foothills and mountains. East of the Cascade Mountains some of the volcanic soils of the Columbia Plateau were magnificent, but the semi-arid climate denied them their full potential. The Indians found in time, however, that the natural grasses of the plateau were a paradise for horses. Southeast and south of the plateau the land shaded off to desert country and to the marshlands of Malheur, Harney, and Klamath lakes.

The mountains of the region are large and rugged. The Coast Range extends fifty to one hundred miles from north to south along the shores of the Pacific. Then across the valleys to the east lies the Cascade Range and finally the Rockies. In the northwest are the Olympics, in the northeast are the Blues and the Wallowas, and to the south, separating Oregon from California, lie the Siskiyous. The mountain chains sheltered game and nurtured timber: cedar and spruce on the coast, Douglas fir on the western slopes of the Cascades, and ponderosa pine along their eastern sides. These dense forests gave wood for fires, planks for houses, bark for clothing, logs for canoes, and food for mystery and mythology.

The Way of the Indians

Although differing in several respects, the major groups of Northwest Indians, who were the first pioneers, shared some common experiences and values. Paramount was the evident and widespread influence of nature. The natural environment gave food, clothing, shelter, implements, and weapons. The Indians created what they needed and shaped the face of the land to their goals. In the Willamette Valley, for example, the newcomers confronted a forested plain which they burned to drive the game and to clear spaces for their villages and routes of transportation. Over time the first inhabitants worked out a system of land management that enabled them both to use and to conserve natural resources.

Nature permeated the religious and philosophical beliefs of the Indians. They did not take their world for granted but sought explanations for its creation and order. Their myths and legends included a system of religious forces that affected the lives of men and women directly and indirectly. The great religious figure was the changer deity who formed the world from preexisting materials. This changer, Coyote, as he was usually depicted, transformed the world out of chaos into animals, people, and landforms. Everything in the world continued thereafter to possess its own living characteristics, its spirit or soul or personality. Indian groups believed that everything had an objective or purpose in life. Salmon, for example, made religious migrations from the sea to provide food for the Indians.

These natural beings, however, dare not be taken for granted. For, as they had their own personalities, they could take offense at mistreatment or neglect and retaliate by failing to give their customary gifts. Every Indian group made certain, then, to conduct proper ceremonies that would insure the continuation of the bounties of nature. The Klamath honored and expressed gratitude to the sucker by catching and cooking the first fish of the migrating season in a formal ritual. The Chinook and other coastal peoples did the same with the first salmon of the year. One was caught, split down the back, and cooked with ceremonial precautions—always before sunset and with care never to be thrown into the water or to the dogs. The first fish represented the entire species and ensured that it would reproduce to maintain the cycle in the years ahead. Other special ceremonies were held when the first roots were dug or the first nuts or berries gathered. If the ceremony were neglected, or carelessly or disrespectfully executed, the sucker or salmon would not return, the bushes and trees would not bear, and the Indian would starve.

Religious life for the Indians was far more than group ceremonials. Every young man, and woman too in some groups, participated at the age of puberty in the spirit quest that was the most intense religious and psychological experience of their life. After careful instruction by an older person, the boy or girl was sent into the wilderness in quest of his or her destiny. Fasting, searching, alone, the youth prayed and thought and hoped until in a dream, hallucination, or vision appeared some dramatic evidence of future vocation and personality. Usually Bluejay or Fox or some other representative of an entire bird or animal species revealed itself to become the lifetime guardian and protector of the youth. If treated with proper respect and ceremony, Bear or Fox or Coyote, whoever had appeared, would thereafter intervene at strategic times to ensure the success of a hunt or military action or marital search. Furthermore the young person chose a vocation based upon the vision. A grizzly guaranteed the strength and might of a hunter; a fox, the sagacity of a chief; a coyote, the cunning of a shaman. But a misinterpretation of the vision, or neglect of the guardian spirit, could result in physical illness, an unsuccessful career, even death.

Indeed care and caution were watchwords for the Indians in other respects as well. It was necessary to be wary when one ventured forth from home, for beyond the village border lay numerous potential perils: wild animals, of course, and also unfriendly spirits and hostile neighbors. There was no such thing as chance in the Indian world. If a man were struck down by lightning or a woman died in childbirth, these misfortunes were not accident but the result of malevolence on the part of the spirit world, the result of neglecting a proper ceremony, or the fatal result of an enemy's magic. So it behooved the young boys or girls to listen attentively when their elders spoke of the virtue of caution and alertness. Even within the bounds of village and family, prudence need apply. Villages were not always happy little communities; there were tensions of rank, personality, and character present even there. This local insecurity arose not so much from physical danger, but from gossip, backbiting, and feelings of guilt.

Security came, first of all, from a consciousness of the superiority of one's own group to that of all other Indians. This "patriotism" undergirded all activities as one took pride in the accomplishments of hunting, war, and domesticity, fully aware that nowhere else were there as able persons as those in the familiar circles. Although in experience this group consciousness was not always justified, it remained as an enduring ideal throughout one's lifetime.

Security also came in the orderliness and predictability of family relationships. First of all, youth learned that longevity equalled virtue. Children respected parents not only because they had given life, but because they had lived long. Children, young adults, and those of the middle years venerated the elderly. Respect for age was no fetish, however; it was based on the very nature of the Indian culture. In the Indian world a person became proficient in the activities of life, from war to canoe making, by long practice. Repetition of tasks ensured proficiency; innovation was discouraged. Thus experience justified, indeed required, respect.

Parents taught children to be self-effacing and to blend their lives with those of their group. Individualism was not always a desirable trait, although there was a good deal of individual freedom in certain aspects of life, as we shall see. In the main, however, nature, religion, and potential enemies dictated a wise conformity, for a culture based upon group activities could not spare time or place for the eccentric, unless the eccentric became a shaman.

The Indians believed that nature and their social organization had made possible a life wherein the desire for material abundance could be gratified. Elders encouraged children to work hard and to acquire as many material possessions as possible. The number of dentalia shells (sea shells from Vancouver Island), implements, bear claws, blankets, or slaves determined not only an Indian's economic status, but also marked him as a being morally superior to his less affluent friends and neighbors. Possessions throughout the Indian country were the hallmark of goodness. But the good person also was generous with his material goods. Hospitality, for example, was a great virtue—no one should be turned away. The miser was as contemptible as the slothful or incompetent.

Indian boys and girls learned the values of their people in diverse ways. Their parents or other relatives were their first instructors, but there were many specialists who taught them proper behavior through example. The shaman, or religious practitioner, conducted group ceremonials wherein the people were reminded of the modes to control nature. Experts led hunting and gathering parties and provided military leadership. Others were respected weavers, canoe builders, and implement makers. In the winter evenings, the storytellers acted out vivid accounts of the exploits of Coyote and other mythical animals, spirits whose adventures and misadventures pointed the way of virtue to the Indians.

Those who failed to absorb the principles of the people were disciplined by the group. The Indians placed little faith in the individual's conscience. Far more effective in keeping people in line, they believed, was group pressure. Adults, parents, and other respected elders, shamed as well as encouraged children to behave. The myths provided everybody, old and young, with horrible examples of what happened to the culture's heroes who strayed from the path of virtue.

Regional Differences

The Indians of the Pacific Northwest were not all alike although they did share broad cultural similarities. Their environment and their history distinguished them in several respects. In the southernmost part of the region, in what is now south central Oregon, resided the Klamath-Modoc Indians, a people adjusted to the high plateau country around Klamath Lake. In this varied environment the Indians moved with the changing seasons in pursuit of food. During the sedentary time of winter they left their boats on Klamath Lake and moved into their semisubterranean earth lodges built within a circular pit one to four feet in depth. When the waters thawed with the coming of spring the lodges were torn down and the people moved into new dwellings without the earth covering and sometimes without the circular pit. Politically the Klamath organized themselves by village groups led by shamans and other influential men. They met in council from time to time to suggest policies that they hoped their people would execute. A similar lack of power marked warfare, for the war leader could only command volunteers, any of whom could depart a campaign at any time.

Klamath society was structured. The basis of the hierarchy was wealth. Leading men had many possessions, several wives, and the right to special ceremonies such as elaborate puberty dances for their children and a funeral cremation wherein the body was decked with many valuables. Those less wealthy had less respect and the poorest were regarded as slaves, derided not only for their poverty but for their poor manners and lack of breeding. There was a sexual division of labor with women taking care of the children, making baskets and mats, and preparing food. Men hunted, fished, and waged war.

Life for the Klamath-Modoc depended upon a variety of natural foods that became available throughout the year. The people collected the eggs of swans and other waterfowl on Klamath Lake. When the suckers and salmon surged up the Sprague and Williamson rivers, the Indians netted, speared, harpooned, and dipped the swarming fish, sometimes fishing with torchlights throughout the night. Their most important single food was seeds, especially those of the pond lily, but they also ate other vegetation: roots of camas, tule, and cattail, as well as berries. In the fall the men cooperated in organizing drives for antelope, sheep, and mule deer.

The only specialist among the Klamath-Modoc was not in economics, but the shaman, who performed the midwinter ceremonies. At these great occasions shamans danced, sang, and demonstrated their "magic tricks." They cured the sick and summoned the spirits of the dead. The ceremonies also reinforced the elders' inculcation of moral virtues: hard work, subordination to group wisdom, consideration of the less fortunate, and, above all, family loyalty.

Living eastward of the Klamath-Modoc were one of the poorest peoples of all of North America. Here in the semiarid, flat, and treeless country of the Great Basin, including parts of eastern Oregon, moved the harassed members of the northern Paiute bands. These men and women sheltered themselves against their harsh environment in caves, rock shelters, or domed wickiups made from poles over which were stretched tule or grass mats. The basic political and social unit of the Paiutes was the nuclear family, which wandered independently under the harsh sunlight of summer in search of insects, roots, and sagebrush. In winter the wanderers gathered together into small villages that averaged less than fifty persons, ranging from two to ten families. Leadership in the larger villages was furnished by a headman whose powers were advisory. Indeed the only organized activity conducted on a level larger than that of the village was the cyclical rabbit or antelope drive

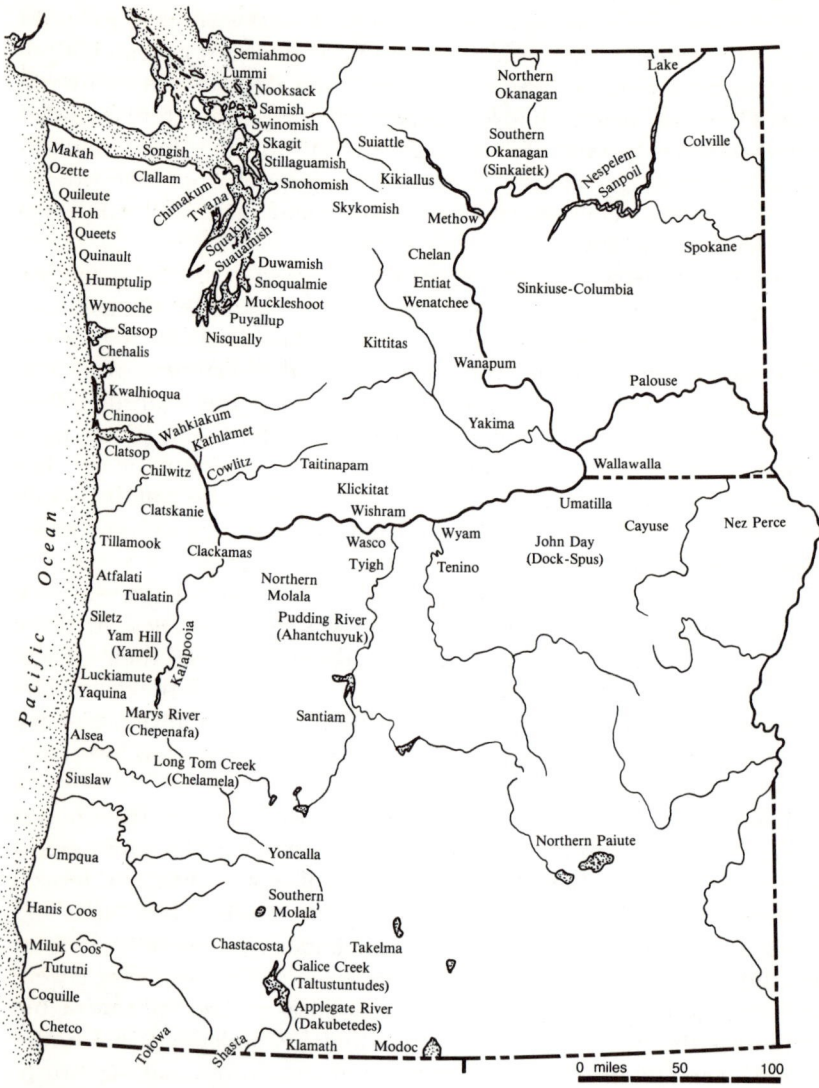

Indian Groups of the Pacific Northwest

held for a two- or three-week period. When meat faltered as a source of food, Paiutes resorted to lower life forms that kept them above the level of starvation. Religious activities included the spirit quest, burial ceremonies, and the use of myths.

North of the Paiutes, living in northeastern Oregon, Idaho, and eastern Washington were the Nez Percé. They were the largest among the many groups of the Columbia Plateau. The Nez Percé range extended over hundreds of square miles, although their wintering base and fishing grounds were the communities along the Salmon, Clearwater, and Snake rivers. In winter, they lived in long houses banked with dirt and in summer they lived in tents. The village and the family were the basic political and social organizations. The village leader was a headman who could counsel but not compel his people in their actions; he ruled by sagacity and respect. So too did the special leaders for war and hunting.

What distinguished the Nez Percé from the other tribes of the Pacific Northwest was their early acquisition of the horse. Beginning sometime in the three decades after 1700 the Nez Percé first obtained horses from their neighbors of the eastern Great Basin. Nez Percé horsemen often organized military campaigns against the western Shoshones, northern Paiutes, and Bannocks, and mounted occasional forays against the Coeur d'Alenes and Spokanes. Sometimes they even crossed the Rockies to attack the Indians of the Great Plains. The introduction of the horse, indeed, made possible acquisition of many facets of the culture of the plains. But warfare could also be more destructive, especially after the middle of the eighteenth century, when the Blackfoot Indians east of the Rockies received guns from British and French fur traders. They pushed westward and for a time wreaked havoc upon the Nez Percé when they were hunting buffalo east of the Bitterroot Mountains.

A major endeavor of Nez Percé males was warfare, the capture of slaves and goods in raids against their foes. Men speared, netted, and trapped salmon along the Clearwater, Snake, and Salmon rivers. Men's hardest work was hunting game by beating through woods or draws, setting snares and deadfalls, and shooting the bison of the plains. Women did the domestic work, sometimes as members of polygamous households that were maintained by men of wealth to enhance their social status. The women also gathered nuts and berries, harvested the wild lily called camas, and dug and cooked the roots of the kouse plant. Women split and dried fish for winter food and for trade.

After its introduction the horse became vital to the economic system. The Nez Percé were among the few Indians of North America to practice selective breeding of animals, a practice that provided them not only the means of war and hunting and an additional source of food, but also a valuable article of commerce.

Trade, indeed, was indispensable to the economic health of the Nez Percé as it was to almost all Indian peoples. At the confluence of the Columbia and Snake rivers, in the Yakima valley, and especially at the great mart of The Dalles, came the Nez Percé to exchange slaves, dried meat, furs, hides, elk teeth, camas, and bear claws for shells, clams, fish oil, wooden implements, and wappato roots of the people of the lower Columbia. They traded eastward across the mountains with the Plains tribes for buffalo robes, skins, beads, feathered bonnets, and stone pipes. One of the great articles of commerce of the Nez Percé was their famous composite bow made from a section of the curled horn of mountain sheep backed by deer sinew. Trade and the horse made the Nez Percé more cosmopolitan. Their culture partook of the plains, mountains, plateau, and lower Columbia. In turn their horse culture had a wide influence among neighboring tribes.

Nez Percé and other interior peoples had many contacts with the Indians of the lower Columbia from The Dalles to the ocean and those living north and south of the mouth of the great river and from the mouth to the falls of the Willamette River. These peoples were the Chinookans. They included the Chinooks proper, the Clatsops, the Wahkiakums, the Kathlamets, and other peoples who died out in the epidemics of the 1830s or merged with other groups. Their culture was similar to both that of the river and ocean Indians (whose region extended from Alaska to the central Oregon Coast) and the Indians of the Columbia Plateau.

They lived in gabled longhouses over deep pits with walls of vertical planks. Houses sometimes extended up to 100 feet in length. The political organization of the Chinooks was based upon the autonomous village. Leadership was in the hands of wealthy people who were selected by all the free males according to a combination of lineage and ability. Chiefs had special economic perquisites and earned them by settling disputes, organizing military affairs, and supervising hunts. Unlike the specialists of the Nez Percé, there were no war or hunting leaders. Physical conflicts were of two kinds, slave raids against outsiders and regulated conflicts among related peoples.

The social structure of the Chinooks was stratified according to classes. Social mobility was possible and men and women were extremely rank conscious. At the bottom of the social structure were the slaves. Chinook slavery was more numerous and more significant than for the surrounding peoples. Slaves were a source of labor, a medium of exchange, and even an instrument of murder. The more numerous free people were divided according to wealth, with power and status flowing to the most affluent. A people as concerned with social distinctions as were the Chinooks naturally had several ways of demonstrating these gradations. The most important was the potlatch, their variation of the ancient ceremony that was practiced throughout the coastal cultures. These were feasts put on by men of wealth at which time gifts were given to the guests as a mark of respect for them. The purpose of the Chinook potlatch was to give formal notice to the world of the class, honor, and distinction of the host and his family. Families also displayed their social credentials by painting distinctive designs on their houses and other property. Although slave women were abased in Chinook society, rich and noble women had a good deal of influence in the society. When a man and woman married, their families exchanged property almost equal in value.

The Chinooks, like the Indians all along the Pacific Ocean, were well-off economically. Their livelihood was based on fishing, hunting, gathering, and trade. The Chinook fishery was a marvel of courage and ingenuity especially for the residents near the mouth of the Columbia. The terrible bar of this river with its tides and currents was the most treacherous on the Pacific Coast. The Chinooks, with their cedar canoes, navigated it in almost all weather to fish for salmon and sturgeon. Chinook peoples also took smelt and clams and oysters. Stranded sea lions and whales were rare but welcome gifts of nature. Skillful hunters took ducks, geese, gulls, pelicans, and snipes by net and bow and arrow. Women gathered cranberries, salmonberries, and other fruits; dug roots, such as ferns; and harvested bulbs, especially the wappato.

But it was trade that especially distinguished the Chinook bands. Their trading canoes carried goods along the coast and all along the Columbia to the great commercial center at The Dalles. For exchange the Chinooks' most valuable commodity was human slaves. These unfortunate women and children—for men were more difficult to capture and keep—had been obtained in slave raids or by purchase from other Indian peoples. The Chinooks also used dentalia as a medium of exchange.

In many ways similar to the Chinookans were the Makah Indians of what today is the state of Washington. They lived in a territory stretching from fifteen miles south of Cape Flattery and Hoko River to about fifteen miles east from Cape Flattery on the Strait of Juan de Fuca. They also occupied Tatoosh Island. They depended on the sea for their food for the most part, but, unlike most fish-eating Northwest Indians, they relied upon the halibut, not the salmon, as their principal source of food. The Makahs were very important trading middlemen. Using their canoes made on Vancouver Island, they were commercial links for Indians from as far south as the Columbia River to those as far north as Nootka Sound on Vancouver Island. Their architecture, religion, government, and social structure resembled that of the Chinooks. The other Indian groups

of the Olympic Peninsula and Puget Sound were also similar in general
to the Makah people.

Continuity and Change

The world of the Indians took shape over millenia. It was shattered in
a few decades, for some Indians in a shorter time. The white persons
who came to the Indian country differed in many ways from the first
inhabitants, but resembled them in some respects as well. The differences
were immediately evident; the similarities appeared only through hind-
sight.

The important differences between the native Americans and the
Europeans were technological, economic, political, and religious. The
whites arrived equipped with steel tools and with firearms as well as with
other products of the Industrial Revolution. The Indians had for centuries relied upon stone, wood, and bone. The European political system
was well organized into the national states that had arisen during the
Renaissance. The Indians had no effective tribal network, although the
whites intentionally or unwittingly forced them—for the whites' purposes—into the tribal mode, which relied upon coercion. Voluntarism
and cooperation had been the bases of Indian political action. The numbers of Europeans were vast compared to the mere thousands of Indians
in the Pacific Northwest. The Christian newcomers recognized an om-
nipotent, omniscient Supreme Being, while the Indians worshipped the
changer and the spirits of nature.

In spite of these distinctions, the two groups were not entirely different in their cultural patterns. The principal resemblance between
them was that whites and Indians shared a dependence upon nature and
a curiosity about it. Both peoples prized nature's riches, both feared its
vagaries. The tragedy of early Northwestern history is that both sides
were unwilling or unable to see their mutual dependence upon nature
as a basis for common understanding in other dimensions of life.

SUGGESTIONS FOR READING

Jarold Ramsay's *Coyote Was Going There: Indian Literature of the Oregon Country*
(1977) reprints some of the myths and discusses Indian values. Samuel N. and
Emily F. Dicken deal with the Indians and the environment in *Two Centuries of
Oregon Geography* (1979–1982) as does D. W. Meinig in *The Great Columbia Plain:
A Historical Geography, 1805–1910* (1968). Indian shelter is discussed in Thomas
Vaughan and Virginia G. Ferriday, *Space, Style and Structure: Building in Northwest
America* (1974). On individual tribes, see Theodore Stern, *The Klamath Tribe: A*

People and Their Reservation (1965); Alvin M. Josephy, *The Nez Percé Indians and the Opening of the Northwest* (1965); Ronald L. Olson, *The Quinault Indians* (1936); Marian W. Smith, *The Puyallup-Nisquall* (1940); and James G. Swan, *The Indians of Cape Flattery; At the Entrance to the Strait of Fuca* (1870). The earliest Indian cultures are described in Ruth Kirk and Richard D. Daugherty, *Exploring Washington Archaeology* (1978). On social and cultural aspects, see William W. Elmendorf, *The Structure of Twana Culture: A Study of Religious Change among the Skagit Indians of Washington* (1974); Wayne Suttles, "The Persistence of Intervillage Ties among the Coast Salish," in Deward E. Walker, comp., *The Emergent Native Americans: A Reader in Cultural Contact* (1971); Angelo Anastasio, *The Southern Plateau: An Ecological Analysis of Intergroup Relations* (1975); and Julian H. Steward, *Theory of Culture Change: The Methodology of Multilinear Evolution* (1955). A valuable handbook is Harold E. Driver, *Indians of North America*, 2d. ed. rev. (1969). Richard White, *Land Use, Environment, and Social Change: The Shaping of Island County, Washington* (1980), is imaginative. An overview for a part of the Pacific Northwest is Jeff Zucker, Kay Hummel, and Bob Høgfoss, *Oregon Indians: Culture, History, and Current Affairs* (1983).

2

Europe Discovers the Pacific Northwest, 1542–1795

The Pacific Northwest is the child of revolution. This revolution developed over many centuries and includes what is known in European history as the Renaissance, the Reformation, the Commercial Revolution, the rise of Absolutism, and the Scientific Revolution, all of which culminated in the seventeenth and eighteenth centuries, the era called by historians the Age of Enlightenment. The "enlightened" Europeans were the heirs of men and women who had been reshaping the face of the earth and recasting the country of the human mind since the Middle Ages.

From the Renaissance men and women had drawn a faith in the boundless capacities of human beings. They exalted their rational capabilities. They believed they could ascend new spiritual heights. They felt they were justified in seeking sensual pleasures. They concluded, all in all, that God had given individuals the opportunity to develop their own abilities to their fullest capacities.

Individualism also underscored the Reformation. This great religious movement, engendered in the religious, economic, and political turmoil of the later Middle Ages, produced a new faith, Protestantism, which emphasized the ability of every person to interpret the Bible and to worship God as he or she pleased. Like the Renaissance scholars, the Reformers based their belief upon the worth and dignity of the individual.

The Commercial Revolution represented the economic side of the European upheavals. As men gained confidence in their powers, and as they escaped from bondage to ancient institutions and customs, they literally sought new worlds to conquer. New economic institutions arose from their medieval roots. Traders developed new transportation routes within and beyond Europe. Financiers created banks. Businessmen began joint stock companies. Inventors contrived new instruments for mariners. Industrialists founded new manufactories. Enterprising individuals undertook the consolidation of agricultural units and forced many peasants off their lands to wander rootless across the face of Europe.

In the swirling upheavals of mind and money, of spirit and senses, politicians, too, reforged the institutions and theories of government. This era was the first great age of European nationalism. Kings and queens extended their authority over larger territories as they crushed the feudal lords. The monarchs—Bourbons in France, Hapsburgs in Spain, Tudors in England—acquired armies, equipped with the latest in arms and armaments, faithful to them rather than to lord or bishop. The monarchs used their new military powers to confiscate the property of their secular and clerical enemies and to redistribute it to new men loyal to them alone. They and their intellectual allies worked out a new political theory, Absolutism, that declared the monarch to be divinely appointed, responsible only to God, and justified in requiring total obedience from his subjects. Gradually these ideas settled into men's consciousness, and what had once been forced now was freely given. People identified their individual welfare with the power and greatness of their king and country.

The dynamic ferment of the European revolutionaries did not confine itself to the Old World. Men with small ships and large visions began to push their way toward the unknown. Prince Henry the Navigator sponsored Portuguese expeditions down the western shore of Africa and around the Cape of Good Hope toward India. Vasco da Gama reached this fabled land in 1498 in the wake of his heroic predecessors. Columbus, meanwhile, sailing westward for India, reached the New World—somewhat to his disappointment. Soon other Spanish mariners followed up his exploits in the Caribbean with explorations, discoveries, and conquests in Florida, Mexico, and South America. British and French seamen were off the coast of Canada and the east coast of the modern United States by the close of the sixteenth century.

The momentous results of the opening of the New World included disappointment and success. The Indians furnished both. They had no gold or silver or precious stones north of Mexico although the treasures of the Aztecs and the Incas were beyond imagination. The Indians welcomed neither European civilization nor Christianity, but they were sources of wonder and amazement to their conquerors in many ways. Their strange customs filled the minds even when their material resources failed to fill the purses of the Europeans.

By the year 1600 Europeans were poised to enter new regions of North America. This effort would be on both sides of the new continent and would involve four powers: England, France, Spain, and Russia. The English, after the failure of Walter Raleigh's two expeditions to Roanoke Island in the 1580s, made the first permanent settlement at Jamestown in 1607. The Pilgrim Colony at Plymouth followed in thirteen years. Samuel de Champlain, the great French colonizer, planted his nation's first permanent North American imperial outpost at Quebec in 1608.

Spain in the Pacific Northwest

A continent away the Spanish were making their tentative approaches to the area that would be called the Oregon Country, and later named the Pacific Northwest. What sent the Spanish northward from western Mexico were two illusions. The first was precious metals, the second, the Northwest Passage. By the 1540s the Spanish were spending profligately the last of their spoils from the Aztecs and the Incas. It seemed reasonable to hope that somewhere else in the Western Hemisphere lay other treasure troves to finance the warfare, arts, literature, and scholarship of the great age of imperial Spain. After 1536 the Spanish came to believe in the golden cities (later called the Seven Cities of Cibola) that supposedly

Nootka Sound habitations. From a drawing by John Webber for Cook's Voyages, Oregon Historical Society

lay in the interior of the continent north of Mexico. Indeed, why should not the Indians of the Pacific Northwest also have gold and silver and precious jewels?

And why should not the northwest be the western outlet of the waterway through North America that everyone was looking for? For it was an article of faith for European scholars, statesmen, businessmen, and mariners that there existed a waterway passage through the continent. This expectation included the subordinate delusion that there was an undiscovered (but fabulously rich) continent lying somewhere between the tips of Africa and South America and the Antarctic. They called this mythic land Terra Australis.

Spain began to act upon these assumptions in 1541. In that year the great viceroy of Mexico, Antonio de Mendoza, dispatched an expedition, commanded by Hernando de Alarcón, up the western coast of Mexico from Acapulco to search for a water route to the Seven Cities of Cibola. Alarcón reached the mouth of the Colorado River and sailed some distance up the river. He found no golden cities. The next year Mendoza sent out another expedition, composed of two vessels, under the command of Juan Cabrillo and Bartolomé Ferrelo. The crews of these fragile ships were the first white men to glimpse the coast of the Pacific Northwest (somewhere about the forty-second parallel), although they did not land. What their impression of the new country was no one knows, for Spain kept the records of its voyages a secret lest they fall into the hands of enemies.

England and the Northwest Passage

The most dangerous of these foes was England. England threatened the treasure ships (called the Manila galleons) bearing Asian goods from the Philippines to Mexico where they were exchanged for silver. Francis Drake was taking Spanish galleons in the Pacific in the 1570s and, while coasting northern California in 1579, may (the records are unclear) have reached the latitude of 43° 21' off the modern city of Coos Bay, Oregon. Other English privateers followed Drake into the Pacific in search of the galleons of gold. The Spanish feared that one of these, Thomas Cavendish, in his course of destruction and devastation up the western slope of the Pacific, may actually have discovered the Northwest Passage in 1587. Although hopeful that the story was untrue, the Spanish crown still faced a dilemma. Should they try to discover the strait, in the hope of preempting the claims of other countries to it? Or should they abandon the search for fear that, once found, their enemies would use it for trade between the oceans or to sail into the central part of North America to disembark a military party which would then march overland to pillage the silver mines of northern Mexico, the most valuable of all Spain's American provinces? Sometimes the Spanish resolved the Northwest Passage dilemma one way, sometimes another.

In any case, more prosaically, it seemed desirable to locate harbors to shelter Manila galleons in distress. In 1602 the Spanish sent Sebastián Vizcaíno and Martín de Aguilar to search for harbors of refuge. This expedition, unlike the earlier ones, was financed by the government, not by private business. Vizcaíno reached 42° or 43° but, discouraged by the winds, the rapid coastal current, and the raw and rainy weather, he turned back without landing on the Northwest Coast.

While these voyages, with their uncertain or disappointing results, were being made, the search for a Northwest Passage continued from the Atlantic side by English mariners inspired by dreams and fantasies. In 1576 Martin Frobisher made a voyage to Canada in search of the passage. He brought back no news of a passage but rather a piece of rock said to contain gold. This ore inspired a businessman, Martin Lok, to organize the Company of Cathay to exploit Frobisher's discoveries. Little happened until 1596 when Lok had a chance encounter in Venice with a Greek mariner, Apostolos Valarianos (whom the Spanish called Juan de Fuca), who had been in the employ of Spain. Four years earlier, he told the credulous Lok, he had sailed a Spanish vessel through a passageway from Pacific to Atlantic for twenty days, passing through a land "rich of gold, silver, pearle, and other things."

Then in 1708 Englishmen read a sensational new book recounting the much earlier voyage of a Spanish admiral through the Northwest Passage. In 1640, the story ran, Bartholomae de Fonte found the western entrance and, more dramatically, met a Boston trading vessel heading west. Fonte continued eastward to the Atlantic and, figuratively, into the mind of a zealous British colonialist, Arthur Dobbs.

Dobbs was a businessman with political connections. He also accepted the stories of Fuca and Fonte uncritically. In 1741 he persuaded the navy to send an expedition to Hudson Bay to search for the passage. The navy found no passage, but Dobbs, a landowner, merchant, and governor of the colony of North Carolina, remained optimistic and persistent. He lobbied through Parliament a reward of £20,000 for discovery of the passage. No one, of course, collected.

In the 1760s the scene shifted to America. A British major, Richard Rogers, stationed at Mackinac Island, picked up a variant on the idea of the Northwest Passage. This was the theory of a River of the West flowing from the Great Lakes area to the Pacific. Rogers sent Jonathan Carver to search for this river in the years 1766–1767. Carver returned without news of the river except for the name the Indians gave it, *Ouragon,* the first entry of this word into the English language, although no one knows the meaning of the word. All of these English ventures had been designed to foster trade and commerce with Asia, but by the late eighteenth century a new dimension was added to the quest.

Enlightenment Science

This goal was derived from the Enlightenment's thirst for scientific knowledge. The great discoveries of Kepler, Galileo, and Newton about the world of nature were popularized widely among literate people across the breadth of Europe. Men and women, as a result of scientific achievements, were confident that they could unravel the fabric of the universe and find the remaining truths about nature and human nature.

Their desire to do so was in part a divine mission. Scientists, scholars, and informed citizens in general believed in the theory of the great chain of being. This theory saw the universe and all the animate and inanimate objects within it as leading downward from the Creator, in an unbroken series of links, to the humblest beings in the universe. The chain of being idea was a call to action as well as a description of the cosmos. One way to understand God was to examine nature, as much of it as possible, from Europe to the most distant, undiscovered portions of the globe. For the nature of nature was the nature of God.

Exploration of the unknown world was also indispensable in fully understanding human nature. Europeans were proud of their accomplishments from art to science. But beneath their smugness lay the shadows of uncertainty. Had not they become too civilized? Had they not gotten too far away from God's handiwork of nature? Might not there be lessons for them elsewhere?

Answers to these haunting questions were available. The age did believe that God had created all mankind, regardless of race or culture, as rational beings and hence, at least in theory, as equal to one another. Perhaps, then, Europeans could learn something from other races, even those they initially considered backward. Perhaps, it was just possible, that the backward races, living close to nature, could teach naturalness, simplicity, indeed divinity to the overrefined, overcivilized Europeans.

These suggestions spawned the ideal of the noble savage. The European came to believe that the primitive African, American, Asian, or South Sea Islander had created a government, economy, and social system that was just and simple, wholesome and happy. To seek out such people was in the self-interest of the civilized, for the primitive could restore them by example to individual and social health.

The best illustration of an institution that reflected the scientific beliefs and hopes of the age of Enlightenment was the Royal Society of Britain. Chartered in 1662, the Society was in the forefront of scientific advances, including voyages to all quarters of the globe. In 1774 the Royal Society revived the plan of seeking a Northwest Passage from the Pacific side. It thus joined to the old commercial objective a scientific purpose in exploring the Pacific Northwest. As a result of the Society's pressure, Parliament in 1775 passed a bill authorizing a naval expedition to the Northwest for both commercial and scientific purposes. On July 6 of the next year the Lords of the Admiralty signed the instructions for Captain James Cook who was to command the expedition.

Spain Tries Again

Before turning to Cook's great venture we must review the hopes and fears of the Spanish in the Pacific Northwest. Spain resumed its voyages to the North Pacific in the late eighteenth century. The reason for this renewed interest was fear of Russian ambitions on the Pacific Coast.

The spirit of the Enlightenment had touched the Russians, backward, suspicious, patriotic as they were. Their great monarch, Peter the Great, knew of the opportunities of the North Pacific, for his people had been probing eastward across his vast land for generations. The traders had crossed the Russian heartland and traversed Siberia in search of fur-bearing animals. Peter wished to know what lay beyond. In 1728 he sent Vitus Bering to explore eastward from Kamchatka. A second expedition led jointly by Bering and Aleksei Chirikov did touch Alaska in 1741. Russian fur traders subsequently began operating in the Aleutian chain in 1743. After that date the Russians sold the sea otter pelts, obtained in trade with the Alaska Aleut, Indian, and Inuit peoples, to the markets of China.

The Spanish feared that the Russians would move down the West Coast of North America, establishing trading posts, military bases, and even colonies. To head off this challenge the Spanish decided to resume their northern voyages in order to spy on the Russian activities.

Viceroy Antonio María de Bucareli commissioned Juan Pérez to carry out this mission in 1774. Pérez got as far north (about 54° 20') as the boundary between modern Alaska and Canada, encountered the Haida Indians in the Queen Charlotte Islands, and discovered the fine harbor at Nootka Sound on the western side of Vancouver island, but he did not land anywhere to claim possession of the region for his country. The next year the disappointed but persistent viceroy sent out Bruno de Hezeta, equipped with three ships and new instructions, to reach 65° north latitude. This voyage was both more successful and more tragic.

Hezeta's men reached as far north as 58°. They landed at four different places to proclaim Spanish sovereignty. Their landfall at Grenville Bay on the Washington coast (July 14) was the first by Europeans in the Pacific Northwest. Hezeta and some twenty officers and men went ashore briefly to take possession of the land in the name of Carlos III. And on August 17, 1775, Hezeta discovered the mouth of a mighty river which he thought might be the strait supposedly found by Fuca in 1592. But he did not enter what was later called the Columbia River. For the Spanish, feelings of satisfaction in their discoveries were not long lasting, however, for in July of 1776 the expedition of Captain Cook was underway.

Captain Cook

James Cook (1728–1779) was born to poverty in northern England. At the age of twenty-two he went to sea as an apprentice in the coal trade of the North Sea, but gave up the merchant marine in 1755 to join the royal navy as an able seaman. He rose through the ranks, serving against the French, but his great fame was as a man of peace, not as a warrior.

In 1768 the navy sent Cook on the first of his scientific voyages. His orders were to observe the transit of the planet Venus across the face of the sun and to explore the South Pacific. Cook fulfilled his instructions, his most notable achievements being the charting of the two main islands of New Zealand, and the discovery of the eastern seaboard of Australia. In the years 1772–1775 Cook made his second Pacific voyage. His charge this time was to conduct a thorough search for the Unknown Continent to frustrate the French who also had this objective. After spending three years circumnavigating the globe as close to the polar cap as possible, Cook proved that the Unknown Continent was a myth.

When Cook's third voyage set sail for North America in 1776, its commander was internationally respected and admired as one of the world's foremost seamen. His mission this time was to prove or disprove the existence of the Northwest Passage. His two vessels, *Resolution* and *Discovery*, passed the Cape of Good Hope and on March 7, 1778, Cook first saw the Oregon Coast at Cape Foulweather. The ships proceeded north—missing both the Columbia River and the Strait of Juan de Fuca, however—and entered Nootka Sound on March 29. They remained at this harbor only until April 26, but the brief visit had momentous consequences.

First of all Cook's men became intrigued with the Indians as human beings and as businessmen. They found the native Americans both attractive and repulsive. The Indians were colorful dancers and singers, good hosts, friendly and brave, in the main. They traded with the whites and respected their goods while inspecting them, although they stole unprotected equipment, including Cook's gold watch. All in all, Cook's people found the Indians, if not noble savages, very worthy men and women.

Captain James Cook. From National Maritime Museum, Oregon Historical Society.

The natural environment was also fascinating. The scenery, especially the snow-crowned mountains and the towering forests, fitted their romantic preconceptions of the beautiful, picturesque, and sublime. The climate was temperate, and game and fish abundant (as were mosquitoes). The soil and rainfall suggested agricultural possibilities.

The greatest benefit of the Pacific Northwest became apparent somewhat later. After leaving Nootka, Cook sailed along the Alaska coast, tried to push through the ice into the Arctic Sea to find the passage there, then retired to Hawaii. In the islands a dispute broke out between some islanders and a party of Englishmen, a scuffle occurred, and Cook was killed in the ensuing brawl. The expedition continued, however, and eventually reached China. Here the sailors learned that the otter pelts, traded with the Indians of Nootka, would bring a rich return. Although the Russians had known for decades of the fur markets of the wealthy Mandarins, their extent and profitability was news for the English. When the reports of Cook's expedition were published in Britain in 1784, businessmen and politicians determined to exploit the fur trade of the Northwest and to assert British sovereignty over the area to do so.

The news of Cook's journeys also produced action and reaction in Spain. The Spanish feared British territorial encroachment in the North Pacific and a contraband trade with Spanish subjects all along the western coast of North America. The first Spanish response to these potential threats was a voyage north commanded by Ignacio de Arteaga who reached Port Etches Bay (60° 19') in 1779.

The French also responded to the publication of Captain Cook's reports. Louis XVI, who became king of France in 1774, admired Cook's scientific achievements and vowed to match them. The person France chose to match Captain Cook was Jean François Galaup, who was born in 1751 into a middle-class family of some wealth. As a boy of fifteen, he entered the navy and served with distinction in the Seven Years' War and in the American Revolution as an ally of the rebellious Thirteen Colonies. Along the way his family had brought him an estate and a title of nobility, Comte de la Pérouse. On July 2, 1785, his two ships, *Boussole* and *Astrolabe*, left their home port for the Pacific.

La Pérouse's instructions were to conduct the broadest and fullest exploration of the Pacific ever made. After making broad sweeps through the Pacific, La Pérouse sighted the Pacific Northwest coast on June 23, 1786, near Mount St. Elias. A few days later he entered Lituya Bay and set up an observatory. He remained there for nearly a month. Realizing that a thorough exploration of the Pacific Northwest would take far longer than he had anticipated, La Pérouse weighed anchor and sailed for California where he reached Monterey on September 14.

La Pérouse's impressions of the Pacific Northwest, gathered on so brief a visit, were mixed. He inventoried the flora and fauna. He saw the agricultural and fishing possibilities and also was probably the first to anticipate the later tourist trade, for he compared the scenery favorably to the Alps and Pyrenees. Yet he implied that any economic future would be distant, and he proclaimed the Indians unpromising—although he welcomed a brisk trade in otter skins—very far from the anticipated noble savages.

In the thrust and counterthrust of European rivalry in the Pacific Northwest, the Russians and Spanish sounded the alarm about La Pérouse's expedition even while it was in the stages of planning and preparation. The Russians employed in 1785 a British mariner with experience on the Northwest coast, Joseph Billings, to chart the territories within the Russian economic sphere. The Spanish responded in a much more elaborate fashion.

In the summer of 1788, two Spanish vessels worked their way north from San Blas. Their commander was Estéban José Martínez; their purpose was to see what La Pérouse had done and to see what the Russians had done about what La Pérouse had done. On this journey Martínez reached Prince William Sound in Alaska and claimed Unalaska for Spain. In the next year, he was northward bound again, this time to strengthen Spain's claims to sovereignty in the Northwest. The viceroy commanded him to plant a pretended colony at Nootka Sound and to examine all the coastline from Nootka to San Francisco Bay.

The year 1789 also saw the launching of the Spanish equivalent to La Pérouse and Cook. After a broad sweep through the Pacific, Alejandro Malaspina came to the Northwest coast on June 27, 1791, at Yakutat Bay. Like La Pérouse, he stayed about one month in the region, but he accomplished far more. He did a good deal of scientific work, including debunking the idea of a Northwest Passage.

While the Martínez and Malaspina voyages were being planned and undertaken, English traders were following up the reports of Cook's men about the fur trade. Cook's reports appeared in 1784; the next year the first English trader, James Hanna, was in the Pacific Northwest. The moving force in the development of the British trade was a London businessman, Richard Cadman Etches. For Etches and his rivals, the fur trade was lucrative but also frustrating. For British traders had to obtain permission from monopolistic corporations to trade. The South Sea Company had the exclusive trading rights in the Northwest; the East India Company had the same rights in China. But in spite of these barriers the exchange of British manufactured goods for the Indians' fur continued at an increasing rate after the middle of the 1780s.

Robert Gray's ship, Columbia, *on the Columbia River, May 1792.* From a painting by Frederick S. Cozzens. Oregon Historical Society

The Nootka Sound Affair

Late in the decade, the rival claims of Britain and Spain to the fur trade and for political sovereignty came to a head. John Meares, a British trader, arrived in Nootka Sound in May 1788, planning to found a fur trading colony. He claimed that the local Indian chief, Maguilla, granted him land and recognized him as "sovereign" of the region. In any case, Meares built a house and a small ship. Later in that year Meares merged his operations with the Etches firm.

In 1789 the new company, called the Associated Merchants, sent James Colnett in command of two ships to Nootka. Then two other Meares vessels appeared. Governor Martínez, the Spanish commander, arrived in early May. Martínez began to build a fort, while worrying about the British trading ships that he regarded as interlopers in Spanish territory. The governor seized, for various periods of time, three of the British ships, one of which he sent to Mexico. Ironically, in the light of the international crisis that followed these confiscations, the viceroy had ordered Martínez (while he was en route to Nootka) to abandon the garrison there. Martínez asked that the order be reversed, meanwhile seizing an American trading vessel, *Fair American.*

When the news of Martínez's actions against the British traders reached world capitols, the nations came to the brink of war. Britain, under the leadership of William Pitt, the prime minister, decided to capitalize on the Nootka seizures. Pitt wanted the Spanish to admit that the British had the right to settle and trade at any area within Spain's territorial claims that the Spanish had never colonized. This claim, if granted, would open up much of Spanish America to British businessmen.

Pitt's timing was strategic. Spain was no match for England. When given an ultimatum by England, King Carlos backed down and accepted a treaty in 1790 that opened to commerce all parts of the Pacific Northwest coast not settled by Spain before April 1789. After this forced concession, the Spanish continued to explore the Pacific Northwest and plan fortifications, trading posts, and colonies. Some of those plans were accomplished, but Spain's interests turned elsewhere and the last Spaniard left the region in 1795. The Spanish legacy was in the filling in of many blank spaces on the map, deeds of courage, the first missionary and farming activity, numerous place names, and, indirectly, the voyages of George Vancouver.

Vancouver's Voyages

William Pitt sent Vancouver to the Northwest in 1791 for three purposes: to take possession of the land returned to British subjects (Meares' fort); to investigate every European settlement in the Pacific Northwest to see if it were founded before or after April 1789; and to search for the Northwest Passage. Vancouver was an apt choice for his complex mission. George Vancouver was born in Norfolk, England in 1757. He began his naval service at the age of fourteen, serving as a midshipman on Cook's second voyage. From 1781 to 1789 he was stationed in the Caribbean before being given the assignment to Nootka.

Vancouver's expedition sighted the shoreline of the Pacific Northwest on April 24, 1792. He voyaged along the coast northward, missing the mouth of the Columbia River before reaching Nootka Sound. Nootka was to be the base of Vancouver's operations for the next three years. During his years in the northwest, Vancouver was sustained by the friendship and hospitality of the Spanish governor, Juan Francisco de la Bodega y Quadra. But in spite of their friendship, Vancouver and Bodega were not able to resolve amicably the diplomatic task of restoring the English property occupied in April 1789. After lengthy negotiations, the two men referred their dispute to their home governments. Ultimately, in another treaty signed in 1793, the Spanish agreed to pay for Meares' property.

Vancouver's great achievement was his search for the Northwest

Captain Robert Gray. Oregon Historical Society

Passage. Of course he did not find it, but the accomplishment of laying the ghost to rest was substantial. His other activities were important, too. Although Vancouver did not rediscover Hezeta's river when he first passed it, he did send a subordinate, William Broughton, many miles along its length after the American trader, Robert Gray, told him of the river. Broughton's voyage did help establish an English claim to what Gray had called the Columbia River. Vancouver's careful explorations, his maps, and his charts were reliable and served mariners well for many decades. Because of his lengthy stay, because of his reputation, and because of the grace of his prose, Vancouver's journals formed an impression of the Northwest for the English that was very influential.

Vancouver characterized the Indians, on the whole, as a worthy people. He found them of real interest simply as human beings. Some of their customs, especially the preparation of food, were repulsive to him, but their music, their seamanship, their carvings, and their canoe-building abilities were among several admirable qualities. Vancouver also found the natural environment of the Pacific Northwest pleasing. As had Cook and La Pérouse, he brought European aesthetic perceptions with him. He found part of the region to be like an English landscape, rounded and on a human scale; some areas resembled cultivated land, like the gardens of his native country. Others were of economic potential, for several times Vancouver noted that the land could easily be converted to farms and villages. He needed to say little of the fur trade for it was already flourishing, and not simply in British hands.

The Coming of the Yankees

Yankee traders sailing from Northeastern ports challenged the British almost as soon as Cook's reports were published. Indeed one colorful American had sailed with Cook on his third voyage, the indefatigable John Ledyard. In 1783, the very year Britain assented to American independence, Ledyard published a report of his journey with Cook. He urged the potential of the fur trade of the Northwest for Chinese markets. Ledyard's dream of a Chinese trade soon found acceptance because of national economic conditions. There were problems as well as pleasures for the Americans who had just won their independence. No longer did they possess the old protected colonial privileges in the markets of the British Empire. There was a postwar depression as men adjusted from war to peace and from colony to independence. In this crisis the Pacific Northwest pointed a way out.

One of the men Ledyard had tried to interest in the Pacific Northwest and China was a Boston merchant named Joseph Barrell. In 1787 Barrell organized a syndicate that dispatched John Kendrick and Robert Gray for China in two vessels, *Lady Washington* and *Columbia*. Three years later, Gray returned to Boston on *Columbia*, the first American ship to sail around the world. Although the voyage was a loss in terms of profit, for the return cargo of tea was spoiled through water damage, the syndicate tried again.

Only a few months after his return to Boston, Gray and *Columbia* sailed for China again. This second voyage (1790–1793) was enormously successful. It made profits for its sponsors. It showed that Americans could organize a trade that stretched from the Atlantic coast to the Pacific Northwest to China and to Europe. It stimulated a stampede of American vessels to the Northwest. And it had political implications. For on May 11, 1792, Gray's ship became the first vessel to cross the bar of the Columbia River. Although he did not take formal possession of the country—he was a businessman, not a government explorer—Gray's action was used later to establish an American claim to the Oregon Country.

SUGGESTIONS FOR READING

Much of the story of the rival powers in the Pacific Northwest, including the development of the Northwest passage idea, is told in Warren L. Cook, *Flood Tide of Empire: Spain and the Pacific Northwest, 1543–1819* (1973). The European visions of America are digested in Howard Mumford Jones, *O Strange New World; American Culture: The Formative Years* (1964). Enlightenment thought patterns as related to exploration are described in J. C. Beaglehole, *The Life of Captain James Cook* (1974). Beaglehole has also written *The Exploration of the Pacific* (1966) and has edited *The Journals of Captain James Cook on His Voyages of Discovery*, 4 vols. (1955–1967). On Vancouver, see Bern Anderson, *Surveyor of the Sea: The Life and Voyages of Captain George Vancouver* (1960). For the Americans, see Frederic W. Howay, ed., *Voyages of the "Columbia" to the Northwest Coast, 1787–1790 and 1790–1793* (1941). A valuable account of a Spanish voyage is Herbert Beals, ed., *For Honor and Country: The Diary of Bruno D. Heceta* (1985).

The Fur Trade, 1793–1846

The American and British maritime fur traders depended on the Indians who caught the aquatic fur seals and sea otters. The native Americans traded pelts of these animals all along the Northwest coast from Alaska to Oregon. Trade was brisk in the last two decades of the 1780s and ultimately so successful that it became ruinous. For neither Caucasian nor Indian took a long view of the business. They hunted the seal and the otter to the verge of extermination, and by the early years of the nineteenth century the maritime trade was largely over. But in spite of their rapacity, the fur trade did not die—it changed its form.

The Beaver Traders

The first men to reshape the fur trade in the Pacific Northwest were Scotsmen and Canadians a continent away from the region. These Montreal merchants organized a company in the 1780s called the North West Company (NWC). Its purpose originally was to compete with the great British monopoly, the Hudson's Bay Company (HBC), organized in 1670 with the exclusive ownership (according to British law) of the eastern third of modern Canada. The new firm invaded the domain of the HBC with trade goods, guerrilla warfare, and Indian allies. The battle was bloody, wasteful of money and furs, and corruptive of the native Americans.

But the NWC also attempted to profit by more peaceful means. It tried to open up unknown country beyond the domain of its older rival. The first of the NWC's imperial explorers was Alexander Mackenzie.

This intrepid Scotsman made a journey to the Arctic Ocean in 1789 in a vain search for furs. In 1793 he tried again, crossing the Canadian plains, over the Rockies, and then down the Bella Coola River to the Pacific in modern British Columbia. Although the journey was difficult, Mackenzie saw it as a first step toward a glorious future.

Mackenzie wanted the North West Company to be the single firm that would control the entire fur trade of North America. The company would receive annual trade goods from England for the Indians at Hudson Bay. It would send other goods by the best overland and waterway route to the Pacific where posts would be built at the mouth of the Columbia River and at other strategic places. Arrangements would be made to open the China market. Mackenzie interested some politicians and businessmen in his plan, but he was never able to persuade his associates in the NWC that a merger with the HBC would be profitable for them. Finally, in frustration, Mackenzie left the NWC in 1800.

This was the year that Spain ceded the huge Louisiana Territory to France. Its acquisition raised up a powerful rival on the western flank of the United States. France now held the mouth of the Mississippi River and could shut off the export lifeline of the American farmers of the trans-Appalachian West. When news of the sale of Louisiana was received in the United States, Thomas Jefferson was president. Jefferson in 1803 was able to remove this western rival in a single stroke with the famous Louisiana Purchase.

Lewis and Clark

The great purchase also involved the Pacific Northwest, although it was not included within the boundaries of Louisiana. The acquisition of Louisiana furnished Jefferson with the opportunity to fulfill an old ambition. Even before he had become interested in politics, Jefferson was intrigued with the idea of exploring the trans-Mississippi West. One expedition he had actually instigated as president of the American Philosophical Society. In 1793 André Michaux had conducted a party down the Ohio River toward the West, but he had been ingloriously recalled when it was discovered that he was a French spy.

Even before the purchase, Jefferson tried again when he asked Congress to appropriate $2,500 to mount an expedition to explore the West. He wanted the expedition to ascend the Missouri River from St. Louis to find the best route over the Rockies to the Columbia River and down it to the Pacific. There were many advantages to the United States, Jefferson indicated in his message to Congress, from such an expedition.

The planned exploring party should take careful note of the flora

William Clark. Oregon Historical Society

and fauna of the region, both for economic and scientific purposes. Jefferson was interested in the farming and fur-trading possibilities of the West, but also cared for scientific knowledge for its own sake. The president also wished to discover all that could be learned about the Indians. Jefferson wanted his explorers to make commercial treaties with the Indians so that they would trade their furs with American citizens rather than British subjects. He also wanted them to discover the best route that fur traders could take in exporting their pelts from the northern Great Plains and the Rocky Mountains. Jefferson had another reason for the expedition, one that did not appear in the message to Congress. The explorers, by crossing the continent to the mouth of the Columbia, would give the United States a claim to the whole watershed of that river by right of discovery. A United States citizen had first crossed the bar at the mouth of the river; now an American would be first to explore the interior of the watershed.

Three months after Jefferson's message, France sold Louisiana to

Meriwether Lewis. Oregon Historical Society

the United States. The expedition went forward as it was not difficult to convince Congress of the validity of western exploration. It appropriated the money, and Jefferson began to organize a military party to head westward. He chose Meriwether Lewis and William Clark to lead it. Lewis took some scientific and medical training in Philadelphia, then went with Clark and others to Wood River, Illinois, at the mouth of the Missouri River across from St. Louis. Here five months were spent in preparing what was called, officially, the Corps of Discovery. It set out up the Missouri River on May 14, 1804, and wintered over the first year at Fort Mandan in what is now North Dakota.

After the winter at Fort Mandan, the Corps of Discovery started again on April 7, 1805. The people who made the immortal trek were a mixed group. Almost all of the thirty-three members were in military service, and military discipline was one reason for the success of the expedition. The civilian members were York, Clark's black slave; Toussaint Charbonneau, a hunter acquired at Fort Mandan; Charbonneau's

Indian woman, Sacajawea; and their baby, Baptiste. York impressed the Indians with his color, and Sacajawea served as a symbol of the peaceful nature of the expedition as the Indians never permitted women and children to accompany a war party.

The route of the expedition was up the Missouri to the second fork of the Jefferson and over the Continental Divide in the Rockies at Lemhi Pass. It then continued along the Lemhi, Salmon, and Bitterroot rivers and over Lolo Pass through the Bitterroot mountain range. On October 16, 1805, the explorers came to the junction of the Snake and Columbia rivers where they entered the Oregon Country for the first time. Lewis and Clark proceeded down the Columbia to its mouth. After camping a few days on the north bank of the river, they set up a wintering post on the south side. They built Fort Clatsop on what is now Lewis and Clark River where the party remained until March 23, 1806.

Lewis and Clark made one of the most successful expeditions in history. With the loss of but a single life (Sergeant Charles Floyd, who probably died of appendicitis), they accomplished most of their objectives. Their scientific and anthropological reports were impressive. Their dealings with the Indians were on the whole successful. Their winter residence at Fort Clatsop strengthened the American claim to Oregon. So far as the Oregon Country was concerned, Lewis and Clark made it clear that there were places where agriculture could flourish and that the Columbia-Snake river watershed was a potential artery to drain the fur trade of the interior to the Pacific Coast.

Lewis and Clark also contributed some facts that were less palatable. Much of the eastern and central portions of the Oregon Country were dry and useless for farming. Their route to Oregon was very difficult in places, requiring crossing of several ranges of mountains, and indeed was not the one that later was used by the fur traders, missionaries, and pioneers. It was obvious, too, that it was Lewis's and (especially) Clark's skill as diplomats, rather than the Indians' natural friendliness, that avoided serious trouble with the aborigines. And the everlasting rainfall of the coast was depressing. But when all was balanced, Lewis and Clark's reports about the Oregon Country had a magnetic effect that was to grow mightily in the American consciousness in the years ahead.

The North West Company

The news of the Corps of Discovery also made an impression in British fur trading circles. It was the final incentive to the North West Company to plant a permanent trading post in the Pacific Northwest. In 1805 the company's great explorer, Simon Fraser, established Fort McLeod at the base of the Rocky Mountains in what is now British Columbia. Fraser continued to found posts in British Columbia and to search for the upper reaches of the Columbia River. In 1808 he mistook the Fraser River for the Columbia and became the first to descend it to its mouth. While Fraser was active, an even greater explorer and cartographer, David Thompson, was founding posts in lower British Columbia, in northern Idaho, and in western Montana. At the trading posts established by the NWC, the manufactured goods of England were exchanged for the beaver skins collected by the Indians. The trader's lot was lonely and potentially dangerous. Without civilized society, surrounded by Indians who seemed too often capricious or lazy, the trader had to have great inner resources to maintain his precarious existence.

John Jacob Astor

Lewis and Clark also had an influence upon American fur traders. The first of these to establish a post for the beaver trade was John Jacob Astor, one of America's greatest entrepreneurs. Astor was born in Waldorf, Germany, in 1763. He took up his father's trade of butchering at age fourteen, but became dissatisfied and decided to follow the example of two of his brothers who had already migrated abroad, George to London and John Henry to New York City. John Jacob Astor worked for his brother George from 1779 to 1783; then he came to the United States in the first year of American independence.

In the next few years, Astor cast his lot with the United States and with the fur trade. His material success was phenomenal. His field of operation expanded from its base in New York City to include much of the Great Lakes fur trade. He formed connections with the fur traders of Canada, including men who were interested in the North West Company. The culmination of Astor's career in the East was his founding of the American Fur Company in 1808.

Two years later Astor was seeking new territory on the Pacific slope. Encouraged by the reports of Lewis and Clark and of the North West Company explorers, he founded the Pacific Fur Company. This firm was to found a worldwide commerce. Astor believed that his two companies could control the fur trade of much of North America, including that of the Pacific Northwest. He intended to collect the furs of the Oregon Country, pay for them with his own trade goods, and market them in China with his own vessels. The base of his operations would be a trading post at the mouth of the Columbia.

To found his imperial venture, Astor projected both a maritime and land expedition to the great river of the West. The ship got off first.

Commanded by a naval officer on leave, Jonathan Thorn, *Tonquin* left New York City on September 8, 1810. It carried a supply of trade goods and some of the personnel to staff the fort. The voyage was anything but a happy occasion, for Thorn was autocratic to the hilt, and it ended in tragedy. The bar of the Columbia was always a terrifying barrier. In attempting to sound out a possible channel, Thorn lost seven men in two days' time, but finally he was successful in crossing.

On the south bank of the river, Astoria arose. While it was being constructed, Thorn took *Tonquin* north to begin the Indian trade on the western side of Vancouver Island. Here he became embroiled in a dispute with the Indians. Carelessly, he permitted a large party of Indians aboard without checking for concealed weapons. Most of the crew, including the captain, were killed almost immediately. The overland expedition also had a multitude of troubles. It left St. Louis, late, on March 12, 1811, under the leadership of Wilson Price Hunt. Hunt was not a very successful leader; his band became lost, two men died, and others became temporarily deranged before arriving at Astoria.

In May 1812, the remnants of the ship's passengers and Hunt's overlanders were reinforced with the arrival of a supply ship. The Pacific Fur Company then was able to consolidate and develop its territory. Astor's fur men trapped in the Willamette Valley. They established important forts at the junction of the Okanogan and Columbia rivers; another near modern Kamloops, British Columbia; and a third (Fort Spokane) near today's Spokane, Washington. At all of these places, the Pacific Fur Company made a good beginning in competing with the NWC and in adjusting to the new fur trade demands of the Pacific Northwest.

Problems of the Beaver Trade

Even experienced traders—and most American and English traders were experienced—had to alter their ideas in the Northwest. First of all, the natural environment west of the Rockies produced fewer beaver and those of lesser quality than in the East. In the Great Lakes country and on the plains, travel was easy through the network of waterways and on level terrain. In the Northwest, much of the country was mountainous, the rivers tumbled through numerous falls, and there were tremendous coulees and canyons.

The Indians' relationship to the traders differed also. In the harsh environment of the East, the Indians became willing partners in the fur trade, eager to absorb European goods. In contrast, the Indians of the Pacific Northwest, living for the most part in a generous environment, were not dependent on European trade for survival. This independence placed the Indians in a strategic position to deal with the beaver traders. They did not need to trap animals for the whites, but the whites needed the Indians' assistance. They needed the Indians to provide them with horses. In an area without bison, the horse was a food supply. Where water transportation was difficult, the horse was required to replace the canoe. Northwestern Indians, in sum, were less an asset, more an obstacle, than those of the central regions.

In spite of these trials of adjustment, and the fiasco of *Tonquin's* destruction, the Pacific Fur Company seemed ready to challenge the North West Company when world events caught up with the trade. News of the outbreak of the War of 1812 reached the Northwest early in the next year. Astor's agents were already considering abandoning their post when this news arrived. They had earlier heard of the loss of their annual supply ship, which left them with no trading goods. Now they feared capture by a British ship which would mean total loss. In the last part

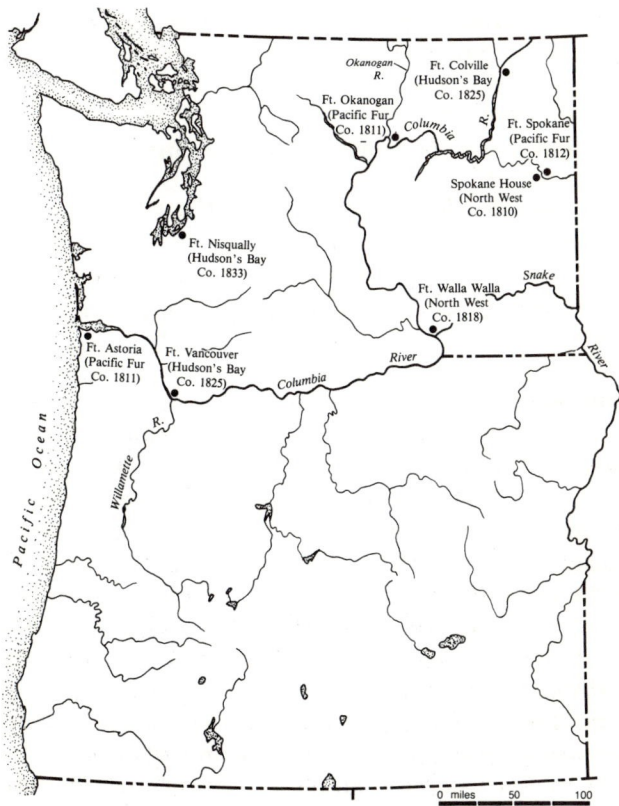

Fur Trading Posts of the Pacific Northwest

of 1813, these two developments were reflected in events at the mouth of the Columbia.

In October, the Pacific Fur Company sold out to the NWC. In December, the British warship *Raccoon* captured Fort Astoria. Although Astor's post was restored to him after the war, he never returned to the Pacific Northwest. He felt the American government could never protect his rights there and he felt he had overestimated the potential of the fur trade. He decided to cut losses and develop other interests elsewhere. These he turned to great advantage, and in the eastern fur trade, real estate speculation in New York City, and other ventures, he became the richest American of his time.

Yet Astor, in spite of discouragement and disappointment, did leave a legacy in the Oregon Country. Through accounts of his work, especially Washington Irving's *Astoria* (1836), the American public learned something not only of the problems of the Northwest, but something of its potentialities as well. Furthermore, the restoration of Astoria to the United States supplemented the earlier activities of maritime traders and Lewis and Clark in fixing an American claim on the Pacific Northwest.

Donald McKenzie and the North West Company

In the short run, however, the British, and especially the North West Company, both capitalized on the failure of the Pacific Fur Company. The company acquired a post (which it renamed Fort George) on the Pacific. It worked out an arrangement with an American company, J. and T. H. Perkins, to sell its furs in China. The NWC spent a good deal of time searching for a major post in the interior that would combine efficient transportation facilities, friendly Indians, and a reliable supply of beaver. It tried in turn Fort Okanogan and Spokane House before settling on Fort Nez Percés (also called Fort Walla Walla) in 1818.

The choice of this fort was one of several important decisions made by Donald McKenzie who assumed the leadership of the NWC in 1816. His great contribution was the invention of a brigade system that revolutionized the western fur trade. Before this time, the fur trade had been based upon the trading post to which the Indian trappers brought their goods for exchange. As the Indians were reluctant to do this work, McKenzie decided to form parties of company employees to go into the field to trap. They would carry their own equipment and supplies on pack horses, be accompanied by their women and children, and be free to follow the beaver wherever supplies were greatest. The brigade provided mobility and flexibility. It removed from the Indian country the tempting target of a well-stocked trading post. It also removed a symbol of advancing white civilization in the domain of the native American. Using this new device, from 1818 to 1821, McKenzie probed for furs deep into the Snake Country, reaching almost as far south as the Great Salt Lake. With all of these achievements, it is not surprising that the NWC underwent a renaissance during McKenzie's leadership. But the company's Oregon operations, like Astor's Pacific Fur Company, became a casualty of distant developments.

The Hudson's Bay Company Appears

By 1821, the government of England was distressed by warfare in central Canada between the HBC and the NWC. The most lurid event in this conflict was the Battle of Seven Oaks in 1816, when a NWC contingent killed twenty-one HBC men in the Red River Valley. Five years later the government took a series of actions to end the conflict. It forced a merger of the two companies under the name of the HBC. This left a vacuum in the Oregon Country, which was filled by the decision to offer a twenty-one year trading monopoly in the region. The license was given to the HBC and carried with it civil and criminal jurisdiction over British subjects.

The newly merged firm was under the direction of George Simpson who was born, illegitimate, in Scotland in 1792. He migrated to London, where he was hired by the HBC and sent to Canada in 1820. Later he became joint governor with responsibility for the Oregon Country. Intelligent, energetic, orderly, economical, charismatic, Simpson was an ideal choice.

Simpson and the directors of the HBC were not at first enamored with all of the Pacific Northwest. The company anticipated profits from New Caledonia to the north, but was doubtful whether or not it should even remain in the Columbia region to the south. But in 1822 it decided to hold onto the area as a buffer zone against the Russians and the Americans. The czar in 1821 had issued a declaration expanding his claim to the coast of Russian Alaska as far south as 51° 40'. The possibility of Russia defending its new claim was ominous.

The American presence was also potentially dangerous. Maritime traders had been on the coast since the time of Gray and Kendrick. Lewis and Clark had publicized the region. Astor's men had occupied at least a portion of it for three years. Congress in 1821 began to debate a bill, introduced by John Floyd of Virginia, that would authorize the construction of a string of forts to Oregon, the granting of land to United States citizens, and the establishment of an American territory.

In the early spring of 1824, it was obvious that Britain, Russia, and

Fort Vancouver, 1845. J. H. Warre, Oregon Historical Society

the United States would soon agree to the line of 54° 40' as the southern boundary of Russian Alaska. This agreement made other decisions possible later in the year. The company sent a vessel to explore the trading opportunities north of the Columbia River. It also decided to move its Oregon headquarters from Fort George (the renamed Astoria) to a site on the north bank of the Columbia as the company anticipated that the river would be the eventual international boundary between the United States and Britain. John McLoughlin and Alexander Kennedy were appointed to command the Columbia District with the title of chief factor.

Meanwhile, between August 1824 and March 1825, Simpson journeyed to the Northwest on a tour of personal inspection. When he returned to the East, he had already begun to put into place the results of his observations. He approved the selection made earlier of the new headquarters post. Its location was eighty miles from the mouth of the Columbia and near the confluence of the Willamette, a site offering plenty of level terrain for trading post, farms, and houses for the employees. It was accessible to the ships that arrived from England. The fort was christened "Vancouver" on March 19, 1825, the day before Simpson left for the East. The governor also decided that the Columbia business must be conducted more efficiently. He ordered each post to grow as much of its own food as possible, thus reducing dependence on expensive imported provisions that had to be packed across Canada to the Columbia.

Simpson determined to enhance the defensive role of the Columbia region by reshaping the Snake River brigade. He put Peter Skene Ogden in control of the brigade to give it a new purpose. Ogden's task was to trap out the entire watershed of the Snake, to render it a fur desert, literally, without a single beaver remaining in it. The desert would become unattractive to the American trappers and traders coming from St. Louis. They would not be tempted to cross the Snake for the Columbia and beyond. They would be confined east of the Rockies on United States soil. But there was a conservation dimension, oddly, to the plan. While Ogden's brigade was swarming through the Snake watershed, older territories would be given a rest, a time to replenish their stock of animals. And a handsome profit might be turned in the Snake region in the meantime.

To complete his plans, Simpson decided to develop a company merchant marine to serve the coast from the Columbia to Alaska. These ships were to compete with the Russians and the Americans for the Indian trade and also carry the furs to China. Simpson, too, wanted an annual brigade to move south from Fort Vancouver to trap in the Willamette Valley and along the Oregon coast. By the time that Simpson left Fort Vancouver for the East after his great tour of inspection, the organization of the HBC was complete for what promised to be a glorious future.

Organization of the Company

The rulers of the HBC were its officers based in the London headquarters. The chief officer was the governor, assisted by a deputy governor. They were responsible to a board of directors of seven men. All of these nine officers were elected by the stockholders in annual meetings. The actual operations of the company in North America were the responsibility of lesser officials in the various geographic regions.

At the top of the American structure were two governors, one for the northern department (which included the Pacific Northwest) and one for the southern. After 1826, however, a single governor ruled all of North America. Beneath them were other officers, divided into two categories: chief factors and chief traders. The twenty-five chief factors supervised districts; the twenty-eight chief traders had charge of single posts or were given special assignments. These fifty-three men received their proportionate share of 40 percent of the annual profits of the company. The officers in America met once a year in the summer at various locations to assess the past and to plan for the future. This gathering became formalized as the Council for the Northern Department of Rupert's Land, presided over by the American governor.

The plans laid by the council were executed by several hundred lesser employees who were arranged according to a strict hierarchy. At the top of this order were the clerks who kept the records and did the correspondence. Their task was one appealing to bright young men on the way up who could look forward, after a fourteen-year apprenticeship, to becoming a chief trader. Then came the men without education who did a whole host of tasks, mostly hard physical labor. They, too, had different statuses and salaries, from the post masters at the top to the voyageurs and laborers at the bottom. The company's officers were mainly Scotsmen—either by birth or descent—the lower ranks were cosmopolitan. They included French Canadians, Indians of mixed blood, and Indians of the country and from the East (mainly Abenakis and Iroquois). Those who came the farthest to sweat and toil for the HBC were the Orkneymen from the Atlantic and the Hawaiians from the Pacific.

Leadership over this heterogeneous but disciplined group of men and their dependents belonged in the Pacific Northwest to Dr. John McLoughlin. An imposing figure, six feet three inches tall, impatient, intelligent, loyal, the chief factor of the Columbia Department was a leader to the core. McLoughlin was born in Quebec in 1784. His mother was a Fraser, of the fur trading family whose relatives had served with the North West Company. McLoughlin gained a medical degree, by the apprenticeship system, at the age of nineteen in 1803. He first began to use his medical skills later in that year when he joined the North West Company as a physician. In 1814 he was made a partner of the NWC which freed him from his medical duties. McLoughlin served the NWC until the coalition with the HBC in 1821. After a year's vacation in France, he spent the next two years in the Great Lakes area until Governor Simpson selected him as chief factor of the Columbia District in 1824.

Activities of the HBC

McLoughlin's headquarters at Fort Vancouver became the center of a whole range of activities largely based upon the plans conceived by Simpson on his visit of 1824–25. These activities, although they overlapped, consisted of four main areas.

First of all, the company conducted an extensive trade north of the Columbia River at a series of trading posts or forts. Here the Indians brought the beaver pelts to exchange them for goods manufactured in

Dr. John McLoughlin. Oregon Historical Society

England or at Fort Vancouver. Fort Colville, located about halfway along the length of the Columbia River, was the most elaborate post, next to Fort Vancouver, in the range of its agricultural and manufacturing operations. In 1827, Fort Langley was built on the Fraser River, and in 1833 the company erected Fort McLoughlin as the chain of posts stretched northward to Alaska. To the east, McLoughlin ordered the construction of Fort Boise (1834) and Fort Hall (1837), both in present-day Idaho.

The second dimension of the HBC was the brigade fur trade that had been pioneered by the NWC. These units operated south and east of Fort Vancouver. The Snake brigade trapped to the east of the Cascade Mountains, while the California brigade worked in the Willamette Valley, the Umpqua watershed, and over the Siskiyou Mountains into northern California. The brigades were led by a chief trader and a clerk or two. The trappers themselves were of two types, company employees who were paid a salary, and the free trappers. The free trappers were outfitted by the company which also paid an agreed sum for each pelt received. The trappers' wives and children accompanied them.

The brigades departed from headquarters in the late fall when the coats of the beaver were at their prime. They moved from area to area, picking up and removing to new territory as the beaver supply became exhausted. When the horses were fully loaded, the men cached the furs. In the early summer the brigades returned to headquarters where the men were paid off, the furs checked and repacked, and reports prepared. Although the brigades were primarily business ventures, they also contributed to geographic knowledge. Ogden's first Snake River party in 1825 swung as far south as the Great Salt Lake before and after traversing much of the Snake and Bear river watersheds. Ogden followed up with five more journeys into regions now part of the states of California, Oregon, and Utah. He was the first explorer to cross the area west of the Rockies from north to south. His reports and maps were printed and publicized throughout America, England, and Europe.

The HBC also became involved in businesses other than the fur trade. These were the export of lumber and salmon. McLoughlin and Simpson took an interest in them not only for the sake of direct profit, but because they would keep out American and Russian competition and give the ships and crews of the company employment when not engaged in the fur trade. In 1828 McLoughlin built a sawmill near Fort Vancouver and he began packing barrels of salmon in salt brine. These products were not as profitable as anticipated, although occasional markets were found for them in Hawaii, South America, and California.

The Maritime Department was indispensable to the success of the company. The ships brought the trading goods from England and sent the furs to China or other markets. If they did not arrive at the wharves at Fort Vancouver, a year's progress might be lost. The department also engaged in a coastal trade beginning in 1825 when the ship *William and Ann* sailed north to Observatory Inlet on a reconnaissance voyage. As in the case of the Snake brigades and the lumber and salmon business, the coastal trade was conducted in part to make a profit directly, in part to drive off competition.

Competitors

The competitors were the Russians and the Americans. In 1825, the *William and Ann* met an American ship *Owyhee* that was engaged in the coastal trade. *Owyhee* and later American ships posed a new kind of threat. They were no longer, as were earlier maritime traders, interested in the aquatic animals. What the new ships wanted from the coastal Indians was beaver pelts, which they in turn received in trade from the interior Indians who formerly sold them to the HBC in their home country. The HBC plan to meet their rivals was to undercut them with a supply of goods that was more reliable, less expensive, and of better quality. The plan was theoretically sound, but developed weaknesses that delayed its success for many years.

First of all, the HBC directors did not place the Maritime Department directly under McLoughlin's supervision. The directors compounded this snarling of the lines of authority by selecting incompetent personnel to command the trading ships. There were difficulties in getting supplies from England. The most serious problem was McLoughlin's halfhearted support of the coastal trading vessels. He favored, instead, a system of permanent trading posts stretching to Alaska to stabilize the trade by making more permanent alliances with the native Americans than were possible with occasional visits by sea. They would also be more economical and reliable than the ships. But the HBC continued to employ both ships and posts throughout its career in the Pacific Northwest. The last American trading vessel appeared on the Northwest Coast by 1837.

On February 6, 1839, the HBC concluded an agreement with the Russian American Company that seemed to seal the end of its competition in the old Oregon Country. The HBC agreed to supply wheat, peas, barley, butter, beef, and ham to the Russians. This arrangement removed them as fur trading rivals south of Alaska and also closed their market to American suppliers. The HBC seemed victorious everywhere, for earlier they had eliminated the two American threats to their interior trade in the Northwest.

American Competition Eliminated

This last story begins in the vivid imagination of a Yankee schoolteacher, Hall J. Kelley. Kelley began to take an interest in Oregon in 1818 and soon became the first American to promote a permanent United States colony in the region. In 1828, he sent a petition to Congress to seek support for a colonizing company he was to organize. This plan, frankly modeled on the HBC's exclusive grant, did not appeal to Congress. Thus in the next year Kelley organized the American Society for Encouraging the Settlement of the Oregon Territory. He tried to recruit settlers and raise capital by writing two pamphlets, *A Geographical Sketch of that Part of North America called Oregon* (1830) and *A Manual of the Oregon Expedition* (1831). In these writings, he stressed the economic possibilities of the Northwest. He planned that his company build a colony based on agriculture, lumber, fishing, and whaling. It would trade with Asia. It would furnish opportunities for unemployed eastern workers. It would help make the Oregon Country American.

In spite of his zeal, Kelley never planted his colony. Two obstacles were insurmountable. One was the uncertain diplomatic situation. The entire Oregon Country was disputed among England, Spain, and the United States. Colonists were reluctant to come with Kelley for they might not know for years into what nation they would fall when the question of sovereignty was finally settled. The second obstacle was propaganda. Both American and British fur traders, fearing Kelley's competition, circulated rumors that he had underestimated the ease of transportation to Oregon and had overestimated its natural resources.

Kelley did influence a Boston businessman, however—his neighbor, Nathaniel J. Wyeth. Wyeth took over Kelley's plan when it became obvious that the schoolteacher had little support. In 1832 and 1834, Wyeth led overland expeditions to the lower Columbia. His purpose was to found a colony to become the nucleus of an international trade in lumber, salmon, furs, and farm products. Wyeth planted his headquarters, named Fort William, on Sauvie Island in the lower Willamette River in 1832. But he could do no business because of the destruction of his supply ship on the Columbia Bar. In 1834 he tried again. This time he founded a second trading post, Fort Hall, in Idaho. But neither Fort William nor Fort Hall was successful. The Hudson's Bay Company simply had the material resources to defeat him, and in 1836 he quit.

Similarly, the HBC destroyed the ambitions of Captain Benjamin L. E. de Bonneville. Bonneville was an army officer on leave of absence to engage in the fur trade from 1831 to 1836. From 1832 to 1835, he conducted business from Fort Bonneville on the Green River and sent parties as far afield as California and Oregon. There is some conjecture that Bonneville was, while on leave of absence, still an active agent of the United States government. In any case, he left the fur trade, but not without publishing a report describing the agricultural attractions of the Willamette Valley.

The Last Days of the HBC

The last activity of the HBC was itself to plant a large-scale agricultural colony. This scheme was based upon economic and political realities and hopes. The company had encouraged, since Simpson's inspection journey of 1824–25, the growing of food at each of the forts. The farms at Fort Vancouver and Fort Colville were quite substantial indeed. By the late 1830s, there was hope that the company could grow enough food to supply the Russian traders in Alaska. Politics also entered in. The twenty-one year trading license in the Pacific Northwest would expire in 1842. To get it renewed by Parliament required adding some concessions by the company. If the company were to engage in a major food-producing operation, then the tax revenues of the British Empire would increase, valuable crops would be grown, and the political grip of Britain on the region would tighten. To meet these hopes, the HBC organized a subsidiary in 1838, the Puget's Sound Agricultural Company. It began a cattle ranch at Nisqually and a wheat farm at Cowlitz Prairie, but was never successful. Problems of securing a labor supply, ungenerous employment terms, and a lack of full commitment to the program by the HBC were the causes of failure.

And failure—in a sense—was the lot of the parent company. By 1846, Britain and the United States at last divided the Oregon Country. With two minor exceptions, their treaty left the HBC with nothing below the forty-ninth parallel. The company's impression was deep on the history of the region, however, in ways other than its profits, for it contributed to geographic knowledge, publicized the economic potential of the area in businesses besides the fur trade, gave Britain a foothold in the region, and propagated the Christian faith. But it could not maintain itself against the coming of the American settlers whose forerunners were the men and women of God.

SUGGESTIONS FOR READING

Two fascinating books discussing exploration and the fur trade are D. W. Meinig, *The Great Columbia Plain: A Historical Geography, 1805–1910* (1968) and William H. Goetzmann, *Exploration and Empire: The Explorer and the Scientist in the Winning of the American West* (1966). The best short account of the Corps of Discovery is John E. Bakeless, *Lewis and Clark: Partners in Discovery* (1947). For Astoria, see Gabriel Franchére, *Journal of a Voyage to the North West Coast of North America*, ed., W. Kaye Lamb (1969). On the North West Company and its rivalry with the HBC, see also E. E. Rich, *The History of the Hudson's Bay Company, 1670–1870* (1958–1959) and John S. Galbraith, *The Hudson's Bay Company as an Imperial Factor, 1821–1869* (1957). For the pioneer American traders, the best sources are Fred W. Powell, *Hall J. Kelley on Oregon* (1932) and F. G. Young, ed., *The Correspondence and Journals of Captain Nathaniel J. Wyeth, 1831–6* (1899) and G. Thomas Edwards and Carlos A. Schwantes, eds., *Experiences in a Promised Land: Essays in Pacific Northwest History* (1986).

The Christian Missionaries, 1789–1847

The decade of the 1820s in America was a dynamic era. Pioneers surged westward toward the sunset. Opportunities for voting and holding office expanded. Intellectuals talked and wrote about a truly American culture, freed from the ideals of the Old World. Men organized banks, capitalized factories, planned roads and canals, plotted land speculation. Individuals strove for social advancement and economic success. The period was one of rampant opportunities for material advancement, but it was also blessed with robust spiritual developments. One of these was the heroic attempt to bring the Word of God to the Indians of the Pacific Northwest.

With Martínez in 1789, tossing in his tiny vessel surrounded by hardbitten seamen, were six priests from Mexico. They were the first to introduce the Christian faith to the Oregon Country. Amidst the awesome natural surroundings of Nootka Sound, themselves testimony to the majesty of God, the priests soon gained a follower. He was a small boy to whom they gave a big name—Estevan Lorenzo Francisco Severo Martínez y Flores—in honor of the Viceroy of Mexico. But no one knows if there were any other converts.

As the maritime and beaver traders in turn penetrated the Indian country, pious men and women at home wondered about the intruders' effect upon the native peoples. As the Indians gave up their furs, might they also lose their souls? Would not some ingredients of the cultural exchange, liquor and veneral disease, leave a heritage of death and destruction? Did not the traders have an obligation to return something priceless to the Indians, the gift of salvation?

These questions also arose in respect to aboriginal peoples elsewhere about the globe. The answers came from a great evangelical movement arising in both England and the United States early in the nineteenth century. It led to the formation or rejuvenation of missionary societies that carried the banner of Christ to the ends of the earth.

In the Pacific Northwest the Indians represented to the traders, however, not souls, but pelts, danger, indifference, and hostility. The fur men did not believe that the fur trade and Christianity could coexist. George Simpson expressed the prevailing view in 1822, when he heard about a missionary plan advanced by a company chaplain: "I have always remarked that an enlightened Indian is good for nothing; there are several of them about the [Hudson] Bay side and totally useless, even the half Breeds of the Country who have been educated in Canada are blackguards of the very worst description, they not only pick up the vices of the Whites upon which they improve but retain those of the Indian in their utmost extent."[1] What Simpson did not say here, but what the traders feared, was that the missionaries would persuade the Indians to abandon the trade to become farmers and that they would report to the British public that the company's servants were introducing vice to the native Americans.

Missionary Work of the Fur Trade

In spite of this opposition, Christianity came with the fur trade. Many of the employees of the North West Company and the Hudson's Bay Company were eastern Indians descended from converts made by the Catholic fathers in French Canada during the colonial era. Two Christian Iroquois, for example, settled among the Flathead people about the year 1814. More organized activity began in 1824 when the British government, responding to pressure from pious subjects at home, ordered the HBC to begin missionary and educational endeavors.

What the company did was to bring two young men from the Northwest to its headquarters at the Red River settlement. Here, in this heterogeneous community of *métis*, Scots, Swiss, and Indians, on the windswept plains of central Canada, in a natural environment vastly different from their own, the two began their education. Presented names honoring their tribes and the governor and deputy governor of the HBC, Kootenai Pelly and Spokane Garry studied English and absorbed the teachings of the Church of England from 1825 to 1829. They then returned to their tribes and did some missionary work in the following years. In 1830, five more Indian boys went to Red River, to be joined by a sixth in 1831.

Missionary Origins

Evangelical Protestantism came to the region soon afterward. In 1810 the Presbyterians, Congregationalists, and Dutch Reformed denominations founded the American Board of Commissioners for Foreign Missions. In 1819 it sent its first missionaries to Hawaii. Both the Hawaiian people and their missionaries were acquainted with the Pacific Northwest, and clergymen began reporting to the American Board headquarters that Oregon might be a fertile field. Jonathan Green in 1829 appeared on the Northwest Coast to survey the region for the American Board. While the American Board considered his report, another evangelical denomination acted first.

One of the most dramatic and mysterious events in the history of the Pacific Northwest was the visit to St. Louis by four Nez Percé men in 1831. They wanted to know something of the religion of the white race. But no one knew then, or knows today, what exactly they were seeking. Were they looking for a fuller description of the Catholic faith? Or of Protestantism? Or for William Clark of Lewis and Clark fame? Or for one of the specific Protestant denominations? Were they looking for missionaries to come to their own country? The record provides no answer.

What it does show is that news of the visit was picked up by eastern religious circles through a letter published by George P. Disoway in the Methodist *Christian Advocate and Journal* on March 1, 1833. Disoway interpreted this visit to be a call for Christian missionaries of the Protestant faith. In the space of three years, both Methodists and American Board missionaries answered this call, a call classically expressed in the missionary hymn:

> From Greenland's icy mountains, from India's coral strand;
> Where Afric's sunny fountains roll down their golden sand:
> From many an ancient river, from many a palmy plain,
> They call us to deliver their land from error's chain.
> Can men, whose souls are lighted with wisdom from on high,
> Can they to men benighted the lamp of life deny?
> Salvation! O salvation! The joyful sound proclaim,
> 'Til earth's remotest nation has learned Messiah's name.

Their momentous response had its roots not only in the campfires of the Rockies where Indians discussed the white man's faith and in the piety and philanthropy of American Christians, but in one of the great moral crusades of United States history that ran its course from 1824 to 1836. It started in a revival movement in western New York where a generation of pioneers had sampled a host of new secular and religious theories. This time, under the leadership of a Presbyterian minister named Charles Grandison Finney, the evangelical Christians stressed the obligation of the convert. To be truly saved meant that one had the obligation to bring the Word of God to the unconverted. This task, in turn, required that the social environment be Christianized so that the unchurched would have the chance to hear the message of hope. These assumptions underlay all the social crusades of antebellum America. Reformers sought to abolish slavery; to teach the deaf, dumb, and blind; to control the liquor traffic; to foster education; to protect Sabbath observance; to remake prisons. And, not least of all, to generate and quicken the missionary impulse, including the search for the souls of the American Indians. The coming of the missionaries to the Oregon Country was stimulated by this moral force.

The Methodists

The Methodists were first. In 1833 Jason Lee and his nephew, Daniel, both ordained ministers of this denomination, were selected by its mission board for the Northwest field. In 1834 they set out, traveling for the sake of safety with the party of Nathaniel Wyeth, the businessman. With them were three assistants, Philip L. Edwards, Cyrus Shepard, and Courtney M. Walker.

Their leader was a big man, in size and in spirit. Six feet three inches tall and of unswerving faith in God, Lee's religious beliefs were those of his Methodist brothers and sisters. The most important was an active search for the will of God through prayer, study, and receptivity to religious experiences. The faithful knew that their lives would not be easy, for temptation was always present, and hardship could come for inexplicable reasons. Adversity required courage. The Christian should work, both in hard and prosperous times, not to gain salvation, but to do good deeds for the love of God. Even though the way ahead was not always clear, Christians believed in the goodness of God and in his personal direction of their lives. In the end, they knew, everything worked together for the glory of God and the welfare of his children.

On September 15, 1834, the Lee party arrived safely at Fort Vancouver to a typical welcome from Dr. McLoughlin. The outward journey had been valuable. It had proved that Lee could get along with the rough and untutored men of Wyeth's company. It had demonstrated the physical strength of his party. At a meeting with the Flathead Indians he had found a real interest in the religion of the Europeans. Indeed his first

Jason Lee's Mission at Salem. From original sketch by Joseph Drayton, Oregon Historical Society

intention was to settle among these people of the interior, who lived in what is now northern Idaho, eastern Washington, western Montana, southeastern British Columbia, and southwestern Alberta.

Once at Fort Vancouver, Lee changed his mind, and rather quickly for such an important decision. He spent only nine days, in prayer, in reflection, and in conversation with McLoughlin and others at the fort, before concluding that his mission headquarters should be planted in the Willamette Valley, not on the plateau and mountains. Why he did this is not known, for he never recorded the reasons for his decision. McLoughlin had told him that the Flatheads were warlike and wandering. Lee had been a farmer and easily appraised the agricultural possibilities of the Willamette watershed where retired employees of the HBC were successful farmers. Good land was important to supply the missionaries with food and to teach the Indians a valuable pursuit. On the other hand, it is puzzling why Lee chose a place where there were so few Indians, for most of the native peoples had been wiped out by disease.

Lee, for whatever reasons, founded the original mission station at Mission Bottom, thirteen miles by river north of the present city of Salem. In 1841 he moved the headquarters to Salem (then called Chemeketa) because of the floods and unhealthy climate at Champoeg. As the years passed, Lee established other mission outposts—at Fort Nisqually, at Clatsop Plains at the mouth of the Columbia, at the falls of the Willamette (now Oregon City), and at The Dalles, which became the largest subsidiary post.

The mission board was generous in supplying Lee with personnel and with equipment. In 1837 two parties arrived and in 1840 appeared the "great reinforcement," comprising fifty-one persons. The missionaries built houses, storehouses, churches, and schools (at Mission Bottom and Chemeketa). They made farms and milled flour and lumber. They expended a good deal of money and a great amount of labor but were disappointed in their results. When the great reinforcement arrived, Jason Lee stated that not one single Indian had been converted.

Things began to go wrong almost from the beginning. The purpose of the Methodist missionary endeavor was clear. It was the traditional Methodist goal for Indians elsewhere in the country—to convert the Indian to Christianity and then to provide for him the features of American civilization. Unlike most Americans, the Methodists did not regard the Indian as racially inferior, thus incapable of Christianity and civilization. They did not propose to found a colony for white persons in Oregon.

But trouble developed when the attempt was made to carry out their purposes. It was wise to send unmarried men to be missionaries. They could move easily through the Indian country following the mobile tribesmen. They need not provide for families and would have to spend relatively little time in producing materials for food and shelter. Yet for a reason not clear, Lee changed his original plan, and requested in 1835 that families be sent. The board complied with this suggestion. Regardless of whether they were single or married, the missionaries were not selected with great care nor very skillfully prepared for their service. Willingness to serve in a lonely and hazardous station and letters of recommendation from local church members were the criteria of selection. No effort was made to provide the missionaries with advance information concerning the Indian culture—indeed, there was probably no one equipped to do so. But it would have been far wiser to take the time—once on the ground—to have the missionaries learn the Indian language than for them to try to teach the Indians English.

Jason Lee, although he recognized some of these problems, was not well suited to handle them. He hated to write reports to his superiors, who consequently lacked information on how best to assist the mission. He hated controversy and thus tried to iron out disputes and settle personality conflicts by delay or consensus, rather than by using his authority. He was not a systematic man: he did not visit the mission stations in a regular manner; he did not organize local congregations when the Indians were converted; and he was poor with accounts, once lamenting in his defense, "I do not understand bookkeeping myself."[2]

Work of the Methodists

In spite of all these handicaps, the Methodists did engage in a great deal of activity during their decade of service in the Pacific Northwest. The first people who attended their services were the Roman Catholic settlers of the French Prairie region. Lee had begun his work a few days after his arrival, preaching at a series of meetings at Fort Vancouver. When he located in the Willamette Valley, he continued to minister to the French Canadian families, opening his school to their children, praying and preaching, even baptizing. But his services terminated abruptly in 1838 with the arrival of the first Catholic priests.

The Indians, although few in number, received devoted attention. It was decided to bring them to live with the missionaries at the headquarters. Here they could learn English, Christianity, and the customs

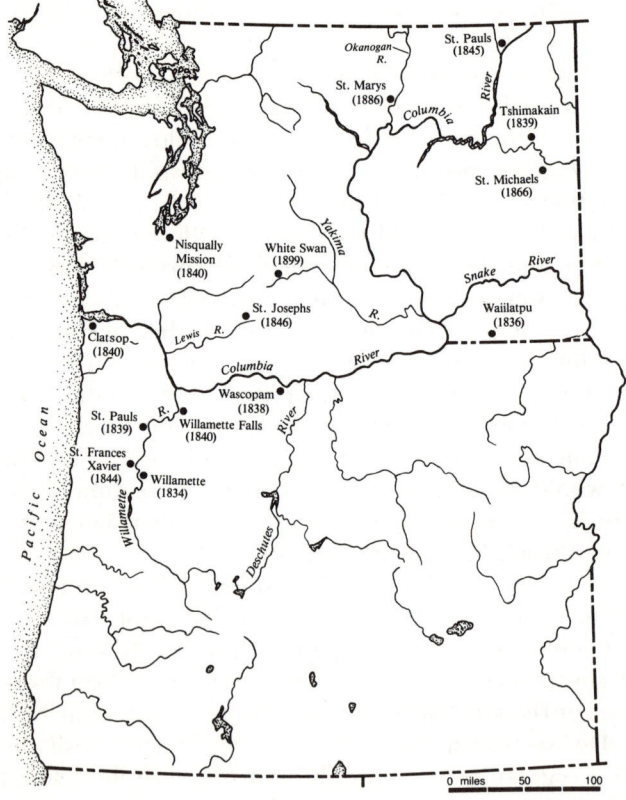

Missionary Stations of the Pacific Northwest

of civilization. The possibility of having the missionaries live with the Indians was rejected because the Indians were mobile and because they would more slowly learn civilized practices in that way. No school was established at the outlying stations. Besides formal education and Christianity, the missionaries also tried to teach the Indians farming, industrial arts, and homemaking pursuits.

Lee and his co-workers had little success in carrying out their programs with the Indians. When the mission was closed in 1844, there were only eight Indian Methodist church members in all of Oregon— all were children living at the Willamette settlement. This paucity of souls resulted from the diseases, carried by Caucasians, for which the stricken Indians had no natural immunity; from the lack of language and vocational training of the mission teachers; from the decision not to settle in the centers of Indian population; and from the hesitancy of Indian parents and children to enroll in the mission schools in the first place. Their initial reluctance was compounded by the teachers' use of corporal punishment. At the outlying stations the work was confined to preaching to the Indians and to seeking their conversion. But there, also, very little was accomplished. The greatest success was obtained at the site of The Dalles of the Columbia. Here under the leadership of Henry W. K. Perkins (who was the only Methodist missionary to learn something of the Indian languages), there were three great revivals in the mission era. But the missionaries were suspicious of the sincerity of the Indian conversions, never organized a local congregation to follow up these conversions, and never trained a native American leadership.

The Whitman Missions

While the Methodists were laboring in the western part of the Oregon Country, American Board missionaries were working in the central and eastern sections. The board decided to follow up the Disoway letter with a preliminary investigation before making a permanent commitment to the region. In 1835 the board sent Marcus Whitman, a medical doctor, and Samuel Parker, a clergyman, to the West. They visited with Flathead and Nez Percé Indians in the Green River country and became convinced that the people were eager to accept Christian doctrine. Whitman returned home, but Parker continued on into the Snake and Clearwater valleys, down the Columbia, and then back to the areas around Forts Colville and Okanogan. He found the country suitable for missionaries, but long before he was home, Whitman was leading a missionary party westward.

This group, which left the East in February 1836, included Marcus

Narcissa Whitman. Sketch by Paul Kane, Oregon Historical Society

and Narcissa Whitman, Henry and Eliza Spalding, and William H. Gray. The party arrived at Fort Vancouver in September, counseled with McLoughlin, and then proceeded to their new stations. Like the Lees, the board missionaries had originally intended to work with the Indians of the eastern plateau and mountains. But while journeying west, Whitman heard that the Cayuse Indians of the central region had asked for missionaries also. Accordingly, two missions were founded in 1836, one at Lapwai (present Idaho) among the Nez Percé, and the other at Wai-ilatpu in the valley of the Walla Walla River. The Spaldings took the first mission, the Whitmans, the second. In 1838 the board sent out other missionaries who founded new posts. Amidst the Spokane Indians settled the Reverends Elkanah Walker and Cushing Eels and their spouses on a site they named Tshimakain, about twenty-five miles northwest of where Spokane now stands. At Kamiah in present-day Idaho were located the Reverend Asa Bowen Smith and his wife in the country of the Nez Percé Indians on the Clearwater River. William H. Gray, a layman, obtained his own station at the mouth of the Yakima River in 1840.

The Board Mission was one of the most courageous and tragic in the annals of American mission life. Much of its work was repetitive and routine, sometimes marked by tedious and angry clashes of personality. Yet a great deal was attempted and many things accomplished. At Tshimakain the missionaries established a school and a farm among the Spokanes, who originally welcomed both. Eighty students turned up in the first year of school and the Indians tried some of their own farms, perhaps at the behest of the missionaries. The importance of agriculture could not be overestimated. Walker himself declared, "We must use the plough as well as the Bible, if we would do anything to benefit the Indians. They must be settled before they can be enlightened." But after the first year, farming was confined to the missionary families. They raised enough food to sustain themselves. The Spokanes' interest in the rest of the mission soon dissipated, too. The years were also barren of achievement in the spiritual realm as the Tshimakain missionaries found not one single Indian worthy of baptism.

At Lapwai the Indians were much more interested. As at Tshimakain, the Indians participated in the first year's farming operations with enthusiasm. Gardens were planted and apple trees set out. In 1837 the farms were ploughed and sown with the aid of sixty or seventy Indian families. By 1839 the Indians were not only dry farming, but had introduced the first irrigation facilities in the Pacific Northwest. By 1843 the Indians had moved out from the mission to establish their own farms; indeed about one-half the Indians had their own farms. There was a sawmill and a grist mill. The mission was self-sufficient in its economy and had 234 students in the school by this date.

The Whitman's mission at Waiilatpu also started out auspiciously, at least in economic matters. Here the Indians farmed through a combination of irrigation and dry farming. In 1843 there were sixty Indians farming their own lands. Here, too, there were mills, houses, and farm buildings in the American mode.

Catholic Missionaries

Catholic priests soon joined Methodist and American Board missionaries in the Oregon Country. In 1838 the Hudson's Bay Company formed its subsidiary, the Puget's Sound Agricultural Company. As part of that company's plan to persuade former HBC employees, all of whom were

Francis Norbert Blanchet. Oregon Historical Society

Catholic, to move from their own farms in the Willamette Valley to the company lands at Cowlitz and Nisqually, it agreed to subsidize the traveling expenses of two Catholic priests. These men were under the supervision of the Bishop of Quebec. When their instructions were written, they included a charge to serve the Indians as well as the Christians of the area.

The two priests selected to make the arduous journey to the Northwest were François Norbert Blanchet and Modeste Demers. They founded their first mission, which they called St. Francis Xavier, on the Cowlitz River. The second mission was their headquarters, St. Paul, located near the Willamette River in the center of the French settlements. From these nuclei the missionaries, joined in time by others, visited the Indians and whites at The Dalles, Walla Walla, Colville, Okanogan, Cowlitz, Nisqually, and Vancouver Island. In 1843 Blanchet became bishop and made his ecclesiastical seat at the falls of the Willamette. At all of these places the missionaries followed the Indians to preach, to instruct, and to civilize. The obstacles were always great, and the results were often scanty.

Problems of the Missionaries

The missionaries' task was far more difficult than that of the other white immigrants: fur traders, farmers, miners, and businessmen. As the others did, they had to make a living from the country. They had to face loneliness, accident, and death. But they had to do something that the others did not have to do. They had to reckon their success in intangibles, not in bushels of wheat, or packs of pelts, or ounces of gold, or number of dollars, but in the salvation of souls. To weigh this type of achievement was most difficult. To be confident of success in it was infrequent.

Some of the difficulties the missionaries placed upon themselves. They knew that they were not saints, but they had hoped to conduct their lives in the spirit of Christian love. But Methodist missionaries Margaret Bailey and the Reverend David Leslie disagreed on the ship to Oregon. Jason Lee tried in vain to moderate or end their quarrel. The young woman, denied the opportunity to teach that she had been promised, protested the injustice and found other faults with the mission operation. Finally, in 1854, she published the first novel in Oregon, *The Grains, or Passages in the Life of Ruth Rover*, an exposé of the mission, whose supporters destroyed all but two copies.

Many of the missionaries wrote back home denouncing Lee's leadership to the mission board. His worst problem was with the unscrupulous Elijah White. When Jason Lee returned with the great reinforcement of 1840 he found White's financial accounts of his mission work to be in disarray. When questioned, White fought back and demanded that Lee resign as head of the mission. Lee brought White to account before a committee of lay and clerical members of the mission who agreed that he had disobeyed the orders of the Church, was dishonest in money matters, and imprudent in denouncing Lee. Whether White then resigned or was dismissed is not clear, but it is obvious that this quarrel was a turning point in mission affairs, causing an irreconcilable split between the members who backed Lee and those who supported White.

Discord was often present at the American Board missions also. One problem was that Henry Spalding was the rejected suitor of Narcissa Whitman, a wound that never closed. Other differences were over matters of principle or place, but they soon became personality conflicts. William Gray, an enormously contentious and egotistical man, wanted his own mission. Whitman and Spalding, the two leading personalities, disagreed over the proper emphasis to be placed upon Christianity or civilization in the mission work and whether or not the missionaries should assist the white immigrants to settle among the Indians. Letters of complaint went back to Boston. The board decided in 1840 to reorganize the work by recalling Gray and the Smiths, dismissing Spalding, and ordering the Whitmans to move to Tshimakain. Lapwai and Waiilatpu were to be abandoned. News of this decision alarmed and dismayed all factions and in 1842 Marcus Whitman made a journey to the East to request reversal of this decision. His appeal was successful, although to save the full mission he had to stress its usefulness in supplying the pioneer immigrants crossing to the Willamette Valley.

Missionary rivalries added to difficulties of converting the Indians. The period was one of violent anti-catholicism, fed by incredible tales of the Catholic immigrants' poverty, lechery, and stupidity. These unflattering impressions, drawn on the eastern seaboard, spread westward. Catholics retorted not in kindness, but in kind. One of Jason Lee's clerical assistants described the Oregon population as follows: "There are about 200 French Canadians in the settlement, all of whom are Papists of the most ignorant and bigoted type; the Roman Catholic priests in the country domineer over them to their entire satisfaction, consequently there is little probability that any Protestant influence that can be exerted upon them will ever convert them from their vain system of relics and image worship, to the true principles of the gospel." Father Demers appraised the Methodist clergy as "men without learning, without education, and you comprehend men of that sort, former sailors, former soldiers, former packing-case porters, . . ." Such religious antipathy went a long way to confuse the Indians, both about religious principles and about how they were actually carried out by their adherents.

The whole matter of the Indian response to the Gospel was confusing. As we have seen, the Indians had religious beliefs—creation, afterlife, tutelary spirits—that could be considered by the missionaries as first steps to Christianity. The Indians, too, at the beginning at least, were receptive to the missionaries. But problems soon emerged. The Indians wanted Christianity for the same purpose as their own religion, to gain a more successful mastery over nature and to increase their material welfare. Unlike Christianity, their faith was not focused upon attainment of the next world.

The Indians were disconcerting in additional ways. Their language was difficult and, of course, unwritten. Only Asa Bowen Smith, who worked out a Nez Percé alphabet, gained much of a knowledge of the native tongues. Communication was in English, difficult for the Indians, as the decision had been made to have them learn this tongue rather than teach the missionaries the native language.

The missionaries faulted the Indians for other aspects of their culture. Some of the native Americans were polygamous; others were suspected of being cannibals. The missionaries believed the Indians to be vain in adorning themselves with necklaces, paint, and headdresses and perverse in slashing their flesh and flattening their heads. What to an Indian was a clever maneuver or economic necessity was to the missionary theft. Given their reformist ideology, the missionaries found slavery and the physical and psychological mistreatment of slaves abhorrent. The Christians regarded the physical labor that Indians assigned to women to be onerous and their subordinate social position to be repulsive. The Indians' indifference, indeed contempt, for the handicapped, shocked their humanitarian visitors.

The problem of Indian mobility was a double one. It became necessary to anchor the Indians to farms in order to be able to minister to them. This was a difficult task in itself, but when the missionaries talked about the Indians' progress in agriculture in reports to their superiors, in lecture trips to the East such as those made by Jason Lee in 1838 and Whitman in 1842, and in private correspondence, they became unintentional agents of American migration. Pioneers who heeded these reports put additional pressure on the Indian land base.

Nature was both opportunity and problem. Its goodness was testimony to the handiwork of God. Not only the agricultural munificence, but the great mountains, including the volcanoes, the broad Pacific, and the immense forests reassured the missionaries of the awesomeness and sublimity of the Divine. Nature, however, had its malign aspects. The Northwest winters were mild but endlessly rainy. Sometimes the natural features seemed not awesome but overbearing. Nature could injure, even kill. Insofar as the Indians were children of nature—identified with the wilderness evils—they revealed its bleaker face.

The gravest problem of all was civilizing the Indians. While the missionaries emphasized the Christian aspect of their endeavors, they could not neglect the necessity of teaching the Indians agriculture. They might, in other circumstances, have avoided teaching English, requiring European clothing, insisting upon American houses. But they did not. They imposed these cultural values, along with Christian teachings, and made the Indians' task difficult. The pace of acculturation also caused disputes within the mission family.

Here two problems intersected to place an additional burden upon the missionaries. For the irony from the beginning was that the missionaries had to serve three constituencies: the Indians, themselves, and other white persons. By the early 1840s, the last were growing thick and fast and placing the entire mission enterprise in jeopardy. The Methodists had served the Catholic community in the beginning. They had a station at The Dalles, which was a major resting place for the overlanders as they neared their ultimate destination.

At Waiilatpu the American board missionaries were even more helpful. Their Christian duty required them to assist the migrants who, by the time they had traversed almost 2,000 miles, needed everything from food and clothing to spiritual reassurance to simply the sight of civilized farms and households. The mission family took in the orphaned and the destitute, temporarily or permanently, as in the case of the seven Sager children whose parents had died on the trail. The able-bodied visitors helped with the crops and other operations and expanded the scope of the mission endeavor. For a time, it seemed possible that assistance to enable the whites to continue their journey to the Willamette Valley would also protect the Indians. Spalding and Walker reasoned that the Indians needed time to be protected from the advance of the Europeans; Whitman may have shared this view temporarily, but soon be became convinced that his primary obligation was to the whites. If he could help attract decent Christian people to the Northwest, the settlement of the area, which he now regarded as inevitable, would be given a proper moral tone. The Indians would benefit indirectly, for their new neighbors could set a proper example for them in the ways of civilization.

More and more, indeed, the Indians dropped out of the missionaries' concern. In part this was because of the literal decline in the numbers of the native Americans due to poor health, and to the other pressures of civilization. In part, it was because some of the missionaries became increasingly disillusioned about the prospect of converting the natives. Others thought the fate of the Indians would be extinction.

The Legacy of the Missionaries

The end of the Protestant missionary era came with suddenness. In 1844, the mission board investigated the Methodist stations in the person of a special agent, the Reverend George Gary. Gary made a careful inventory of the property, purposes, and personnel of the mission and concluded to close it. Lee, who had been recalled a year earlier, was commended by the board for his labors and assigned a new station. He died in 1845.

The end of the Whitman mission came not by reasoned calculation, but by an act of fury. The Cayuse had seen the whites arrive in large parties since the emigration of 1843 which brought more than 800 people to Oregon. They knew that population pressure sooner than later would mark the end of their way of life. They resented the missionaries' criticism of that way of life and they did not find that Christianity and civilization were providing them the material prosperity that they had originally anticipated. The Indians felt that Dr. Whitman had not protected them against sickness, especially a measles epidemic of 1847; some believed that he was poisoning them to clear their land for the invasion of the whites. The end came on November 29, 1847, with a surprise attack upon the Waiilatpu mission. The Indians slaughtered Marcus and Narcissa Whitman and twelve others on the spot. Of the forty-seven captives taken, three died, all children. The terrible news spread to the other missions which were quickly abandoned. No thought was ever given to regrouping, and the pioneer mission era in present-day Oregon and Washington ended forever.

Yet the missionaries had a greater influence on the development of the region than any preceding group. They did convert some Indians, and they planted the seed of Christianity among the Indians that would flower in later generations. They set an example for their countrymen of a belief in racial equality. They laid the foundation for an American colony, although this was not their original intention. They publicized the region, on the basis of their own experience, as a place for a viable economic future for their countrymen.

NOTES

1. Frederick Merk, ed., *Fur Trade and Empire*, rev. ed. (1968), p. 181.
2. Cornelius J. Brosnan, *Jason Lee: Prophet of the New Oregon* (1932), p.263.

SUGGESTIONS FOR READING

D. W. Meinig in *The Great Columbia Plain: A Historical Geography, 1805–1910* (1968) deals with the missionaries and the environment. Cornelius J. Brosnan, *Jason Lee, Prophet of the New Oregon* (1932), is still the most recent biography. A controversial interpretation is Robert J. Loewenberg, *Equality on the Oregon Frontier: Jason Lee and the Methodist Mission, 1834–1843* (1976). A sounder one is Robert J. Decker, "Jason Lee, Missionary to Oregon: A Re-evaluation." Ph.D. diss., Indiana University, 1961. The Whitman party efforts are described in Clifford M. Drury, *Marcus and Narcissa Whitman and the Opening of Old Oregon* (1973). On the Catholics, see William N. Bischoff, *The Jesuits in Old Oregon* (1945) and Carl Landerholm, ed., *Notices and Voyages of the Famed Quebec Mission to the Pacific Northwest* (1956).

People of a New Colony, 1840–1880

The American settlers who followed the explorers, fur traders, and missionaries to the Oregon Country were a vigorous and conservative people. They tried to preserve or improve their traditional patterns of life. Their philosophy was based upon the past: their own experience, that of their ancestors, and the national heritage. The westward movement was probably the most compelling ingredient in that history. The pull of agricultural land and personal freedom drew their forebears to America, impelled them across the Appalachians, embroiled them in Indian wars, and, to no small extent, contributed to the tensions with Great Britain that culminated in the Revolution. The currents of population movement released by independence flowed rapidly across the Middle West and the Gulf plains and crossed the Mississippi by the decade of the 1820s.

Manifest Destiny

In the late teens and early twenties, politicians and citizens alike began to take a renewed interest in the Pacific Northwest. They digested their memories of Robert Gray, of Lewis and Clark, and of John Jacob Astor. In 1817 the British consented to restore Astoria to the United States. They agreed that it had been captured and, under the terms of the Treaty of Ghent, that it had to be restored to the Americans. In 1818, in the process of clearing up several longstanding disputes, Britain and the United States negotiated the joint occupation treaty. This agreement was, in a sense, an agreement to disagree. It postponed the question of sovereignty in the Oregon region, as neither side was strong enough or willing enough to force a showdown. The matter of the boundary between the two nations in the Pacific Northwest was left to the future. The treaty itself was to run for ten years.

In this era also Americans began to write a new chapter in the book of what later would be called Manifest Destiny. This powerful ideology taught that God, or Nature, or Fate had decreed that the United States, representing political democracy, economic opportunity, social mobility, and religious freedom, would expand its boundaries to the Pacific—some said even beyond—so that the Stars and Stripes would float over a region that would shelter her citizens' posterity for countless generations. Manifest Destiny justified ejecting the Spanish from Texas and the area north of California by 1821. In that same year, it took legislative form with the introduction of a bill into Congress by Senator John Floyd of Virginia, a distant cousin of Charles Floyd, the only person who died on the Lewis and Clark expedition. Floyd proposed that the government of the United States should take a hand in strengthening the American claim to Oregon. The form of this assistance was to establish an American colony in the region. Government could assist this project by building a line of military posts along the Lewis and Clark route to Oregon to protect pioneers heading to the lower Columbia and Willamette valleys. Why would settlers be bound there? Because Floyd would have the United States, in defiance of the joint occupation treaty, grant land and establish a government and forts in Oregon. Floyd's bill threatened to ignite a war with England over a region that most people believed was not yet needed for settlement. Congress buried it (and a similar bill introduced in the next year by Francis Baylies) in committee.

Later in the decade, St. Louis traders began to probe the fringes of the Oregon Country, diplomats renewed the treaty of joint occupation in 1827, and Kelley began his propaganda. In the 1830s came Nathaniel Wyeth and the Protestant and Catholic missionaries, all of whom were emigrants of a sort. The resources, the route, the ideology, and the interest were all present by the end of that decade.

Motives for Migrants

The need appeared in the 1840s. For each person who went, the motive was as simple or complex as the individual himself. It was a great folk movement, the crossing to Oregon, but it was not simply a mass psychological stampede. Rather it was composed of thousands of hopes, hesitancies, withdrawals, and fears until the individual decision crystallized. For all who went willingly, adventure surely played a part.

Others, not by nature daring, found Oregon—or at least the thought of Oregon—a chance for a new life. These were the escapists, dodging debts, shedding spouses, fleeing fever. The burden of health in the Middle West was terrible, for death had a vast arsenal from which to choose: influenza, scarlet fever, measles, smallpox, erysipelas, opthelamia, cholera, milksickness, tuberculosis, and malaria. For these there was no known cause and no known cure. Both treatment and lack of treatment killed, as disease and doctors were equally destructive of bodies already weakened by poor diet, lack of sanitation, and heavy drinking.

Some, in pouring over letters from family members who had migrated, in perusing newspapers by fireside or candlelight, and listening to missionaries and adventurers in the little town halls and churches of the Middle West, concluded that patriotism required their departure. They must save the Northwest from Britain. Why? Because Britain represented the union of church and state, tolerated chartered monopolies like the Hudson's Bay Company, and supported an hereditary aristocracy and a dynastic monarchy. America stood for religious toleration, unfettered capitalism, social mobility, and a republican and democratic government.

For most pioneers, however, Oregon personified a better material life. Not that the soil of the Middle West was unproductive, nor markets

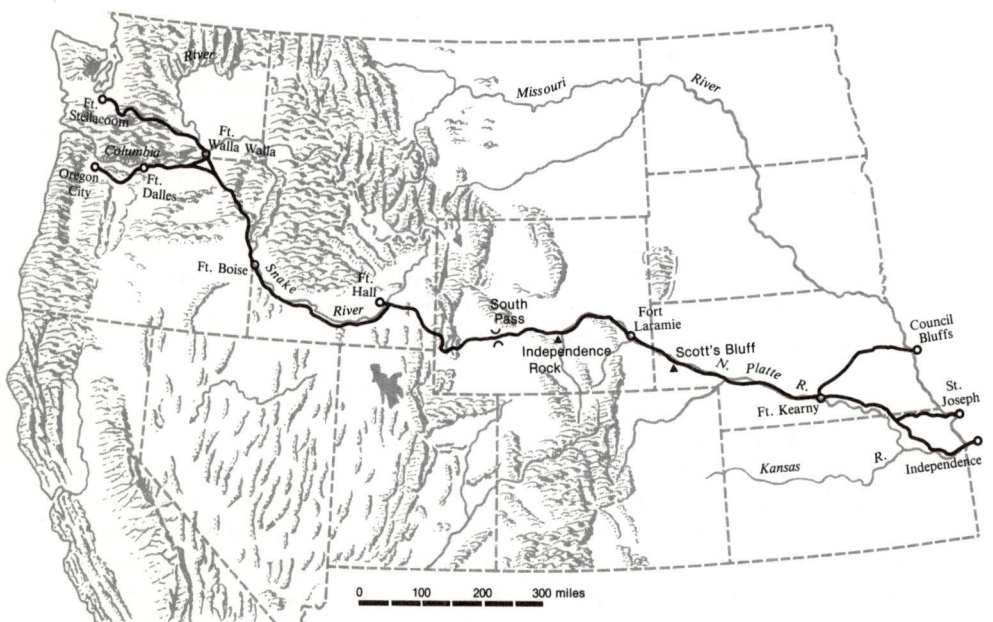

The Oregon Trail with Forts and Landmarks

lacking for farm products. But there were limitations on economic progress. The land was filling up. Even those who had established farmsteads found their labors heavier with the passing years. The winters seemed colder and longer, the snows deeper, and the winds sharper. It became more troublesome and expensive to raise and store the fodder for winter feed and to build and maintain barns for protection of the stock. Nature sometimes sent floods, the worst occurring in the years 1836, 1844, and 1849. The swirling waters took, in days, sometimes hours, the labors of a year.

Nature was not the only force beyond the control of the pioneers. Economic conditions often were as merciless. The worst depression in American history to that date struck in 1837. Banks failed, governments went bankrupt, dreams evaporated. Farmers could find no markets, were unable to meet their payments to land officers or to bankers. What made the situation more serious was that the hard times came on the heels of a great (if unsound) boom, a decade of rising land prices, unsecured loans and currency issues, and a fever of land speculation, canal building, and railroad construction.

In spite of all these problems, most Midwesterners stayed home. And most Eastern and foreign people who took up land came to the Middle West, not the Pacific Northwest. For example, more went to Iowa alone from 1850 to 1870 than to both Oregon and Washington from 1850 to 1900. There was some special quality about the small minority of pioneers who became Northwesterners that sent them across the trail and around the Horn to the Oregon Country.

The Pioneers

The people whose lives were affected by the troubles at home and the pull of the Oregon Country, the men and women whose ancestors had moved many times before, were almost all rural people living in the great river valleys of the Middle West: the Missouri, the Mississippi, and the Ohio. As such, they derived their ancestors from two main American streams which in turn had come from one source. Their mother country was the British Isles, from whence their forebears had come to the Atlantic Coast in the seventeenth and eighteenth centuries. Those who landed in the South, and their descendants, moved in time to the Piedmont, then over the Appalachians to Kentucky and Tennessee before making their way to the Middle West. The immigrants who touched American soil first in New England sent an exodus to the hill country of the region, thence to the Appalachian plateau of New York, Ohio, and Pennsylvania, and finally the Great Heartland.

Along the stops of their exodus, these families, both Yankees and Southerners, had refined a pioneer culture that, for all its precariousness, had served them well. If they felt an institutional dependence upon God, it was expressed through Protestant evangelical denominations: Baptists, Methodists, Campbellites, Presbyterians. They had a strong sense of pride in their country, in its history and its destiny. But the influences that could never be escaped were nature and the family. Both furnished an abundant certainty and uncertainty alike.

Nature was capricious. It provided the confidence of the changing seasons, a time to plant, a time to nurture, a time to harvest. The cycle of the year, with its allotted tasks, sanctioned by the folk wisdom of millenia, never changed. People mostly did what farmers had done for-ever, it seemed, and took their losses and gains with curses or stoicism, with joy and thankfulness. They remembered the good years, time when the corn and wheat flourished, the stock proliferated, the fevers mod-erated, and the markets strengthened. It was then that hope fed on success, just as despair battened on the crop of failure.

The family was the shield against the vagaries of nature. So much as possible it furnished the security of routine, of appointed tasks, of knowing one's place in the domestic circle. The job of children was easily defined: they were to become like adults as soon as possible, with a minimum of argument and complaint. One thing they surely learned, by precept some and by example more, was that their fathers and mothers had more than physical differences. From their mothers, who were re-sponsible for educating both boys and girls until about the age of ten, children came to understand that the work and character of men and women was distinct although interlocking.

Men's sphere was outdoors and public. The men did most farm chores and made the decisions about how and when to accomplish them. They were necessarily not only tillers of the soil, but also carpenters, businessmen, architects, railsplitters, meteorologists, soil scientists, and experts in animal husbandry. Beyond the boundaries of the farmstead, men also engaged in work. They met together at someone's farm to assist one another in tasks too costly or backbreaking for a single family. Men also enjoyed the companionship of other males without the excuse of communal labor. Some of these gatherings were avowedly social, almost all of them reflected the rough cruelty of the frontier. Militia drills, cockfights, and bearbaiting were favorite recreations. Hunting and fish-ing were both pastime and necessity.

Politics also was largely an outdoor, competitive, masculine sport. True, it provided officeholders to run the country; but of equal or greater importance, it furnished entertainment. The candidates came to the county seats or swung around the circuit of the small towns. Electioneering involved speechmaking, betting, torchlight parades, and the final drama of the vote when the citizen called out publicly his choice for office.

The adult males and older boys who engaged in their pursuits developed a set of enduring values. Men were to be physically and mentally strong, never to show emotions of fear or sadness—competitive, tough in every sense of the word. They needed these characteristics, for the public burden of society was upon them. They were the decision makers in home and nation.

The world of women was private and noncompetitive. Women were wives, mothers, teachers of the young. Although they did tend a kitchen garden and feed the animals, their primary sphere was indoors. In a lifetime they would bear five or six children; how many survived would depend on the will of God. The women made the cloth for the family clothing, cut and sewed it into garments. They cooked over fires in the dark, small, and smoky cabins. They served other women as midwives and their families as physicians. Their recreation was indoors, too, by and large in the company of other women. In this sense, the quilting bee was the feminine equivalent of logrolling.

At these times, as well as from their female relatives, girls learned the characteristics of true womenhood. They were to be a moral force, to be the conscience and soul of society. Women were expected to be physically fearful, if morally strong. They were to be, however, cheerful and self-disciplined in the face of life's adversities. They were to be cooperative and resilient and the purveyors of harmony within the family circle.

Together, then, with their complementary labor, men, women, and children made a family-centered culture. Although the trials of domestic life and of rural society were great, the Middle Westerners were not without hope. The devout prepared for heaven. Irreligious and pious alike agreed that a solid homestead was the foundation of a secure, prosperous, and virtuous nation. The pioneer generation determined to carry this culture and this ideology 2,000 miles to the shores of the Pacific, to transplant the world of their parents to Oregon.

Life on the Oregon Trail

They gathered in jumping off places in the river ports of the Great Missouri Valley. Favorite points of departure were St. Joseph, Omaha, and the Mormon town of Kanesville, later named Council Bluffs. Here they encountered a bustling town life, some for the first time, where they worried about what kind of supplies to lay in, how much to carry, with whom to associate on the trail.

This task of finding people who were like oneself was not difficult. Most, of course, were farmers. Most had been born in the Middle West and almost all were residents of that section. In the census year of 1850, the 10,811 Americans living in Oregon bore out these generalizations. The three states of Arkansas, Missouri, and Iowa were the birthplace of 23 percent of them, with Missouri having the largest number (18.5 percent). The five states of the old Northwest (Ohio, Indiana, Illinois, Michigan, and Wisconsin) were the birthplace of almost 22 percent. In 1850, of the country's entire population, 67 percent lived in the Atlantic and Gulf states, but only 19 percent of Oregon's population came from these areas.

Once equipped, the settlers chose their traveling companions for the long journey. Many of the wagon trains were organized under fairly elaborate regulations governing choice of officers and the moral conduct of the emigrants while on the trail. As a minimum, each expedition had a captain, with overall responsibility, and a pilot (if at all possible one who had been over the trail before) who pointed the way and negotiated with the Indians. Over all the preparations, the delays, and the achievements, hung the great uncertainty: Could the settlers make it?

Faith sustained them in their hour of worry. For the religious there was a faith in God. For many there was a faith in the future based upon their belief that it was America's destiny that they go on to the Pacific Coast. For others it was the consolation of their countrymen that they and their companions were the salt of the earth.

At last they were underway, the oxen, horses, or mules pulling the covered wagons in trains of twenty to twenty-five wagons. The settlers expected danger and adventure. Their principal weapon against danger was the security of tradition, which they interwove into every aspect of their daily lives on the 120- to 180-day journey to their new homes. Tradition began within the family circle.

Men continued to lead outdoor lives. They drove the wagons. They took care of the stock and formed the guard against the Indians. Except for the last, this work somewhat resembled their familiar farm chores. The men also continued to make the public decisions. They chose the time of departure, the route, and their officers. In the daily operations, they determined the pace, located camps, picked the fords, and even changed the officers. Their recreation was also traditional—fishing, swimming, and hunting.

Women's work on the overland trail was as separate from that of men as before. It was also somewhat traditional. Women as always cooked the food, but outdoors was a new and unpleasant experience, and cooking in high altitude was even worse. Mothers and sisters watched the younger children, trying to guard them against rattlesnakes, wagon wheels, drownings, and other accidents. Unlike men, women's social life was greatly constricted. They had very little time for visiting other women because they were always either traveling in isolated wagons or, at noon or evening stops, cooking and cleaning up.

Other trail experiences were also caught between the desire for conservatism and the necessity for innovations. Law and order were carefully preserved. Before a journey started, the pioneers met to select leaders and establish written rules and regulations. They demoted their officers when disagreements festered, at times breaking up into separate parties if the disputes proved irreconcilable. They accused, tried, and convicted criminals based on their knowledge of the procedures of civilization. Without courts, judges, or many lawyers, they respected the rights of property.

Respect for law was a security against the possibility of anarchy. Other dangers required other remedies. Disease was feared as much as the Indians. The most prevalent diseases were cholera (which struck especially hard in the years 1850 and 1852), mountain fever, and scurvy. There were no preventive measures that could be taken for most diseases and no cures. Physicians provided help, free to those who could not pay, but their aid could only be psychological. Too often the scenes were as this one: "We pitched our tent but soon found we were in a distressed crowd. Many Oregon families. One woman & two men lay dead on the grass & some more ready to die of cholra [sic], measles, and small pocks."[1]

There were many problems encountered on the trail, some in the objective environment, some of the pioneers' own making. Of these, the most feared, after disease, was the Indians. On the trail itself, the Indians turned out somewhat differently from the stereotypes. In many ways they proved helpful. They knew the country, where the grass was greenest, the fords safest, the buffalo thickest. They could serve as guides through the wilderness of plains and mountains. The Indians carried letters from party to party, from trail to civilization. They operated ferries. Their supplies of horses were at times invaluable for transportation, or in the leanest of times, for food. They sold other foods and clothing and moccasins to refresh and shelter the wearying bodies of the emigrants. But there is some truth, too, in the historic image of racial conflict, of the encircled wagon trains firing heroically back at the mounted Sioux, "the fiery centaurs of the Plains." One modern historian has reckoned that on all the overland trails, in the years 1840–1860, 426 Indians and 362 whites died in racial strife.

Unlike the Indians, the whites could ask for help beyond their own resources. The federal government had always been an ally of pioneers who had no hesitancy in calling upon it for aid. The government provided forts from which mounted soldiers patrolled routinely and sallied forth in emergencies. As the overlanders proceeded westward, they looked forward to reaching the forts—reassuring symbols that in a land without civil government, Uncle Sam had not forgotten them.

The government also negotiated treaties with the Indians in the time-honored manner. The most significant of these agreements, reached amidst splendor and ceremony at Fort Laramie, with 10,000 Indians in attendance, was the treaty of 1851. The Indians, in exchange for $2,500,000, agreed to the establishment of a reservation and to the building of roads and forts in the Indian country. The list of additional services is long. The government contributed information about the best route to take and about trail conditions. Military explorers filled in spaces on the map nearly every year. Army doctors provided medical aid at the forts. The post blacksmith shod horses and oxen lamed by the trail and fixed tires and other broken parts of the wagons. For the overlanders who could not solve their own problems, the army officers gave advice and even settled disputes by the formal processes of justice. Government carried the mail, too.

Nature itself, beyond its human occupants, was a challenge of inconceivable magnitude. Geographical distance alone was beyond the ken of American experience. People began their trek with the expectation of the American Great Desert, publicized by army explorers, Zebulon Pike and Stephen H. Long, but the reality of the combination of treelessness, aridity, and flatness was amazing. The lack of timber meant it was difficult to repair axles and wheels. It forced the pioneers to the distasteful task of gathering buffalo chips. Even though precipitation was limited, crossing the rivers was perilous. The Platte, and its numerous branches, the canyon of the Snake, and, the worst at the last, the waterway journey from The Dalles of the Columbia to Fort Vancouver, all claimed their drowning victims. The mountains, too, were an agency of accident and death. The pioneers learned to fear above all the Snake River country and, as a grim alternative to the Columbia toward the end of the trail, the terrible passage on the Barlow Road around the south face of Mount Hood.

The immensity, capriciousness, and goodness of nature were epitomized in the bison. These awesome creatures, both anticipated and unpredictable, resembled the Indians. Surely no one who had glimpsed the enormous herds or had lived through a stampede would ever forget. "Buffalo extended the whole length of our afternoon's travel," one emigrant wrote, "not in hundreds but in solid phalanx . . . thick as sheep in a pasture. . . . I estimated two million. . . ." Another man was caught in a stampede: "As these huge creatures came booming along, their beards being pendant from their jaws and almost sweeping the ground, their long naked but tufted tails sticking straight out behind, their great brawny necks and shoulders covered with long flowing hair and mane . . . with their eyes rolling and fiery, they looked like a most noble and formidable enemy."[2]

These problems were present always. The emigrants, courageous and resourceful, could cope with, but not evade them. Other difficulties the pioneers brought upon themselves. The nineteenth-century American was both armed and careless. Familiarity with firearms indeed bred contempt. Loaded guns, set off mistakenly, doubtless caused more trail injuries than Indians. Children, escaping the protective eyes of their mothers, died under the rolling wheels of wagons or of the bite of poisonous snakes. In the swearing, struggling, and sweating of the river crossings, the occasions for accidents were rife.

In a way it was unfortunate that the trail did not offer more opportunities for danger and excitement. For much of life was dull routine: rising to the insistent call of the bugle, plodding for miles in the dust of the wheels ahead, eating the same food, hearing at waking the same

Covered wagon on flatboat. Beacon Rock, Columbia River. Oregon Historical Society

complaints. Setting up and taking down camp with sore muscles, scanning the horizon with sore eyes, nursing grievances with sore hearts, the pioneers' festering psychological and personality conflicts sometimes burst in awful scenes of screaming, hitting, swearing, and murder. The fruits of monotony were as often self-pity as self-control.

Once it happened this way: "Two men who prepared their outfit in company at Independence, had frequent quarrels in regard to their traveling and camping arrangements. Going into camp near Chimney Rock, the quarrel was renewed . . . in the heat of passion, they drew out their hunting knives and closed in mortal combat. In a few minutes one fell and almost instantly died; the other, fainting from loss of blood, was carried in the shade of a tent where, within an hour, he too expired; and with the same grim irony of fate, at sunset they were laid side by side in the same grave."[3]

If one of these men had lived, we do not know what his fate might have been. For the lot of people accused of crime varied. Few could be tried with all the procedural guarantees of an American law court. Yet in most cases the spirit and forms of traditional law were preserved and employed. A terse report of one case touches the essence: "Young shot Scott dead. The company had a trial and found him guilty. They gave him a choice to be hung or shot. He preferred being shot, and was forthwith."[4]

A problem much more pressing than crime was food and other supplies. Almost until their destination the overlanders worried about it. Their concern was that their limited space on wagon or pack trains was inadequate for both the needs of the trail and the requirements of their future homes. Most learned that they did not have enough for both. When sustenance ran short, those who were without depended upon their neighbors' charity. There are no instances of the hungry being turned away. Those with money were expected to pay. But where could money be spent?

Pioneers could buy from their fellow overlanders, from the Indians, from the military posts, or from the businessmen who attached themselves to the army forts or set themselves up at other strategic places along the trail. They could barter goods for food, with all of these people and, if they were absolutely sure that it had been abandoned, they might acquire a bit of property that someone had left behind.

In spite of the infinite variety of hardships, most who crossed the trail survived it. And as they drew near their new homes, their hearts were warmed by their welcome. For the pioneers were objects of desire. The West Coast residents sought them avidly. Businessmen, editors, ordinary people, all would stop at little to make sure that the newcomers settled in their town or county. At Fort Hall (in present-day Idaho) Oregonians and Californians held out the blandishments of their respective regions. The same pleading occurred at all other important trail junctions. Oregonians also contended with Oregonians in this furious quest for the new settlers. Communities planned for new roads and cutoffs from the old trails so that the overlanders would wind up in their territory. A people who survived were doubly worthy of admiration. They were proud that they had made it. They were pleased that others thought them worthy neighbors.

So when the great adventuresome journeys were over, what remained? What was left to do immediately, what was the long-term psychological significance of the crossings for those who completed them? For each of the thousands who came to the new land, the answers would differ. But we might generalize about them. The overlanders gained a sense of power by the successful crossing. They made a great decision and justified it. They also made a series of lesser individual decisions. They not only chose to leave home, but they also selected their jumping off places, their traveling companions, their officers and guides. They made their own rules and regulations for the journey and enforced them. They made their government responsive to their needs. They fought the Indians and nature. They were courted when they arrived at their destination.

But the emigrants' sense of power was also enhanced in other ways. The tradition of cooperation was strengthened. Nationalism, faith in the American government, was confirmed. Confidence was boosted—for what challenge would be too strong for those who had mastered the trail? Finally, in a host of ways, the crossing of the plains and mountains justified and maintained the conservative philosophy of the pioneers. The American system of politics and law, at least in rudimentary fashion, had worked. Social life survived—few walked alone to Oregon. Racial attitudes also continued, for however helpful the Indian was, he remained inferior. Sex roles did not alter except for emergencies; men and women did the same things on the trail as at home. The conquest of the wilderness was done again as all gloried in the victory of survival over nature. They had also fulfilled the historic role of Americans, played their part in the march of civilization to the setting sun.

A Different Kind of Migrant

In their time, in numbers, in myth, and in history, the overlanders were the most important migrants. But there were other new Northwesterners who did not cross the trail or, if they did, were not of white, rural, Midwestern background. Among those who came to the Willamette Val-

Oregon City, 1845. Sketch by Henry Warre, Oregon Historical Society

ley or the shores of Puget Sound were bright, young men whose background and intention was urban. They came from New England or the Middle Atlantic states seeking a new opportunity in transportation, merchandising, or banking. Unencumbered by families, they could move quickly and adapt easily. They hoped to settle down in time, but for the moment they wanted to develop and to build the country. When they did marry, their wives and daughters became community builders, too, although in a different way. They were the moving spirits in developing schools, art museums, libraries, and other cultural institutions.

A few of the urban newcomers were German Jews. Some had come to California to seek gold and then had joined the argonauts of Southern Oregon in the early 1850s. Most of the early Jews were merchants not miners, however. By 1852 there were seven Jews in Jacksonville, all connected with merchandising. Almost all of the arrivals were young, single men who continued their familiar pursuits—from the Old World or the settled parts of the United States—of peddlers and storekeepers. In this respect, they were similar to the New Englanders who came in the same years to pursue the same occupations. The German Jews integrated rapidly into Northwestern communities without prejudice. They lived wherever they wished to. They joined benevolent organizations like the Elks and Masons. Some won political office. Joseph Simon, a lawyer, was Oregon's most powerful Republican politician by the middle of the 1870s. Portland had two Jewish mayors in succession, Bernard Goldsmith (1869–1871) and Philip Wasserman (1871–1873).

In time, the migrants married Jewish women from home, and family life required new institutions to preserve their culture. Both men and women participated in this institution building. The first was Portland's Mt. Sinai Cemetery Association dating from the mid-1850s. The first religious organization was Congregation Beth Israel (1858), which constructed its first building six years later. The second congregation was Congregation Ahavi Shalom formed in 1868. B'nai B'rith was a national organization formed for sociability and mutual benefit insurance. It obtained its first Oregon lodge—in Portland—in 1865. The first Jewish women's group in that city was the Hebrew Ladies Benevolent Aid Society, a relief organization founded in 1874.

The United States settlers, rural or urban, already found a settled economic community, indeed three, in the Oregon country. The fur traders and missionaries, as we have already seen, were the first businessmen and farmers. Both of these endeavors also touched the lives of the French Canadians. As the life of the mountain men grew harder, as the beaver supply diminished, as the grueling labor for the HBC or PSAC seemed harsher, as they themselves became older, the life of the farmer beckoned. For these worn-out trappers and *voyageurs*, the Tualatin

Valley and the region near present-day Salem (the French Prairie was named for them) provided a gentle, pastoral routine of contentment and order. They were a unified community, tied together by British nationality, the French language, and kinship. They intermarried, compounding the unions of French and Indian women that had begun without benefit of clergy in the mountains. They were Catholic in religion, turning first for services to the Methodist missionaries, then to the priests, Blanchet and Demers, after their arrival in 1838. The French Canadians also clung together because of prejudice in the years ahead, for their new Protestant American neighbors looked down upon them. The *coup de grâce* for the French Canadian community in America came with the great flood on the Willamette River in 1861 which destroyed the Champoeg settlement and dispersed most of the settlers.

The Pacific Northwest population of the pioneer generation included several nonwhite persons. Those who came the farthest were the Chinese. In the China of the nineteenth century there were troubles of every dimension. In Kwantung Province of southern China there were political turmoil, economic deterioration, natural disasters, and resultant breakdown of law and order. It was this province that sent the most Chinese to North America, migrants lured by the tales of gold in California.

It did not take them long to spread northward. In 1851 there were Chinese in the Rogue River gold fields of southern Oregon. In 1860 the first Chinese settler reached Seattle, and later in the decade large numbers of them panned gold in eastern Oregon around John Day, Auburn, Granite, and Union. In 1862 they were at the mouth of the Methow River in north central Washington and from there they spread all along the Columbia River for 400 miles northward from Walla Walla.

When the mines ran out, the Chinese took up other pursuits. In 1871 George Hume, a salmon packer, first introduced the Chinese to the salmon canneries. On the Columbia River and on the coastal streams they did the slimy, dangerous work of cutting, cleaning, and packing the fish into cans. After the fishing season they moved back to Portland or San Francisco to spend the winter months. Chinese also practiced farming. They cleared land by cutting trees and grubbing up stumps; some were employed as ranch hands; others harvested, as in the hop fields around Puyallup in Washington. Still others risked exhaustion and boredom, let alone life and limb, in the construction industry. The bravery and brawn of hundreds of Chinese built the Oregon Central Railroad, the Oregon and California, and the Northern Pacific branch from Kalama to Tacoma. In the urban areas, Chinese were cooks, other domestic servants, and laborers in the iron and woolen mills. A favored few moved into the ranks of the business or professional classes, serving white clientele, for example in laundries, or providing the services that their countrymen required in the Chinatowns.

Chinese cultural life was built around family relationships if at all possible. Since the early settlers were almost all single men, however, other cultural institutions substituted for the consolations of a nuclear family. Cultural cohesion was maintained through the Chinatowns, where the familiarity of race and culture comforted the sojourners who had no desire to assimilate with American culture. Another community institution was the tong, which acquired (in part deservedly) an evil reputation among whites. They were organizations of small families, which, like so much else of Northwestern culture, came from California. There, rival tongs contested for control of prostitution, crime, and gambling, and their internecine strife caused trouble for the police for many years.

The tongs had other purposes. They were groups that provided sociability, a place for neighborly chatting. They were also sources of illegal recreation: gambling, drugs, and women. They provided protection for single men who had no family or governmental agency to assist them, men who were uncomfortable or unwilling to seek the assistance of white charity or church. Their members received aid when jailed or protection or retribution when rival tongs were bent on mischief.

But the Chinese paid a price for separation. Their distinctiveness stood out. They were convenient targets for those who resented them—for insults, blows, arson, and racist legislation. Wild stories circulated. With a knowing wink, the Caucasian repeated tales of opium dens, tong wars, exotic diets. There was something of the truth in all of this, but exaggeration ran rampant. The Chinese created formal cultural institutions such as theaters and temples in the 1870s. The Christian churches also worked with the Chinese. In Portland both the Methodist Church and the YMCA opened Chinese schools in 1869 to teach Christianity and the English language. In 1874 the Portland First Baptist Church established a mission school that became the nucleus of the oldest continuous Chinese church in the Pacific Northwest. For some the opium pipe, the prostitute, and the saloon provided consolation.

Also represented in the Pacific Northwest were the Hawaiians. In 1788 the first Islander reached the region. Others followed in both the maritime and beaver trades. With their seafaring background in their native country, the Hawaiians quickly adapted to the fur trade as canoemen, sailors, and shipbuilders. They worked for all the great firms, including the Pacific Fur Company, the North West Company, and the HBC. Their qualities that were most admired were willingness to work hard and acceptance of low pay.

The Hawaiians, in the Northwest as in their homeland, came in

Unidentified Chinese. Britt photograph, Oregon Historical
Society

contact with the missionaries. The missionaries found the Hawaiians to
be a very valuable supply of labor. They took up the slack that the Indians
left, for there was labor that the native Americans were not interested
in performing. Hawaiians did construction work at the Methodist missions and also worked on the mission farms and in the kitchens.

The American Board missionaries also used Hawaiians. The Whitmans, Smiths, and Spaldings all employed Hawaiian laborers, and all
found them to be infinitely superior to the Indians. They praised the
Islanders' energy and loyalty (once a Hawaiian stepped between Spalding
and an enraged Indian to protect the missionary's life). In spite of their
general excellent reputation, however, the Hawaiians never developed
a cultural foothold in the Northwest. They adapted to the prevailing
culture, whether fur trade or missionary, rather than establishing their
own institutions. The reasons for this were three: they were small in
number; most were single men determined to go home after making a

competence; and they suffered racial prejudice brought by the white pioneers.

With the white migrants also came blacks. Indeed blacks had arrived in the earlier eras of maritime exploration and the fur trade. The first black person who is known to have set foot in the Pacific Northwest was Marcus Lopius who served with Robert Gray as a cabin boy on Gray's first voyage. He left his blood and body for this honor, for as a member of a watering party Lopius was killed by a band of Tillamook Indians in 1788. Gray gave Tillamook Bay the name Murderers' Harbor as a memorial to this tragedy.

Other important blacks came as the continent began to be explored. York, the slave of William Clark, was a useful member of the Corps of Discovery, impressing the Indians with his hair, color, and physical strength, and serving his fellows as a hunter of prowess. There was a black cook aboard Astor's *Tonquin* and Francois Duchoquette, of mixed French and Canadian and black ancestry, worked for the Pacific Fur Company as a blacksmith. The Hudson's Bay Company at Fort Okanogan employed Duchoquette's son.

The period of colonization was one in which blacks participated in a variety of roles. One of the wagon trains of 1844 illustrated this racial participation. The guide was Moses "Black" Harris, a mulatto, who had served as a fur trapper for the famous St. Louis businessman, William H. Ashley. His experience gave him the customary qualifications to pilot a wagon train. Among those he guided was a white man, Nathaniel Ford, who brought with him three black slaves, Robin, Polly, and Mary Holmes. Of greater influence was George Washington Bush. Before he came overland in 1844, Bush had acquired a family and a good deal of property in Missouri. He was concerned about racial prejudice and discrimination and started for Oregon in the hope that he would receive equitable treatment there. But he also had a reserve plan; if he were not treated as a free man in the Northwest, he intended to go to California or New Mexico, possessions of Mexico, where racial prejudice was less prevalent than in the United States. After looking over the country, Bush settled down in an area near Tumwater (now Olympia), Washington, that soon came to be known as Bush Prairie. Here he became a landed patriarch and he and his descendants honored citizens.

George Bush is an exception. He is exceptional because of his status and because of his economic circumstances. He is exceptional also because a good deal is known about him. For most blacks in the Northwest— and there were only a handful—their strivings and frustrations were known to themselves and to their neighbors, not to posterity. Here and there a name appears, but little more. The first black resident of Seattle was Manuel Lopes who opened a barbershop in 1852, later adding a restaurant. These occupations were the principal ones of the early black businessmen. Not much is known about institutional life except that the church was first. In Portland there was a People's Church (1862) and an African Methodist Episcopal Church Zion (1869); the first formal institutions in Seattle did not come until the next era. What is known about blacks, like those of most nonwhites, is not their achievements, but rather their trials at the hands of prejudiced whites.

For racial prejudice was one of the principal ingredients of the cultural baggage of the whites. All of the nonwhite groups suffered from it. It began in the Middle West, although it was almost certainly rooted farther back. All of the states of the Middle West had laws prohibiting slavery and the residence of free black persons. Blacks in the Northwest also felt the weight of this type of law. The Organic Law of the Provisional Government in 1843 prohibited slavery and denied the franchise to free blacks and to Indians. In 1844, the arrest of James Saules, a black man who was married to an Indian, triggered further racist sentiment. For Saules threatened to incite his wife's people to a great interracial war against the whites unless he was released. Government's response was swift. Later in 1844 it again prohibited slavery and also added a prohibition against the residence of even free black persons. Slaves were to be freed and they, along with those already free, had to leave the territory within three years on pain of the lash. The exclusion law was repealed in 1845. The antislavery statute was renewed by Congress when the Oregon Territory was created in 1848, and the exclusion law was reenacted from 1849 to 1854. Both of these racist provisions were contained in the constitution for the new state adopted in November 1857. The effect of these measures is difficult to gauge. In 1851, Jacob Vanderpool, a resident of Salem who owned a boarding house and a saloon, was adjudged in violation of the exclusion law and ordered from the territory. No one knows whether or not he departed.

A few other instances of racial prejudice appeared. The Portland Public Schools System opened a segregated school for blacks in 1867. In 1871 Pendleton converted its public school into a private academy to prevent the enrollment of blacks. What the exact psychological effect upon blacks of being classed as inferior is unclear. It could hardly have been salutary. It probably kept blacks out of Oregon (and Washington Territory, created in 1853, which had similar statutes). In the longer perspective it confirmed a racial prejudice that has yet to die in the Pacific Northwest.

Hawaiians also felt the racist sting. The antiblack legislation of 1844 was applied by implication to Hawaiians. In 1845 they were attacked directly when the legislature of the provisional government enacted a law taxing employers of Hawaiian labor the sum of $5.00 each for each new Hawaiian introduced and $3.00 a person for those already resident. The territorial government refused to allow Hawaiians to vote. The final insult came in 1850 when Congress passed the Oregon Donation Land Act. In one provision of this statute, Hawaiians were prohibited the free lands open to whites. This final straw denied the Hawaiians a future in the Northwest and forced them to leave.

The Chinese also suffered from racial prejudice. It followed them north from California. One of the first laws in Washington territory denied them the vote. The constitution of the state of Oregon in 1857 prohibited Chinese from voting, from holding real estate, and from working mining claims. In the same year a law laid a special tax on Chinese miners. Washington denied Chinese the right to testify in court in 1863, and applied a special tax on their employers in 1864. Portland passed ordinances taxing laundries and prohibiting Chinese from using any building as a residence. Many other examples could be given.

The Chinese, unlike blacks and Hawaiians, also felt mass opposition. In 1867 a meeting in Lake Oswego passed a resolution against Chinese being employed by the Oregon Iron Company; two years later the same expression of outrage took place in Oregon City against the employees of the Oregon City Woolen Manufacturing Company. In 1873 agitators founded the Oregon Anti-Chinese Association. In 1875 a group of Indians in the Methow River Valley in Washington attacked a camp of Chinese miners.

But Indians were much more apt to be victims than victimizers. The displacement of the Indian is the saddest chapter in the history of the American frontier. In Oregon it came swiftly and in the usual manner. The Indians were quickly weakened by the white man's diseases, to which they had no natural immunity. In the years 1830–1833, for example, influenza, typhus, and especially malaria, all brought by the traders, killed 75 to 90 percent of the Indians residing below The Dalles of the Columbia. The whites moved into a region slowly; the Indians did little. More came, and faster, and incidents multiplied. The settlers called on informal forces, then state or territorial militia, finally federal troops.

Wars and Treaties

Congress responded to their constituents' desires with arms and treaties. There were several Indian wars throughout the Northwest from the close of the Cayuse War in 1850 to the late 1870s. They occurred in most of the geographic areas of the region. In southern Oregon, gold was the cause of the Rogue River War (1850–1855). Miners going to California after the discovery at Sutter's Mill fell afoul of the Indians of the Rogue

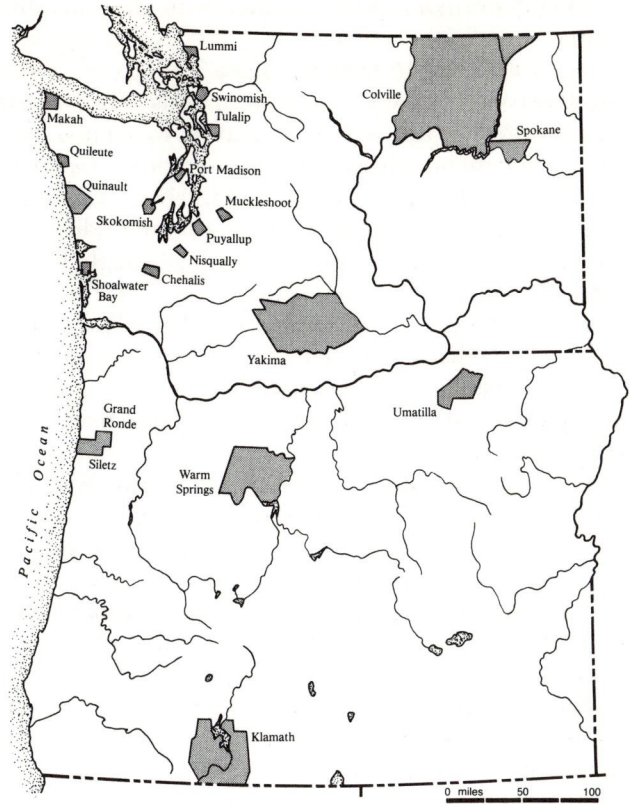

Early Indian Reservations of the Pacific Northwest

country. More clashes occurred when miners rushed into the Rogue Valley itself in 1853. Skirmishes were succeeded by battles, and battles by treaties. The treaties forced the Indians onto the Coast Reservation created in 1855 along Oregon's coast shoreline.

In Washington Territory (created in 1853) the first governor, Isaac I. Stevens, was the federal government's chief negotiator and warrior. Stevens moved to his tasks against the background of increasing Indian-white violence on the Oregon Trail and loss of life near Seattle and at Bellingham Bay in 1853–1854. He was aware, too, of the distant bloodshed in southern Oregon. In 1854–1855 he made a treaty with the Nisqually and Puyallup Indians of Puget Sound. The treaty gave settlers the land "bounded by the Cascade Mountains, Puget Sound, the present southern suburbs of Seattle and Skookumchuck River," a total of about 2,500,000 acres. The entire treaty-making process took only two days.

In January 1855, Stevens concluded treaties with the remaining Indians of Puget Sound.

Negotiations with the Indians of Puget Sound were relatively easy compared to those east of the Cascade Mountains. The western Indians were accustomed to the whites, indeed gravely weakened by them, but the eastern Indians still largely enjoyed their original precontact culture. Because the eastern tribes' territory crossed the border between Oregon and Washington, Stevens and Joel Palmer, superintendent for Oregon, were jointly responsible for these negotiations, although Stevens was the unquestioned leader.

The first council held in the East was at Walla Walla beginning on May 21, 1855. The Indians represented were from the Nez Percé, Cayuse, Walla Walla, Umatilla, and Yakima tribes. Stevens and Palmer spoke, the Indians responded, offers and counteroffers were made. The Indians were internally divided, some recognizing the inevitability of the coming of the whites to their domain, some denying it. Three separate treaties were ultimately signed, similar to those of the Puget Sound region. The Indians agreed to go onto reservations in exchange for cash payments, subsidies in goods, and the services of academic and vocational teachers, and physicians. The chiefs received houses and gardens. In time the reservation lands were to be divided into individual plots.

As elsewhere on the American frontier, the treaties crumpled in the rush of settlement. In both Oregon and Washington farmers and miners were in this vanguard. As they moved into the Indians' domain, threats and counterthreats escalated into isolated incidents that in turn evolved into wars. All over Oregon and Washington, the 1850s was a decade of .conflict. In the Puget Sound region the settlers, the army, and the militia skirmished with the local Indians. The Yakima War broke out in central Washington in 1855 and dissident Yakima, Klickitat, and Cascade Indians attacked the Cascades settlement in January 1856. There were rumors that the Yakimas were intriguing with the Puget Sound Indians to join in an assault upon the settlers of Seattle. In 1858 gold was again a cause for prolonging the war when miners went into the Colville region of northern Washington. Clashes between them and the Palouse and Spokane Indians resulted in the calling of the army. After initial failure, the army under Colonel George Wright defeated the Indians in 1858, and in the next year Congress approved the Stevens' treaties. Under their provisions separate reservations were established for the Umatillas, Walla Wallas, and Cayuse in Oregon; for the Nez Percés in Idaho; and two for the Yakimas in Washington. Some reservations were not born of warfare. In the 1850s Warm Springs Reservation was established for the Wascos and part of the Walla Wallas (who were joined by a portion of the Paiutes in 1864). In 1864 others of the Paiutes, Modocs, and Klamath Indians were gathered on the Kalamath Reservation in southern Oregon.

After the peaceful decade of the 1860s, the 1870s saw three Indian conflicts. The Modoc War in 1873 was caused by the refusal of Indians to stay on their reservation. After futile parlays, the assassination of two peace commissioners, and war on the lava beds, the Indians gave up. In 1877 a portion of the Nez Percés, objecting to going onto their tribal reservation, sought refuge in Canada in one of the most dramatic incidents of American Indian history. After a masterful retreat, the Indians were forced to surrender a mere thirty miles from safety in Canada. Chief Joseph's people spent the next dozen years in Kansas before being returned to the Colville Reservation in Washington. In 1878 the Bannock War raged briefly over Idaho and eastern Oregon. It was the last military conflict in the Pacific Northwest. The defeat of the Indians all along the frontier led to their placement on reservations, and to the long story of their willing or forced encounters with Europeans and Americans.

On the reservations the Indian people were expected to emulate white men and women. They were to become Christian, learn the English language, dress like whites, live in frame houses, and prepare for white vocations. Above all, they were to settle down and become farmers like the majority of the American people. The Indians, reluctant to change in any case, had little help from the representatives of white society. The government sent agents and teachers. The churches sent missionaries. But the agents were usually political appointees who were usually uninterested or incompetent. Most of the good agents left quickly because of discouragement over poor pay or Indian resistance to acculturation. The missionaries were somewhat more successful in gaining conversions, but the Indians had little enthusiasm for abandoning their old religion. Lack of interest, poor teachers, or unsuitable land made the Indians' agricultural experiences unhappy. Some resented being placed on reservations with members of other Indian groups. The remarkable thing is that so much of Indian culture remained for a better day that lay ahead.

NOTES

1. Merrill J. Mattes, *The Great Platte River Road: The Covered Wagon Mainline from Fort Kearney to Fort Laramie* (1979), p. 84.

2. Mattes, *The Great Platte River Road*, pp. 254, 256.

3. Mattes. *The Great Platte River Road*, pp. 78–79.

4. Mattes. *The Great Platte River Road*, p. 79.

SUGGESTIONS FOR READING

On Manifest Destiny, see Frederick Merk, *Manifest Destiny and Mission in American History: A Reinterpretation* (1963). For life in the Middle West, see William A. Bowen, *The Willamette Valley: Migration and Settlement on the Oregon Frontier* (1978) and John Mack Faragher, *Women and Men on the Overland Trail* (1979). For the trail experience, excellent studies besides Faragher are John D. Unruh, *The Plains Across: The Overland Emigrants and the Trans-Mississippi West, 1840–60* (1979); Julie Roy Jeffrey, *Frontier Women: The Trans-Mississippi West* (1979); and John Philip Reid, *Law for the Elephant: Property and Social Behavior on the Overland Trail* (1980). For representative books on nonwhites, see the suggestions for reading in chapter one for the Indians, and Robert M. Utley, *Frontiersmen in Blue: The United States Army and the Indian* (1967); Stephen Dow Beckham, *The Indians of Western Oregon: This Land Was Theirs* (1977); G. Thomas Edwards and Carlos Schwantes, eds., *Experiences in A Promised Land: Essays in Pacific Northwest History* (1986); Robert E. Wynne, *Reaction to the Chinese in the Pacific Northwest and British Columbia, 1850 to 1919* (1978); Lorraine B. Hildebrand, *Straw Hats, Sandals and Steel: The Chinese in Washington State* (1977); Nelson C. Ho, *Portland's Chinatown: A History of an Urban Ethnic District* (1978); Esther H. Mumford, *Seattle's Black Victorians, 1852–1901* (1980); Elizabeth McLagan, *A Peculiar Paradise: A History of Blacks in Oregon, 1788–1940* (1980); and Janice K. Duncan, *Minority without a Champion: Kanakas on the Pacific Coast, 1788–1850* (1972). On the Indian treaties and wars, see Kent D. Richards, *Isaac I. Stevens: Young Man in a Hurry* (1979).

Pioneer Politics, Economics, Culture, 1840–1880

American pioneers of every frontier were never anarchists. They wanted law and order, the protection of life and property. When there was no official government, no effective government, or no government at all, they provided one. This political tradition arose from the Mayflower Compact in 1620, was nurtured by informal governments developed in Kentucky and Tennessee, and spread to the agricultural claims clubs of the Middle West. It was carried to Oregon and applied there.

The Oregonians who adopted it in the 1830s and 1840s found themselves in a region with few settlers but several communities. The largest and most powerful at the beginning of this era was the HBC headed by the indefatigable Dr. John McLoughlin. It had the sole right by act of parliament in 1821 to rule over the British subjects in the area, but it also had to grapple with political problems that would overlap those of the residents who were not its employees. These persons included the former HBC employees who had retired from the fur trade to enter farming. They were French Canadian in culture, Catholic in religion. Their leader was Father (later Archbishop) Blanchet. Somewhat similar to them, both in prior and present occupation, were the American ex-mountain men such as Joseph Meek and Robert "Doc" Newell. Until its closing in 1844, the Methodist mission was a powerful institution, with economic holdings and political goals, as well as its spiritual endeavors. Last of all were the American farmers and businessmen, especially the first, who became the most numerous and influential group by the mid-1840s. The interplay of these various groups created the remarkable Oregon Provisional Government.

The Provisional Government

This process began with the joint occupation treaties of 1818 and 1827. These agreements between Britain and the United States postponed the question of sovereignty. So far as government was concerned, British subjects had the protection of the HBC, but the Americans were left to their own devices.

For a time the HBC, the French Canadians, the missionaries, and the mountain men coexisted reasonably well. For example, when Ewing Young, a former trapper, wanted to manufacture whiskey in 1836, McLoughlin and Jason Lee persuaded him to drop the project, but joined him to bring up stock from California in 1837 to begin the cattle business in Oregon. But in the last years of the decade, the Americans began to act on their own politically.

In 1838 the Methodists took two political steps. They appointed a justice of the peace and a constable from their own ranks. More important, they sent a petition to Congress asking for the application of American laws. Some French Canadians also signed this petition which stressed the need for government so that decent, hardworking American citizens would wish to come to Oregon.

In 1841 a need for American government became more apparent when Ewing Young, who had become prosperous, died without a will and without known heirs. How to dispose of his property? In February the Methodists chose a committee to call a general meeting to make laws and elect officers. Some French Canadians joined the committee, but no laws were adopted and only one officer was appointed, Ira Babcock, who served as probate judge until 1843. He was to administer the laws of New York state. In June of 1841 the French Canadians dropped out of the lawmaking process, under pressure from the HBC which feared the new government would be hostile to its interests, and government making languished until 1842.

Elijah White, the former missionary, returned to Oregon in September of that year with the position of sub-Indian agent given him by the president. The Methodists, who had dismissed him earlier, were fearful that he wanted to become governor of a new territory. They pushed forward their plans to organize a government themselves.

By 1843 their concerns, rumblings of discontent on the part of the Cayuse and Nez Percé east of the Cascades, and the arrival of several overland settlers in the previous year forced the issue. To the Methodist desire for a moral community, the pioneers added their passionate beliefs in popular self-government, in the agrarian myth of the superiority of farm life, and in Manifest Destiny. By this date, too, the Methodists were hostile to the HBC because of its lucrative mill site at Willamette Falls. Other Americans also resented the economic power of the great British firm.

In February and March 1843, several Americans and Canadians attended meetings to discuss raising money to pay bounties for wolves that were killing stock. By the March meeting it was agreed to form a government at a later time. This goal was accomplished in May. On the second of the month, at Champoeg, about one-half the adult population of the Willamette Valley conferred. The majority decided to "organize themselves into a civil community, and provide themselves with the protection, secured by the enforcement of law and order."[1] A committee was appointed, and later in the month, and in June, it drew up a constitution (the Organic Law) and several statutes. The laws created the familiar separation of powers into judicial, legislative, and executive (although there was not a governor, but a three-man executive committee) branches. The Oregon Country was divided into four counties, the traditional division of powers. Every settler was allowed to have a land claim of one square mile. Taxes were voluntary. The mission was permitted to have a claim of six square miles in extent. On July 5, 1843, at Champoeg, the Organic Law and the statutes were adopted.

The new government was pulled and hauled until its death in 1848. In 1843, over 800 settlers crossed the Oregon Trail. They made their political influence felt in the next year under the leadership of Peter Burnett. In May the newcomers took over the government by electing new officers. For expedient reasons, the HBC and the French Canadians joined the government to protect their land claims. In June the new coalition rewrote the laws by adding the power to tax; by requiring that newcomers register their land claims within twenty days of arrival; and by creating the position of governor, which was first filled by George Abernethy. The HBC was restored its land claim at Oregon City and the Methodists lost their special claim.

In 1845 the government continued in the hands of the American settlers who were willing to cooperate with the HBC. The central issue of the year was whether to establish a new constitution for an independent country or to continue with a government that was truly "provisional," that is, temporary until the boundary question was established and official United States jurisdiction extended to its part of Oregon. In June the settlers defeated a provision for a constitutional convention. The legislature, under the leadership of Jesse Applegate, revised the Organic Law to remove all the statutory legislation from it. It also worked out an accord with the HBC whereby the company agreed to pay taxes on all its goods brought into Oregon for resale. The new organic law also created a county (Vancouver) north of the Columbia River in which the HBC would control appointments for judge and sheriff.

The record of the provisional government was a mixed one. It kept the peace. It provided a rudimentary record of land titles. It was flexible enough to accommodate or mediate the interests of different groups. It provided a mechanism for the transfer of power from the Methodists to the American farmers. But it was not able to handle the problems of Indian relations. The provisional government, indeed, never attempted any program to facilitate the adjustment of Caucasian and native American. Thus when the Whitman massacre occurred, all the government could do was to wage the unsuccessful Cayuse War against the Indians. Its army's campaigns were complete failures. The only way the hostages were recovered and the murderers surrendered was by the provisional government begging the HBC to act for it. Peter Skene Ogden accomplished the job without loss of life and without payment. The Cayuse War fiasco was the last straw for the provisional government. Its citizens welcomed the treaty of 1846 and the organization of Oregon Territory in August 1848. They were giving up full self-government, but gaining a traditional structure of government that they hoped would soon lead to statehood.

Oregon Territory

The territory as a unit of government in the United States had a long history. The first territory was created in the Northwest Ordinance of 1787 that set the pattern of a government that was part appointive, part elective, part paternal, part democratic. In the federal territories Congress paid the salaries of officials, provided a territorial library, and financed public buildings and military affairs. Congress also had to approve all laws of the territorial legislature. The president of the United States appointed the territorial governor, secretary, and three judges. The voters of the territory (white males and half-whites over twenty-one years of age) elected a two-house legislature (the assembly and the council) and a nonvoting delegate to Congress who functioned more as a lobbyist to the various branches of government than as a legislator.

Joseph Lane, an Indiana Democratic politician, frontiersman, and general in the Mexican War, was Oregon's first governor. The issues he faced were weighty but not numerous. The most pressing was the question of land ownership. When Congress created the territory, it upheld the existing laws of the provisional government with the notable exception of the land laws. Pioneers worried extensively over this concern.

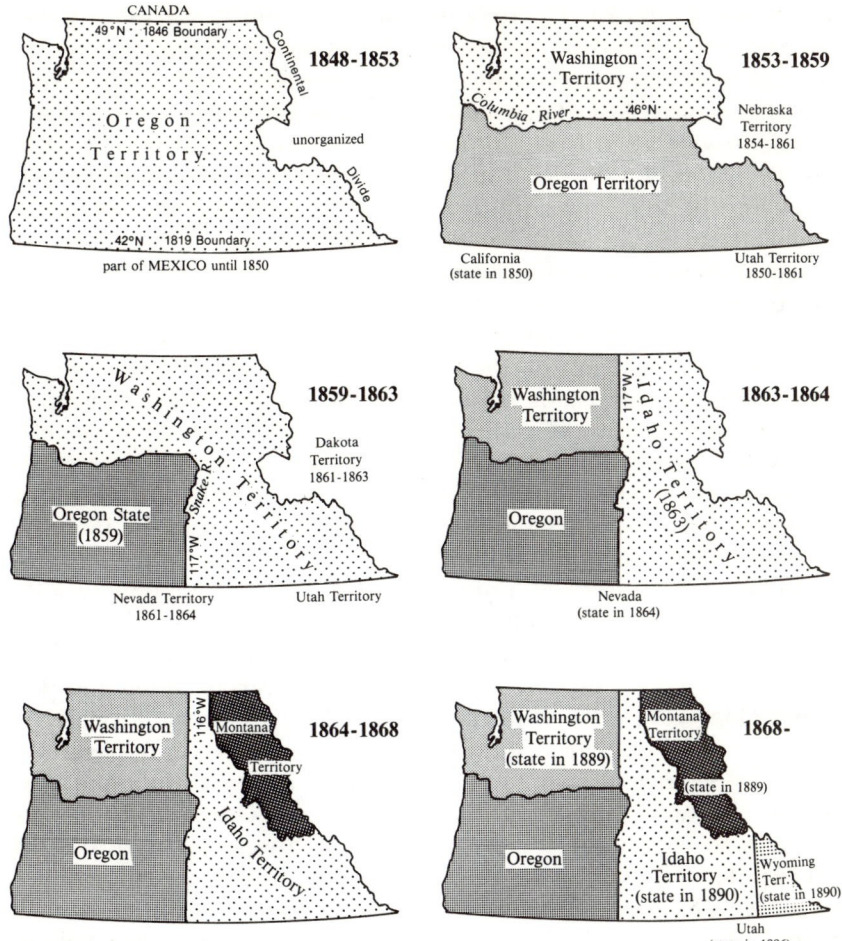

From Territories to Statehood

Only Congress could grant land from the public domain. Oregonians and future Oregonians hoped that Congress would ratify the promises of politicians, both within and without the territory, who had long argued that its settlers should be rewarded by grants of free land for the dangerous work of extending the frontier. Fortunately, there was a precedent, a statute of 1842 that gave free homesteads to occupants of the Florida frontier.

Congress, indeed, did recognize the contributions of the settlers of the Pacific Northwest. The Oregon Donation Land Act of 1850 applied both to the past and to the future. A man who had cultivated a land claim for four consecutive years before December 1, 1850, was given 320 acres in his own right. If married, or if he married within a year, his wife received another 320 acres. Those who came between December 1, 1850, and December 1, 1853, got 160 acres, with their wives receiving another 160 acres. In 1853, the law was extended to those arriving before December 1, 1855. Although hailed by the settlers, the Donation Act led to new difficulties with the Indians.

In Oregon, as elsewhere on the frontier, the public domain was not to be disposed of until the Indian title was cleared. In the early 1850s, first a group of commissioners, then Oregon superintendent of Indian affairs, Anson Dart, made treaties with the Indians of the Willamette Valley. These agreements put the Indians on reservations, but included the sensible provision that the reservation would include part of the ancestral domains. But because this policy would place the Indians in close proximity to the whites, Congress, at the request of the pioneers, rejected the treaties and Dart resigned.

While the settlers south of the Columbia River were opposing the treaties and fighting the Indians in the Rogue and Umpqua valleys, they were peaceably reducing their domain to the north. At Monticello (later Longview) on November 25, 1852, settlers met in convention and petitioned Congress for a new territory north of the Columbia River. Their neighbors south of the river were quick to endorse the request. The territorial legislature and Joseph Lane, now territorial delegate, supported partition. They did so for three reasons. Oregon's chances for becoming a state would be greater if the area were reduced to a size smaller than the largest existing state. Oregonians hoped that a new territory (and eventual state) would increase the power of the Pacific Coast in Washington D. C. and further the chances for greater military appropriations and a transcontinental railroad. A smaller region would also relieve Oregon of the problems of HBC claims north of the Columbia. Congress and President Franklin Pierce concurred in the Oregonians' wish and Washington became a territory in 1853.

Its first governor was Isaac I. Stevens. A man of energy and decision, Stevens was of New England roots and educated at West Point where he graduated first in his class. He had served in the Corps of Engineers and was on the fields of battle in the war with Mexico. Now he had arrived in the Pacific Northwest, not only as governor, but as superintendent of Indian affairs for the new territory. Furthermore, he arrived as engineer in charge of surveying a northern route for a transcontinental railroad from the Great Lakes country to Puget Sound. As we have seen he also received and discharged the task of liquidating Indian title to the land.

Governor Isaac Ingalls Stevens. Oregon Historical Society

Political Issues in Oregon Territory

The Oregon territorial government had to address a range of issues. Governor Lane and the first legislators grappled with the question of federal-state relations. Oregonians wanted the national government to pay the costs of the Indian wars. They lobbied Congress, successfully as we have seen, to pass a law securing title to land. They urged the president to appoint better qualified territorial officials. Legislators considered the position of nonwhites, as had their predecessors in the provisional government. In this matter, racism continued to prevail. Congress, in organizing the Oregon Territory, had prohibited slavery. The territorial legislature in 1849 prohibited the residence of free black persons, but in 1854 this law was by error placed on a list of statutes to be repealed. Attempts to reenact it were never successful.

But the most urgent issue was none of these. Rather, the great concern was statehood. Citizens of every territory of course hoped eventually to become citizens of states free and equal to others within the union. The controversy was over when statehood would occur and, more specifically, when statehood would be to the advantage of which political party. For Oregonians had not only built their provisional government on traditional bases, and had been eager to replace it by a federal territory, they were also conservative in importing political parties. Indeed both the institution of the political party itself and the particular parties were traditional. Asahel Bush, a young newspaperman and lawyer from Massachusetts, had been the moving force in creating the Democratic party in 1852. It was the dominant party for most of the decade. In the next year the Whig party was organized. Two years later the Free Soilers were on the scene and in 1857 the Republican party formed. For most of the 1850s the parties contested elections in terms of personalities and patronage—not issues, and certainly not national issues like slavery expansion, which could easily become divisive.

Statehood

Statehood was a typical partisan issue. Democrats favored it because more offices were elected in a state than in a territory and, as the majority party, they anticipated winning these offices. Whigs favored retaining territorial status because, whenever there was a Whig president, he would appoint Whig officeholders. The voters rejected a call for a state constitution in 1854, 1855, and 1856. But in 1857 they decided to form a state because all parties joined in this cause. The reason they changed their mind was national politics.

Oregonians had always opposed slavery. Almost everyone in the nation agreed that states could permit or forbid slavery. The great political issue of pre–Civil War America was slavery in the territories. By early 1857 the Supreme Court in the Dred Scott case had declared that territories had no right to exclude slavery. Thus if Oregon were to keep clear of slavery, the voters had best to move promptly for statehood.

In August 1857, a constitutional convention was held at Salem. It took almost exactly one month to write the constitution. The sixty delegates created a document that was drawn from the constitutions of the middle western states with which they were most familiar. There was almost nothing new in it, again proof of the conservatism of the voters. The explosive issues, two racial matters, were kept out of the main body of the constitution and referred to the voters in separate questions. In

November the people spoke. They approved the constitution and voted to prohibit slavery and the residence of free black persons.

But it took fourteen months for Oregon to be admitted to the Union. One reason was national politics. Northern representatives and senators objected to the residence clause, Southerners, to the antislavery provision. Republicans were hostile to the admission of a Democratic state. Other northern territories, Minnesota and Kansas, were also applying. Another objection was nonpolitical. Oregon did not reach the required population until at least 1870. Finally, on February 14, 1859, Oregon by a narrow vote became the thirty-third state.

National politics in the late 1850s also shifted the party balance in Oregon. The dominant Democrats divided. The Republicans, incorporating members of other parties, gained. As in the nation as a whole, the Democratic split was over slavery expansion. Some Democrats (in Oregon led by Asahel Bush) favored the view of United States Senator Stephen A. Douglas that the people of each state or territory could decide the slavery question. Prosouthern Democrats (in Oregon, Lane was their spokesman) joined President James Buchanan in arguing that the United States Constitution required Congress to make slavery lawful in every territory. Division between Douglas and Buchanan Democrats mounted as the presidential election of 1860 drew near. Three major candidates were in the race in that campaign: Abraham Lincoln (Republican); Stephen A. Douglas (northern Democrat); and John C. Breckinridge (southern Democrat). A curiosity about the last candidate is that he selected as his vice-presidential choice Joseph Lane who took, as a matter of principle, the unpopular course in his own state of running with a proslavery, pro-states' rights, and implicitly secessionist candidate.

Abraham Lincoln won the state but without a majority of the popular vote. His platform planks opposing slavery expansion into the territories, advocating a Pacific railroad, and endorsing free homestead legislation, and his staunch unionism, carried the day. Republican Edward D. Baker, an Illinois friend and law partner of Lincoln, was chosen as one United States senator, and James W. Nesmith, a Douglas Democrat, as the second. Again in these contests support for the Union was triumphant.

In Washington Territory, too, the pre–Civil War years saw a party realignment. Governor Stevens was the most prominent Democrat, but there was not a machine like the Salem Clique. The Republicans organized in 1857. They gained strength as the Democratic division deepened over the Buchanan-Douglas slavery controversy. Stevens was elected delegate in 1857 and 1859 and served the Breckinridge-Lane ticket as campaign manager in 1860. But the Republicans and Unionist Democrats controlled the territory after the outbreak of the Civil War in 1861.

Oregon was also pro–Union during the war, although there were some neutralists and even prosouthern citizens (the federal government suppressed several newspapers in Oregon). But the Pacific Northwest was the region least affected by the Civil War. Two prominent citizens joined the Union army and gave their lives in the early years of the war: Edward Baker, who had resigned from the Senate, at Ball's Bluff; and Isaac Stevens, who had resigned as delegate, at Chantilly. For most Northwesterners, however, the war had little effect. Citizens joined military units that were mustered into federal service, but they were assigned to military posts within the region to release the regulars for fighting the Confederates. Women made bandages and clothes for the war effort and citizens contributed money to the cause. Unless one had a friend or relative in combat, the Civil War was literally and figuratively a distant event.

Urban Life

The first settlers of the old Oregon Country gathered in both urban and rural areas. Founding towns went hand in hand with the creation of farms and occurred at almost the same time in the regions that would become Oregon and Washington.

The beginnings of town life in Oregon went back to the efforts of both Methodist missionaries and the Hudson's Bay Company. John McLoughlin laid out Oregon City at the falls of the Willamette in 1842. The Methodists established Salem (then called Chemeketa) when they moved their headquarters from Mission Bottom in 1841. The ruling Democratic party made it the territorial capital in 1851. The origin of Portland was a land claim made by William Overton and Francis W. Pettygrove in 1845. Other men dreamed of great cities arising at Milwaukie, St. Helens, Linnton (near St. Johns), and a dozen other sites along the Willamette and Columbia rivers.

Residents of the small villages and towns had one main task to perform before they could achieve their dreams of growth. This task was somehow to join the wheat belt of the Tualatin River to the Columbia for export to the outside world. Of course the hopes and dreams also had to include the development of markets in that world. Indeed, until the 1840s, there were no markets for farmers and merchants in Oregon except for the arriving pioneers and (infrequently) the posts of the Hudson's Bay Company.

All of this changed dramatically at the end of the decade. Gold was discovered in California. The Pacific Northwest was the closest source of lumber, wheat, flour, and beef as the gold miners had neither time nor inclination to provide their own food or shelter, although California had the abundant potential for both. Puget Sound, with its immense stands of trees adjacent to its splendid harbors, captured the California lumber market.

Portland took charge of the rest of the business. The city became the metropolis of the new territory, indeed of the entire Pacific Northwest, because of two developments. First, ship captains determined that the city was the reliable head of navigation, although in good years ships could go as far as Eugene another 169 miles. (Any passage beyond Oregon City, however, required expensive transshipment around the falls at that place.) Second, Portlanders built a crude wagon road over the hills into the Tualatin valley to tap the wheat trade. Its rivals were too far away from the valley, or on the wrong side of the Columbia, or blocked off by mountains, or lacking in ambition.

The gold rush provided great benefits to the Northwest. It furnished the first reliable export market. It gave the region its first sound money supply, gold dust. It diversified the population by adding more businessmen to the stock of farmers. It stimulated citizens to seek further development principally by transportation improvements. By 1851 George Abernethy, now a local merchant, had a line of sailing vessels

S.W. Front Street, Portland, c. 1852. Oregon Historical Society

"Wide West," Oregon Steam Navigation Company. Oregon Historical Society

running to San Francisco, and Robert Aspinwall, a national shipping magnate, had scheduled steamships to San Francisco, with connections to New York from that place.

Portland, the chief beneficiary of this economic progress, became the main supplier of the next gold rush, that to southern Oregon. After 1851 people hurried from California, Oregon, and Washington to the banks of the Rogue River. From Jacksonville to Gold Beach instant communities emerged. Chinese and blacks mingled with Caucasians and all skirmished with the Indians. The expanding population needed supplies of all types. Much of what they required came from Portland, down the Willamette Valley on the backs of mules and horses. When the Rogue River gold fields faded out in 1854, the town's hopes turned to supplying the soldiers fighting the Indian wars around the Northwest and to continuing as wholesale and retail centers for the farmers, and for the miners rushing to strikes in northern Washington around Colville in 1856 and to British Columbia in 1858.

In 1860 news arrived in the western cities of gold strikes in eastern Oregon and eastern Washington, and then of other discoveries in what is now Idaho and Montana. Miners hastened to the new diggings, but the chief gainers, as always on the miners' frontier, were the suppliers: farmers, merchants, transportation men. New towns sprang up to cash in on the mineral rushes, but the old ones profited most. Walla Walla was given new life as a secondary supply center, but Portland was the principal supplier.

Its businessmen, led by John C. Ainsworth, Simeon G. Reed, and Robert R. Thompson, founded the Oregon Steam Navigation Company in 1860. Its fast, well-maintained steamships connected Portland with the gold fields of Montana and Idaho. Profits from the OSNC and from other Portland businesses serving the miners formed the base of regional enterprises more enduring than the mines. As mining pulled the Northwest out of economic doldrums, many of the foundations of regional industry were laid in the decade of the 1860s.

Washington Towns

North of the Columbia River, Michael Simmons and a few other settlers laid out the first town, New Market (later called Tumwater) in 1845. Nicholas Delin, a Swede, placed the first claim in what would be Tacoma in 1851. George Washington Bush, the black pioneer, established Bush Prairie thirty miles northeast of Olympia in 1845. Another black resident, George Bush, founded Centerville, later Centralia, in 1850. In 1851 Port Townsend was settled and in the same year a little group whose leader was Arthur Denny, came to Elliott Bay to become the pioneers of Seattle. In all of these communities, the initial hope was to group together for companionship, but then hopes turned to market and supply centers, mill towns, and governmental sites. Henry Yesler, the Seattle sawmill owner, was typical of many whose income was derived from the chief business of Puget Sound, lumber. All over the Sound nature had provided a paradise for lumbermen. The towering forests of fir and spruce grew to the water's edge. The harbors were deep all the way to the shore. Transportation costs from stump to ship were minimal as logs could be dragged to mills and to docks. (The tracks to Yesler's mill in Seattle was the world's first "Skid Road.")

For many years Seattle was but one of many small communities on Puget Sound. But in 1865 its fortunes changed. Men found coal at Issaquah across Lake Washington to the east of the little community on Elliott Bay. Seattle became the supply center for the mines. It also rose above its rivals because its central location made it the focus for supplying lumber camps around the Sound. As the mining and lumber trades grew, the city's commercial hopes increased with the development of plans to throw a wagon road across the Cascades to Walla Walla, to build local railroads to expand the territory, and, above all, to gain the great prize of the western terminal of the transcontinental railroad. But this important decision would not be made until the next era.

Meanwhile, in Tacoma to the south, citizens also built their commercial hopes upon a variety of possibilities. Portland investors, starting in 1868, began pouring money into the land along the shores of Commencement Bay. Their hopes were in traces of bituminous coal found in the adjacent hills; in the forested hinterland that promised fortunes in lumber; and in the deep waters of the harbor. Commencement Bay made Tacoma a potential site for the northwestern transcontinental. The harbor, the abundant and flat shore facilities for wharves, and the availability of cheap land led the Northern Pacific Railroad to select Tacoma for the terminal in 1872 and in the next year the line from Kalama on the Columbia to Tacoma was completed. But this was a short link; another decade was to pass before the railroad connected Kalama with the Middle West.

Industries and Transportation

The earliest, longest lasting, and, for many years, most dynamic industry in the Northwest began at the time of the California gold rush. The huge trees, dense forests, and deep harbors of Washington were the ingredients that nature had provided for the lumber business. Most of the first lumbermen came from New England. These entrepreneurs connected the forests of Washington with the markets of California by a fleet of sailing vessels. Although there were many companies in the lumber business, a few large ones dominated. They included the Puget Mill Company based at Port Gamble, an enterprise funded by Pope and Talbot of New England in 1852; the Washington Mill Company in 1857; the Meigs firm founded in 1860; the Port Blakely Mill Company begun in 1863; and the Tacoma Mill Company organized in 1869. The majority of the successful firms shared four characteristics: they were created and controlled by San Francisco capital; they broadened their market base with the passing years; they had their own California yards and their own ships; and they modernized their production facilities from mechanized equipment to company towns.

All along the Columbia and at the mouths of the coastal rivers salmon canneries sprang up. Led by John West and the Hume brothers, William, George, and Robert, businessmen linked the great Chinooks, American fishermen, Chinese cannery workers, and British markets. For a few decades it seemed that both the supplies of fish and the appetites of industrial workers in the English midlands were limitless. Australia, New Zealand, and South America also furnished markets.

The paper industry began in Oregon City in 1866 with the mill of W. W. Buck. Other entrepreneurs soon joined him in employing local

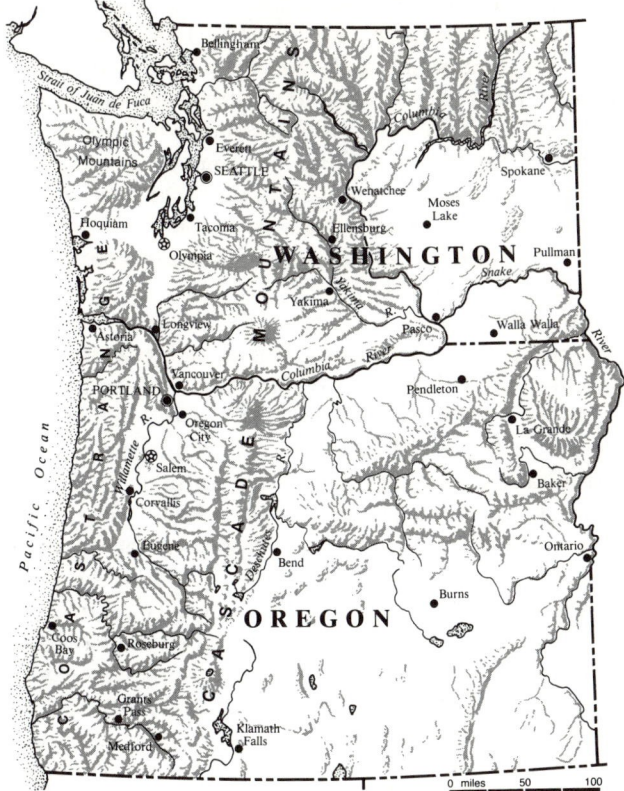

Major Cities and Towns of the Pacific Northwest

women and Chinese migrants for labor. China, too, furnished some of the supplies of rags from which paper was made. Although papermaking was not very profitable in those years, the basis for one of the Northwest's great industries was laid. This was the case also with the woolen business. The Willamette Valley was sheep country but the animals had hitherto found only a local market. Now capital was available to furnish the expanding population with wool and cloth. The first mill was put into operation at Salem in 1857. As in so many cases in the Pacific Northwest, the technical knowledge and the machinery itself in the new business came from the East or from abroad. By 1870 there were six woolen mills in the region, all of them in Oregon.

Others' hopes for economic modernization rested on the iron industry. A few miles south of Portland lay Sucker Lake (now Lake Oswego). Near its shores were discovered iron ore deposits and William S.

Ladd, one of the founders of the Oregon Steam Navigation Company, formed the Oregon Iron Company in 1867. The company worked off and on until 1894 when it failed. Its problems were those of any colonial manufacturing enterprise. The iron deposits were spotty in quantity and low-grade in quality. There was a shortage of skilled labor. The problem of fuel was serious as coal was lacking and charcoal was expensive. Ladd and his fellow investors were reluctant to risk much capital as safer investments, especially real estate, beckoned. Above all, the markets were uncertain: the local one was too small and the cost of transportation to distant ones was prohibitive.

Besides the OSNC, this was a period of ventures in transportation and communications. Businessmen projected wagon roads to link the great arteries of the Columbia and Willamette to expanding hinterlands. Roads were planned to central Oregon and to the coast as the population of these regions increased. Grants of land were given to their promoters by government, land that was to be sold for construction costs. Land was often sold, but frequently corruptly, and few miles were built. The railroad also came in this era. One of the reasons for Seattle's rise was the building of small local lines to the coal mines and lumber camps.

The growth of Portland led in 1867 to the formation of a stage line, the Oregon and California, which ran from Portland to Sacramento. In the following year Ben Holladay appeared in the Pacific Northwest. He was a transportation magnate, an imperial figure in the stage and express business of the Trans-Mississippi West. Holladay secured a land grant from the Oregon legislature to build a railroad down the east bank of the Willamette toward California. The legislature also chartered a rival corporation headed by Joseph Gaston, a Portlander, to follow the west side of the river. Through political pressure and the outright buying of votes, Holladay persuaded the legislature to consolidate the grants under his direction. Actual construction was slow, as the railroad had only reached Roseburg by 1873. Finally, communication was facilitated by the construction of a telegraph line from California to Portland in 1864.

In spite of the desire for industrialization, the promotional literature, the commercial meetings, the letters to the editor, and other publicity for it, the Northwest economy was basically agricultural.

Farmers and Farming

Like any venture, farm making and farming was composed of scores of decisions. In a new country there were even more than usual. But one thing was certain to the pioneers—they must rely on their immediate family. Just as the influence of kinfolk was decisive in choosing to come to the Northwest, and vital on the journey itself, so too did people tend to settle among the lands of their kinsmen in the new country.

If the immigrants were fortunate, they or their relatives had made a selection of a farmstead that would endure for generations. This choice involved more than the selection of an area of good soil. The heart of the farm was prairie land, free of trees because of hundreds of years of natural conflagrations or burning by the Indians. But farms also needed to be located near the groves of trees that were dotted through the prairies. Trees were important because they provided a stock of lumber for houses and outbuildings, the only source of fuel and fencing, food for human beings, and food for the swine that rooted up the camas that grew in the forests and that gorged upon the fallen acorns.

Experience back in the Ohio or Missouri valleys also taught them what land to avoid. Dense woods were anathema. The hill country should be avoided. And the land of the river banks, even though it was rich soil and close to transportation routes, was unpromising also. It brought back too many harsh memories of floods and malaria. It also was found to be soil hard to break and lacking in springs, which the settlers preferred to river water for drinking.

After land selection, the pioneers planned their planting. Although conservative in most respects, the early settlers were adventuresome in crop selection. They tried almost everything from flax to tobacco. But their great hopes were in the two traditional frontier crops, wheat and corn. Wheat was most important. It grew abundantly, it was easy to raise, it kept and shipped well. It provided not only food for local people, but also a valuable export. Oats were the second most important crop. A third staple was potatoes, mainly an article for home consumption as it could not be safely shipped long distances. If wheat, oats, and potatoes were the great successes, corn was an abysmal failure. Here the climate of the Northwest failed the pioneers as the nights were too cool and the growing season too short.

Farm life was based in large part upon animals for power and for food. In 1837 Ewing Young, with financial aid from Lee and McLoughlin, had brought from California the first herd of cattle to the Pacific Northwest. These Spanish cattle proliferated in the Willamette Valley on the free range of wild grasses. Tough and sinewy, they provided beef and milk for the first generation settlers who supplemented them with stock drives across the plains. Gradually some farmers built up the bloodlines of their herds, agreeing to the extra work of fencing and feeding in exchange for the greater profitability of high quality herds.

Horses were almost as easy to obtain as wild cattle. They were acquired from the Cayuse, Nez Percé, and other horse Indians of the plateau country. Farmers argued the merits of the horses and oxen as draft animals, but the supply of both was ample. Some farmers had flocks of sheep, too. Swine were a farmer's ideal animal. They ran wild, eating camas and acorns, gleaning in the fields after harvest, and were fed whey and skim milk from the household. They bred prolifically and their meat was easy to preserve.

Agricultural techniques in the Pacific Northwest in the pioneer generation were primitive. By modern standards—indeed by progressive contemporary standards—they were careless and wasteful. The reasons for this "wasteful" farming was not that Oregon farmers were evil men and women, contemptuous of the environment and scornful of the welfare of future generations. Rather it was a matter of dollars and cents. Land was cheaper than labor. Why be a conservative farmer when the market provided a profit without hiring the expensive labor necessary to farm carefully?

The Economy East of the Cascades

Although most pioneers settled in the Willamette Valley and around Puget Sound, a small number of particularly adventurous men and women opened up other parts of the Pacific Northwest. The main economic components of this development were mining, farming, and stockraising. Miners were in the foothills of Oregon's Blue Mountains in 1861. To meet their needs merchants created the town of Auburn in the next year, the first urban development in the northeastern part of the state. Other towns sprang up to serve the miners going to the diggings of Idaho and Montana in the 1860s.

Farmers appeared in the river valleys of central Oregon in the 1860s also, and on the high benchlands north and south of the Columbia a decade later. Other farmers came to the Powder River valley of Northeastern Oregon in the 1860s and to the Wallowa River country in the 1870s. By the latter half of the 1870s the vanguard of farmers was in the Palouse Country of eastern Washington.

Sheepmen in the late 1860s and 1870s came to the region south of The Dalles, to the area between the John Day and the Deschutes rivers, and to the Umatilla River country. The cattlemen advanced into central and southern Oregon in the 1850s and 1860s because the flat terrain and the nutritious bunchgrass gave them a free hand. In northeastern Oregon cattlemen sought out the Grande Ronde River valley and the Powder River valley in the early 1860s and the Wallowa Country in the late 1870s. In Washington cattlemen first ran their stock on the north bank of the Columbia and in the Yakima Valley in the 1850s; by

1870 they were in the Kittitas Valley and in the scablands of southeastern Washington north of the Snake River.

Towns arose to serve the surrounding regions as markets and supply centers for them. The most important in Oregon were The Dalles and Prineville in the central part of the state; Klamath Falls in the south; and Pendleton, Baker, La Grande, Joseph, and Enterprise in the northeastern section. Washington's most important communities established before 1880 were the old fur trade and mission center, Walla Walla; Yakima City in the central region; and Colfax in the Palouse River country.

Pioneer Cultural Life

The pioneer generation of Oregon and Washington repeated familiar cultural patterns. They copied their homes and churches and mills from their former places of residence. Thus architecture in the Willamette Valley or Puget Sound resembled that of the middle western frontier, which in turn was derived from the Atlantic South, New England, and French Canada. In religious life both Protestants and Catholics introduced nothing new in church doctrine or church government. In Oregon, as we have mentioned, the Methodist mission became a settled church. Its first congregation was formed in Oregon City in 1844. First churches of other denominations were Congregational (1847), Episcopalian (1851), Presbyterian (1854), and Baptist (1872), all in Portland. Temple Beth Israel, the first Jewish congregation, was founded in 1858 in Portland. A Methodist congregation at Steilacoom in 1853 was the first religious foundation in Washington.

As on earlier frontiers, the churches engaged in educational activities. Religious education began with the Methodist missionaries in 1834. Other denominations followed. The first public school in Oregon was started in Portland in 1851 with John Outhouse as teacher. Secondary education remained in the hands of the churches or of private academies until the first public high school came to Portland in 1869. Denominations also initiated college education, the Methodists' Willamette University tracing its roots to the year 1842. Other early Oregon colleges included Pacific University (1849) founded at Forest Grove and the University of Oregon, the first state-supported university, established in 1876.

In 1852, while Washington was still a part of Oregon Territory, the first public school was founded north of the Columbia at Washougal. The Washington territorial legislature authorized local public schools in 1854. The first public high school opened in Dayton in 1880. At the college level, the first institution was public, not private. Arthur Denney and other Seattle founders gave the land for the University of Washington which opened in what is now downtown Seattle in 1861. The first private college, what later became named Whitman College, admitted its first class at Walla Walla in 1865. Most of the early educational endeavors, private or public, were primitive by the standards of the East or the Middle West. College curriculum and facilities measured up no better. In some form the pioneers would work to give their children instruction in reading, writing, and arithmetic. The tiny minority that went on to high school or college was suspect as pretentious and parasitic. At these levels most public institutions were supported grudgingly.

One great frontier educational institution was the newspaper. Readers found their newspapers written in vitriol. The news columns as well as the editorials reflected the prejudices and opinions of their owner-editors. Papers concentrated on biased reporting of local politics, leavened by outpourings of local verse, advertisements, and letters to the editor. News from beyond the region was months late, but nonetheless eagerly devoured. The first of the region's newspapers was the *Spectator*, founded at Oregon City in 1846. More important was Asahel Bush's *Statesman*, established at Oregon City in 1851, but moved to Salem in 1853. It was the mouthpiece of the state Democratic machine. Similar political service for the Whigs and later the Republicans was furnished by Thomas J. Dryer's *Oregonian*, started in 1850 in Portland. Washington's first newspapers were the Olympia *Columbian* (1852) and the Steilacoom *Puget Sound Courier* (1855).

Beyond the church, the school, and the newspaper there was little formal culture. It is too much to expect anything of quality in a poor, underdeveloped region. Local people did attempt verse, fiction, and drama, but not a single one was of national standard. Two were, however, enormously controversial. One was Margaret Jewett Bailey's *The Grains, or Passages in the Life of Ruth Rover*. The other was Whig editor William Adams's play, *Treason, Strategem, and Spoils*, published in 1852. It was a satirical attack upon the Democratic Salem clique as grasping and ruthless political hacks and spoilsmen. The clique attempted to acquire the entire press run to destroy it, but a few copies escaped.

A Colonial Region

On the eve of the greatest development in the economic history of the Pacific Northwest, the coming of the transcontinental railroad, the region was expanding but it remained a colonial area. It was an exporter of raw materials, like wheat, or of partially finished goods, like lumber. There was very little manufacturing of finished goods. In return for raw materials, the Northwest imported the products of a rapidly industrializing United States. Colonialism also meant the importation of labor and most of the population growth of Oregon and Washington from 1850 was due to migration. Capital also flowed in from around the country. Very little was raised locally—the Oregon Steam Navigation Company and some of the investments in the salmon canning business were exceptions. The federal government also supplied capital in the form of monies to finance Indian wars and the expenses of territorial government, and of land grants for military roads and railroad corporations. Perhaps most important of all, the plans, projects, and dreams for the burgeoning colonial economy came from men sitting at desks hundreds of miles away from the Pacific Northwest.

Thus it was that most residents of the Pacific Northwest, in political, economic, and cultural affairs, were psychologically divided. On the one hand, they prided themselves on their heritage. They were free and independent citizens of a growing region. Their farms, towns, and cities were progressive and growing. Their cultural institutions were taking root. But along with their confidence and pride went a sense of inferiority. The people were in many aspects of life not decision makers. They were indeed colonial subjects.

NOTES

1. David C. Duniway and Neil R. Riggs, eds., "The Oregon Archives, 1841–1843," *Oregon Historical Quarterly*, 60 (June 1959): 236.

SUGGESTIONS FOR READING

The political history of the Northwest is told in Robert W. Johannsen, *Frontier Politics and the Sectional Conflict: The Pacific Northwest on the Eve of the Civil War* (1955); James E. Hendrickson, *Joe Lane of Oregon: Machine Politics and the Sectional Crisis, 1849–1861* (1967); Kent D. Richards, *Isaac I. Stevens: Young Man in a Hurry* (1979); and Eugene H. Berwanger, *The Frontier Against Slavery: Western Anti-Negro Prejudice and the Slavery Expansion Controversy* (1967). On urbanization, see Roger Sale, *Seattle: Past to Present* (1976); Murray C. Morgan, *Puget's Sound: A Narrative of Early Tacoma and the Southern Sound* (1979); and Arthur L. Throckmorton, *Oregon Argonauts: Merchant Adventurers on the Western Frontier* (1961). Economic life is discussed in Throckmorton and in Oscar O. Winther, *The Old Oregon Country: A History of Frontier Trade, Transportation, and Travel* (1950); Eugene E. Snyder, *Early Portland: Stump Town Triumphant; Rival Towns on the Willamette, 1831–1854* (1970); Paul W. Gates, *The Farmers Age: Agriculture, 1815–1860* (1960); and John R. Finger, "Henry L. Yesler's Seattle Years, 1852–1892," Ph.D. diss., University of Washington, 1968.

The People of
the Northwest, 1880–1920

As the decade of the 1880s opened, the Pacific Northwest awaited the transcontinental railroad. It was expected with eagerness, indeed with tremendous hope. It was the symbol of progress, wealth, and modernity. It also became the agent of great changes across the broad spectrum of life in the region. It ushered in forty years or so of economic growth that continued until after the First World War. These four decades also witnessed enormous changes in cultural affairs and in politics. The people who lived through this era were a more cosmopolitan group than had resided here before.

The Indians' New World

For the oldest inhabitants, the native Americans, the times necessitated continuing adjustments to pressures from the white world. The changes came from a new direction taken by federal Indian policy. Always before the government had expected that the Indians would adjust communally to the Caucasian world. There were reservation farms, reservation shops, reservation ranches. There was no individual ownership of these economic assets. By the 1880s many white Americans, interested in the welfare of the Indians, became convinced that the poverty, degradation, and ill health of the Indians was caused by their lack of individual responsibility for their property. The reformers, aided by pressures from Westerners who coveted reservation lands, prevailed, and in 1887 Congress passed the Dawes Act. This law permitted the president of the United States, at his discretion, to break up Indian reservations into individual land holdings (division "in severalty") which could not be sold for a period of twenty-five years (the trust period). When a reservation was divided, the Indians were forced to choose their individual allotment. If they did not do so, the allotments would be chosen for them. Citizenship came with the allotments.

The severalty principle was applied to several reservations in the Northwest under provisions of the Dawes Act or similar statutes. Its advocates compared the Dawes Act to the freeing of the slaves and called it the Act of Indian Emancipation. But their high hopes were dashed. For the Indians lost their land promptly after the trust period was over. Some Indians had spent the trust period leasing their land to whites, not in learning economic skills as individuals. Some sold their land after the trust period ended. Others lost their land for failure to pay taxes. Still others settled on poor land, or had poor land chosen for them, and could not make a living.

In the Dawes Act era some Indians tried pursuits other than farming land individually. Many continued casual employment on and off the reservation, working as cooks, maids, and handymen in homes of reservation employees or of white persons in adjacent towns or distant cities. Some entered the freighting business, while a fortunate few were able to raise cattle. Others practiced occupations from precontact days: hunting, fishing, trapping, gathering foods, and making baskets. On the far side of the law there were those who supplemented their income by logging the reservation lands illegally.

The Dawes Act also was intended to bring Indians into the mainstream of political life. It granted the Indians, along with their allotments of land, citizenship and its rights and privileges, including that of voting. In practice, the states restricted the right to vote and in 1906 Congress revised the Dawes Act to accord citizenship only after the end of the trust period.

In spite of these frustrations the native Americans did gain some experience in democratic political life. One result, at least on all large reservations, was that the politically minded Indians organized themselves into factions that disputed policies of the government or the actions of their agent. One issue (that divided whites as well as Indians) everywhere was the nature of education, which dissolved into two large questions. Should education be classical or vocational? Should education, regardless of the curriculum, be conducted at day schools on the reservation or in boarding schools such as at Chemawa in Salem, Oregon, or Carlisle in distant Pennsylvania? Some said education at home was humane and maintained the family unit. Others argued that parents and grandparents dragged their children back into Indian ways and that boarding school was the way to liberating integration and into the world.

Chief Joseph's camp at Nespalem, Colville Reservation. Eastern Washington State Historical Society

Some said Indian education should be vocational to bring them into the economic mainstream. Others said such training would relegate Indians to manual pursuits forever.

In cultural and social matters the tension between the old and new worlds continued. The forces for assimilation included the pressures of the agent and his subordinates: teachers, blacksmiths, carpenters, doctors, interpreters, and clerical workers. They and their families were the most immediate models. Those who worked off the reservation also obtained more than a glimpse of the Caucasian world. The schools affected not only the children, but also their parents who, whether or not they favored the new education, had to react to it by acceptance or rejection, for the whole point of the schools was to teach children to abandon their parents' ways.

The church continued to be a force for assimilation. Indeed, for a time, church and state were combined on the reservation as a result of action taken by President Ulysses S. Grant. The president became convinced that the way to root out corruption and incompetence among the Indian agents was to appoint them from the ranks of the clergy. This policy, in effect from 1869 to 1877, among other things, aided religion. A classic example of the blending of Indian tradition and Christianity in the religious realm occurred in the founding by the Indians of the Shaker Church. From the date of its inception in 1881 near Olympia, the Shaker faith spread among the Indians of Puget Sound. Like many new sects it suffered persecution as the Indian agents tried to stamp it out. Finally, in 1892, it again became lawful. As in the preceding era, the pressures of assimilation continued at the same time as the elders were able to pass on to some of their children the cultural heritage of the past.

A Black Community Develops

The railroad had a large influence upon the blacks. In a real sense the railroad made the black community a permanent part of the life of the Pacific Northwest. For it was after the arrival of the transcontinental that the black population expanded and became rooted in the region. In Oregon the number of blacks rose from 487 in 1880 to 2,144 in 1920; in the same period in Washington the increase was from 325 to 6,883.

Many economic opportunities for blacks were in the railroad business or in allied occupations. Black men worked in the car shops, the roundhouses, and the yards of Portland, Roseburg, La Grande, Seattle, Tacoma, and Spokane, important terminals or division points. They worked as waiters, porters, and cooks aboard trains and in similar positions on ships and in hotels. A black community developed in the Washington coal mines of Roslyn, Franklin, and Newcastle after 1888. About the only opportunities for women who wished to work outside the home was in domestic service and as elevator operators. Some were able to take in laundry in their own homes.

A small number of Northwestern blacks won places in the ranks of businesses and the professions. Many businesses catered to blacks themselves, who were prohibited by segregation laws or customs from patronizing restaurants, saloons, beauty shops, barber shops, and hotels with white clientele. Some blacks invested in real estate, ran employment agencies, became contractors, operated hauling businesses, and a handful secured federal or municipal jobs. Concerning professional people, J. A. Merriman became in 1903 the first black physician in Portland, and in the same year McCants Stewart was the first black attorney to pass the Oregon Bar. Robert O. Lee was the first black admitted to the Washington State Bar in 1889. Joshua Runsnowden in 1880 was Washington's first black physician. Blacks also owned newspapers. There were seven in Seattle from 1891 to 1901. The first was Brittain Oxendine's *Seattle Standard,* founded in 1891, although Horace Cayton published the longest-lived one, the *Seattle Republican* (1894–1915). Three journals appeared in Portland: the *New Age* (1896–1907); the *Advocate* (1903–1933); and the *Portland Times* (1918–1923).

Newspapers are an indication of a stable community. Indeed, after the coming of the railroad, black men and women put down their roots in the Northwest. Black community institutions provided security and pleasure and opportunity for their members. Churches were the social and cultural as well as the religious pillars of black communities. In Portland, for example, new black churches were the African Methodist Episcopal Church (1895) and the Mount Olive Baptist Church (1890s). The first churches in Seattle were the African Methodist Episcopal Church (1890) and the Mt. Zion Baptist Church (1894). Spokane's first two black churches were both begun in 1890. The churches not only conducted services and provided the usual auxiliary activities such as Sunday schools, youth groups, temperance chapters, and women's circles, but they organized oratorical contests, put on plays, and provided children's activities. The minister was a man of influence who was spiritual leader, of course, but also served as employment counselor, political adviser, and welfare mentor.

Social benefits were an important reason for men or women to join a lodge. In 1867 there was formed a relief organization, the Portland Colored Benevolent Association. With the rise in black immigration following the railroad came the Masons, the Odd Fellows, the Elks, the Knights of Pythias, and their women's auxiliaries. There was the sleeping

Horace Cayton, Sr. Special Collections Division, University of
Washington Libraries

car porters' club in Seattle in the 1890s. As a lodge member, a person's
benefits were not only good fellowship, but monetary grants to the sick,
the disabled, and to widows and orphans of members. Recreation was
provided not only in lodges, but through baseball teams, music clubs,
and literary societies. Women also organized clubs. Seattle women founded the Ladies Colored Social Circle in 1889. In 1912 Portland women
organized the Colored Women's Council which secured its own clubhouse
two years later. Nine Portland women's clubs banded together in 1917
to found the Oregon Federation of Colored Women's Clubs.

One thing more was needed to establish a complete community.
This was political action, required both to secure advantages and to
overcome racial discrimination. Throughout the period, most Oregon

blacks were Republicans, grateful to the party of Lincoln for emancipation and for the policies of the Reconstruction era. In the 1870s Portland blacks organized the Sumner Union Club and the Bed Rock Political Club.

In Washington, Owen Bush, son of the pioneer, was elected a member of the first state legislature. In 1889 a public accommodations law was passed, but it was made ineffectual in 1895 when the penalty clause was removed. Most blacks in Washington were Republicans. Their first political organization was founded in 1888, the Colored Harrison and Morton Legion, named for the Republican presidential and vice-presidential candidates. Daniel K. Oliver, a businessman, was elected to the city council in Spokane in 1896, the first black to hold elective office in that city. There were a few black Democrats. Their first organization was founded in Seattle in 1891, the Colored Democratic Club. There were local affiliates of national civil rights organizations, also. In 1890 Seattle blacks organized a branch of the Afro-American League. In 1899 a Seattle chapter of the National Council of Afro-Americans was formed. The National Association for the Advancement of Colored People was mainly concerned with politics. Founded nationally in 1909, it had chapters in Seattle, Tacoma, and Portland by 1914. One of the organizers of these chapters was Nettie Asberry, a black woman.

There was much for these organizations to do to alleviate the lot of black citizens. The Pacific Northwest remained an extremely prejudiced region, although Washington, unlike Oregon, had no antiblack laws. There seemed to be discriminatory barriers everywhere. The exceptions to this pattern were housing (although in 1919 Portland realtors adopted a segregation policy) and education, which in the cities (although not in the towns) was open to all wherever they could afford to live. In other respects there were difficulties. It was almost impossible to obtain a job outside the lowest paid positions in the transportation industry or in domestic service. Unions prohibited black membership. Businesses did not hire blacks for white collar jobs. Literally only a handful of black professional people existed because blacks lacked well-paid jobs that opened up expensive higher education.

Blacks with an income had trouble finding nonsegregated places to spend their earnings. Hotels and restaurants were often closed to them. Insurance rates were prohibitively high. Theaters had Jim Crow sections. Whites made sneering remarks or ignored black citizens. In Oregon, although not in Washington, blacks and whites could not intermarry. Discrimination increased after the turn of the century, for example, in the restaurant business.

Although small in numbers, poorly paid, ignored or despised by whites, black people resisted their unfortunate condition. In 1894 the

New Port Republican Club secured the appointment of the first black policeman in Portland, George Hardin. In 1905 Oliver Taylor refused to accept the requirement that he buy a ticket to the segregated section of a Portland theater. He sued the manager for $500 in damages, but lost the case. Three black children attempted to integrate the public schools of Coos Bay in 1903, but were given a separate room and teacher instead. In 1893 Portland black activists sponsored the first attempts to amend the Oregon constitution to remove the provisions prohibiting blacks and Chinese from residing in the state and from voting. These attempts continued until 1900 when the legislature approved placing the removal of the exclusion clause before the voters as a constitutional amendment. It was defeated in a close vote. In 1916 the citizens voted on a proposed constitutional amendment to repeal the constitutional ban on voting. It, also, was defeated by a narrow margin, 100,701 to 100,027 votes. An attempt to repeal the law prohibiting intermarriage was made in the 1893 legislature. It failed as did a similar effort in 1917.

The most evident activism of Oregon blacks in the political arena concerned a famous motion picture. In 1915 one of the masters of American film technology, D. W. Griffith, produced a movie called *Birth of a Nation*. Although it introduced many novel techniques of film making, the movie also depicted the South of the Reconstruction era as a place where blacks were morally corrupt, politically arrogant, and culturally childlike. The Portland chapter attacked the film in 1916 when it was first scheduled to be shown in the city. With other members of the black community, the NAACP persuaded the city council to pass a law prohibiting the showing of any film that would instigate racial hatred. Such political victories were few indeed.

The Chinese

The 1880s ushered in an era of terrible hardship for the Chinese. Foreshadowed in the discrimination of the earlier years, anti-Chinese bigotry now reached endemic proportions. Congress passed a law in 1882 excluding most Chinese from emigrating to the United States. The Chinese became scapegoats for the economic downturn after 1883. White workers became convinced that the Chinese were undercutting their standard of living.

Whites also applied other stigmas to the Chinese. They were regarded as peculiarly prone to prostitution, gambling, and opium. They were accused of criminality and their tongs were equated with lawless gangs. They were considered ultraprolific; alarmists depicted the Chinese as "the yellow peril," a race inevitably to become the majority of the

American population within the following decade or two. They stuck together, which was not good; and if they desired to leave the ghettos, that was worse, because the Chinese could never adopt American customs, could never become assimilated. Finally, the Chinese were considered an economic drain, for the money they earned was sent to China for their relatives.

In the Pacific Northwest the whites, almost all members of the working class, acted violently against the Chinese who bore these stereotypes. The violence began in 1885 in rural Washington with the murder of two or three Chinese hop pickers at Squaw Valley. Whites burned down the quarters of Chinese miners at Coal Creek. Later in the year Chinese were expelled from Tacoma and Puyallup and the Tacoma contingent was placed forcibly on railroad cars and shipped to Portland.

In the same year the worst agitation began. In Seattle laborers marched and demonstrated against the Chinese and urged the government to expel them. Some Chinese left the city out of fear; technically they left voluntarily. On February 7, 1886, a mob forced 196 Chinese to leave for San Francisco. By the end of the month almost all had been forced to leave. In 1887 ten Chinese miners were killed on the Snake River at a place called Log Cabin Bar.

Oregonians were as prejudiced against the Chinese as Washingtonians. The intent was the same: expulsion. In February 1886, as the Chinese were leaving Seattle, there were demands in Portland that the Chinese leave town in forty days. Conservative people opposed the move and mobilized the city militia as well as the police to protect the Chinese. On February 21, Chinese laborers in the woolen mills in Oregon City were evicted by white workers; they took refuge in Portland. From late February through March 12, three other incidents occurred in Portland or adjacent communities. The Chinese were driven out of Albina; Chinese woodcutters were evicted from Mount Tabor; and the Chinese homes at Guild's Lake were raided and the occupants expelled.

Besides the conservative populace, the courts provided some defense for the Chinese, although even they became less protective of their rights. Before the passage of the Chinese Exclusion Law the territorial and supreme courts of the Pacific Northwest in most civil and criminal cases upheld the Chinese. After that date, they ruled against them in most instances.

Although spectacular, violence was not the most enduring of the Chinese experiences in the Northwest. Besides their jobs, they expanded their community institutions. The size of the Chinatowns grew. The tongs continued both their lawful and illegal activities, the most dramatic of which was the violence among rival tongs. Less sinister were the family and district associations that gained importance as men brought wives or daughters when they made their commitment to settle down in the new land. They helped provide jobs or housing; they kept people in line morally; and they provided the same type of protection as did the tongs. Dinners, card games, and parties were also encompassed within the work of the family association. To tie together the various associations the Chinese Consolidated Benevolent Association was formed in the 1890s.

Religious organizations continued to be important. As in the previous era, they were both Christian and Asian. The Portland Chinese Baptist Church continued; the Portland Chinese Presbyterian Church was founded in 1885. Others were also established. They all served not only to Christianize, but to Americanize—introducing the English language and customs of the new land. Not all Chinese favored this acculturation—in fact some dreaded the loss of the ancient language and took steps to protect it. In 1908 a Chinese language school was founded in Portland. Although the children did not relish this additional work after the close of public school and on Saturday mornings, their elders considered it a necessity to maintain the community's heritage.

The economic basis for the Northwest Chinese community shifted somewhat in these years. Because of these changes, coupled with the racial terror of the 1880s, the size of the Chinese communities declined. In 1880 the Chinese population of Oregon was 9,510; by 1920 it had declined to 3,090 persons. It had also changed its location to become more centralized in Portland. In 1880 Washington's Chinese totaled 3,186 persons; in 1920 they numbered 2,363 with more than one-third living in Seattle.

The most striking development in the ranks of employed persons is the increase in the numbers of business and professional people. But most of these persons served the Chinese community which was far less prosperous than the white society. The wealthiest of Chinese entrepreneurs had succeeded in the real estate, mercantile or contract labor occupations.

Those less fortunate economically continued to work as migrant farm laborers, salmon canners, construction laborers, and domestic servants. As the farms were cleared and the railroads built, and as the fishing industry progressively declined, Chinese were forced into urban pursuits or forced to leave the region. Their economic problems were accelerated by discrimination, less violent than that of the 1880s, but still formidable. Labor unions, reflecting their historic fear that the Chinese would lower the Caucasian standard of living, discriminated against them. Unions favored the exclusion of Chinese immigrants and refused to admit to organized labor those who were already residents. In an era where unskilled labor often had no organization of any kind, there was little that the Chinese could do.

By 1920 the Chinese of the Northwest were certainly far better off materially than in 1880. Violence against them had disappeared. Those who wished to were free to move out from Chinatown ghettos to other portions of the city of Portland, especially to the southeast portion of the city. Portland was the first city in the nation to see this exodus made possible, to see the barriers of residential segregation breached. The reason for this is that the Chinese family structure in Portland resembled that of the typical American nuclear family more so than elsewhere. There were far fewer unmarried Chinese in Portland than in other portions of the country.

The price of acceptance, grudging as it might be, was high, especially in the realm of psychological pressure. Generations seemed to split apart. Children, pressured by church and school to reject the culture of their parents, became more affected by white society. The young people rejected the traditional arranged marriage (often with an unknown person in China). They abandoned ancestor worship. They found it inconvenient to share their household with parents or grandparents. They tried to conform, even when the majority culture frequently would not let them. For the individual, cultural and family tensions often led to frustration, mental illness, even suicide. For the survivors, especially the second generation, the future looked—if not bright—at least more hopeful than the past.

The Japanese

By the last quarter of the nineteenth century, Japan had taken the initial steps to become a modern nation. The Japanese opened their lives to the influence of Western civilization. Population increased rapidly, too rapidly to be comfortably absorbed, as jobs were lacking for the rising generation. Into this world of promise, of change, and of disappointment came rumors of economic opportunities in the United States, 4,500 miles across the Pacific.

In 1880 there were three Japanese citizens living in the Pacific Northwest. During the next few years a trickle of immigrants came to the region: to Astoria (1882), Port Blakely (1883), Sumner and Spokane (1884), and Tacoma (1885). They wanted to make enough money to return to their native land, there to live in comfort, if not in wealth. Those who did so made a great impression. One villager remembered: "According to what people said, in America money was hanging from the trees and one could rake up treasure like fallen leaves."[1]

Raking these leaves turned out to be arduous work. Backbreaking work building railroads was one of the first opportunities. A man could

Japanese work camp near Hood River, Oregon, c. 1920. Oregon Historical Society

sign a piece of paper with a labor contractor in his native village that would bring him across the ocean to a job in the Pacific Northwest. The contractors were fellow countrymen, who began in 1891 to arrange jobs for Japanese workers. The jobs they arranged in the 1890s paid $1.15 a day for a ten-hour day (whites received $1.45). The men lived in shacks, and followed construction camps from spring to fall. In the winter months of unemployment, when weather prevented construction, the men gathered in the ghettos of Seattle, Tacoma, Portland, and Spokane.

Some Japanese also worked in the coal mines of the Pacific Northwest, such as the Loader mine east of Tacoma, but the work was so dangerous and the union opposition so vigilant that few entered this pursuit. A much more congenial occupation was oystering. The Japanese became active in this pursuit in the late 1910s, working at Mud Bay, Oyster Bay at Olympia, and North and South bays near Seattle. It was dangerous work, night and day, standing in cold water or working from a boat. Rheumatism, arthritis, drownings were the prices paid.

Best of all was farm work. It was not dangerous and it was familiar to the immigrants. It was also an occupation that encouraged family life, for it was stable and family members could participate in it. In 1897 Japanese citizens began to farm in the Hood River valley in Oregon, a natural paradise for fruit growers. The first Japanese went into the fertile Yakima River valley in 1902 where they opened up large farms. Living in tents under the burning sun, they cleared the land of sagebrush and dug irrigation wells to bring it to life. They planted potatoes, wheat, and alfalfa.

Most Japanese farmers were truck gardeners. They lived in Washington, Marion, and Multnomah counties in Oregon, and around Seattle and Tacoma. Almost all kinds of fruits and vegetables were raised to find their markets in the growing urban centers. Those who owned their land were the fortunate ones whose incredibly difficult labor produced their own farms. Some found in America only a life of day labor for others, clearing trees and brush, grubbing stumps, digging potatoes, picking strawberries and hops. Truly they were sustained only as one immigrant's poem declared:

> Alien hardships
> Made bearable by the hope
> I hold for my children.[2]

On the opposite extreme of the economic scale were the business and professional people. Most had made their beginning as labor contractors for their countrymen or as merchants supplying specialized foods or drugs demanded by the immigrants. Others ran restaurants, hotels, saloons, and houses of prostitution for the same clientele.

The cultural institutions of the Japanese settlers reflected the range of human activities. The most dramatic change occurred when single men began, about the turn of the century, to settle down and bring wives from Japan. This commitment furnished even more stable institutions than those that existed in the "bird of passage" phase.

The early male migrants had little time or inclination for organized religion. As the years passed, however, Christian missionaries organized congregations for the Japanese. In 1891 and 1892, respectively, in Portland and in Seattle, Japanese ministers began teaching Christianity to the young people. The first formally organized congregation was the Portland Japanese Methodist Church (1893), organized by the Reverend Teikichi Kawabe. In 1899 the Seattle Japanese Baptist Church was founded and two years later there began the Seattle Buddhist Church with the accompanying Young Men's Buddhist Association.

Buddhism was one attempt to preserve the old culture from assimilation to the new. Another was the children's language school. The first of these schools was founded in Seattle in 1902. A haiku society was formed in Seattle in 1906 and a literary society three years later. Organizations of broader scope also commenced. In 1891 the Tacoma Japanese Association began and nine years later came the Seattle Japanese Association which communicated with its members by means of a mimeographed newsletter. In 1902 its broader scope was reflected in its change of name; it became the Washington State Japanese Association. Also indispensable for cultural retention were newspapers, the first being the daily *Japonica Portland* founded in 1899, followed by the *Asahi Shimbun* established in Seattle in 1905. By 1920 Japanese had all the institutions of Americans except political ones, for Congress had never made the first generation eligible for citizenship.

Lack of political rights was particularly felt as prejudice and discrimination arose against the Japanese. Incidents of violence were widespread. In 1898 a band of whites, armed with rifles, assaulted four track layers for the Southern Pacific Railroad and gave them thirty minutes to leave Portland. In 1907 a mob in Bellingham attacked a Japanese restaurant. One victim remembered "the persecution from young roughnecks which was repeated continually day in and day out. I am [was] one of the victims of their daytime attacks. Police were troubled by this, too, and finally they started saying, 'Since there are many *judo* experts among Japanese, just protect yourselves.' "[3]

Other forms of prejudice, as cruel if less physical, were legion. Pickets urged white persons not to patronize Japanese-owned businesses. "White only" signs confronted Japanese in stores, restaurants, and barbershops. Public beaches and swimming pools were closed to Japanese. They had to take seats in the balconies of theaters. Unions refused to admit Japanese citizens and persecuted white employers who hired them.

The roots of these sentiments were complex. Whites in the Northwest had a long tradition of bigotry. The Japanese were industrious, far more than many whites, who saw them as competitors. Rumors circulated of the Japanese inevitably acquiring most of the agricultural land of the region. Japanese were assailed as clannish, as dirty, and as heathen. But bigotry had not yet been translated into political action.

The British

Many subjects of Great Britain continued to come to the Northwest. Here they assimilated with ease. They knew the language; they were familiar with democracy and urban-industrial capitalism; and they were educated. With these advantages they were welcome additions to the region, people who moved more quickly than any other immigrant group into skilled industrial jobs, white collar work, and the professions. With no discriminatory laws or customs to impede them, and with no sense of cultural loss, the British immigrants felt little need to form the benevolent societies required by less favored minorities. They soon made a place for themselves in American politics also. Because of their Catholic faith and relative lack of education, the Irish had a harder time economically and in community acceptance than did the English or the Scotch, but they too came in large numbers.

The Nordics

The Nordics (people from Sweden, Norway, Denmark, Finland, and Iceland) began their migration to the United States in the middle of the nineteenth century. Many came to gain religious freedom. They had no desire to pay taxes to an established church if they were not members of it; members of some denominations were even prohibited from worshipping. Others came to escape the draft. The class system was rigid. But most people left because of growing pressure upon natural resources. As population increased, children found their family farms inadequate, both in size and soil.

Many who came to America had no intention of remaining. They were single males who hoped to return home again with a stake in the old country. But by the 1870s the migration had become a family one. The first stop of most Nordic migrants was the American Middle West or the Great Plains. In time, many of these persons came to the Pacific Northwest, from the Dakotas, Illinois, Iowa, Minnesota, and Wisconsin. They formed nuclei of settlements which drew others of their heritage. Most of the Nordic migrants settled west of the Cascade Mountains, both in the cities and in rural areas. They came because these were regions of economic growth and because the natural environment was similar to that of the Nordic lands.

In the Northwest the Nordics worked in farming, fishing, lumbering, and logging. In the cities they were largely employed as day laborers or in street or sewer construction. If possible, they worked together in Nordic communities such as Astoria, Ballard (then an independent city adjacent to Seattle), and Junction City, Oregon. In Portland the Nordic centers were never as long lived as in Seattle, as the people moved rather rapidly from neighborhood to neighborhood within the metropolitan community. In 1910 the Nordic population of the Pacific Northwest was the largest of all the groups of foreign extraction in the region.

Most of the first generation Nordic male migrants remained in their original pursuits of skilled and unskilled labor in the trades, in lumbering, and in fishing. Women worked in domestic service and in the apparel trades. Lack of capital or formal education, plus unfamiliarity with the English language, precluded most Nordic immigrants from careers in business or the professions.

The vast majority of Nordic immigrants were not "birds of passage." This meant that they quickly put down institutional roots. Included among the many groups were the Sons of Norway, the Vasa Order of America, and the Danish Aid Society. These fraternal or benevolent organizations were economic and cultural necessities in the period of adjustment. So too were the churches, in addition to providing for the cure of souls. The churches indeed were the first Nordic institutions established in the new land. In America the Nordics brought with them the Lutheran Church, established in their old homes, now justified in America—which had no union of church and state—solely upon its merits. In the Northwest, as in the rest of America, the Lutheran church split into different synods based on language. Many Nordics also joined American denominations, principally Baptist, Methodist, and Congregational. The congregations of these denominations also soon broke into separate groups based on language, a development that perhaps inspired the Congregationalists from the first to organize their churches on the basis of country of origin.

As the Nordic people quickly merged into American life, the need for political blocs and ethnic candidates was slight in the Pacific Northwest compared to other regions of the nation. By 1920 the Nordics were either assimilated or on the path to assimilation. They had few barriers to this course, language alone being an obstacle. They were Christian, literate people who shared the majority's beliefs in social mobility, material success, hard work, and representative democracy.

The Germans

The Germans were the other major northern European ethnic group. They came from a region of many kingdoms only united in 1871. Before unification, there were waves of political agitation in the German states based upon the spread of the libertarian ideals of the American and French revolutions. There were unsuccessful liberal revolutions in some of these states in 1830 and in 1848, the last of which sent an important element to the United States, "the Forty-Eighters." Most who came to America had experienced the hard times of the 1840s, "the hungry Forties," when crops failed and lands were consolidated. As Germany's agriculture became more precarious, the displaced peasants relocated in the cities. If the factory failed them, America was the last resort.

The first major German penetration of the Northwest was both spectacular and unique. This was the founding of the Aurora colony twenty-eight miles south of Portland. Its leader was Wilhelm Keil who had founded a communitarian settlement, Bethel, in Missouri in 1844. In 1855, Keil led a group of his followers over the trail to Washington but soon moved to Oregon. The Aurora Colony formally operated until 1883, only six years after Keil's death. It was an interesting experiment, but most German migrants came as individuals.

Diversity marked the Germans' economic pursuits. They lived in both the country and the city. In the city they followed many occupations because the majority of them had a level of education and a supply of capital that was quite high. Many were able to become brewers, millers, and owners of other businesses. Others entered the professions or politics. Their cultural institutions came, too. Although some abandoned the established churches of their home country, many remained loyal to Lutheranism or Catholicism. The first German churches appeared in 1882 in Washington: the German Evangelical Lutheran Trinity Church in Tacoma and a German Lutheran Church in Seattle. In Portland the initial German church was the First German Evangelical Reformed Church which was founded in 1874. The first Portland German Catholic Church, St. Michael's, dates back to 1890.

Germans were active in educating mind and body as well as soul. Like other ethnic groups, they pressed for schools to maintain the old language. In Portland the Independent German School (1871) and the Anglo-German Institute were the first German language schools established. The most famous German cultural group that was brought to America was the Turn Verein. It dedicated its members to the ancient Greek ideal of a sound mind in a healthy body. The Portland Branch was established in 1857. American lodges, as in the case of the Scandinavians, established German branches, but the Germans also created indigenous groups. The oldest and most comprehensive of the German groups in Oregon was the General German Aid Society. Founded in 1871 it, and its auxiliary German Ladies Relief Society, located jobs for Germans, afforded medical and insurance benefits, built a home for the aged, and in these good works provided a social bond for its membership.

Newspapers as well as social groups bound the German peoples together. The first paper in the region was founded in Portland in 1867, the *Deutsche Zeitung*. Portland also had the paper with the largest circulation in the entire region (14,000 by World War I), the *Pazifik Nachrichten*. The pioneer German language newspaper in Washington was *Die Washington Tribuene* founded in Seattle in 1883.

With one exception there were no occasions for separate German political action until the outbreak of the First World War. The exception was prohibition, which the temperate but beer-drinking Germans fought in vain. Prohibition came to both Oregon and Washington in 1914. But other than on this issue Germans did not run for office or vote as members of a bloc.

Regardless of their occupation or social or political affiliation, the Germans were given a hearty welcome to the Northwest. They fit in because they shared the values and characteristics of the native born. They were apt to be literate, although in an alien tongue. They valued public education. Most were Protestants who believed in the separation of church and state. They had some familiarity with democratic political philosophy and perhaps, at least at the local level, with actual participation in politics.

The "New Immigrants"

Immigrants from Northern Europe were not the only Europeans to arrive in the region after the railroad. Many came from the southern, eastern, and central portions of the continent, from Italy and the Austro-Hungarian and Russian empires. They were often referred to as the "new immigrants." They confronted problems that the northerners had in lesser degree or not at all. These difficulties revolved about their greater differences from the majority of American citizens. Most of the new European immigrants were Catholic and Jewish. Almost none had political experience and few in any case expected much positive from government. For them, government meant taxes, war, conscription, trouble in a variety of ways. The new immigrants were illiterate for the most part. Thus altogether they lacked acquaintance with four bastions of the American system: the Protestant church, local government, the public school, and the free press.

The most numerous of the new immigrants were the Italians. Their motivation in coming was economic. The soil and forests of the old country were depleted or destroyed. Agricultural depression was related not only to these conditions but to tariff barriers erected by other nations. The cities could not absorb them. Some were able to stay in farming only as sharecroppers. Others had no choice but to emigrate. In the 1890s began the great outflow.

Although most Italian immigrants resided in eastern cities, some crossed the continent by train to the Pacific Northwest. Most of these migrants were from northern Italy. Once at their destination they lived among their countrymen. In Oregon their favored places were in Portland and its surrounding countryside. In Washington the centers of settlement were Seattle, Tacoma, Spokane, and their immediately adjacent areas. The first migrants who came to these regions were apt to be married or unmarried males. Married males came alone because they could afford passage money for themselves but not for their families. Unmarried men were likely to come because they were unencumbered by job or family. Some wanted to reside permanently in America. Others wanted to make enough money to return home to live in comfort.

Familiar with farm work, the peasants would have preferred agricultural pursuits in America. Few could find them, however, although truck gardening and dairying near the large cities offered some opportunities. Italians found fertile plots of land in East Portland, in the Fife area north of Tacoma, and in Kent south of Seattle. Walla Walla, too, was a center of Italian truck gardening.

The majority of Italians also worked outdoors but not in agriculture. They took up the heavy pursuits within the construction industry. They worked on the railroads all across the region. Gangs of Italians, usually under the leadership of a boss or foreman of their own nationality, joined other immigrants (although each group was segregated in its own quarters) in mobile camps of construction cars.

An even more difficult job was coal mining. In Kittitas, King, and Pierce counties in Washington Italian miners, men and boys, labored in the pits as miners and greasers and on the surface as screeners. In Washington's Roslyn, Black Diamond, Issaquah, Ravensdale, and other districts, the miners lived a life largely controlled by their employers. The mining companies not only set their conditions of employment, but they required employees to buy their own tools and powder. They lived in company bunkhouses, traded in company stores, and, if single, ate in company mess halls. The company provided medical care and leased houses or lots to family men. Besides mining and construction, there were a handful of men in almost every profession or occupation, but the first two pursuits predominated. Women were not urged to leave the household, but if they had to work they were apt to be waitresses, dressmakers, laundresses. For both men and women the language barrier kept them from better paying jobs. By 1920 a few had, however, made the arduous climb to the professions.

People needed protection, in these difficult days, from the rigors of unemployment, disability, and loneliness. Immigrants' own organizations, rather than government, attempted to cope with these problems. Being small in numbers, and mobile, the Italians had little political strength in the Northwest as an ethnic group, although Portland's Italians formed the Italian-American Republican Club in 1916. The Catholic Church was the center of cultural life. St. Michael's in Portland, Mt. Virgin in Seattle, and St. Francis in Walla Walla were among the pioneer parishes. These centers not only provided the sacraments, but a variety of social services ranging from church suppers to sewing circles. Other means of keeping communities together included ethnic newspapers, benevolent societies, and occupational groups that provided a range of benefits from funeral expenses to disability insurance.

Greeks were another Mediterranean people who found shelter in the Northwest. The first Greek settlers were two sailors who settled down in Seattle in 1870. Others followed for many of the same reasons that sent the Italians to the New World. Resource depletion, population growth, and lack of urban opportunities were the reasons for migration. In addition, many people of Greek culture were citizens of the Turkish Empire who fled to America to escape conscription into the imperial army.

The railroads were their magnet to the Northwest. They came after 1900 to live in the mobile ghettos composed of bunk cars, dining cars, and kitchen cars. Most of the Greeks were single males, "the birds of passage," itinerants who were looking for a stake, in the old world or the new, and willing to take almost any job to get one. Like most other migrants, foreign or citizens, the Greeks would have preferred a farm for their livelihood. But the opportunities were of the city: shoe shine parlors, restaurants and saloons, and tobacco, fruit, and candy stores. The favorite form of restaurant was the coffee house, which, with the church, the saloon, and the benevolent society, comprised the cultural centers. There was prostitution and gambling in some coffee houses, but almost all served as more lawful shelters against an indifferent or hostile world.

The Greek Orthodox Church commanded the allegiance of almost all of the first generation. The first church in the Northwest was in Seattle; its priest also served the Portland Greek community until 1909. In that year Holy Trinity Church obtained its own resident priest two years after the congregation was formed. Social and benevolent societies followed the church. In 1912 Portlanders organized the Hellenic Social Club. In the next decade the Greeks organized—in the usual North-western imitative way—two chapters of national organizations: the American Hellenic Educational Progressive Association, dedicated to Americanizing the immigrants, and the Greek American Progressive Association, which was concerned with preserving as much as possible of the Greek heritage during the assimilation process.

Slavic people also made their escape from the hardships of the Austro-Hungarian Empire and from Russia. Numbers of South Slavs, Slovenes, and Serbo-Croats, migrated to Washington after the turn of the century. Their motivation for coming typified those of both Christian and Jewish migrants to America from central and eastern Europe.

Their principal economic occupation at home was that of a small farmer, either tenant or landowner. In addition, some worked as fishermen in small craft on the waters of the Adriatic. By the late 1800s, both pursuits were suffering the neglect of centuries as the soil was depleted and the fisheries declining. As the Austro-Hungarian Empire prepared for war, taxes increased and, simultaneously, improved health conditions made for a larger population to further pressure the resource base. Plant diseases and forest conservation measures injured the vineyards and restricted goat herding, respectively. Citizens resented compulsory military service and censorship of the press, especially by a government that was composed of alien German speakers who had occupied the Slavic homeland. Migration to America was a natural result of these grievances.

In the Pacific Northwest the center of Slavic life was in western Washington in the Puget Sound and Olympic Peninsula regions and on the slopes of the Cascade Mountains, both east and west. The most fortunate migrants were the fishermen, because they alone could preserve their former occupation in America. They settled in all the ports in the state to engage in the great salmon fishing industry, although the largest number settled in Bellingham.

Lack of farming opportunities meant that nonfishermen had to turn to a variety of industrial pursuits. Most went into coal mining, but some also took heavy jobs in lumbering and construction. Only a tiny minority of the first generation secured positions in business or the professions because of the language barrier.

Cultural institutions reflected the usual tension of the immigrants between the old and the new. The first generation, because of its small numbers, relied mainly upon the family for support and joined American Catholic churches rather than forming their own. However, they did found benevolent societies; the first Croatian one was at Roslyn in 1897 and the first Slovene one at the same place in 1902. The initial activity of the lodges was always to raise money for funeral expenses and to buy cemetery lots. Political opportunities were limited to city council positions.

Another Slavic group, the Russians, also came in small numbers to the Pacific Northwest. At the time of the outbreak of the First World War in 1914, there were somewhere between fifty and two hundred Russian settlers in Oregon. The majority were single males seeking better economic opportunities which they found in the unskilled pursuits in the region. Only one institution was founded in Oregon, a short-lived Russian Baptist Church which lasted between 1901 and 1903.

There were more Russian Slavs in Seattle, a sufficient number to be located by an Orthodox missionary priest in 1892. In 1895 the first formal

Russian Orthodox congregation, St. Spiridon, was founded in Seattle. But as in Oregon, the Russians of Washington were largely anonymous people in this era.

The Jews of Oregon

The Jewish population by 1920 was quite diverse. The first German Jews were community leaders. Many had fine homes, several settling by the 1890s in northwestern Portland. Most continued as clothing merchants and successful traders. Their children were by now entering the professions. Although they were welcomed into political, economic, and some social institutions of the broader community, the German Jews also founded—out of necessity or desire—some separate social organizations. It was in this era that arose the Council of Jewish Women, the Concordia Club, and the Tualatin Country Club.

The largest number of Jews were from Eastern Europe, from the Russian and Austro-Hungarian empires, fleeing religious persecution and economic hardships. The earliest began coming from Poland in the 1870s. Unlike the first German Jews of the midnineteenth century, they came as family members, not as single males. Poor and uneducated, knowing no English, their time of adjustment would have been difficult except for the aid of Jewish residents. Under the leadership of Ben Selling, Portland Jews formed a chapter of the national Industrial Removal Office to settle East European Jews by giving them temporary financial assistance.

German and East European Jews also cooperated in many ventures. One was the B'nai B'rith Building Association (1910) which built a community center (later called the Jewish Community Center in 1938 and renamed the Mittleman Jewish Community Center in 1977). Another was the Portland Hebrew School (1916). In the wider community Jews contributed much. Rabbi Stephen S. Wise was active in the Consumer's League in its fight against child labor. Joseph Teal, Jr. was one of Oregon's first conservationists. Joseph Simon was a Republican political leader as a member of the state senate, as United States senator (1898–1903), and as mayor of Portland (1909–1913). Ben Selling was the Republican candidate for the United States Senate in 1912. Sol Hirsch was minister to Turkey from 1889 to 1892. These successes certainly manifested widespread acceptance and appreciation of Jews in regional society. But there was some prejudice and some discrimination. Portland's B'nai B'rith established an antidefamation committee in 1916 to combat Jewish slurs in the press and on the stage.

Washington's Jews

Washington's Jews were both similar to and different from those in Oregon. The first Jews, Ashkenazim like those of Oregon, were merchants from northern Europe who came as single men. They formed the first Jewish congregation, Bikur Cholia, in 1891, which obtained its first synogogue seven years later. They created a Jewish Welfare Society in 1892. Many more German Jews came to Seattle to take advantage of the mercantile opportunities created by the Alaska gold rush in the late 1890s. Most owned pawnshops, junkyards, secondhand stores, and jewelry, clothing, and household furnishings shops. By 1914 there were three Ashkenazim synogogues, one reform and two orthodox, to serve a population of 8,500. As in Portland (and in the United States), most of Seattle's Jews by 1914 were rooted in eastern Europe. Poorly educated and poor, members of family units when they migrated, they came to Seattle after an interlude on the East Coast. Slowly they built their institutions and their incomes.

What was unusual about the Seattle Jewish community was the large number of Sephardic Jews who came after the turn of the century. The Sephardic Jews were descendants of Jews expelled from Spain in 1492. Most had taken refuge in Greece and the countries of the Near East. Seattle's first Sephardic Jews arrived from the Island of Marmara in Turkey in 1903. Most Seattle Sephardim came from three locations: the Rodosto district in Turkey and the islands of Rhodes and Marmara. By 1914 there were 1,500 Sephardic Jews in Seattle. Disruptions of the First World War brought others. Taking the humble economic occupations at first, mainly ownership of fish and fruit stores, the Sephardics slowly built community institutions. This was a difficult process for the three groups were divided in liturgy, language, and customs. Still each group first created a mutual aid society, then religious congregations. By the outbreak of the First World War a positive and constructive community life was underway.

So it was for most non-Anglo Saxon Protestants. Certainly the major cities of Seattle and Portland had a high percentage of foreign-born people throughout the era after 1880, men and women who added to what had been a most homogeneous population when the period opened.

Caucasian American Citizens

The most numerous of the migrants of the era were white American citizens of rural background who came to the area mostly from the Middle

West. Their desire was to become more prosperous farmers in their new homes. But most were disappointed in this pursuit. Although there was some good land available for settlement in eastern Oregon and Washington until the turn of the century, there was not a lot of it. The area west of the Cascades was by this time settled, although a few migrants tried in vain to make a living in the early years of the century in the cutover area of western Washington and in the semiarid region of central Oregon. Almost all failed for lack of capital, proper agricultural experience, or knowledge of soils and crops. The prospective farmers had to work in the lumber camps, in the mines, in the mills, and in a variety of urban pursuits. The least fortunate or energetic of the Americans became migratory workers, the "bindle stiffs," who rotated from farm to lumber camp to city skid row as the seasons changed. The most successful were people of business or professional background who pursued the same vocations after coming to the Northwest.

The Americans were, if anything, almost all Protestant in religion. They believed in education and supported it more willingly than had their parents. They continued to buy a wide range of newspapers and periodicals. Although most saw little value in the higher culture, wives and daughters of the upper classes were the mainstays of the urban symphonies, libraries, and museums. The main link between the new generation and that of the pioneers was their mutual faith in material progress and their shared belief that it was more readily available in the Pacific Northwest than any place on earth. Their main difference from the parents' lives was the setting—with each passing year the city became more populous.

Urbanization

The urban population of the Pacific Northwest grew enormously from 1880 to 1910. Portland's population increased in these years 107 percent. That of Seattle rose 66 percent. Spokane went up 297 percent, Tacoma 75 percent. Portland began the era as the regional metropolis. When it was over, Seattle dominated, although Tacoma and Spokane in these decades had also attempted to become the major city of the Northwest.

Seattle rose to prominence because of the coming of the Great Northern Railroad in 1893 and the stimulus of the Alaska gold rush that started in 1897. Seattle's ascent was caused by its successful expansion of commerce not only to Alaska, but to California, Europe, and England, and to the other communities of Puget Sound. Wheat and lumber were the major exports to these destinations. Although men talked of adding manufacturing to this commercial base, Seattle never became a great manufacturing center. Distance from major national markets, scarcity of iron and coal, and lack of venture capital (most businessmen invested in real estate or the extractive industries) were insuperable barriers. In spite of this disappointment, commerce made Seattle the metropolis of the region by 1900.

The other cities were envious but impotent to stop its rise. Portland was too distant from the sea and had too small a populated hinterland compared to Seattle to hold its earlier commercial supremacy. Its business and financial communities were too timid or too conservative to try alternatives to traditional pursuits. Its investors sunk money into real estate development or streetcar franchises rather than manufacturing. But even if they had been bolder, the same obstacles applied as in the case of Seattle. The third port city, Tacoma, slipped farther behind. Tacoma lacked the financial base of Portland that had been built in the gold rushes to California and the Inland Empire. It was farther from other seaports than Seattle. Its hinterland was not as productive as Seattle's, nor did it have much industrial potential.

Spokane, the principal inland city, had developed as a railroad hub. It had hoped to add flour and lumber milling to its assets, but it was frustrated in becoming a great manufacturing center. It lacked the diversified export base of its port rivals and also the population strength that could make it a great magnet for imports. Spokane's forested hinterland was not as great as that of the port cities, nor was its agricultural hinterland as large as that of the middle western milling centers. Its period of dynamic growth was largely over by 1910, as was that of Tacoma and Portland.

East of the Cascades men dreamed of many another community to make them rich. Few were successful, but those that survived were on the railroad, in mineral regions, or in the center of logging or farming regions. In Central Oregon the railroad created Bend in 1904. In northeastern Oregon arose Halfway (1887), Unity (1891), Richland (1897), Imnaha (1901), and Troy (1902). In Washington the settling of the Palouse country revived Colfax and created Palouse City and Pullman in 1888 and 1882, respectively. Davenport became the most important community in the region of the Big Bend of the Columbia when it was founded in 1880. The Kittitas Valley was the scene of commercial struggle among North Yakima (later simply Yakima), Ellensburg, and Prosser.

In money, population, political influence, and cultural accomplishments, Seattle hereafter reigned supreme. Yet Seattle's growth was only the most impressive of these years, for almost all cities grew, a process of development based upon new economic possibilities that in turn created fresh political problems and remedies and also yielded cultural and intellectual harvests.

NOTES

1. Kazuo Ito, *Issei: A History of Japanese Immigrants in North America* (1973), p. 18.
2. Ibid., p. 497.
3. Ibid., p. 94.

SUGGESTIONS FOR READING

Robert H. Ruby and John A. Brown, *Indians of the Pacific Northwest* (1981) is a survey, as is Cecelia S. Carpenter, *They Walked Before: The Indians of Washington State* (1977). Theodore Stern, *The Klamath Tribe: A People and Their Reservation* (1965) is excellent. Thelma D. Cliff, "A History of the Warm Springs Reservation, 1855–1900," M.S. thesis, University of Oregon, 1942, is useful. On blacks, see Elizabeth McLagan, *A Peculiar Paradise: A History of Blacks in Oregon, 1788–1940* (1980); K. Keith Richard, "Unwelcome Settlers: Black and Mulatto Oregon Pioneers," *Oregon Historical Quarterly,* 81 (1983); Robert A. Campbell, "Blacks and the Coal Mines of Western Washington, 1888–1896," *Pacific Northwest Quarterly,* 73 (1982); and Esther H. Mumford, *Seattle's Black Victorians, 1852–1901* (1980). On the Chinese, introductory studies are Lorraine B. Hildebrand, *Straw Hats, Sandals and Steel: The Chinese in Washington State* (1977) and John R. Wunder, "The Chinese and the Courts in the Pacific Northwest: Justice Denied?," *Pacific Historical Review,* 52 (1983). For the Japanese, a compendium is Kazuo Ito, *Issei: A History of Japanese Immigrants in North America* (1973). A scholarly account of the Jews is William Toll, *The Making of An Ethnic Middle Class: Portland Jewry over Four Generations* (1982). For other groups, short surveys are David L. Nicandri, *Italians in Washington State: Emigration, 1853–1924* (1978); Bruce Le Roy, *Lairds, Bairds, and Mariners: The Scots in Northwest America* (1978); Dale R. Wirsing, *Builders, Brewers, and Burghers: Germans of Washington State* (1977); and Albert Adatto, "Sephardim and the Seattle Sephardic Community," M.A. thesis, University of Washington, 1939. Also valuable are Paul C. Merriam, "The 'Other Portland:' A Statistical Note on Foreign-Born, 1860–1910," *Oregon Historical Quarterly,* 80 (1979) and G. Thomas Edwards and Carlos A. Schwantes, *Experiences in A Promised Land: Essays in Pacific Northwest History* (1986).

Economic and Cultural Life, 1880–1920

Members of the pioneer generation had lived and worked within the context of a colonial economy. Their life was in many ways satisfying, for some prosperous, but it was out of the mainstream of the economic life of the nation. In the decade of the 1880s the coming of the transcontinental railroad ushered in a modernizing period that inextricably bound the Northwest into a national economy.

Ever since the time of Isaac I. Stevens in the 1850s, residents of the Pacific Northwest had looked forward to the coming of the railroad. It promised rapid communication with loved ones, an easy passage to the new country, and abundant imported goods. Most important, it was the key to a prosperous export economy. The first railroad construction of consequence began, as we have seen, with the line between Portland and California in 1868. Small lines were built in the 1870s from Seattle and Portland toward their hinterlands, but all regarded these roads as preliminary to the transcontinentals.

The first railroad to connect the Middle West with the Pacific Northwest was the Northern Pacific. The road was organized in 1864 with the aid of a large grant of land by Congress. It began construction at two points: westward from St. Paul, Minnesota, and northward from Kalama on the Columbia River west of Portland on the Washington side. In 1873 the Kalama-Tacoma portion of the railroad was completed. National depression in 1873 halted construction of the westward section at Bismarck in Dakota Territory. When work eventually resumed, attention in the Pacific Northwest centered upon the choice of the terminal. Practically every community on Puget Sound made an effort to secure the prize, but Tacoma was the victor. The railroad selected that site because of the splendid harbor at Commencement Bay, the level lands surrounding it, and the cheapness of those lands. Men talked also of the forests and the mineral deposits in the hills surrounding the bay. Little could be done until the business depression lifted, however, and when it did there was a new leader at the helm of the Northern Pacific.

Henry Villard was a German immigrant, a journalist who had originally come to the United States as an agent of German bondholders of Holladay's Oregon railroads. By 1879 he had obtained control of the old Oregon Steam Navigation Company. In the same year he began building a railroad along the south bank of the Columbia River to its junction with the Snake and reorganized his water and rail interests into a new corporation, the Oregon Railway and Navigation Company, which also bought the Oregon Steamship Company that provided service from Portland to San Francisco. He planned to make Portland the outlet of the trade of the Northwest from east of the Cascades. In 1883 Villard completed the first transcontinental link when he obtained control of the Northern Pacific and connected it to the OR and N.

In the following year, however, Villard lost control of the two lines, which then went their separate ways. Taking advantage of his departure, the Puget Sound interests, who now controlled the Northern Pacific, built a link from the Snake River over the Cascades to Tacoma in 1887, thus bypassing Portland. The efficiency of this route was enhanced in the next year with the construction of Stampede Tunnel through the mountains. In the same year the Northern Pacific extended a line from Tacoma to Seattle.

Villard made a comeback in 1889 when he organized the Oregon Transcontinental Company. It took over the Northern Pacific and shared ownership of the OR and N with the Union Pacific. The Union Pacific had been the second transcontinental to reach the Pacific Northwest. In 1884 the Union Pacific had built a line (called the Oregon Short Line) from Granger, Wyoming, on the main line from Omaha to California, to Huntington on the Snake where it connected with the OR and N, dropping south from the Columbia.

The other partner with the Union Pacific in building the first transcontinental, the Central Pacific, had become by the 1880s the basis of a vast western railroad called the Southern Pacific. The SP had absorbed Holladay's Oregon and California and had completed the railroad from Portland to Sacramento in 1887. About this same time another momentous development occurred in the railroading history of the Northwest: James J. Hill arrived.

Hill was a storekeeper in St. Paul who had entered the railroad business in 1878 when, with some Canadian associates, he acquired the St. Paul and Pacific Railroad. Since the mid-1880s he had realized that

James J. Hill. Oregon Historical Society

his line had to build to the Pacific Northwest or to acquire the Northern Pacific or to reconcile itself to remaining a regional railroad forever. The major reason for expansion was that the Pacific Northwest, indeed the entire country, was now joined into a national economy. Hill also needed a Northwest connection to compete with the Northern Pacific that was invading his territory in the Middle West and on the Canadian Plains.

In 1889 Hill committed himself to a road to the Pacific Northwest. He did not know if he and his associates had the financial resources to best Villard, but did know that a newly constructed, properly engineered and financed road would be far more profitable than the ramshackle Northern Pacific. Thus was born the Great Northern Railway.

As construction proceeded, interests in the Pacific Northwest waited hungrily to see if their town or city was to be on the right-of-way of the new railroad. The biggest prize of all was the western terminal. Hill chose Seattle for it. Seattle was the wholesaling and retailing center of the Sound; it had a system of local railroads; and suitable land was available along the waterfront for terminal facilities. The Great Northern's golden spike was driven on January 6, 1893, but through-passenger service did not reach Seattle until June. By that time the nation was plunging into its worst depression to that date.

After a four-year pause, business again picked up. But the Northern Pacific had not survived under Villard's leadership. It had paid out its surpluses in dividends rather than in reconstructing its lines; its spur lines were often poorly located; and it had been badly built. The railroad was reorganized under the financial leadership of J. Pierpoint Morgan, the banking titan. But James J. Hill was the man in effective charge of the line. By the turn of the century he planned to obtain control of the railroads of the Pacific Northwest.

This favorable picture, however, was soon blurred by the emergence of the Union Pacific Railroad, under the inspired leadership of Edward H. Harriman, as a threat to the monopoly of the Hill lines. The Union Pacific controlled the ORNC which had the water level route along the south bank of the Columbia River from its confluence with the Snake to Portland. Hill needed access to Portland along this easy route, either by cooperating with the ORNC, or by building a new line on the north bank. Harriman, in turn, needed a connection to the port cities of Tacoma and Seattle over the Cascades. He could obtain this connection either by cooperating with the Hill lines or by building a new line through these mountains.

There was another point of competition between the two railroad magnates. This was their rivalry to control the Chicago, Burlington, and Quincy Railroad. This road, which originated in Chicago, had a connection to the Pacific Northwest from Nebraska to Billings, Montana, where it joined the Northern Pacific. It also had the potential to acquire railroads running to the Southwest. Hill and Harriman, backed by the giants of Wall Street, fought a financial battle to buy the Burlington in the year 1901. Prices of its stock rose spectacularly, but in the end Hill and his ally Morgan won out. They formed a new corporation, the Northern Securities Company, which controlled the Burlington, the Great Northern, and the Northern Pacific. Although broken up by the United States Supreme Court in 1904 as a violation of the Sherman Antitrust Act, the three companies continued to cooperate.

They soon had a new competitor. The Chicago, Milwaukee, and St. Paul Railroad decided to build to Puget Sound in 1901. It was completed in 1909 to Seattle, with a portion of its line throughout the Rockies being the first electrified line in the region. Yet one more railroad was to come. James J. Hill decided at last to build a line along the north bank of the Columbia River. Construction began on the Spokane, Portland, and Seattle in 1906 and was completed in 1909. The road ran from Spokane

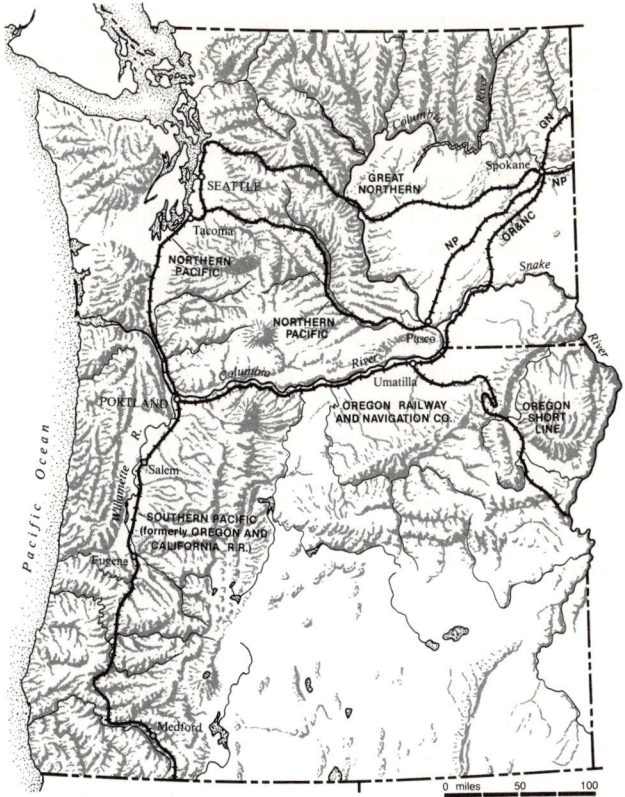

Major Railroads of the Pacific Northwest, c. 1893

to Portland, indeed, but then on to Astoria to meet Hill's coastal steamships. It was not extended to Seattle.

The results of railroad construction in the Pacific Northwest were momentous. The railroad enormously expanded the territory tributary to the port cities of Portland, Tacoma, and Seattle. Although these cities fought over the trade of the interior, they increased it immensely over the days of the Columbia-Willamette route. Now the wheat, lumber, and wool of the interior could flow to the sea unimpeded by the barriers of nature. The railroad encouraged the flow of immigration to the region. Most of those who produced the great population increase of these years and contributed to its greater homogeneity were relieved in body and pocketbook to come by train rather than by covered wagon or by ship.

The railroad also brought goods as well as people. The region remained colonial and depended on the outside world for its supply of manufactured goods. From the cities and factories of the East Coast and the Middle West came tons of consumer goods, farm machinery, and construction materials to supply the growing farms and cities of the Pacific Northwest.

The railroad of course sent out exports. It made transportation facilities cheap enough for the lumbermen and farmers of the Northwest to be competitive with the pine forests of the South and the wheat fields of the Great Plains. Railroads not only were beneficial in themselves, but they forced the steamship companies to lower their rates.

The railroad advanced the economic development of the region, as well as its own, by publicizing the opportunities of the area. Both the Northern Pacific and the Great Northern had publicity bureaus. The Northern Pacific distributed literature throughout the eastern part of the United States and in Europe. It sent special cars to the East with publicity exhibits. It sold its land inexpensively, realizing that the real profits for the railroad would come from the transportation of crops, not from the sale of the land.

The railroad changed the land use patterns of the region. For example, in the area east of the Cascades, both in Oregon and in Washington, the railroad made possible the transportation of wheat to markets in large quantities. The coming of wheat farmers was, however, at the expense of the cattlemen. Now it was no longer possible to run herds on the open range and to conduct the long drives to the markets of the Great Plains. The railroad dotted the landscape with farms and drove the ranchers from their old ranges. In southeastern Oregon the railroad replaced cattlemen with sheepherders, for it was more economical to transport a pound of wool by rail than a pound of beef on the hoof.

The railroad also created new communities. A classic instance is Spokane which became a true railroad hub. In 1881 the little village of Spokane Falls was chosen for a site on the Northern Pacific because it was at the terminus of the best route over the Rockies. Beginning in 1887 Spokane began to prosper. In that year in the Coeur d'Alene region of Idaho, just eastward across the boundary, miners discovered rich deposits of placer gold. A local capitalist, Daniel C. Corbin, built a railroad to the diggings to supply miners with food, clothing, and equipment. Shortly afterward miners rushed northward to the Colville region of Washington in 1888 and to the Kootenay country of British Columbia in 1891. Again, Corbin built the railroad to these regions.

The railroad also helped Spokane become an agricultural center. In the middle of the 1880s farmers moved onto the virgin soils of the Palouse region of Idaho and Washington. The Northern Pacific reached down to this area and attached it to Spokane's orbit, taking it from the grasp of the Union Pacific which had hoped to direct its traffic to Portland. In the late 1880s the agricultural frontier reached the Big Bend region, where the Columbia River makes a massive turn to the west, and the railroad also drew the wheat exports of this country to Spokane.

Soon James J. Hill's Great Northern Railway was approaching the Northwest. Hill bargained judiciously with the Spokane city fathers, who were eager for a place on the newest transcontinental, and he extracted the promise of a free right-of-way and other concessions from the city in return for selecting it. In 1892 the Great Northern reached Spokane. It opened up new parts of the Big Bend and the Okanogan regions as tributaries of Spokane. It also temporarily lowered freight rates while the Great Northern was in competition with the Northern Pacific. This last advantage, however, dissipated when the interests of the Great Northern and the Northern Pacific were joined in 1901.

Many other communities were affected, positively or negatively, by the railroad. Walla Walla, which had a connection to Wallula on the Columbia River, suffered when the Northern Pacific began its Cascade route to Puget Sound. This line, in drawing traffic to the Sound away from the Columbia River, also injured the trade of Portland. But the Rose City fought back by gaining federal appropriations to widen and deepen the Columbia River, although there was no denying that in wheat exporting, Portland did lose traffic to Seattle. On the other hand, not only Spokane, but cities such as Ellensburg, Yakima, The Dalles, and Umatilla either began or took a new lease on life with the coming of the railroads.

Waterways transportation also improved in this era. The great bottleneck of the Columbia River had been the falls and rapids extending from the Cascades to Celilo, a series of menacing obstacles known to the whites since the time of Lewis and Clark. To farmers and merchants seeking an alternative to the railroads along the Columbia, it seemed an eternity until the federal government finally completed two canals. The one at the Cascades was opened in 1896, that at The Dalles in 1915. Faced with competition from the railroads, steamship companies dropped their rates. This reduction not only facilitated wheat shipments to traditional markets like California, Great Britain, and the East Coast, but revived dreams of the "limitless markets of Asia," dear to the American imagination since the time of the clipper ships. James J. Hill was one of the most ambitious of those in quest of the China trade. In 1890 Hill made an agreement with a Japanese steamship company to link Seattle with Yokohama, the first regularly scheduled connection between the Pacific Northwest and Japan. In 1900 he ordered the construction of two massive twin-screw steel steamers to serve this route, but their technology was outmoded by the time that they were launched.

Other men ardently longed for the opening of the Panama Canal. Begun under American auspices in 1904, the canal was opened in 1914. It proved an enormous benefit in time, but its most important result before the First World War was in the governmental realm. Portland founded its Public Docks Commission in 1910. Seattle established a port commission in 1911. Both were public bodies created in anticipation of a great general volume of commerce that the canal would engender.

The most important industry affected by these transportation changes in the region was lumber. Indeed lumber was the most important regional enterprise and the principal export. But in spite of its continuing importance throughout these forty years, the industry changed its nature during the period. The coming of the railroad was important to the lumber industry in several ways. It created a market for railroad ties as the main and branch lines were being constructed. The mill companies opened up hundreds of miles of local logging railroads to tap timber that had been inaccessible to ox or horse teams. The first logging railroad constructed was the Tenino and Olympia in 1881. The great cost of logging lines meant that railroad companies had to acquire their own blocks of timber to justify their construction.

The railroad was not the only technological change of the 1880s to have an effect upon the lumber business. In the woods the steam donkey engine was invented to pull in the logs by cables. Crosscut saws and double-bitted axes were introduced. Dams and flumes appeared to bring the logs to the mills by water in support of the logging railroads and the steam donkeys. In the mills, workmen used the bandsaw with the mechanical-driven carriage. The double circular saw replaced the single circular saw and inventors devised a means to replace broken teeth in the saws without replacing the entire saw. Mechanical blowers sped the disposal of sawdust from the mills.

Out of the mills came new products to meet changing markets. Rough, green lumber was now not the only product. Planing mills and dry kilns produced finished lumber as box shooks, mouldings, doors, and sashes. One important market for this new output was in southern California where there was tremendous growth as men and women flocked into the area as part of a "health boom" that drew invalids from the Middle West. As the lumber products of the Northwest became more sophisticated, they found markets in England, the East Coast, Europe, and South Africa. To meet these markets, the construction, loading, and rigging of the lumber vessels was improved.

The end of this cargo trade came in the great depression of 1893. No attempt had ever been made to organize production as large and small units saturated the market. Prices plunged in the late 1890s and millmen failed by the score. But the pioneer lumbermen and their cargo trade had contributed to regional development by bringing in capital, opening up areas unsuited for mining and agriculture, and diversifying the economic base.

The twentieth century lumber industry was born out of the destruction of the Great Lake forests and the devastation of the depression of the late 1890s. The turn of the century saw a great migration of lumbermen from Mid-America to the Pacific Northwest. But other Midwesterners went to the South where they sought the native pine. In order to compete with them, the Northwest needed to overcome its distance differential from the South. This was accomplished in two ways, one by human ingenuity, one by a simple fact of nature. The Northwest lowered its production costs by mechanization. What made this process more valuable in the Northwest than in the South was the quality of the natural resources. The trees on the slopes of the Cascades and on the Olympic Peninsula are large and are gathered in thick stands. A dollar invested in a machine in Oregon or Washington paid higher dividends in lower labor costs than one spent in Georgia or Louisiana.

After the turn of the century lumber prices rose. But the costs of timber and of machinery were high. New capital flowed into the region to supplement the California investors who survived from the cargo trade era. One example is Frederick Weyerhaeuser, a Midwestern lumberman, who bought 900,000 acres of timber from the Northern Pacific Railroad in 1900. Other Midwesterners, David M. Clough and Roland H. Hartley, financed by Easterners such as William C. Butler, formed the Clough-Hartley Company, with headquarters in Everett.

Following lumber, the second most important product exported from the Pacific Northwest was wheat. Farmers benefited from the fall in railroad freight rates. Nature also helped them reduce their production costs to a point lower than anywhere else in the United States. The virgin soils of the region enabled farmers to grow crops that were singularly free of pests and plant diseases for a generation. After that time, mechanization played its role in reducing costs. Its costs, however, forced smaller farmers out of business and increased the size of the remaining farms. By 1910 most of the wheat country had been occupied and agriculture had begun to lose its dynamic role in economic development.

Farmers moved into the eastern and central parts of the Pacific Northwest after 1870. Although rainfall was lighter than the new settlers were used to in the humid areas of Puget Sound, the Willamette Valley, and the Middle West, farmers first found crops could be grown in the river valleys and then on the bench lands behind the rivers. By 1890 the wheat growers were entrenched in the Palouse, Big Bend, and Yakima regions of Washington and in the John Day, Deschutes, and Umatilla valleys in Oregon. After 1890 the Big Bend country made the most spectacular growth of all of these areas, but the latecoming pioneers also filled in the open spaces elsewhere in the region.

The advance of the farmers was made possible not only by the railroad, but by other national and international developments. Northwest wheat was now finding an increasing number of markets overseas, especially in Great Britain. The land laws of the United States were generous, providing either for homesteads or cheap land. The railroads also sold land inexpensively. Railroads and chambers of commerce publicized the area in the Middle West and abroad, and publicized it in fairly accurate terms. Agricultural colleges and extension agents contributed advice to inquiring settlers.

The expansion of wheat raising affected not only farmers, but also city dwellers. Men were needed to unload and reship grain at the ports. Others manufactured sacks and farm implements. Still others labored in white collar jobs to record the details of worldwide wheat commerce.

The wheat farmers' gains were others' losses. Most severely hurt by the advance of the farming frontier were the beef raisers. In the 1870s and 1880s the sagebrush and grasslands east of the Cascades in both Oregon and Washington drew the cattlemen. The cattlemen's markets were the growing cities of the Northwest; the mines of Nevada; San Francisco; and, greatest of all, the ranges of the northern Great Plains where the herds would be held for fattening for eastern cities. The ranch owners, capital, techniques, and cattle were all California imports, including the successful Peter French, who controlled 100,000 acres of range land in central Oregon.

These halcyon years ended in the 1880s. The railroads were now available to send the farmers' products to market. Wheat was cheaper to export than beef. The farmers' greater numbers gave them political power and vigilante strength to defeat the cattlemen. Peter French, himself, was a victim of their growing might—he was murdered by a settler, Ed P. Oliver, in 1897. His assailant was acquitted by a farm jury.

Most cattlemen who wanted to continue their business had to modify it in one of several ways. They could abandon the open range and the long drive in favor of supplying the regional cities. Or they could simply leave the region to move their open range enterprise to Idaho, Montana, or the Dakotas. Others took the ignominious but necessary route of becoming sheepmen. Finally, some could seek grazing permits from the United States Forest Service after 1906 to run their cattle in the national forests.

The sheepmen survived the advent of the railroad and the farmer better than did the cattle raisers. Sheep could be herded easily and thus driven to shelter better than could cattle. They flourished on the exotic plants that succeeded the native grasses. And they furnished raw material for the booming wool market of the 1880s, a period in which beef prices reached low points. Sheepmen continued in some areas because their product, wool, was valuable in respect to its bulk. Others stayed because they adapted to the changing environment, both natural and social, and became efficient businessmen and astute politicians.

The greatest of the Northwest sheep raisers was the Baldwin Sheep and Land Company of Hay Creek (Crook County), Oregon. Dr. David Baldwin, a California physician, began sheep ranching in this area either in 1873 or 1874. In 1883 Baldwin sold his ranch to two brothers, Charles A. and Judson P. Van Houten, from the wool region of New York State. In 1887 they and other investors took a symbolic step: they incorporated the first agricultural enterprise in the Northwest since the Puget's Sound Agricultural Company.

The Baldwin Company took advantage of its site and of developing markets after the depression of the mid-1880s by importing Merino sheep, which gave it an animal that grew thick and high quality wool. The company took its share of the grazing reserves on the national forest land after the permit system was introduced in 1906. It continued to be managed efficiently. But its success, and that of other prosperous sheep grazers, was also due to developments outside the region. As America industrialized, markets arose for wool and for mutton to clothe and feed the urban workers. In the eastern states in these years, also, land costs were appreciating, and farmers there turned from wool to more valuable crops such as corn, wheat, beef, and pork. In Oregon the rise of the wool industry centered in the market town of Shanaiko which became one of the largest centers for wool collection in the nation. Later Pendleton became the great exporting city.

A few sheepmen also expanded into farming. The most successful of these survivors were the McGregor brothers of eastern Washington. They had come to the state in 1882 to farm, but soon entered the open range business. When the railroaders and the homesteaders closed the open range, the McGregors rebounded. They bought and leased land, upgraded the quality of their animals, and learned to care for them scientifically. In 1905 the brothers formed the McGregor Land and Livestock Company and in the same year began to raise wheat. During the First World War the firm benefited from high prices on wheat and wool and they also began raising lambs for urban markets at this time.

The salmon canning industry rose and fell in the Pacific Northwest from the Civil War to the First World War. The industry had begun on the Columbia River in 1867 and then spread to Puget Sound, the Oregon coastal rivers, and to Alaska. Capital for the enterprise came from Californians initially, with the first entrepreneurs being the Hume brothers who had pioneered the salmon-canning industry on the Pacific Coast, beginning on the Sacramento River in 1864. Workers in the canneries, doing the disagreeable jobs there, were Chinese. The fishermen were Americans, Finns, and central and southern Europeans.

A flaw in the industry was apparent by the turn of the century, however. Very few were interested in conservation measures (the major exception was Robert D. Hume of Oregon's Rogue River). Methods of artificial propagation were not widely practiced. Seasonal limitations were either nonexistent or ignored. The industry was highly competitive. And a high degree of mechanization was accomplished which further depleted the resource base. Among these mechanical innovations was the so-called "Iron Chink" machine that cut, cleaned, and packed the fish into cans. Nets were lengthened and strengthened and boats made larger and more efficient. All of these mechanical improvements were too expensive for the majority of the small cannerymen. Most went bankrupt or were absorbed by large concerns like the Columbia River Packers Association (1887) or the Alaska Packers Association (1893). Even they were not successful in maintaining the fisheries of the Columbia River and Puget Sound and had to yield primacy to Alaska by 1910. By that date the fishing industry was of relatively minor importance in the Pacific Northwest.

Manufacturing

The fact that the regional exports were largely raw materials or semifinished goods was disappointing to many citizens of the Northwest. They wanted to advance in the same way as the dynamic regions of the country (the East and the Middle West) toward a sophisticated manufacturing economy. Chambers of commerce, newspapers, labor unions, all proclaimed the virtues and necessity of manufacturing. This faith led to conventions, pamphlets, speeches, letters to the editor. But few results came from these exhortatory works. The iron plant at Oswego, Oregon, operated sporadically until 1894. There were shingle mills scattered throughout the region. There were manufactures for the area's growing cities: breweries, bakeries, building materials, and light machinery, for example. But in spite of numerous optimistic claims, no northwestern city became a new Pittsburgh or Chicago or Minneapolis.

In Seattle there were some potential assets for manufacturing. There were local, regional, and transcontinental railroads. Population was growing rapidly after the mid-1880s. There was a plethora of lumber and coal deposits within easy range. And there were some people willing to take the plunge into manufacturing. In 1886 a British iron and steel man, Peter Kirk, visited the Seattle area. After canvassing several sites for a steel mill, Kirk decided to lay out a new town, called Kirkland, on the shores of Lake Washington. With the support of eastern shareholders, Kirk began construction of the mill in 1891. A scant two years after groundbreaking, the nation was devastated by the depression of 1893. Eastern banks began calling in their loans. At Kirkland the eastern investors began to default on their stock subscriptions. In 1895 Kirk gave up, even before his mill was completed.

Peter Kirk was a failure, but he had the courage to try. Most businessmen, while talking up manufacturing, avoided it. They preferred to invest their capital in the safer, more lucrative ventures of real estate in the urban areas. Many people, for example, profited from the rebuilding of cities after the great fires in Portland (1873), Seattle (1889), and Spokane (1889). In spite of their optimistic talk, most investors realized that Seattle manufacturing possibilities were limited by a shortage of iron ore and of coal, the lack of a skilled labor force, and the city's geographical isolation from the rest of the nation.

Much the same thing happened at Everett. A Wisconsin lumberman, Henry Hewitt, Jr., came to Port Gardner Bay in 1888. He interested James J. Hill, prominent shareholders of the Northern Pacific Railroad, and John D. Rockefeller in the surrounding area. The town of Everett was laid out, founded upon hopes for sawmills, shipyards, smelters. But the depression of 1893 ruined these plans. After recovery, the city did enjoy a prosperous future, but based upon lumber, not heavy industry.

Spokane, also, suffered from delusions of manufacturing grandeur. Citizens argued that the ample water power of the falls of the Spokane River, its railroads in all directions, and its proximity to wheat and lumber would make it a flour and lumber milling metropolis. These claims were in part valid, but great manufacturing did not arise. Dreams for industries fell before the reality that Spokane lacked fuel, capital, and raw materials.

By the end of the first decade of the twentieth century the Pacific Northwest's economy was growing, prosperous, and dynamic. Population had increased vastly in the past three decades. Cities were the principal beneficiary of this uban growth. Yet the area remained largely commercial, for its industrial development was weak. Even the commercial side was becoming less varied. Exports of minerals and salmon were less important in 1910 than in 1880. Wheat was valuable, but had reached its geographic limits. Only lumber remained a growth industry.

Labor

The manufacturing enterprises that existed in the Pacific Northwest were built upon harsh conditions of labor. But the workers were not passive;

Spokane, c. 1885. Eastern Washington State Historical Society

some turned to organized efforts to better their conditions. Both the American Federation of Labor and the Industrial Workers of the World offered relief. The first successful labor union in the Northwest was the American Federation of Labor. Its first organizing efforts took place in Portland in 1883. By 1910 the union movement was strong in both Portland and Seattle, but it was largely confined to skilled workers in these cities. It had won for them the eight-hour day and wages and dignity sufficient to make its members consider themselves solid—if not conservative—citizens. Left out were the unskilled and those, regardless of job, who worked in the forest products industry. The AFL was pragmatic, not ideological. It had no plans to transform society. It certainly did not want to replace capitalism. Its goals were once summed up by a high official: "We have no ultimate ends, we are going on from day to day."[1] What it did do was to try to organize skilled workers for the important but limited goals of better pay, improved working conditions, and shorter hours.

Its opponents were not only the employers, but also, after the turn of the century, the Industrial Workers of the World. Founded in 1905 in Chicago, and led by William F. "Big Bill" Haywood of the Western Federation of Miners, the IWW was radical. It proclaimed a philosophy of "industrial unionism" that would give the workers the ownership and management of the economic system from production of goods and services to their distribution. The IWW's vision is captured in the preamble to its 1908 constitution: "The working class and the employing class have nothing in common. . . . Between these two classes a struggle must go on until the workers of the world organize as a class, take possession of the earth and the machinery of production, and abolish the wage system."[2] In practice the IWW frequently supplemented this large scheme with more typical labor goals like those of the AFL. The tactics of the IWW, regardless of its goals, were largely unorthodox.

The Wobblies (no one knows the origin of this nickname) tried to organize all the workers, unskilled as well as skilled. They participated in spontaneous strikes that they believed would one day culminate in a massive general strike—national or even worldwide in scope—resulting in the overthrow of the old system and the substitution of industrial unionism. They scorned political action to achieve their apocalyptic vision; they did not vote, run for office, use the courts, or lobby before governmental bodies. They were opposed to all international wars as capitalistic plots. They advocated relentless propaganda activity—newspapers, soap boxes, pamphlets carried their messages. The Wobblies made the "free speech fight" famous (or infamous, depending on one's view). Whenever a community made the IWW or other radical message unlawful, the Wobblies courted arrest and publicity. They defiantly broke the law by speaking anyway and filled the jails to overflowing. There were so many, and the prison board charges rose so high, that the authorities had to free them to repeat their fight at the next town. Finally, they occasionally practiced sabotage to bring the capitalists to heel.

The IWW first appeared in the Pacific Northwest in Portland in 1907, when its members paraded to protest the trial in Idaho of Bill Haywood for the murder of former governor, Frank Steunenberg. In 1911 they held rowdy street meetings in the city and in the following year heckled Robert Baden-Powell, the founder of the Boy Scouts, which in Wobbly eyes was a militaristic organization. The mayor responded by prohibiting meetings of the IWW in Portland. Spanish American War veterans responded when the Wobblies fell into the habit of holding meetings at the war memorial in Lownsdale Park. Resenting this "desecration" of their monument, the veterans began attacking the Wobblies throughout the city. In January 1914, a period of unemployment in the Northwest, IWW members joined in a march of the unemployed from Portland to Eugene.

IWW members also participated in strikes. The first lasted for three weeks in the lumber mills of Portland in January 1907 over wages and hours. It failed miserably. So, too, did an attempted strike of Wobbly construction workers building an interurban railroad line at Eugene. None of the other workers there joined the Wobblies in walking out. In May and June of 1913 a Wobbly strike failed in the logging camps at Coos Bay. When world war broke out, in the next year, the IWW would become far more notorious if not more successful.

Cultural Life

The cultural life of the era between 1880 and 1920 was much more complex and sophisticated than in the pioneer era. Higher regional income, the growth of a small leisure class, improved communication with the rest of the nation, and a more heterogeneous population were contributing factors. So too was a conscious desire to emulate the cultural life of the older regions. As earlier, the Pacific Northwest remained culturally conservative.

Architecture

Architectural developments illustrate this last point. The great influence on Victorian architecture in America was Andrew Jackson Downing, whose "pattern books" of architectural plans could be followed easily by housebuilders. Downing urged that a house express its function in the design of the rooms and in its relationship to the natural environment. Northwesterners applied this philosophy with a bewildering array of architectural styles, often in rich combination.

These diverse influences were represented in the growing cities of the Pacific Northwest. Although classical buildings of the Greek Revival form survived the Civil War, residents slowly adopted newer forms from the East, usually a generation after their introduction in that region.

Gothic Revival was marked by gables, pointed arches, appliques, and asymmetry. It was easy to master and could be applied, in pure or modified form, to the older cottages with relative ease. Stick Style was wood architecture at its best. People of wealth favored, beginning in the 1870s, the French Empire style, which encompassed mansard roofs, wooden quoines and keystones, and flush board siding. Other members of the aristocracy had architects draw their plans in the Italianate Villa style. People of daring tastes had no compunction about blending the various modes into sometimes attractive, sometimes bizarre assemblages.

After its American premiere at the centennial exposition in Philadelphia in 1876, the Queen Anne Style crossed the continent. It was eclectic, referring to no particular historical era, but blending together a rich selection of traditions. In the 1890s Pacific Northwesterners adopted the Romanesque style of H. H. Richardson, a New York architect who had become popular in the East in the 1870s. Richardson Romanesque featured open floor spaces, vaults, and rounded arches. Colonial Revival houses followed close behind in popularity in this decade.

For people of middle class and working class status, homes were, of course, more modest. In the crowded areas of the cities, and even in the new suburbs, the houses were rectangular, wooden, two-story dwellings resembling the cottages of fifty to seventy-five years earlier. There was somewhat of an exception in the Puget Sound region where Shingle Style bungalows, an adaptation of Queen Anne, were prominent. The architects who provided the houses, banks, churches, and factories were often competent men, even distinguished, but they were not innovators.

The Press

Journalism in the Pacific Northwest partook of national trends and characteristics, but included some distinguished newspapermen. The most prominent newspaper of all, a real teacher to Oregon, and a journal of national reputation, was the Portland *Oregonian*. The *Oregonian* had begun as a weekly in the 1850s, but in 1870 fell under the editorship of Harvey W. Scott who, with the exception of a few years, remained its editor until his death in 1910. Scott was born in Illinois and had crossed the Oregon Trail in 1852 at the age of seventeen.

Scott was a product of the frontier and of the metropolis, a man who bridged the transition in the Pacific Northwest from the rural economy to the new urbanism and industrialism. Throughout his long life he tried to retain the individualism of his youth in the vastly different metropolitan circumstances of his maturity. This effort stamped him as representative of conservative causes. He fought against free public high schools, arguing that the state should educate the young in citizenship and basic education only through the elementary grades. In the political struggles of the times, Scott staunchly defended the cause of business against all critics. He supported the gold standard and the high protective tariff. He opposed woman suffrage. Yet his editorials were solid, erudite, even brilliant.

In Washington the opposite numbers of the *Oregonian* were the *Washington Standard* and the *Post-Intelligencer*. The publisher of Olympia's *Standard* was John M. Murphy. He hewed to the conservative position through the years of controversy over statehood. Seattle's *Post-Intelligen-*

cer, especially under the editorship of Erastus Brainerd (1904–1911), was an accurate, conservative paper, dedicated editorially to "booming" the city in opposition to its rivals, Tacoma and Portland. On civic matters it stood for decency, law, and order.

There were some progressive newspapers, too. In Pendleton, Sam Jackson had published the *East Oregonian* for many years as the voice of ranchers and farmers of the cross-Cascades region. In 1902 he established the *Oregon Journal* in Portland as a formidable opponent of the *Oregonian* on almost every issue. The *Journal's* major concerns were those of the progressive movement in city and state. It supported the drive for the initiative and referendum and for woman suffrage and worked for home rule for cities, municipal cleanliness, and regulation of the liquor traffic and the railroads. Spokane had a fine progressive paper, W. H. Cowles's *Spokesman-Review.* It fought for local progressives and national leaders like Theodore Roosevelt, who were battling to regulate the unrestrained forces of modern industrialism. In Seattle there was a unique journal, the *Union Record,* the only daily newspaper in the United States published by organized labor. In Oregon, Abigail Scott Duniway, the woman suffrage leader, published a spritely and profitable paper, the *New Northwest,* from 1871 to 1887.

Regardless of their ideological orientation, all of these papers were old-fashioned in the sense that they were personal newspapers, the reflection of their editors' personalities, philosophies, and prejudices. There were other papers that represented newer journalistic trends in the nation. As the century turned, the metropolitan newspapers of America, for the most part, lowered their standards. Papers cost less and publishers believed that the new urban reader wanted light fare. Comics and sports captured space from news. As newspapers gained more circulation, advertising increased. When that happened, editors feared to publish controversial matters or to take unpopular stands. In many cases, papers were joined together into chains by journalistic entrepreneurs like William Randolph Hearst and Joseph Pulitzer.

The chief northwestern representative of the new mass newspaper was Alden J. Blethen, owner of the Seattle *Daily Times.* Blethen was a sensationalist, a political chauvinist, and an advocate of vice and corruption as being good sources of business profits. He pandered to what he conceived to be mass taste by printing lurid stories, the most famous of which was illustrated by a composite photograph of a political opponent allegedly depicted in a homosexual embrace. Its emphasis upon low life gave it a nickname, the *Daily Crimes.* Other newspapers, business journals, religious organs, and weeklies continued, but they too reflected the national patterns in their respective spheres.

Art and Music

The world of art in the Pacific Northwest was a very small one. Portland, with its tradition, wealth, and New England cultural background, was in the forefront of artistic endeavors. There was a tiny Bohemian community where artists gathered in the Little Club and the Oregon Society of Artists. In these groups, and informally, they discussed their own works and the great movements of modern art that were revolutionizing the Western world and first impressing Americans in the Armory Show in New York in 1913.

Patronage of the arts was confined to wealthy people. The Ladd family was the chief force in founding the Portland Art Association in 1892 with a room in the city's public library. In 1905 the Association erected a museum building which also became the headquarters for an art school. In this building there worked for decades two heroic figures whose brilliance, devotion, and energy compensated for the limited cultural atmosphere in which they labored.

Anna Belle Crocker, born in Milwaukee, Wisconsin, and educated as a secretary, was director of the museum from 1909 to 1936. Crocker was a tactful fundraiser, an able administrator, and a splendid teacher to the community. She not only exhibited local artists' work and the few old masters donated by local patrons, but she educated the public to the newest art modes. In 1913, for example, she brought to the museum Marcel Duchamp's painting, "Nude Descending a Staircase," and always kept abreast of developments in Europe and New York. One of her greatest accomplishments was in bringing Harry Wentz to the art school as teacher.

Wentz was a local man, but not a parochial one. He assumed the influential position of being the principal educator at the only art school in Oregon. To the school came men and women, young and old, part-time night students with daytime jobs, and people who took the day classes. From Wentz they learned not only techniques, but something of the international dimension of art, for their teacher had a vast curiosity that he periodically refreshed by visits to New York City. Above all Wentz was important because he exemplified art as life, urging upon students the truth that art was integral to the human experience, not a portion of it; it was central, not an avocation.

In Seattle progress was slower and in the other regional cities confined to self-taught amateurs. Artists founded the Seattle Fine Arts Society in 1906. Although it had difficulty in finding a headquarters, it began holding annual exhibitions of regional artists in 1916. This small band was supplemented late in the period by the arrival of Nellie Cen-

Nellie Centennial Cornish. Special Collections Division, University of Washington Libraries

tennial Cornish in 1914 and Ambrose Patterson in 1918. Cornish was a pianist and a music teacher. She was also an inspiration. Born in 1876, a recent resident of Salt Lake City, she had come to a turning point in her life when she decided to found the Cornish School of Allied Arts in Seattle. Here visual arts were taught, as well as music and dance. Ambrose Patterson, unlike Cornish, was an established figure when he arrived in Seattle. He was an Australian by birth, had studied and exhibited in Europe, and was a practitioner of modern art. He continued to paint in Seattle and also contributed to the art scene by establishing the School of Painting and Design at the University of Washington in 1918. Out of all of this came exhibitions of local artists, the establishment of collections at the art association and the university, and a few painters that were known outside the region. These included John Butler, E. Frere Champney, Paul Gustin, and Roi Patridge.

The story of music is also one of labored progress. The moving force were men and women of wealth. The Portland Symphony was founded in 1895, but limped along for many years. Amateur musicians organized the Seattle Symphony Orchestra in 1903 which received an institutional patron, the Seattle Symphony Society, in 1907. In neither city was there sufficient interest to create a professional orchestra nor to bring to their citizens musicians of national or international acclaim.

Religion

Church members faced two overriding issues in the Pacific Northwest in these years, as they did across the nation. One problem was intellectual, one institutional. In the post-Civil War years the doctrines of Darwinian evolution spread across the continent. Many church people felt themselves caught in the dilemma of either repudiating the new science or denying the biblical account of creation as described in Genesis. Others, a prominent example of which was Thomas Condon, retained faith in both science and God. Condon, a Congregational minister, and a professional geologist who served on the faculty at the University of Oregon, was the author of a geologic work on central Oregon entitled *The Two Islands and What Came of Them* (1902) that gained national reputation. He abandoned the literal Genesis interpretation of creation, but argued that the complexity of evolution was an even greater testimony to the creative power of God than the biblical one.

The second pressure may be broadly described as urbanization. The problems of the urban poor; of working conditions, pay, and hours (especially of women and children) of factory workers; and the impersonality of city life challenged the clergy. One who responded was Thomas Lamb Eliot, Unitarian minister and civic leader in Portland for sixty-nine years who either founded or was the moving spirit in the establishment of the Oregon Humane Society, the Home (for orphans), and the Boys and Girls Aid Society of Oregon. He pushed for enlightened aid to the criminal and the insane. Rabbi Jonah B. Wise of Portland was a supporter of laws restricting the worst conditions of tenement life. Mark Matthews, a prominent Presbyterian clergyman in Seattle, waged a long fight against the alliance among the political boss, the vice lord, and the saloonkeeper in that city. Two Catholic clergy, Father Edwin V. O'Hara and Sister Caroline Gleason, gathered data and presented it to the Oregon legislature in such compelling form that the state passed the first effective minimum wage law in American history in 1913. The Methodists in the

Puget Sound area took over Seattle General Hospital in 1900 and did settlement house work in the inner cities.

Church membership remained low in spite of this activity. When a religious census was taken in 1906, 39.1 percent of Americans had a denominational affiliation, but only 25.3 percent of Oregonians and 31.2 percent of Washingtonians were so connected. In the Northwest, as in the nation, the largest denominations, in descending order, were Roman Catholic, Methodist, and Baptist. Size produced distance as well as growth. The ministers of the urban churches became administrators as much as pastors, the supervisors of lay specialists who took over various areas of the church such as Sunday schools and missions. The urban clergy also were higher paid than their rural colleagues and came to dominate district and conference sessions.

Literature

With few exceptions regional literature was undistinguished. Edmond Meany of the University of Washington explained why for his area: "No, Puget Sound has no literature . . . there is nothing that can drive the thoughts of literature from a man's mind so completely as the impetuous, eager, absorbing chase for gold. . . ."[3] But the quest for wealth is not the only explanation for literary backwardness. Besides the lack of money to support a leisure class to write or to patronize literature another reason was the generally conservative, tradition-bound nature of the population including its intellectuals.

For whatever reason, novelists and poets concentrated upon historical novels of the pioneer era and upon natural beauties of the region. The best works, although far below the highest national standards, were written by women. Eve Emery Dye's *McLoughlin and Old Oregon* (1900), *The Conquest* (1902), and *McDonald of Oregon* (1906); Ella Higginson's *Mariella* (1904); and Abigail Scott Duniway's *From the West to the West: Across the Plains to Oregon* (1905) are the best illustrations of this genre. Frederick Homer Balch in *The Bridge of the Gods* (1890) was the first author to take the Indian seriously as a literary source, but the plot and characterization of his book are painfully inadequate. The glorification of the pioneers and the celebration of nature are also the major themes of poetry. The most popular poets were Sam Simpson, author of "Beautiful Willamette," Minnie Dyer, and Joaquin Miller. These poets were also similar to the novelists in other ways. They avoided the new literary trends. In the United States this was a period of the heady, new freedom of the naturalist and realist movements. Novelists and poets, in reaction against the prevailing romantic mode of the Genteel Tradition, celebrated a new "reality" (that often was equated with the darker side of life). But the realist credo had few believers in the Northwest.

The only distinguished poet was Charles Erskine Scott Wood. Born into a prominent and wealthy family, Wood had attended the United States Military Academy and then had become an attorney in Portland. He became a wealthy corporation lawyer, but also a defender of the disadvantaged and of radical causes. From his first visit, he had become enamoured of the beauty of the Oregon Desert and spent several summers in the ranching country of Malheur county. His poetic masterpiece, "The Poet in the Desert," was first published in 1915 (with several later revisions). Wood's work ends with a call for proletarian revolution, but is mainly a lyrical evocation of the beauties of the desert.

The writing of history and the social sciences was somewhat higher in quality than the works of fiction and poetry. Historical writing was not confined to the pioneer era, nor to amateurs. Yet the best historian was not professionally trained. Frances Fuller Victor, poet and journalist, wrote a history of early Oregon around the career of Joe Meek, the colorful frontier politician, which she entitled *The River of the West* (1870). She later moved to San Francisco and wrote four complete works in Hubert Howe Bancroft's *History of the Pacific Coast:* the two volumes on Oregon; one on Washington, Idaho, and Montana; and one on Nevada, Colorado, and Wyoming; and probably portions of four others. Although not without bias—she was unfair in her treatment of the missionaries and unsympathetic toward the Indians—her books are based upon careful research in original documents, generally objective, and clearly written.

Another self-taught historian was Elwood Evans, a Washington lawyer and politician, who published his *History of the Pacific Northwest: Oregon and Washington* in 1869. This two-volume work was written mainly by Evans who also edited the contributions of others. Although the pioneer Jesse Applegate wrote Evans that his book would "do duty in the privy or light the kitchen fires," it is well documented and objective, although the style is wooden. Far less temperate is William H. Gray's *History of Oregon* (1870). The former missionary was an ax grinder, who blamed the Catholic Church for inciting the Indians to murder the Whitmans, who was violently prejudiced against the Hudson's Bay Company, and who took other outrageous positions that vitiated his history as of any serious value.

University professors were also beginning to write history. Their ideal was the new scientific history that was the fashion in the eastern United States and in Europe. Its practitioners believed in rigorous factual accuracy, in using original sources, and in concentrating upon the development of institutions, particularly poliltical ones. Joseph Schafer of the University of Oregon, for example, was in this category. His *History of the Pacific Northwest* (1905), the first one-volume synthesis of regional history, was well received and still is worth consulting. His colleague, Frederic G. Young, also broke away from a sentimental concentration upon the pioneers. Their importance for him was as a guide to the future. The pioneers' virtues, their practice of liberty, equality, and democracy, provided a benchmark that modern society could use to solve its own problems. Young also served history as editor of the *Oregon Historical Quarterly* and published the journal of Nathaniel Wyeth.

Somewhat comparable to Young was Edmund S. Meany, professor at the University of Washington, who in 1909 published the first edition of his *History of the State of Washington*. Meany had a graduate degree in history from the University of Wisconsin, but also partook of the old antiquarian, romantic glorification of heroes of the pioneer era. His *History* did go beyond the formative period, however, to take in the events of the territorial and early statehood years. He also came to appreciate the culture of the Indians and was adopted into the membership of three tribes. Meany's other services to history came in helping to establish the Columbia Historical Society (one of the forerunners of the Washington State Historical Society) and in the founding of the *Washington Historical Quarterly* in 1906. Although neither a profound writer nor a distinguished scholar, Meany did contribute to historical knowledge in addition to his scholarly labors by helping amass a manuscript collection and the Pacific Northwest Collection in the library at the University of Washington and by lecturing to popular audiences.

In social sciences the only notable figure in the region was J. Allan Smith, professor of political science at the University of Washington. Smith was a reformer, an heir of Jefferson, who believed passionately in democracy and equality. In his writings, Smith dealt with political problems such as urban legislative representation, municipal home rule, and regulation of utilities. His masterpiece, however, explored a broader theme. In 1907 Smith published *The Spirit of American Government*. This pioneering work was a critical examination of the formation of the constitution of the United States in which he argued that the founding fathers created an instrument that was undemocratic even in the context of 1787. The book also discussed current institutions ranging from academic faculties to the legal profession. Throughout, Smith emphasized the economic motives that, he claimed, lay beneath the lofty rhetoric of American politics. His book received a varied reception within and without the region, but remains a splendid illustration of progressive scholarship.

More than a progressive, indeed the most famous Northwestern advocate of radicalism, was John Reed. This brilliant and generous writer was born to wealth, but to a family that demonstrated iconoclasm in several of its members. Reed attended Harvard and then entered journalism through the patronage of the great muckraker, Lincoln Steffens. After college, Reed moved to the Bohemian center of Greenwich Village where he wrote for conventional magazines and for the radical organ, *The Masses*. He turned out fiction, articles, plays, poems, and short stories, but his true genre was reporting. He became a radical, staged a pageant in Madison Square Garden in 1912 to suport the IWW strike in the textile mills in Paterson, New Jersey, and covered the IWW strike in Lowell, Massachusetts. He accompanied the Mexican revoluntionary, Pancho Villa, on his raiding expeditions and wrote a stirring report of them for *Metropolitan Magazine*.

But Reed's great adventure was the Russian Revolution. He was, of course, a sympathizer with the Bolsheviks and an eyewitness to the revolution of 1917. He also was engaged in diplomatic work for the new government, but his principal service to the Left was *Ten Days that Shook the World* (1919), an account of the revolution that the distinguished diplomat and historian George F. Kennan described as follows: "Despite his exuberant and uninhibited political bias, Reed's account of events of

John Reed. Oregon Historical Society

that time rises above every other contemporary record for its literary power, its penetration, its command of detail. It will be remembered when all the others are forgotten."[4] Reed did not live long enough to enjoy the acclaim for his book, for he died in Moscow of typhus in 1920. Communists at once enshrined him as a martyr and he is buried in the Kremlin's Wall.

Education

In elementary, secondary, and higher education the citizens and academics were content to emulate Eastern models. In 1865 Whitman College was opened as a seminary in Walla Walla. The Jesuits established two enduring institutions on the familiar lines of their order: Gonzaga University in Spokane in 1881 and Seattle University in 1892. Methodists founded the College of Puget Sound (1888); Presbyterians, Whitworth College (1890); Lutherans, Pacific Lutheran College (1890); and Seventh Day Adventists, Walla Walla College (1892). In the public realm the University of Washington, which opened its doors in 1861, first began to offer real university work in this period. So, too, did Washington State College, founded in 1892 as an agricultural and mechanical college.

In Oregon the private colleges of the pioneer era were joined by the Presbyterians' Albany College (1867) and the Methodists' Columbia University (1891), which became the Catholics' University of Portland in 1901. Amanda Reed, wife of Simeon of OSNC fame, left in her will a sum of money that was used to found Reed Institute (now College) in 1911. The University of Oregon (1876) and Oregon State College (1885) continued their separate ways in these years. The rise in the new number of public schools and their increasing quality led to the founding of teacher-training institutions in both areas: in Oregon, at Ashland and Monmouth in 1882; and at Cheney (1890), Ellensburg (1890), and Bellingham (1893) in Washington.

Conditions improved for elementary and secondary students in both states. Teachers were better qualified and somewhat better paid in 1920 than in 1880. The high school was a normal feature of urban life. Public education was made available and compulsory to all students through the elementary grades. Taxpayers, in other words, paid for the bare minimum of education for children. They did so for basic vocational and citizenship purposes. But they grudged supporting anything more. Their attitude toward education was typical of their approach to cultural life in general. Culture was necessary, but not very important. And whatever support was given to it demanded a return in traditional nonthreatening forms, not in innovative ideas or institutions.

NOTES

1. David Brody, ed., *The American Labor Movement* (1971), p. 1.

2. Joyce L. Kornbluh, *Rebel Voices: An IWW Anthology* (1964), pp. 12-13.

3. George A. Frykman, "Edward S. Meany, Historian," *Pacific Northwest Quarterly*, 51 (October 1960): 161.

4. George F. Kennan, *Russia Leaves the War* (1967), pp. 68-69.

SUGGESTIONS FOR READING

Three excellent comprehensive accounts of the railroads of the Northwest are Robert Athearn, *Union Pacific Country* (1971); James B. Hedges, *Henry Villard and the Railways of the Northwest* (1930); and Albro Martin, *James J. Hill and the Opening of the Northwest* (1976). A masterful history of changing land use is D. W. Meinig, *The Great Columbia Plain: A Historical Geography, 1805–1910* (1968). On the lumber industry, see Thomas R. Cox, *Mills and Markets: A History of the Pacific Coast Lumber Industry to 1900* (1974) and Ralph W. Hidy, Frank E. Hill, and Allan Nevins, *Timber and Men: The Weyerhaeuser Story* (1963). A splendid account of sheep and wheat in eastern Washington is Alexander C. McGregor, *Counting Sheep: From Open Range to Agribusiness on the Columbia Plateau* (1982). Cattle are dealt with in James O. Oliphant, *On the Cattle Ranges of the Oregon Country* (1968). On salmon canning, see Gordon B. Dodds, *The Salmon King of Oregon: R. D. Hume and the Pacific Fisheries* (1959). For urbanization, see Norman H. Clark, *Mill Town: A Social History of Everett, Washington* (1970); Murray C. Morgan, *Puget's Sound: A Narrative of Early Tacoma and the Southern Sound* (1979); and Roger Sale, *Seattle: Past to Present* (1976). On economic life, see G. Thomas Edwards and Carlos Schwantes, *Experiences in a Promised Land: Essays in Pacific Northwest History* (1986). The story of the IWW is told in Robert L. Tyler, *Rebels of the Woods: The IWW in the Pacific Northwest* (1967). Architecture is dealt with in Thomas Vaughan and Virginia G. Ferriday, *Space, Style, and Structure: Building in Northwest America* (1974); Rosalind L. Clark, *Architecture: Oregon Style* (1983); and Sally B. Woodbridge and Roger Montgomery, *A Guide to Architecture in Washington State* (1980). The best biography of John Reed is Robert A. Rosenstone, *Romantic Revolutionary: A Biography of John Reed* (1975). For C. E. S. Wood, see G. Thomas Edwards and Carlos Schwantes, *Experiences in a Promised Land: Essays in Pacific Northwest History* (1986). Various other dimensions of cultural life are dealt with in Thomas L. Vaughan, *The Western Shore: Oregon Country Essays Honoring the American Revolution* (1975).

Politics, 1865–1889

The quarter century after the Civil War saw a whole constellation of political issues confront the citizens of the Pacific Northwest. They had to deal with a party structure shattered by the war; the coming of the transcontinental railroad; the advent of the Chinese immigrants; the growth of organized labor; and the rise of political corruption. They formed a new state from old Oregon. In their attempts to deal with these myriad challenges the voters flirted with reform movements, but in general they remained loyal to the two-party system and conservative policies.

Oregon Politics

The Democrats faced a major remodeling task in both Oregon and Washington. The party had divided on the eve of the Civil War. During the conflict most of its members had joined in coalition with Republicans (forming a Union Party) to support the Lincoln administration, although some had sympathized with the South. After the war these opponents of black equality and advocates of state rights would be heard from again. In Oregon their leader was James O'Meara, a journalist; the Unionist forces were led by Lafayette Grover and James Kelly. Somehow these factions had to be blended into a unified party. By 1868 the Democrats were winning some elections, the first since a decade earlier. Although Republican presidents carried the state after 1868, the two-party system in Oregon continued strong into the 1890s in races for Congress and state offices.

The return of the Democrats resulted from national issues. After 1866 the party capitalized upon its conservative supporters' opposition to the reconstruction policies and programs of the congressional Republicans. The old antiblack prejudices emerged again as a winning issue. In 1866 the Oregon legislature did ratify the Fourteenth Amendment that made the freed persons citizens. But the amendment passed in the lower house by a mere two votes. Opposition to the amendment helped the Democrats enormously. In 1868 they won both the House and the Senate. These gains were made because many Democrats who had backed the Union party during the war now returned to their old fold. Conservative Democrats opposed the national Republican positions of granting the right to vote to the freed slaves; the military reconstruction of the South; the retention of wartime taxes after the war; and the Republican strengthening of the federal government.

Once in power the Democratic legislative majority acted on their own convictions. They rescinded the state's ratification of the Fourteenth Amendment even though it had already been adopted by enough states to go into effect. In the same year they asked, in vain, the state's two Republican United States senators to resign. In 1870 the state legislature defeated the Fifteenth Amendment, which guaranteed the freed slaves the right to vote.

The Republicans also assumed their old name after the war, shedding the Union party designation. For as long as possible they campaigned as the party that had saved the Union, branding the Democrats as sessionists, slaveholders, and traitors. Although the party did receive credit for the Union victory, it had to contend not only with a revived Democratic party, but also with pressing current issues. And these issues became less important nationally and more important locally.

The railroad was the paramount issue. Democrats and Republicans alike campaigned for federal aid to railroad construction both to and within the state. Congress gave a land grant, but authorized the Oregon legislature to bestow it. Ben Holladay obtained the grant. In 1868 he began building his Oregon Central Railroad down the east side of the Willamette Valley. It had a rival line on the other side of the river. Holladay's efforts to thwart his competition was a subject of political controversy. It was said that he bribed legislators to gain the land grant. Some detested him for employing Chinese labor to construct his lines, arguing that the Chinese were unassimilable and were undercutting the standard of living of native Americans. Others assailed Holladay for the alleged slow progress of his railroad construction and for high freight rates when it was completed. Still others condemned him for not quickly disposing of his land grant at cheap prices.

Holladay's railroad was not the only transportation issue in politics.

Ben Holladay, railroad magnate. Oregon Historical Society

Farmers were increasingly agitated by the costs of shipping their grain on steamship lines and the charges for storing grain in elevators while awaiting transportation. By 1870 there were transportation monopolies on both of Oregon's major rivers. The steamship companies controlled, directly or indirectly, the grain elevator companies. The farmers' remedy was typical of Oregon history: import an institution. Farmers Clubs had been formed as early as 1858 in Illinois; by 1872 there were enough of them in California to form as association. They had spread to Oregon by April 1873, when a state union was formed in Salem.

The purposes of the union were economic. It favored farmer-owned warehouses and river vessels. It also favored farmer manufacture of farm implements. Oregon agrarians also acted politically. They formed a third party, the Independent party, which won impressive victories in the election of 1874. When the legislature assembled, the Independents supported bills forcing railroads to fence their rights of way; regulating freight rates and fares; and encouraging construction of new railroads by giving them privileges and subsidies.

Only the subsidy issue was even partially resolved. The legislature did assist the founders of the Willamette Valley and Coast Railroad and the Portland, Dalles, and Salt Lake Railroad. But these railroads were never built. The reason for the slight legislative accomplishments include the division of power among Independents, Republicans, and Democrats, which meant that no party had its own majority; the lack of tradition and familiar, trusted leaders among the Independents; and the money and influence of Ben Holladay, who was able to forestall the fence and rate bills. After this setback, farmers either returned to the Republican or Democratic ranks or switched their reform efforts from the political arena to the activities of the Grange.

The Grange, officially named the Patrons of Husbandry, was another transplant from the East where it had been founded in 1867 in Washington, D. C. The Oregon State Grange was organized at Salem in September 1873. The Grange conducted a political lobby. In 1875 and for many years thereafter it petitioned the federal government to construct a portage road, or a canal, at The Dalles to circumvent the monopoly of the Oregon Steam Navigation Company and its successors at that strategic place. Session after session it asked the Oregon legislature for laws regulating rates and preventing transportation companies from giving lower rates to large shippers. None of these efforts bore much fruit for many years, but there were some gains. In 1876 the legislature created a canal commission with power to compel reports from the company operating the locks at the falls of the Willamette River. In 1887 it passed two bills favorable to the Granger cause: one to regulate the rates of corporations entering the state and the other to establish a two-person railroad commission appointed by the governor to investigate the annual reports of railroad companies. In 1889 the commission was expanded to three persons appointed by the legislature.

Another reform cause that took on new emphasis after the Civil War was woman's rights, especially the right to vote. All over the country women demanded that they receive the vote, suffrage which had recently been extended to the former black slaves in the Fifteenth Amendment to the United States Constitution (1870). National woman suffrage groups sprang up with local affiliates. The leader of the suffrage cause in Oregon was Abigail Scott Duniway.

Abigail Scott was born of a pioneer family in Illinois in 1834. She participated in the greatest pioneer experience—the westward movement across the trail to Oregon in 1852. Shortly after arriving, she married Benjamin C. Duniway, a rancher, and assumed the heavy tasks of frontier wife and mother. After her husband was injured, Abigail took up the millinery business, a necessity required by her husband's loss of money through endorsing a debt of an injudicious friend. The need for a livelihood also forced the family to move from Albany to Portland in 1871. In Portland Abigail began to publish a weekly newspaper, *The New Northwest,* which for the next sixteen years offered general news, literature, and editorials and articles devoted to the cause of woman suffrage. Also beginning in 1871 Duniway became a lecturer for woman suffrage all over the Pacific Northwest. Traveling by every possible means of conveyance, from train to horseback, Duniway and her associates carried the message of woman suffrage and other woman's rights throughout the region.

For many years results were meager, but there were enough achievements to keep the cause alive. In 1872 Duniway became the first woman to address the Oregon legislature. The subject was woman suffrage and the bill almost passed the house of representatives, failing by a single vote. In the same year the legislature adopted a bill which permitted married women to retain their property without liability for their husband's debts. In 1878 Oregon saw the enactment of the Married Woman's Property Act that gave wives the right to keep their wages and to sell or will their property.

But the major political issue of the 1880s for women was the suffrage. In 1880 Duniway and the other suffrage advocates decided to support a state constitutional amendment to obtain the vote. Amending the constitution required passage of a measure at two separate legislative sessions and then approval by the voters in a referendum. The woman suffrage bill passed in the legislative sessions of 1880 and 1882 and came before the people in 1884. Duniway's campaign was based upon the principle of equality. She said that woman suffrage was right in itself and should not be supported as a means to any particular moral reform. This argument was particularly important because many reformers, especially prohibitionists, hoped that women, who were regarded as keepers of moral virtue, would use their votes to control or eliminate the liquor traffic.

The campaign was hard fought, but when the votes were counted, the amendment was defeated—18,176 against, and 11,223 in favor. Although support came from all the rural counties, the voters of Portland and Multnomah County defeated it.

Other blows followed. In 1887 the Oregon legislature defeated a state suffrage law and the United States Congress defeated a woman suffrage constitutional amendment. Two other events affecting woman suffrage happened in that year. The Washington woman suffrage law was declared unconstitutional and Duniway sold, at a good profit, *The*

New Northwest. There followed a hiatus in the woman suffrage movement in Oregon for several years, until the progressive movement of the 1890s.

Temperance

Another reform movement in the 1870s and 1880s was temperance. In 1874 the Woman's Christian Temperance Union was founded. In the same year a Portland branch was opened. The first actions of the Portland branch were dramatic. Its members began to picket the Webfoot Saloon and then engaged in a sit-in. They sang hymns and prayed both inside and outside the saloon, but no enduring results were obtained from the war on the Webfoot. Thereafter WCTU members began to urge a prohibition law before the legislature and a constitutional amendment. They attempted to join forces with those of woman suffrage, arguing that the enfranchised women would use their votes to enact prohibition. The attempt failed. Prohibition did not gather much support among the citizens until the 1890s.

The Politics of Business

Other Oregon citizens were not interested in reform at all. Their concern was to use the power of government to improve their economic status. In so doing, some operated honestly, but others gave the state a reputation for corruption that was unsurpassed elsewhere.

One legitimate need was for wagon roads to connect the developing centers of the state. The railroads could not go everywhere, and roads were needed to connect them with smaller towns even after the railroads were built. In the 1860s Oregonians petitioned the federal government for lands to be given to wagon road companies. These petitions were extremely successful. Congress gave 2,490,890 acres of land for roads in Oregon in the 1860s, two-thirds of all land granted by the federal government for this purpose. Most of this land was wasted for the purpose of the grant. Either the companies built no roads or the land passed into the hands of speculators. Congress was aware of the situation and by 1870 had cut the state off from this source of revenue.

Frustrated, Oregon politicians and voters turned to another source of land for wagon road construction. This source was the federal Swamp Land Act of 1850, that gave swamp lands to the state, provided the state sold them to people who would reclaim them. For a decade Oregon had done nothing about this statute, but in 1870 it passed a law accepting the federal swamp land offer. For buyers the state set a purchase price of one dollar an acre, the amount to be claimed was unlimited, and only a 20 percent down payment had to be made. What followed demonstrated the inept and corrupt state of Oregon politics in the post–Civil War decade.

All of the state land laws were administered by the State Land Board, which was composed of the governor, secretary of state, and the state treasurer. The board permitted the swamp land claimants to survey and claim their own lands without the intervention of state surveys. This casual decision opened the way for individuals and corporations to claim as swamp land vast amounts of land that were absolutely dry. To compound the problem, beginning in 1872 the legislature began appropriating money for the school fund and for wagon roads payable out of the swamp land fund. The state began to pay the wagon road companies in warrants (in effect, IOUs) that would be redeemed when money was paid into the treasury from the sale of swamp lands. As the 1870s wore on, more and more warrants were given to more and more road companies. But the roads were never built, as their officers diverted the warrants into their own pockets, ever hopeful that they would become rich when the state redeemed the warrants. The legislature passed a law that attempted to tighten up land sales in 1878, but interpretation of the statute by the State Land Board nullified it. The legislature also attempted to get the state to negotiate with the federal government a final agreement on what actually was to be classified as the state's swamplands. This issue was settled in 1891, but it came too late. When the final accounting was achieved in 1895 the sale of swamp lands—a free gift to the state of Oregon—had netted the state $8.76, so thorough had the corruption been.

Washington's Party Politics

After the Civil War the parties faced new issues that forced reorganization and reappraisal. The Democrats had to recover from the charge of secession and treason, although few of the party were actually guilty of these crimes. Yet they seemed to court electoral disaster by hanging on to the past during the Reconstruction years. They favored immediate readmission of the Southern states, fought giving the freed slaves the vote, and opposed other Republican measures of reconstruction. As the years went on, the party tried to adopt more positive positions but was rarely successful in defeating the Republicans.

The Republicans, after the war, took full credit for the Union victory. They "waved the bloody shirt" ("Every man who fired a Confederate gun was a Democrat") by accusing the Democrats of treason. They also indulged in emotionalism and personal attacks within their own ranks, a divisiveness that gave the Democrats one of their few victories. In 1872 dissenting Republicans condemned the territorial delegate, Selucius Garfielde, for building a political machine. They broke away to form an Independent Republican party that cooperated with the Democrats to elect Obadiah B. McFadden delegate and gave the Democrats and Independents twenty-two of thirty seats in the territorial legislature. But by 1876 the Democrats lost their last legislative majorities until statehood.

One issue that crossed party lines was woman suffrage. Inspired by the example of suffragists nationally and in Oregon, Washington women (with some male allies) persuaded the territorial legislature to give them the right to vote in 1883. But the experiment was short-lived. Opponents of woman suffrage contended—as some supporters of it hoped—that it would lead to temperance or prohibition legislation. They went to court, and the territorial Supreme Court declared woman suffrage unconstitutional on a technicality in 1887. The law was reenacted in 1888, but again declared unconstitutional later in the same year when the Supreme Court ruled that Congress had not intended to give the territorial legislature the right to enfranchise women.

The Chinese issue was a major concern of Washingtonians. It resulted in violence in Tacoma and Seattle in the 1880s, and it produced a good deal of agitation that the state legislature should "do something" about the Chinese presence. But no one could develop any measure that was both constitutional and politically feasible. Various individuals made their reputations as enemies of the Chinese, such as Mayor Jacob Robert Weisbach of Tacoma, while others were cursed as their friends. In the last category was Governor Watson Squire who called out the territorial militia to protect the Chinese at the time of the Seattle riots in 1886. An anti-Chinese party won several electoral victories in Seattle in 1886. Shortly after the expulsion, with the return of prosperity and the departure of many of the Chinese, the issue largely faded away.

Another issue that arose in violent form in the 1880s, but did not fade away, was labor conflict. In Washington it began when the Knights of Labor sought to improve wages, hours, and working conditions in the coal mines of the company towns of Roslyn and Newcastle. In 1888 the miners went on strike at Roslyn and the operators tried to break the strike by bringing in black miners from the Midwest. The operators hired a private army to protect the strikebreakers and tried to persuade Governor Eugene Semple to use federal marshals and state militia to do the same.

At Newcastle there had been a strike in 1886, but trouble occurred again in 1888 when a member of the company union was hired to replace a member of the Knights who had quit. This led to a strike, and the company called on Semple for militia aid to protect its property. The governor said he had no authority to protect property of the mining companies at either Roslyn or Newcastle, and the strikes, occasional violence, and community ill will engendered by labor-management troubles festered on into the statehood era.

So, too, did railroad problems. As in Oregon, Washingtonians had a love-hate relationship with the railroads. They hungered for them to boost their economy, but they objected to high rates and to the railroads' slowness in selling their land grant to the public. Railroads which bypassed communities earned the enmity of local citizens. In Washington the sequence of farmers' clubs and Grangers developed to try to regulate the railroads, but nothing was accomplished in this era. The railroad was also a factor in political life in other respects. Jealous that the Northern Pacific had begun to favor Tacoma after 1884, the business community of Seattle struck back at the railroad by supporting an issue popular with large numbers of citizens. This was to demand that Congress cancel the railroad's land grant, to force it to disgorge the lands that it had not already sold. In the election campaign of 1884 the Democrats took up this issue and elected Charles Vorhees as territorial delegate. Vorhees won again on this issue in 1886, but his victory and Democratic President Grover Cleveland's appointment of Eugene Semple as governor were the only important offices won by the Democrats. The railroad land grant issue, like the labor one, was put off to the statehood era. The territorial legislature remained solidly Republican since the pre–Civil War years.

Statehood for Washington

The great issue of Washington's territorial era was statehood, as it had been earlier in Oregon. Citizens chafed at a lack of population that condemned them to a subordinate form of government. This inferior status became particularly galling in 1874 when Congress passed a statute that unified the laws applying to the territories. Among other provisions, this new law removed the right of Washingtonians to elect the various members of the executive branch (except the governor) that the first territorial legislature had enacted in 1854. Territorial citizens also continued to resent their lack of voting representation in the United States Congress. The immediate cause of the first serious statehood movement, however, was none of these longstanding grievances. It was the desire of prosperous, civilized Walla Walla, with its grain-shipping connection down the Columbia River to Portland, to be annexed, with its hinterland, to Oregon. Senator James Kelly of Oregon in December 1875 introduced a bill to this effect.

In order to head off this loss, western Washington rallied to the statehood cause. In 1876 the voters called for a constitutional convention by a vote of five to one, although only a little less than 20 percent of the voters cast their ballots. The convention met at Walla Walla in 1878. There were fifteen delegates, eight Republicans and seven Democrats, half of whom were lawyers. The document they worked to shape reflected, to a surprising extent, the reform sentiment of the 1870s that was fearful of corporations and eager to support new causes.

Thus the delegates heard a speech by Abigail Scott Duniway and agreed to send a separate woman suffrage article to the voters. They also reflected the new temperance movement by consenting to a separate article allowing counties the option to prohibit the sale and consumption of alcoholic beverages. In five articles the delegates drafted restraints on corporations, reflecting disenchantment with banks and railroad companies.

While it was distinctive in its economic provisions, the constitution was a rather typical one in its governmental structure. It had a separation of power among governor, judges, and legislators. It had a division of power between the state government and the counties. There was a bill of rights that contained the usual guarantees, but also included some innovations. Except for the vote, women's rights were included; three-fourths rather than a unanimous vote was required for a conviction in a criminal case; the grand jury was to be composed of seven members, with five votes required for an indictment.

There was also an innovation concerning the election of state legislators. Voters could cast as many votes for one candidate as there were representatives in the district or they could distribute the votes among the candidates. This proportional system was designed to ensure minority party representation in the state legislature.

The delegates were distrustful of governmental expenditures. Salaries for state officials were low; for example, the governor's salary was $1,500. The state debt was limited, and the legislature had the duty to fix the debt limits of counties.

The vote on the constitution was taken in November 1878. Most of the state newspapers favored the constitution, and the voters adopted the main body of the constitution by a two to one margin, 6,642 in favor, 3,231 opposed. But the separate articles on woman suffrage and local option for prohibition were too radical for the voters, who rejected them. Overall the railroad was the decisive issue in the campaign. The counties that had not been chosen by the Northern Pacific for its lines voted against the constitution. Areas where the Northern Pacific had its greatest political influence also produced a vote against the constitution because of its corporation control measures.

When the constitution was submitted, Congress rejected it for two major reasons. The vote on the constitution was low, compared to the total number of votes cast in the 1878 election for other issues and for candidates. Second, Washington was a Republican territory, while Congress was controlled by Democrats who feared an influx of Republican federal legislators after statehood.

Statehood Attained

Agitation for statehood continued and finally succeeded in reaching its goal in 1889. In the election of the fall of 1888, Washington had elected a Republican governor and legislature at the same time the nation had chosen a Republican president and Congress. There was now no political barrier against the admission of a Republican state. Population size had also increased dramatically in the 1880s, beyond that of several states already in the Union.

Congress passed an enabling act and the constitutional convention met in 1889 at Olympia. The debates were more spirited than in 1878 and the issues more varied. The delegates, of course, all had some stake in the selection of the state capital. This choice would affect the local economy, with the payrolls of legislators and other state officials being a boon to local businesses. The contenders for the capital were Olympia, North Yakima, and Ellensburg. Seattle and Tacoma businessmen supported North Yakima or Ellensburg, as they had large real estate investments as well as commercial connections with those two communities. Olympia, however, was the victor. The actual provisions of the constitution were influenced by four factors: the constitution of Oregon; the constitution of California; the abortive Washington constitution of 1878; and a draft constitution prepared by W. Lair Hill.

On economic issues, there was less anticorporate activity than in 1878. Eastern and western parts of the state divided over the question of public indebtedness. The east wanted a provision limiting public debt to 5 percent of the value of taxable property. The one exception in the east was Spokane, which joined Seattle in desiring a high debt limit because of the need to rebuild their communities after respective fires in 1889. The limitation was set at 5 percent.

Other cities had their particular economic axes to grind. Walla Walla wanted a constitutional provision that would permit cities and counties to grant subsidies to corporations. This was a very controversial proposal rooted in the city of Walla Walla's grant of $80,000 to the Northern Pacific Railroad to build a line—competing with that of the Union Pacific—from Walla Walla to Wallula on the Columbia River. Times had

Inauguration of first governor of state of Washington (1889). Special Collections Division, University of Washington Libraries

changed, however, and the Northern Pacific and the city now agreed that the railroad should return the $80,000. For its part, the railroad promised to build a branch line into the Grande Ronde Valley and on to Dayton if Walla Walla would give it a new subsidy. The constitutional provision was beaten, however, because of the opposition of the Union Pacific.

The Northern Pacific, however, won another battle. The railroad was able to defeat a move to write a railroad commission into the constitution. Large business interests also prevailed regarding land. Speculators overcame delegates who wanted to lease the school lands that had been provided by the federal government as an endowment fund for the public schools. Instead it was agreed that these lands would be sold. Speculators also won out on harbor and tideland issues. After enormous controversy, the delegates agreed that the state was to own the beds and shores of all navigable waters up to the line of ordinary high water.

The political sections of the new constitution were not innovative. One observer noted that most of the committees had little to do: "They are following very closely the provisions of the California constitution, and little is required of them beyond such knowledge of the English language [as] will enable them to make intelligent changes in phraseology."[1] The bill of rights was taken from the Oregon constitution and a draft constitution drawn up by W. Lair Hill, a former Oregon resident, which in turn was largely adapted from the constitution of Indiana. The legislature was traditional, its provisions adapted from the California and Wisconsin constitutions. The judiciary was similarly familiar, its sources being the Hill constitution as adapted from California.

What was somewhat new was the provision for the executive branch. The single executive of the 1878 constitution was replaced by several elected officials. In this sense, however, the executive branch was familiar, for it resembled that of the territorial era. The only exception—an innovation in American state government—was the creation of an officer in the executive branch to deal with the public lands of the state. The constitution as a whole reflected the times in its great length, in the powers of legislature and executive, and in opening the way for corporation opportunities. It was not innovative for the most part and the delegates handled new issues separately from the main part of the constitution. Thus articles on woman suffrage and on prohibition were sent separately to the voters.

The convention adjourned on August 22, 1889. The voters considered the constitution on October 1, 1889, and adopted it by a vote of 40,152 to 11,879. The separate clauses were turned down by large majorities. When the constitution was forwarded to the nation's capital, a Republican Congress and a Republican president had no trouble in accepting the admission of a Republican state. The date of admission was November 11, 1889, the same day as Montana and North and South Dakota joined the union.

Statehood for Washington was one of the few decisive events in the political history of the post-Civil War era. In most respects the picture was confused. Neither Democrats nor Republicans had clear philosophies or programs that differentiated the two parties. Personalities predominated. Even when concrete issues like railroad regulation appeared, neither reformers nor conservatives could resolve them decisively. By the late 1880s voters were still groping for ways to adjust traditional institutions to new conditions. They did not know that they were on the verge of a new period of greater political clarity and commitment.

NOTES

1. "Drafting Washington's State Constitution," *Pacific Northwest Quarterly*, 48 (January 1957): 22.

SUGGESTIONS FOR READING

There are several works on Oregon politics in these years, but relatively few dealing with Washington Territory. Old but still valuable is Walter C. Woodward, *The Rise and Early History of Political Parties in Oregon, 1843–1868* (1913). See also Robert W. Johannsen, "The Oregon Legislature of 1868 and the Fourteenth Amendment," *Oregon Historical Quarterly*, 51 (1950). Also excellent is Eugene H. Berwanger, *The West and Reconstruction* (1981). On Washington, see Keith A. Murray, "The Movement for Statehood in Washington," *Pacific Northwest Quarterly*, 32 (1941); Alan Hynding, *The Public Life of Eugene Semple: Promoter and Politician of the Pacific Northwest* (1973); and Richard E. Frisch, "A History of the Democratic Party in the State of Washington, 1854–1956," Ph.D. diss., University of Oregon, 1975. On woman suffrage, see Ruth B. Moynihan, *Rebel for Rights: Abigail Scott Duniway* (1983).

10

Progressive Politics, 1889–1914

By 1889 the sores created by industrialism continued to fester. The railroad had integrated farmers into world markets. While wheat prices fell, farmers's fixed debts for land, equipment, and taxes remained. They blamed, in most cases, not the market, but the railroad for their calamitous position. Small businessmen, and even some large industrial shippers, also attacked the railroads for not providing enough cars to ship their produce. Unions, too, were discontented. They wanted improved wages, hours, and working conditions. They hated the employment of professional strikebreakers. They feared foreigners, especially Chinese, arguing that they undercut the standard of living of American citizens by accepting long hours, low pay, and poor working conditions.

Citizens had some noneconomic grievances also. Some wished to prohibit or regulate the use of alcoholic beverages. Others sought the state's aid in furnishing free textbooks to school children. To get their substantive reforms accomplished men and women focused upon changes in the political structure: the Australian (secret) ballot, the initiative and referendum, and woman suffrage.

The first bright flowering of the new reform spirit was a convention held at Salem in August 1889. Present were representatives of the Grange, the Knights of Labor, prohibitionists, and the Farmers' Alliance. The Alliance had strength in the South and the Middle West because of its platform of cheap money and railroad regulation and had recently carried these doctrines to Oregon and Washington. At Salem the reformers created a new political organization, the Union Party. It came out for prohibition, for a railroad commission to set rates, for free textbooks, and for laws against strikebreaking. It favored equal pay for equal work for both sexes and demanded that Congress require a period of ten years' residence before immigrants could become citizens.

The principal vehicle for reform, both in Oregon and Washington, was the Populist party. It grew out of the Farmers' Alliance in other regions. It was founded in 1890 and became famous (or notorious) with its national convention at Omaha in 1892. At this gathering the Populists (a nickname for the official title, the People's Party) presented a thorough-going program of specific reforms. Later in that year Populist parties were organized in Oregon and Washington.

The two most famous Populists in the Pacific Northwest were John R. Rogers of Washington and Sylvester Pennoyer of Oregon. Rogers, who had lived in many places, had been active in reform politics in the Middle West. He was a man of intellect and vision who articulated the Populist philosophy and program in books and articles. He looked backward to a golden age when the family farmer was the most important person in society. He believed in individual worth and dignity and in a person's natural right to the land. Rogers was elected to the Washington legislature in 1894 and chosen governor in 1896.

Sylvester Pennoyer was elected governor of Oregon in 1886. He had moved to the state in 1855 and had become wealthy in the lumber business. Like Rogers, Pennoyer was an intellectual. He had published articles on public problems in prestigious national magazines such as the *North American Review.* He believed in the labor theory of value, structural reforms in politics, and Asian deportation and exclusion. Although first elected as a Democrat, he ran on a joint ticket with the Populists in 1890 and in the next year repudiated the Democratic connection.

Oregon Populists went into the 1892 campaign as confident as did the national Populists who nominated James B. Weaver of Iowa as their candidate for president of the United States. The Oregon platform stood for free silver to increase the supply of money in circulation. It demanded that the national government improve the navigation of the Columbia River by dredging the mouth of the river and by channel improvements. It urged that Congress build a railroad along the north bank of the Columbia. Both of these last measures were designed to provide competitive rates and services to the private steamship and railroad corporations which had hitherto dominated the great artery of commerce.

The platform asked the state for a good deal, too. It called for state liquor stores. It sought the prohibition of the hiring of strikebreakers by corporations. It suggested that the state publish textbooks and supply them free to school children. In Portland, too, there was a Populist ticket asking a broad range of reforms including free municipal lodging houses for those without homes.

From 1892 to 1896 the Populists campaigned hard at these various levels of government. But they were not very successful in Oregon. Governor Pennoyer obtained a good deal of publicity. He was abusive in his remarks about the Chinese, labeling them as partly responsible for the great depression of 1893. He pardoned criminals in unprecedented numbers. He gave money to the poor from his own pocket and operated his mills even in depressed times to give work to his employees. Yet neither the governor nor Populist legislators could fashion any important laws. Even though Populists won some victories in the state senate and house, they never controlled either body. They were unsuccessful in allying with Democrats or Republicans to make up a majority. In Portland, too, they were failures.

Lack of success was largely due to internal splits. The Populists could not decide whether to hold fast as a third party or to merge with Democrats or Republicans in a common effort to win elections on the silver issue at the price of dropping the other radical planks in their platform. The controversy over this "fusion" issue never was resolved. In spite of these problems the Oregon Populists turned out a large vote for Weaver in the 1892 presidential election. He won 16 percent of the popular vote, a surprising accomplishment for a third party. One of the state's electors also balloted for him in the electoral college, contributing to the twenty-two votes he gained nationwide in that body.

In Washington the Populists fared better than in Oregon. They fused with the Democrats and Silver Republicans (mostly from Spokane). Weaver won 21.79 percent of the popular vote in the 1892 election. And at the state level there were even greater gains. Populists won several legislative seats in 1892 and 1894. After the advent of the depression in 1893, in cooperation with Democrats, they saw some legislative achievements. In the 1895 session their most famous accomplishment was a new tax designed to supplement the permanent school fund income; in combination the two sources of revenue would produce a tax to the amount of six dollars a year for each school child in the state. The Populists also gained a statute requiring safety devices in shingle mills and one that established a state Bureau of Statistics. The last agency was to gather data that would be used to provide additional legislation in the interests of farmers and industrial workers.

After the adjournment of the legislature, politically minded citizens looked ahead to the 1896 contests. At the presidential level this was one of the most exciting races in national history. The Republicans nominated William McKinley on a platform advocating the gold standard. The Democrats, who nominated William Jennings Bryan, adopted the old Populist free-silver plank as their leading issue to free the country from the grip of depression. Many Populists supported Bryan out of expediency, although others rejected fusion as "selling out" the rest of the Populist agenda. In a close race McKinley won the presidency. In the Pacific Northwest he carried Oregon, but Bryan won Washington. John Rogers also won the governorship of Washington.

When the legislature convened at Olympia, Governor Rogers looked forward to securing Populist legislation. He was not disappointed, although he did not gain all that he expected. The legislature passed a law giving itself the power to regulate railroad rates. It passed another law that exempted the personal property of homeowners up to $1,000 from attachment and sale for debt. Another measure granted tax-exempt status up to $500 for personal property and improvements on land; the same measure also increased the tax on railroad corporations. Another statute made it easier for school districts to distribute free textbooks. Industrial workers also gained. Laws were passed regulating working conditions in coal mines, creating a state Bureau of Labor with inspection powers and authority to enforce the state's labor laws, giving workers a lien on employers for wages, and prohibiting employers' property from exemptions for wages owed their workers.

There was something in this collection of laws for almost every disaffected interest group. Yet many were disappointed that more was not gained. The Populists had no one but themselves to blame for much of their frustration. Some Populist legislators sniped at Governor Rogers, putting their own personal ambitions ahead of the party program. Others lacked knowledge of parliamentary procedure while still others took dogmatic, uncompromising positions in the legislative maneuvers. These self-inflicted wounds were salted by conservative legislators and their newspaper allies, who labeled the Populists as hayseeds, radicals, or demagogues. Furthermore, Democrats and silver Republicans who had supported the Populists during the campaign now deserted the party.

By the late 1890s it was all over for the Populists. They vanished in the fusion confusion, in self-destruction, in the return of prosperity in 1897, and in the Spanish American War. And they also disappeared because they were, although considered radical by their enemies, in a way backward looking. They envisioned a period in which the family farmer and the artisan would be restored to their imagined freedom and dignity of the days of yore. They did not fully understand that the corporation and the city were here to stay. But their political death was by no means the end of reform.

Northwesterners in the War with Spain

Foreign affairs intruded briefly upon domestic politics around the turn of the century. The United States went to war with Spain in April 1898.

Four months later Spain surrendered and the peace treaty of the following year gave Puerto Rico, Guam, and the Philippines to the United States. Fighting continued for three more years in the Philippines where the inhabitants thought the war would result in independence, not in a new colonial master. The state of Oregon received a good deal of indirect publicity in the war when the battleship *Oregon* made its 15,770-mile voyage from Bremerton, Washington, to Key West to support the American fleet in the Caribbean. This voyage, unequaled by any battleship, caught the world's attention. So far as fighting went, the Twenty-Second Oregon Regiment was the only one from the state to engage in combat. It fought in forty-two battles, engagements, and skirmishes in the Philippines. Sixty-four of its members died in service. The First Washington Regiment fought in twenty-nine engagements and skirmishes in the Filipino insurrection with the loss of twenty-four lives.

The Progressive Movement

The reform movement symbolized by the Populists broadened into the Progressive movement. Progressives welcomed the conflict with the old order in a spirit of joyous combat. One reason that they could feel this way was that their era of reform, oddly, took place at a time of prosperity rather than depression. More important, the reformers were confident about gaining their desires because they were confident about humanity. They believed that men and women were all endowed by birth with reason and with goodness. People could thus shape their future, individually and collectively, in a direction that would be fulfilling to them.

The progressives also believed, paradoxically, in a kind of determinism, in the power of the social environment to mold individuals. If a person's environment were constructive, he would be free and independent; if his environment were negative (e.g., marked by poverty, drunkenness, lack of education), then his future would be forever disadvantaged and unfree. As William S. U'Ren, the most famous Oregon Progressive, once put it, "Things make men do bad things . . . conditions that can be changed."[1] For the Progressives the important side of the paradox was the liberating power of humanity, not the deterministic power of the environment. And the way for people to shape the environment was, according to the progressives, to change the machinery of government. After the framework of government was changed, useful social and economic legislation would follow.

The people in the Northwest who subscribed to the progressive ideology were extremely varied. They included farmers worried about railroad rates and their general loss of status in an industrializing society;

William S. U'Ren. Oregon Historical Society

small businessmen resentful of the power of outside corporations; clergy upset by the linkage between vice and politics; workers fearful of strike-breakers and corporate oppression; citizens concerned about immigration from strange and distant countries; city dwellers wanting home rule; men and women of all ideologies desiring to abolish political corruption; and ideologists advocating panaceas for the ills of society.

U'Ren of Oregon combined many of these grievances. Born in Lancaster, in Wisconsin, trained as a blacksmith, he had lived in Colorado, Hawaii, and California before moving to Oregon in 1889. He brought with him two faiths that he never abandoned.

One was the idea of the single tax that had been conceived by the California economist, Henry George. In order to restore national prosperity, George advocated a confiscatory tax on unearned income from land or gain through speculation on land. Land would thus flow into the hands of the landless. U'Ren endorsed the single tax wholeheartedly. He realized, of course, that large landholders such as the railroads would resist the single tax. He knew of the corporate influence in the state legislature. His solution was to amend the state constitution so that the intiative and the referendum would become a part of it, although these ideas were not his inventions.

As early as 1884, A. D. Cridge, editor and labor organizer, publicized the initiative and referendum in a Salem paper, the *Oregon Vidette and Anti-Monopolist.* Other people in labor circles picked up the idea and publicized it, but it was U'Ren who first formed an organization to secure it. In 1893 U'Ren founded the Joint Committee on Direct Legislation (renamed the Non-Partisan Direct Legislation League in 1897). His group began with farmers and a few industrial workers, then expanded to include small businessmen, well-known editors and politicians, and other leaders of public opinion. U'Ren came quickly to realize, in other words, that prominent people were required to give credibility to a political crusade.

But why should they? What were the conditions that impelled people to progressive reform? And why should they succeed when earlier reformers had failed? There were several reasons that made reform possible.

One was a split in the ranks of the hitherto dominant Republican party. This division was in part over personalities, in part over issues. There were two factions, one led by John H. Mitchell, the other first by Henry Corbett, then by Joseph Simon, boss of Portland. The divisive issue was the old panacea, free silver. Mitchell had always supported free silver until 1896. When he abandoned it, he antagonized his long-time ally, Jonathan Bourne. With the traditional Republican party sundered, there was an opportunity for reformers to maneuver.

They also gained by the skillful way that U'Ren propagandized his cause. He played up the mechanics of his reforms. They were tools, he said, to enable the people to craft whatever legislation they desired. He played down the single tax, a controversial issue, although it was his real goal. This was a wise decision, for many saw in the initiative and referendum not the single tax, but a way to achieve their particular objectives.

U'Ren was a good speaker and a superb organizer. He was committed to the initiative and referendum and used whatever means were necessary to gain them. He had first ventured into elective politics when he was chosen as a Populist to the state house of representatives in 1896. He became their leader in that body. This position gave him his golden opportunity in the legislative session of 1897. Prior to the adoption of the Seventeenth Amendment (1913), the state legislatures chose the members of the United States Senate. John H. Mitchell was a candidate for re-election. His opponents now included his erstwhile ally, Jonathan Bourne. U'Ren and Bourne struck a bargain. Bourne would promise future support for the initiative and referendum amendments if U'Ren would persuade the Populists to stay away from the legislature so that it could not be organized for lack of a quorum and so Mitchell could not be elected. This agreement was carried out, the legislature did not meet, no laws were passed, and the citizens were denied one voice and one vote in the United States Senate for a year.

In 1898 U'Ren took his first step toward success. The initiative and referendum amendments were passed by the legislature. They passed again in 1900 and were approved by the people and made a part of the Oregon constitution in 1902. This action was the first time that the constitution had ever been amended. The popular vote for it was overwhelming (62,029 to 5,668); it carried in every county. In 1904 a direct primary law amendment also carried in every county, an amendment that made it possible for candidates for the state legislature to declare that they would vote for the United States Senate candidates who received the highest number of votes in an advisory referendum. Other changes in political machinery were the recall of elected officials (1908), the presidential preference primary (1910), and the creation of a public utility commission (1911).

The Oregonians used these political changes to bring about social and economic legislation. But these laws were progressive, not radical. Voters in counties were given the right to decide whether or not they favored prohibition. The legislature or the people (via initiative or referendum) adopted an eight-hour day for public works and a ten-hour day for women workers in certain occupations. They adopted a minimum wage law for women. Laws were also enacted that raised taxes on public utilities and public carriers (railroad car companies and telephone and telegraph companies). It became illegal to employ convicts privately. The voters abolished capital punishment. Oregon had been one of the three states in the Union not to have a board of health; it obtained one in 1903. In the same year Oregon passed its first child labor law. The people behind it were humanitarians who wanted to protect the young and the weak, and union officers who feared child labor was undercutting the wages of adult workers. One of its provisions fostered education by requiring compulsory school attendance of all children until age fourteen. Also in these years the Oregon forestry conservation movement began;

in 1905 the legislature established a state forest commission. Finally, prohibition came to Oregon in 1914.

Although certain interests were overjoyed at these statutes, and there were gains among them for almost every occupational group, what was not done shows as much about the character of the state as what was accomplished. The people accepted change, but not radical change. In 1912, for example, the People's Power League proposed a constitutional amendment that would have drastically reorganized the state government. Drafted by U'Ren, the measure would have abolished the state senate, had the legislators elected by proportional representation, extended the initiative and referendum to towns, and declared that only the governor could introduce appropriation bills. It was beaten overwhelmingly.

The greatest irony of all in the defeat of radical proposals was the fate of the single tax. This measure, dearest of all to U'Ren's heart, was on the ballot in 1910, 1912, 1914, 1916, and 1920. It never passed—with one near exception. In 1910 U'Ren got a single tax measure on the ballot, but it was not a comprehensive measure and was one that came in false colors to boot. It applied to the counties, not the entire state. The first words of the proposed amendment read, "No poll or head tax shall be levied or collected in Oregon." It then went on to spell out the single tax in the body of the amendment. Doubtless many people thought they were voting against the poll tax (which did not exist in Oregon anyway), while in reality they were supporting the single tax. The measure passed, but was repealed in 1912 after it had been exposed.

Four other points about Oregon progressivism need to be noted in addition to its restraint. One was that it was nonpartisan, working through the two traditional parties. Republicans and Democrats combined to elect progressive majorities in the legislature and progressive governors like Oswald West and George E. Chamberlain. The second important characteristic of Oregon progressivism is that it was inexpensive. The ordinary taxpayer paid little for the structural changes in government. The burden of social and economic legislation was placed on the employers. But the people not only defeated the single tax, they also never favored a sales tax, or income tax, or any other kind of revenue-producing measure that struck the individual. Third, the voters spoke very clearly, usually passing or defeating measures by overwhelming majorities that included people of all classes, occupations, and regions. Finally, the progressive faith in an informed electorate produced the nation's first *Voters Pamphlet* (1907) to give arguments for or against direct legislation measures (extended to candidate biographies in 1909) and the first comprehensive guide to state government, the *Blue Book,* first published in 1911.

The pattern of progressivism in Washington at the state level was similar to that in Oregon. Here there were the same complaints about political corruption, corporate control of the economy, and lack of access to the political machinery. The advocates of change were both rural and urban. They included members of the Grange and the American Federation of Labor, but also numbered many business and professional people. As in Oregon, Washingtonians accomplished reform by working through the two old parties, although the progressive governors were Republicans in Washington, rather than Democrats as in Oregon.

The example of Oregon was useful to Washingtonians in achieving structural reforms, but there was some difference between the two states in the order of change. In Washington some important legislation preceded the initiative and the referendum. In 1907, for example, the state legislature passed a railway commission law by overwhelming majorities. Child labor laws were adopted in 1903 and 1907. Women received the eight-hour day in 1911. The same year saw the passage of a workman's compensation law. In 1913 came a minimum wage law for women and children. But prohibition was adopted in 1914 in Washington as it was in Oregon. Changes in political machinery, too, occurred in a different pattern than in Oregon. The direct primary and the advisory primary for United States senators came first, in 1907; next was women suffrage in 1910; and finally the initiative, referendum, and recall in 1912.

Woman Suffrage

One issue that shows a good deal about Northwestern progressive politics is woman suffrage. It had been talked of extensively in the earlier era, especially by Abigail Scott Duniway, and had a faithful group of supporters for several decades.

Washington adopted woman suffrage in 1910, Oregon in 1912. The Washington victory was important nationally, for the state was the first state or territory to adopt the vote for women in fourteen years. But the tactics and strategy were derived from earlier experiences—productive or frustrating—in Oregon, especially those formulated by Abigail Scott Duniway.

The leaders of the rejuvenated woman suffrage forces in Washington were Emma Smith DeVoe and Dr. Cora Smith Eaton, a physician. Both were residents of Seattle. They realized that they had to have an organization in eastern Washington, too, and selected for this work one of the most memorable figures in the history of the Pacific Northwest. Mary Arkwright Hutton was rich, but not elegant. "She went about the house,"

Mary Arkwright Hutton. Eastern Washington State Historical Society

said one relative, "like a lusty slattern, great bosom, unconfined beneath her sleazy calico, her globular contour bisected by an apron string, shoes and stockings awash about her generous ankles."

Hutton's life, clothing, and personality all reeked of color. She had been a cook in a small mining town in Idaho, had married a railroad engineer, and then she and her husband had literally struck it rich in the mines. Mary Hutton gave of her money and her time to the poor and the unfortunate, especially orphans and unwed mothers. Woman suffrage became one of her crusades for justice. Her assistant east of the Cascades was another rich woman, LaReine Baker.

The quartet of leaders used the years 1906–1908 for organizational purposes. They founded suffrage clubs all over the state, most of which were headed by women of gentility or professional women of the middle classes. In making their appeal the woman suffrage leaders decided upon tactics that had been designed by Abigail Scott Duniway. Instead of trying to convert everyone, the suffrage leaders concentrated upon the leaders of public opinion whom they approached quietly for the endorsement. They also were successful in uncoupling suffrage from other, potentially divisive issues. Chief among these was prohibition. As in any political campaign, door-to-door electioneering, monetary contributions, and speeches were also employed.

The ideology of the suffragists was an appeal to both justice and expediency. Women, like men, suffragists proclaimed, were participants in society and in American history. Our national heritage was born in resistance to taxation without representation. It was based upon government of the people, by the people, for the people. The expediency argument went back further into American history and was muted in Washington. If women were given the right to vote, this argument went, then all types of social reforms would follow. Women were guardians of the home and especially endowed with moral virtue. When they went to the polls they would elect officials who would seek laws versus prostitution, drinking, and gambling. Women would also press for laws in their own immediate interest such as equal pay for equal work.

The campaign opened in the legislative session of 1908. George Cotterill, a progressive senator, devised an important strategic move. It was to leave the matter to the voters, not to make the final decision in the legislature. This would relieve the legislators of pressure and would fit in with the progressives' belief in letting the people decide important

Abigail Scott Duniway at the polls. Oregon Historical Society

political matters. Finally, in 1910, the vote was taken and woman suffrage was adopted.

Two years later woman suffrage came to Oregon. The strategy and tactics were the same as in Washington. In Oregon the vote was close, 61,265 to 57,104, but support came from all segments in society. In carrying the campaign to victory, Abigail Scott Duniway broke away from the prohibitionists in the 1890s. In 1894 she organized the Oregon State Equal Suffrage Association. She always insisted that the state group remain free of direction from the national suffrage groups, not only because she was personally distrustful of some of their leaders, but because she knew of "colonial" Oregonians' dislike of advice from residents of a "mother country." The free and independent Oregon group made its appeal to the citizens mainly on the basis of justice, especially through an appeal to history. In this tactic, Duniway was aided by her impeccable credentials as an 1852 participant in the great epic of American history, the crossing of the Oregon Trail. She grounded the woman suffrage cause, as she said on one occasion, "wholly upon the fundamental right of self-government, that inheres in the individual, which the Declaration of Independence and the Constitution of the United States had taught us to revere."[2] One of her co-workers, Eve Emery Dye, the novelist, also used the past for the cause. It was Dye who converted Sacajawea into the "guide" of the Lewis and Clark expedition. The young Indian woman became a symbol of the role of enlightened women who were guiding men and women to the goal of woman suffrage.

Duniway also carefully balanced her view of woman's equality with men with her belief in sexual attractiveness. She promised over and over again that women would not use the right to vote to emasculate men. "Show me a woman who doesn't like men," she once wrote, "and I will show you a sour-souled, vinegar-visaged specimen of unfortunate femininity, who owes the world an apology for living in it at all. . . ."[3]

One result of women's increased political role was the election of women to political office. In 1912 in Washington the first two women legislators, Nena Jolidon-Croake and Frances Axtell, were chosen. In the same year the voters elected Josephine C. Preston state superintendent of public instruction, the first woman to hold statewide office. Oregonians chose their first woman state legislator, Marion B. Towne, in 1914.

Progressivism in Portland

The progressives moved to reform the evils of urban life. Their philosophy was the same as on state and national levels and was played out in all of the larger cities in the region. In Portland the reform coalition

Harry Lane, mayor of Portland. Oregon Historical Society

embraced white collar liberal Democrats, progressive Republicans, blue collar Democrats, clergy like Thomas Lamb Eliot, and the newspaper publisher Sam Jackson of the *Oregon Journal*. The forces of conservatism included the *Oregonian* (edited by Harvey Scott until his death in 1910), the businessmen who enjoyed the material fruits of control of city government, the Republican city machine led by Joseph Simon, with George H. Williams, President Grant's attorney general as front man, and those temperamentally distrustful of reform.

The years of the progressive challenge to the old order were 1905–1915. The chief political symbol of this crusade was Dr. Harry Lane, "Doc" Lane to friends and enemies alike. He was the grandson of Joseph Lane, the ante-bellum Democratic politician, and the son of Lafayette

Lane, who served Oregon in the House of Representatives from 1875 to 1877. Harry Lane had first demonstrated his concern for society's unfortunate as head of the state asylum for the insane. Lane had also served as city health officer, doing some practical work, but also gaining notoriety for exploding the Chinese residents' unsanitary pots of night soil with rifle shots en route to his day's work. Lane's honesty made him unusual for municipal politics, as did his unprepossessing appearance, his inspiring oratory, and his avocation of bird-watching.

The reformers elected Lane mayor of Portland in 1905 and reelected him in 1907. His goal was to preserve the natural environment and improve the social one. Mayor Lane tried with limited success to check private control of public property. He vetoed a law transferring a street railway franchise from one private corporation to another because the city stood to gain little from the company for the franchise. The council overrode the veto. James J. Hill's United Railways secured a city franchise for a railroad track down Front Street. In 1908 Lane urged the city council members to sue the railroad for failing to fulfill the terms of its charter. The council refused.

The council also declined to repeal the franchise of the Southern Pacific Railroad on Fourth Street even though the tracks had been granted for passenger service and were now being occupied exclusively by freight trains. The council dealt Lane another defeat when it overrode his veto of an ordinance that would permit the Spokane, Portland, and Seattle Railroad to execute a cut through an established neighborhood in North Portland. One victory Lane did win against the railroad interests was extracting land for a new fire station from the Northern Pacific Terminal Company. His power in this matter was his knowledge that the company was occupying portions of the two city streets with no right to do so.

Portland reformers were not much more successful in fighting the prostitution interests than they were the railroads. The progressives, with their belief in human dignity, had long opposed this social evil. They knew of its relationship with another of their enemies, the saloon keeper, and his master, the brewery interests. The liquor business owned houses of prostitution for the profits made in selling drinks within them. Others, including many members of Portland's most socially prominent families, leased their buildings to madams and pimps.

Lane ordered the police to raid the illegal houses. He tried to get the council to cancel the liquor licenses of saloons that combined their business with prostitution. Mayor Lane's efforts were not of enduring success. Nor were those of the progressive governor Oswald West, who began a cleanup campaign in Portland in August 1911.

On certain issues Mayor Lane and the city council could cooperate.

As a physician with public health experience, Dr. Lane was able to get a reorganization of the health department and appointed Esther Pohl Lovejoy as head. Dr. Lovejoy subsequently became one of the famous women physicians in the world as head of the Women's Hospital Association. The mayor succeeded in exposing some instances of shoddy work by unscrupulous contractors. He was able to assist in the passage of bond issues for a water system, parks, municipal dock land, a new bridge across the Willamette River, and other needed services. Sometimes these measures were supported by Lane's opponents, but they never abated their objection to him.

In 1909 the Democratic party denied him renomination for a third term. He ran anyway as an Independent Democrat, but Republican Joseph Simon was elected. Simon's administration was conservative, but not as reactionary as many progressives had feared. He faithfully carried out measures that the council or voters had already approved, but he initiated few new proposals. One of the last was to initiate a "city beautiful" fund to raise the money to pay for a comprehensive municipal plan. But the voters found Simon's contributions inadequate and defeated him in 1911 when he ran for reelection.

His successor was A. G. Rushlight, a plumbing contractor. During his tenure was completed one of the most interesting of the proposed progressive reforms. This was the "city beautiful" plan developed by Edward H. Bennett of Chicago. Bennett envisioned a great metropolis, its industrial area segregated from the residential section, with a civic center, abundant parks, and a ring of boulevards encircling the city. It was typical of Portland voters that they would authorize the development of such a plan, which they did in 1912. It was also typical of them that they carried it out in bits and pieces in the years ahead. The plan was too spacious, the cost too great for Portlanders even in the progressive era.

At the municipal level the progressives also talked of structural reform in politics. The focus of this effort was a new city charter that incorporated the latest device in municipal reform. This was the commission form of government. It incorporated several main elements. There was a mayor and four commissioners. Each administered a city department. Elections were held on a citywide basis, thus abolishing the old ward units. Candidates did not run on a party basis, but were chosen in nonpartisan elections under a system of preferential voting. In 1913 the new charter narrowly passed in Portland, a significant victory for reform, although only 22 percent of the voters participated. Later in the year Portland's last reform mayor of the Progressive era was elected, H. Russell Albee, an insurance man, along with a majority of reform-minded commissioners. During his term of office, however, Albee's achievement was mainly to bring to completion projects begun earlier: the opening of the municipal dock commission's first public dock and the construction of a public auditorium and a public market.

Progressivism in Seattle

The progressive years were ones of great material progress in Seattle. The coming of the Great Northern Railway and the Alaska gold rush made the city the metropolis of the Pacific Northwest. Prosperity created geographic expansion and cultural ornaments. The very shape of the city changed as engineers leveled the hills and businessmen built skyscrapers. But growth brought problems as well as pride, both derived from the same sources: the hunger of individuals and corporations for profits and the conflict between this quest and the need for efficient social services for a burgeoning population. In resolving these conflicts men and women talked in abstractions: community pride, socialism, justice, the "Seattle Spirit" (for boosterism), but they acted concretely and pragmatically rather than ideologically in terms of working for what was attainable rather than for some grand scheme. Yet humanitarian values derived from the Judaeo-Christian tradition were at the core of reform. It is significant that three clergymen, Samuel Koch (Reform Judaism), Mark Matthews (Presbyterian), and Sydney Strong (Congregationalist), were important leaders of Seattle progressivism.

Municipal services furnish an apt illustration of progressives' concerns. Seattle needed a supply of fresh water from the Cedar River. The private Seattle Power Company wanted the job, but the citizens thought otherwise and in an election in 1895 it was decided that the city would build and operate the water line. Another comparable issue was the production of hydroelectric power. The matter followed logically from the expansion of the city. The city needed electric streetcars which required a source of electric power for them. Seattle's great city engineer, Reginald H. Thompson, the force behind leveling the hills and municipal water power, was also the leader in the fight for city production of power from the falls of the Cedar River. In 1902 the voters overwhelmingly decided in favor of a city power plant. The operation, called City Light, was first used for lighting the streets and municipal buildings, but in time was expanded for other purposes.

The city also developed a park and boulevard system, far better than that accomplished in Portland or anywhere else in the Pacific Northwest. The moving spirit in designing these beautiful public places was J. C. Olmsted of the famous New York City landscaping firm. The people supported these developments, although many of the sites were given by private individuals. In 1910 there was a move to take the park-boulevard system even farther. This was the work of the city's Municipal Plans Commission which hired a local engineer, Virgil Bogue, to draw up a municipal plan that encompassed a noble city of space and grace. But, as in Portland, the voters never put the plan into execution.

Seattle's reformers also waged war against vice. The first target was prostitution. Many in Seattle were heirs of the gold rush to Alaska and of the earlier frontier. They saw no need for this type of civic virtue. Others saw no need for it as they were the owners of houses of prostitution. But the stable citizens, who dreamed of progress, became advocates of driving out the prostitutes.

Hiram "Hi" Gill wanted to leave the prostitutes alone. As an advocate of an "open city," he was elected to the city council and then elected mayor in 1910. His theory was to confine prostitution to a restricted district supervised by his police chief, Charles W. Wappenstein ("Wappy"). The first price of "restriction" was corruption, as owners of brothels contributed a percentage of their profits to the police and to Gill's political allies. The second price was failure, as the prostitutes spread from the restricted districts or remained in their original quarters outside it. Citizens soon refused to pay either price, and Gill was recalled from office in 1911. Wappenstein went to jail, contenting himself with becoming a proficient feeder of chickens at the prison farm.

Progressives had other victories, too. In 1906 they amended the city charter to allow for the institution of the recall. They also elected at this time William H. Moore as mayor over the opposition of the conservatives. In 1912 progressives supported George Cotterill for mayor. Cotterill was a civil engineer, who represented the antiprostitution, proprohibition element of reform. Gill ran again, for vindication, but Cotterill defeated him. Unknown to them, however, this was the last progressive victory in Seattle.

Cotterill became entangled in the prohibition issue which divided the reformers. The middle-class people favored it. The working class, which had been the staunch ally of middle-class progressives on the municipal ownership and corporate regulation issues, opposed prohibition. Times were changing as the city became less optimistic about human virtues and human nature. The first political beneficiary of the new spirit was Hiram Gill who was elected mayor in 1914 and again in 1916 and who had to confront the issues of the First World War.

The exceptions to nonradical change were few but interesting. In the state of Washington several secular, utopian, radical, communitarian experiments arose between 1885 and 1915. The largest were the Puget Sound Cooperative Commonwealth at Port Angeles; Equality Colony in Skagit County; Freeland on Whidbey Island; Burley Colony on Southern

George Cotterill. Special Collections Division, University of
Washington Libraries

Puget Sound; and Home in the same region. All failed to change society; indeed, all failed to endure. They did not succeed because their leaders failed to understand human nature and because their members lacked the necessary commitment to the ideals of the colony. Outside opposition was not much evident, occurring only at Home, and cannot be the explanation of the collapse of the utopian visions when put to the test of practice. Oregon had only one somewhat lasting community, New Odessa, founded by Jewish radicals near Roseburg. It lasted from 1882 to 1887. Besides the radicals of the IWW, the anarchists of the region included a Portland group which published a newspaper, *The Firebrand*, from 1895 to 1897. However, even proponents of moderate change, let alone radicalism, became suspect when the world went to war.

NOTES

1. Lincoln Steffens, *Upbuilders* (1968), p. 291.
2. Abigail Scott Duniway, *Path Breaking: An Autobiographical History of the Equal Suffrage Movement in Pacific Coast States,* 2d ed. (1971), p. 114.
3. Ibid., p. 157.

SUGGESTIONS FOR READING

There is a substantial literature on reform politics. The following works are among the best: Mansel G. Blackford, "Reform Politics in Seattle during the Progressive Era," *Pacific Northwest Quarterly,* 59 (1968); Norman H. Clark, *The Dry Years: Prohibition and Social Change in Washington* (1965); William T. Kerr, Jr., "The Progressives of Washington, 1910–12," *Pacific Northwest Quarterly,* 55 (1964); Keith A. Murray, "Issues and Personalities of Pacific Northwest Politics, 1889–1950," *Pacific Northwest Quarterly,* 41 (1950); Robert C. Woodward, "W. S. U'Ren and the Single Tax in Oregon," *Oregon Historical Quarterly,* 61 (1960); and Thomas W. Riddle, "The Old Radicalism in America: John R. Rogers and the Populist Movement in Washington, 1891—1900," Ph.D. diss., Washington State University, 1976. Woman suffrage is discussed in Ruth B. Moynihan, *Rebel for Rights: Abigail Scott Duniway* (1983). A valuable specialized work is Donald G. Balmer, *State Election Services in Oregon* (n.d.). On city politics, see Carl Abbott, *Portland: Planning, Politics, and Growth in a Twentieth-Century City* (1983); E. Kimbark MacColl, *The Shaping of a City: Business and Politics in Portland, Oregon, 1885–1915* (1976); Murray C. Morgan, *Puget's Sound: A Narrative of Early Tacoma and the Southern Sound* (1979); and Roger Sale, *Seattle: Past to Present* (1976). On radicalism, see Charles P. LeWarne, *Utopias on Puget Sound, 1885–1915* (1975) and Carlos A. Schwantes, "Free Love and Free Speech on the Pacific Northwest Frontier," *Oregon Historical Quarterly,* 83 (1982). See also G. Thomas Edwards and Carlos A. Schwantes, *Experiences in a Promised Land: Essays in Pacific Northwest History* (1986).

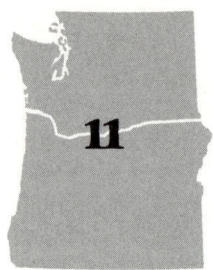

The First World War, 1914–1918

The First World War influenced the Pacific Northwest in ways beyond the loss of life and limb of many of its citizens. The federal government grew more important; manufacturing for the first time became significant; and the progressive spirit diminished. The war was a point of transition between the optimism, faith, and civility of the Progressive Era and the suspicion, nationalism, and fear evident in many aspects of the culture of the 1920s.

Support for the War Effort

World war was a shock for most Americans, a staggering blow for the progressives. It came when the world had long been at peace and it undermined the progressive faith in human reason and human goodness. Arbitration treaties, the World Court, plans for international organizations failed to avert the bloodbath. After shock, emotions flowed free. Most Americans wanted the Allies to win; even more, they wanted the United States to remain out of the conflict. The Socialist party, the Industrial Workers of the World, and the pacifists opposed entry as a matter of principle. One of the reasons President Wilson won reelection in 1916 was his campaign slogan, "He Kept Us Out of War."

Wilson was unable to fulfill his campaign pledge as Germany tightened its U-boat noose around the United States. The president tried to restrain Germany from its submarine campaign. One method was to ask Congress to arm American merchant ships sailing through the war zone. A small group of senators filibustered the bill, arguing that, contrary to

Wilson's intentions, his plan would drag the country into war. Wilson denounced these senators, one of whom was Harry Lane of Oregon, as a "little group of willful men, representing no opinion but their own," who had made the government "helpless and contemptible." Oregon's other senator, George Chamberlain, backed Wilson's preparedness campaign, arguing that the nation armed could better stay out of war than the nation unprepared.

Lane and Chamberlain represented the division of opinion throughout the Northwest. Lane, indeed, voted against the declaration of war, one of only six senators who did so. Many of the public attacked him viciously, assailing both his judgment and his patriotism. Most citizens gave the war effort enthusiastic support. Those who went into military service numbered 43,358 Oregonians and 66,870 Washingtonians. They served in all theaters and combat zones. Oregonians suffered 360 dead and 997 wounded; Washingtonian casualties numbered 764 dead and 2,172 wounded. The region had high rates of enlistment and purchase of war bonds. Oregon, indeed, led the nation in per capita contributions in both of these areas. People volunteered their services on draft boards, worked for the Red Cross, took soldiers and sailors into their homes, sewed garments, and made bandages.

In spite of these positive endeavors, there were those who defined patriotism not as support of the United States, but as hatred of Germany. Many citizens regarded Germany as pursuing a master plan for world conquest. More than that, they regarded Germans as inhuman.

Hatred of Germany was transferred to German Americans. In Portland the City Council changed the name of Frankfurt Street to Lafayette, Frederick to Pershing, and Bismarck to Bush. A small Portland boy, Frank Robert Wilhelm, "taunted by the jeers of his schoolmates who called him Kaiser," changed his legal name to Frank Roberts Minor. Carl Haberlach, a Swiss immigrant who managed the co-operative creamery at Tillamook, Oregon, was tarred and feathered because his Swiss cultural background was confused with German. The state of Washington banned the teaching of the German language in the public schools. Germans and German-Americans were also scrutinized by federal authorities. A proprietor of a shoe shop in Yakima was arrested as an espionage suspect; one charge was that "he spent much time hunting and killing rattlesnakes for some mysterious purpose. . . ."[1] Germans and German-Americans took defensive measures to prove their loyalty. Churches of immigrants converted their services from German to English language. The Chehalis German Lutheran Church, for one, decided to conduct its services in English. People of German background took out newspaper advertisements proclaiming their loyalty to the United States. Others ostentatiously bought war bonds or joined the colors.

Anna Louise Strong. Special Collections Division, University
of Washington Libraries

Besides the individual citizens, cities, states, and the nation made
sure that the war effort moved forward unimpeded by the evident dissent
of some members of the public. In Seattle, Anna Louise Strong, daughter
of a prominent Congregational minister, was serving on the school board
when the war broke out. She was also a pacifist who had agitated to keep
the United States out of the war. Once the country joined, she opposed
the draft and publicly defended the radical opponents of the war. These
positions cost her her position on the school board in March 1918 when
the voters recalled her by a margin of 27,157 to 21,824.

In Portland similar circumstances prevailed. M. Louise Hunt was a
member of the staff of the Multnomah County Library. She was also a
pacifist. When the library employees were asked to buy war bonds, she
refused. She opposed the Germans, wanted their enemies to win the war,

and was willing to sell war bonds. But she would not buy them. When her position became known, citizens led by Major George L. Baker and County Commissioner Rufus Holman demanded that the library board fire her. The board hesitated, but Hunt resigned, and left the state.

The federal government conducted its struggle against dissenters not only through its historic powers to move against traitors but also through the Espionage Act (1917) and the Sedition Act (1918). In the wartime atmosphere it became impossible to enforce these statutes with justice. J. Henry Albers, a rich and prominent miller in Portland, was sentenced to three years in prison and fined $10,000 for singing German songs while in drunken revelry. Floyd Ramp, a Eugene farmer, served eighteen months in jail for telling a troop train of soldiers that they were fighting to protect the capital of John D. Rockefeller. The federal government also attempted to control enemy aliens by proclamation. The president prohibited their presence, "within one-half mile of any Federal or State fort, camp, naval vessel, etc."

Economic Consequences of the War

When the Central Powers (Germany, Austria, and Turkey) and the Allies (France, England, Russia, and Italy) went to war in 1914, they provided new markets for the farms and factories of the Pacific Northwest. These markets, although interfered with by German submarines and British naval blockade, were lucrative. After the United States entered the war against Germany in April 1917, a domestic demand joined the needs of the Allies.

Ships were essential to feeding and equipping the Allies and to transporting United States soldiers overseas. This demand produced a major merchant shipbuilding industry in the Pacific Northwest, the first large modern manufacturing industry in the history of the region. During the war there were twenty-eight shipyards building wooden schooners and nine constructing steel ships. As capital flowed into the yards from private sources and from the federal Emergency Fleet Corporation, and as workers gathered from all over the country, the industry began its surge toward meeting production targets. By the conclusion of the war it had delivered 297 ships for America and its allies.

In the countryside the war produced a boom. The Allies and the nation needed wheat and meat for their soldiers and sailors. The United States government for the first time in its history subsidized the price of food products. Wheat production in the region doubled as prices rose. Beef, sheep, and hog raisers also saw their incomes increase dramatically. Sometimes the war even aided those who lost their overseas outlets. The producers of apples—which were not considered vital to the Allied war effort—were able to make such gains in the domestic market that their profits were far in excess of their prewar income.

The old industry of fishing and fish canning also flourished. On a downhill course since 1895, the peak year on the Columbia River, the salmon producers benefited enormously by the world war. The United States government bought practically every can. Federal purchases also were a boon to the industry in an indirect fashion as government inspectors checked the quality of the pack. Most of it was satisfactory, an endorsement that the packers made use of in postwar markets.

The Fortunes of Labor

The world war had mixed effects upon those who attempted to represent working people. The conflict helped the organization of working men and women if they became affiliated with traditional unions. But it was an era of destruction for radical labor like the Industrial Workers of the World.

In the lumber industry the advent of war was marked by labor strife. Conditions in the mills and logging camps were abominable. Men worked long hours at the risk of their lives for low pay and poor food. The employers treated them as a commodity, hiring and firing according to

Seattle workers leaving the shipyards to begin the general strike. Special Collections Division, University of Washington Libraries

the dictates of the lumber market which they found impossible to stabilize even when they tried.

During and immediately after the war the IWW became embroiled in controversies that had long-term consequences for labor. The two most sensational events occurred in Everett and Centralia in 1916 and 1919, respectively. In Everett the shingleweavers had organized a union in 1901. In 1915 the owners had cut their wages. This blow was a double one. The wage loss was bad enough, but it was compounded by the insult that the wages for shingleweavers in the rest of the state were going up because of wartime prosperity. The strike began on May 1, 1916. The response of the employers was bloody and spectacular.

They hired armed vigilantes, deputized and led by the county sheriff, to break the strike. The posse severely beat about forty Wobblies who were on the picket line. In retaliation the Wobblies decided to lead a free speech fight in Everett. They called for allies from Seattle. The call was answered when a contingent of about 250 Wobblies arrived in Everett harbor on November 5 aboard the ship *Verona*. The employer's force of some 300 deputies was waiting. A shot rang out. In the battle that followed five Wobblies died and thirty-one were wounded. Among the deputies, the casualties were two dead and twenty wounded. The Everett Massacre ruined the Wobbly effort in the city. It only temporarily postponed the strike, but when it was resumed the cause was lost.

The Everett strike was but a prelude to the Northwest's great lumber strike in 1917. It took place against the background of interunion rivalry between AFL and IWW; the long history of the exploitation of workers; and American entry into the war which made striking by any group injurious to the war effort. The strike began in July 1917. The goals were the traditional ones of improved pay, better working conditions, and shorter hours. The effect of the strike differed in Oregon and Washington. Oregon was a relatively small producer of lumber products and the unions did not put much effort into hindering production. They did strike the Columbia River logging camps and the mills of Portland and Astoria, but the effect of the strike was felt only for about two weeks.

In Washington where lumbering was vital not only to the state's economy, but to the national war effort, the strike assumed great significance. As it wore on, the federal government played its hand to keep war production going. The United States Army was used to work in the lumber industry. The members of the Spruce Division were originally sent to maintain quality production, but they soon necessarily became strikebreakers. The division, under the command of Brigadier General Brice P. Disque, organized a company union, the Loyal Legion of Loggers and Lumbermen. It included almost all the civilian employees in the industry, who bound themselves not to strike or boycott their employers.

The war ended in November 1918. Among many of its consequences was the formation of a new veterans' organization, the American Legion, founded early in the next year. It had a post in Centralia. The Wobbly presence had been in the town since November 1918. Its ideology and tactics were unpopular with the townspeople, both labor and employers. They drove out the Wobblies, who returned in 1919 when they hired a hall. On Armistice Day 1919 the Legionnaires paraded down Tower Avenue past Wobbly headquarters. Someone fired a shot. In an exchange of gunfire, two Wobblies and four Legionnaires died. The Legionnaires poured into the hall and destroyed most of its contents. Several of the Wobblies were arrested. That night, Wesley Everest, one of the prisoners, was lynched. The other Wobbly prisoners were not brought to trial until 1920. Seven of the ten were adjudged guilty and given lengthy prison terms.

A third spectacular event in Washington's labor history occurred after the war. It was the general strike in Seattle, the first and only one of its kind in American history. The immediate cause of the strike was the postwar downturn in the economy. The workers in the shipyards protested that their wages were being cut. The government pay board agreed with them, but the company did not. The workers planned a strike and caught up the entire city's labor movement. When the shipyard workers went out on strike, the rest of the city's workers joined them. For five days Seattle was quiet. No work was done except for essential services. The general strike in that sense was a complete success, except that no one was sure what its outcome was to be. As the strike wore on, citizens became more apprehensive about its goal. They were not reassured by Anna Louise Strong's editorial in the labor press that "no one knows where" it would lead. But the strike evaporated overnight, almost as quickly as it had arisen.

After the Seattle general strike and the Centralia Massacre most citizens made the simple identification of organized labor and radicalism. They saw the conservative unions as equivalent to the IWW or even to the Bolsheviks who had taken power in Russia in 1917 and attempted a revolution in Germany in 1919. The AFL unions changed in the public eye from a respectable or neutral cause to a dangerous one. This postwar mood was also expressed in legislation.

In 1919 Oregon passed a criminal syndicalism law. It was aimed at the IWW as were similar laws in many other states and territories at this time. The Oregon statute made it illegal to use or advocate violent means to bring about political change or industrial change. In Portland the police raided the local headquarters of the IWW. In the same town a news vendor was arrested for selling the *Western Socialist*, but he was soon released. There were few other arrests, fewer convictions, and the law itself was repealed within a few years.

Walter M. Pierce, Oregon governor and congressman.
Oregon Historical Society

Progressivism Survives

The syndicalism law was symbolic in the context of the new postprogressive conservatism. Its lack of enforcement and its subsequent repeal demonstrated that the progressive movement did not entirely die out during the war years. There were several other instances of the survival of progressivism.

In 1914 prohibition had come to both Oregon and Washington. In 1916 farming interests founded the Oregon State Taxpayers' League. It was designed to shift the burden of financing state government from the property tax to the income tax, from rural areas to urban corporations. Since it was impossible to get an income tax at that time, an expedient was adopted. This was a constitutional amendment—also gained in 1916—that limited tax increases for all governing bodies, without a vote of the people, to 6 percent of the average of the tax roll for the preceding three years. This measure would limit property taxes and the cost of increased governmental services until the citizens were ready to pay for them with an income tax.

In 1917 progressivism continued to make its mark in the Oregon legislature. Walter Pierce, an eastern Oregon legislator, sponsored a bill that became the state grain standards law. It required the inspection of grain and hay and of nitrates and other fertilizers. Farmers also participated in one of the last vestiges of progressivism when the Non-Partisan League came to the Northwest from North Dakota. It advocated state ownership of business in the interests of agriculture. Although too radical for most voters—one of its organizers was arrested in Walla Walla in 1918—its candidates did attract some rural votes in the elections of 1918 and 1920. In the aftermath of the war, Oregon legislators passed one bill to benefit returning war veterans. It allowed state payments for veterans' education. But for the most part the heritage of the war was to severely diminish the people's faith in the power of government to enhance their lives and livelihoods.

NOTES

1. Dale R. Wirsing, *Builders, Brewers, and Burghers: Germans of Washington State* (Tacoma: The Washington State American Revolution Bicentennial Commission, 1977), p. 49.

SUGGESTIONS FOR READING

Good accounts of the home front are Annette M. Bartholomae, "A Conscientious Objector: Oregon, 1918," *Oregon Historical Quarterly*, 71 (1970); and Roger Sale, *Seattle: Past to Present* (1976). On Germans and German-Americans, see Dale R. Wirsing, *Builders, Brewers, and Burghers: Germans of Washington State* (1977). The IWW is treated in Robert L. Tyler, *Rebels of the Woods: The IWW and the Pacific Northwest* (1967). A good history of labor is Jack E. Triplett, "History of the Oregon Labor Movement Prior to the New Deal," M.A. thesis, University of Oregon, 1958. On Centralia, see John A. McClelland, Jr., "Terror on Tower Avenue," *Pacific Northwest Quarterly*, 57 (1966). Everett is described in Norman H. Clark, *Mill Town: A Social History of Everett, Washington* (1970). Robert L. Friedheim deals with an important event in *The Seattle General Strike* (1964). For progressivism, see Arthur H. Bone, ed., *Oregon Cattleman/ Governor/Congressman: Memoirs and Times of Walter M. Pierce* (1981).

The Twenties

A slump followed the First World War. The economy fell off, the politics of idealism disintegrated, and moral standards eroded. People sought intellectual ease and material comfort. The values of progressivism were on the defensive. Conservatism, even reaction, rode high. Fear and mistrust replaced hope and progress as the dominant mood. Yet suspicion and irrationality did not completely destroy the dreams of men and women who believed in reason, progress, and economic and social justice.

Party Politics of Washington State

Washington was largely a one-party state throughout the decade of the 1920s. The period opened with Republican Louis Hart in the governor's chair in Olympia. Hart, a Tacoma businessman, was an accidental chief executive. He succeeded Democrat Ernest Lister, who had died of a heart attack in 1919. Although not a strong progressive as Lister had been, Hart coupled the old progressive belief in efficiency in government with the emerging conservative passion to cut taxes. Taxation, indeed, was the major issue of the decade, linked with the allied concerns of the growth of government bureaucracy and the conflict between public and private electric power. But prohibition, racism, religious bigotry, and antiintellectualism also flourished in the corridors of the state capitol and among the citizens.

In the twenties, the taxpayers placed their faith for solution of public problems almost exclusively in the Republican party. Washington was very nearly as much a one-party state as were those of the solid South. The Republicans swept all the offices elected statewide in the decade with the exception of one United States Senate seat. They controlled both houses of the state legislature by huge majorities. Most local officials were invariably Republican.

The dominant Republicans, like all political parties, were not unified into a coherent whole. They encompassed diverse regions, occupations, and personal factions. The first regional alliance was between a Tacoma group led by Hart and Clark Savidge and the rural Republicans of the farming-logging-fishing area of the southwest and the farmers and ranchers of the dry country east of the Cascades. The second faction composed the party members in Seattle, Everett, and the coastal logging regions of Puget Sound and the Olympic Peninsula. The leader of the lumbermen was Roland Hartley. Spokane's Republicans stood somewhat apart from both factions.

The cement for this coalition was one of Washington's most experienced politicians, Mark Reed, a wealthy lumberman from Shelton. Reed's power was based in part upon his ability to hold together different factions. But this authority in turn derived from his powerful intellect, his genial personality, and his willingness to compromise. Reed also had power because he was not a zealot or ideologist. Although conservative, he had, for example, helped create and defend a state workman's compensation law, a program that was considered anathema by most of his fellow lumbermen.

The Democratic party also had some able leaders, but few followers when the votes were counted. Similar to the Republicans, it was also ridden with factionalism. The oldest and most conservative political group was known as the "Bourbons." In Washington their leaders were the Stephen Chadwicks, father and son, both lawyers in Seattle. The older man, Judge Stephen T. Chadwick, had been active in the constitutional convention and had gone on to a considerable fortune. His son, Stephen F. Chadwick, was young, gregarious, and charismatic, a veteran of the world war and a founder of the American Legion. The Chadwicks and their friends were conservative in several respects. They felt most change was for the worse, and opposed the progressive reforms of state and nation. Woodrow Wilson's domestic program was special anathema to them. They had no use for the income tax, prohibition, labor laws, and the whole spectrum of progressive reform. Their vision of the ideal government was simply that of a custodian of life and property. It had no role to play in providing a freer or more abundant life for the citizens.

The progressive Democrats admired, even loved, President Wilson's program. They pointed with pride to the changes at the state and municipal levels made in the progressive era. They tried to keep the reform

Senator Mark Reed. Washington State Historical Society

cause breathing in the new conservative era closing around them. The most popular old progressive Democrat was George F. Cotterill. The most popular young one was Scott Bullitt. The most popular of all was Clarence Dill.

George Cotterill was born in England, but raised in Seattle. He became a surveyor and plunged into the early progressive movement in that city. He had supported the creation of a city-owned light and water system. In 1906 he was elected to the state legislature and six years later he became mayor of Seattle. Cotterill was an ardent supporter of Woodrow Wilson and a defender of civil liberties. As such he was detested by conservatives. By the 1920s Cotterill had become chiefly identified with the maintenance of prohibition.

Scott Bullitt was a relatively recent migrant to Washington. A lawyer by profession, he was personable, handsome, and articulate. Bullitt was progressive but as pragmatic in his party as was Mark Reed among Republicans, striving for what could be accomplished as well as what was the ideal. He concentrated upon attempting to adjust the progressive experiment with prohibition to the growing public disenchantment with it.

Clarence C. Dill of Spokane had been elected to Congress in 1914 as a progressive Democrat. He had voted against the declaration of war against Germany, a stand that cost him reelection in 1918. But he had returned to Washington, D.C., in 1922 when elected to the United States Senate, defeating incumbent Miles Poindexter. A resident of the eastern part of the state, Dill pushed for a large national role in reclamation and power projects and was one of the principal early sponsors of a federal dam at Grand Coulee. Like Bullitt, he attempted to salvage something of the progressive legacy in the postwar years. Another powerful figure in the state was James Geraghty, the boss of Spokane, whose sole concern was Democratic victory at the polls, not ideology.

The conservative twenties did not entirely kill the hope of a third party devoted to reform. For a time the Farmer-Labor party hung on. Created in the war at both national and state levels, it was not able to win many successes at the polls. The party did not have the support of the state AFL or the state Grange. Another progressive party was the Washington Conference for Progressive Political Action founded in the state in 1919. Five years later the WCPPA joined with like-minded people nationally to support the presidential candidacy of independent Senator Robert M. La Follette of Wisconsin who stood for the nationalization of banks, public utilities, railroads, and mines. His loss destroyed progressivism as a third force in national politics.

During the twenties the Republicans were the principal gainers from the interparty and intraparty strife. They had several advantages over their Democratic and progressive foes. The state was traditionally Republican; by 1920 the Democrats or third parties had elected, since statehood in 1889, only one United States senator; one representative who served two terms; and two governors, both of whom were reelected. They had never controlled the state legislature. The Republicans, although they had some internal strife, had more money than their opponents. Their period of rule from 1889 through the 1920s was one of prosperity and growth. The Republicans were able to accommodate their internal feuds and preserve a united front.

In the 1920s the state Democrats were weakened by divisions over prohibition, by disputes over the choice of progressive or conservative presidential candidates, and by their inability to gain the support of organized labor and agriculture in any consistent manner. Because the

Republicans were the majority party the state Federation of Labor tried to influence their choice of candidates and their platforms; it did not bother with the Democrats. The Washington State Grange, the principal farmers' group, did not ordinarily endorse candidates of either group. The Democrats were beset by a large number of ideologists in their ranks—from prohibitionists to socialists—men and women who would rather fight for a cause than win it. Finally, many Democrats never got over their disillusionment with the policies of the last two years of the Wilson administration. They lost faith because of the fight over the League of Nations; the persecution of radicals during the Red Scare; and the growth of racist policies.

Political Issues

Republican dominance did not mean that there were no hotly contested issues among the citizens. One of the most controversial was public power. As far back as the early days of the twentieth century some municipalities in the state, Tacoma and Seattle among them, had established municipal plants to supply their citizens with power. As the municipal plants proved their worth, sentiment developed to extend their services. In the 1923 legislative session, Homer Bone of Tacoma, a Farmer-Labor progressive, introduced a bill that would permit municipal utilities to sell power outside their city limits. Many rural people favored the measure because they saw no hope that their counties would ever adopt public power or even get electricity at all. On the other hand, there were some rural residents in the counties where the new municipal plants and distribution facilities would be located who objected violently to the Bone Bill. Governmental units like power plants were exempt from taxation and they saw no reason to see their taxes rise when land in their counties became exempt.

Mark Reed became their champion in the legislature. Reed was not merely negative, however; he proposed a compromise to the legislators. The Reed bill would create a 5 percent tax on the gross income of public power plants; if municipal power facilities were extended, he declared, they would have to pay their fair share. As it turned out the legislature adopted both the Bone and the Reed bills and referred them to the electorate. The voters defeated them both at the polls in November 1924. Public power did not disappear as an issue at the state level, but it did not become important until the next decade.

Taxation, however, remained very much a live issue. The principal source of revenue for the state was the property tax. It fell upon all interests: farmers, ranchers, lumbermen, private utilities. In the 1920s there was a call to reduce taxes, which most property owners endorsed. There were also some attempts to redistribute taxes. One was by adopting a state income tax, a measure endorsed by a group called the Washington Tax Limit League. In 1923 the legislature defeated an income tax. Four years later taxation again was a major legislative issue. The Tax Limit League tried a new twist. It wanted a constitutional amendment that would permit the legislature to reclassify property for tax purposes. It was pushed by farmers and opposed by lumbermen who feared that a farmer-dominated legislature would raise taxes on timberland. The amendment passed in the legislature, but was defeated by the people in the fall of 1928. One short-lived tax reform was effected; a five-dollar poll tax was passed by the legislature in 1921 but repealed in a referendum in the next year.

Of course another way to cut taxes was to make state services more efficient or to reduce them. The first was the tack of Governor Hart, who had succeeded in consolidating all of the various state agencies into ten departments, the heads of which would be appointed by the governor. Hart had relied upon Mark Reed to push the measure through the legislature in 1921, and the results seemed to justify the statute.

A far more heavy-handed approach took place under the administration of Governor Roland Hartley, who was elected in 1924. A lumberman from Everett, Hartley was the most controversial politician in the state. He had gotten into politics in the 1910s and soon earned a reputation as a reactionary. He was a bitter opponent of the IWW, opposed the federal government's role in improving the lot of loggers and mill workers during the war, and resisted the passage of the workman's compensation law. He showed his true colors as reactionary, not conservative, in his inaugural message to the legislature in January 1925.

In this address he proposed slashing taxes on everything. He was particularly opposed to educational expenditures. To reduce them or to punish educators or to enhance his own power—or all three—he wanted to centralize the state's educational system under his own control. He asked the legislature to replace the independent boards for each of the state institutions of higher education with a single board to be appointed by the governor. Hartley also wished this new consolidated board to oversee the state's elementary and secondary schools. Although this bill was not enacted into law, Hartley did gain one spectacular success in his antiintellectual crusade.

Henry Suzzallo was president of the University of Washington, brought by the regents in 1915 from Columbia University. Suzzallo's presidential tenure was controversial. He antagonized some faculty and citizens by moving too fast, by seeming too articulate, by acting with arrogance. He antagonized many more people—including the future

Governor Roland Hartley. Washington State Historical Society

Governor Hartley—by his wartime career as head of the State Council of Defense. Suzzallo had been among those who favored improved working conditions in the lumber industry. Hartley, a lumberman, was one of those most adamantly opposed to this type of interference in private business. After Hartley became governor, he became further enraged at Suzzallo when the president fought his educational consolidation plan. "I was born in America, and not in Italy,"[1] Hartley declared in a nativistic outburst. (In fact, he was born in Canada and Suzzallo in California.) In 1926 Hartley packed the university board of regents with his own appointees, who fired Suzzallo. There was an immediate public outcry by Suzzallo's supporters and an attempt to impeach Hartley, but it failed.

Hartley became embroiled with many citizens other than university supporters. Mark Reed labeled his cost-cutting inaugural address as "the most destructive message that was ever presented to any legislature during the history of this commonwealth."[2] Other lumbermen took offense at Hartley's proposals. The governor baited them. He said that the state forests had been sold at bargain prices to lumbermen, a thrust at Reed's ally, Savidge, who was state land commissioner. He proposed a bill to make state timber cruises—which determined sale prices—public. He also proposed a bill to make logging railroads common carriers. If this were done, individual companies could not tie up choice timberland adjacent to their property by refusing to ship their competitors' logs. It was not passed, but was another divisive issue among the majority Republicans.

After the war an emotional antilabor, antiprogress, antiforeign spirit arose. The opposition of many labor groups to American entry into the war, wartime strikes, and acts of sabotage by the IWW identified unions with radicalism. Labor had little success in the twenties except that it convinced Mark Reed to persuade the legislature in 1923 to increase workmen's compensation benefits by 25 percent. Otherwise, for labor, organization flagged, union membership fell, discouragement prevailed. The legislature adopted a criminal syndicalism law in 1919, a statute born of hatred of the IWW that essentially made it illegal to attempt to change the capitalist system or political democracy by means of force.

A final manifestation of the fears of the postwar years was passage of an alien land law. In 1921 the legislature made it illegal for persons ineligible for citizenship (Asians) to hold land in the state. The Japanese were considered unassimilable, filthy in habit and morals, and, above all, too acquisitive. Citizens feared that the Japanese would soon own all the agricultural land of the state. The effect of the law upon the Japanese was oppressive. Some lost their land; others had to transfer it to their children who were American citizens. The psychological impact of this racist measure was also obvious and enduring. Land had been the only means of security for a people who had never had the safeguards of citizenship. Now it, too, was in peril.

Washington and National Politics

Washington produced no political figure of renown on the national scene in this decade. When the decade opened, the United States senators were two Republicans, Wesley Jones and Miles Poindexter. Poindexter was much the better known; he had been a senator since 1910, and indeed he had something of a national reputation as a progressive.

Poindexter's progressive zeal slumped, however, during and after the war, then evaporated. He became a super-patriot and a red baiter.

He became a convert to the creed of business growth, growth that he saw increasingly hampered by high taxes and governmental controls. When Poindexter came up for reelection in 1922 he had a formidable opponent. Clarence Dill, like Poindexter, was from eastern Washington. He was a progressive Democrat whose strength lay in the cities of Spokane and Seattle. In his campaign Dill picked apart Poindexter's record. More positively, Dill continued to stress the progressive faith in governmental power, particularly the need for large federal irrigation projects, especially at Grand Coulee. He won the race, a victory that encouraged progressive Democrats to expect successes in the near future. This hope seemed valid when in a special congressional election in eastern Washington in 1923 the Democratic candidate, Samuel B. Hill, won.

The elections of Dill and Hill gave their party some hope for the selection of a progressive western Democrat for president in 1924. But the convention's choice was a conservative easterner, John W. Davis. His nomination led many Washington Democrats, along with old progressives and radicals of other parties, to support the independent candidacy of Robert La Follette. His platform was full-blown progressive, calling for nationalizing of banks, railroads, and private utilities. But it was out-of-date. Imbued with the resurging probusiness spirit and the return of agricultural and industrial prosperity, the voters of state and nation carried Republican candidate Calvin Coolidge into office with a resounding victory, although La Follette ran far ahead of Davis in Washington. Only Sam Hill, reelected to Congress, survived the Republican sweep.

In 1926 the Democrats again fought the Republican tide. Scott Bullitt challenged Wesley Jones for the Senate seat. Stephen F. Chadwick ran in the election for the Seattle seat in Congress. Bullitt waged the most dynamic election campaign in Washington history. He favored the McNary-Haugen bill to raise farm prices; he assailed the Republican federal statute of 1926 that cut tax rates disproportionately for the wealthy; and he suggested modification in the enforcement of prohibition. Chadwick's major issue was prohibition revision; otherwise his views were as conservative as the majority of Republicans. In spite of intelligence, charisma, and energy, both Bullitt and Chadwick lost. Only Sam Hill won a national office for the Democrats.

In 1928, year of the last major election of the prosperous twenties, the Republicans prevailed easily. Bullitt waged another vigorous campaign as the gubernatorial opponent of Roland Hartley. He moderated his prohibition views of two years earlier and concentrated upon Hartley's attacks on Suzzallo and upon education in general and on his criticism of the land board in its timber sales policy. Hartley responded in his typical *ad hominum* manner by assailing Bullitt as a rich man and as a Kentucky carpetbagger. He was victorious.

The only Democrat to win major office was Senator Clarence Dill. His defeat of Kenneth Mackintosh was impressive. Dill's victory—in a Republican state and in a year of prosperity—showed that not all voters were content to bury progressivism under the shovels of conservative Republicans. These progressives would increase their appeal in the decade of depression that lay ahead.

Oregon Politics in the Twenties

South of the Columbia River there were political phenomena similar to those in Washington State. Neither party was monolithic, although Republicans won most of the elections. There were personality clashes. And many of the issues were local, not national ones.

The Party Strength

Oregon's Republicans were led by Ralph Cake, national committeeman, and Charles Linza McNary, United States senator. Cake was to the right, McNary to the left of the center of the Republican spectrum. The party remained strong in all sections of the state, but its greatest power was in Portland, the coast, and in the Willamette Valley. Cake was the behind-the-scenes leader, a Portland attorney and director of the Equitable Savings and Loan Association, who conciliated egos and formed factional and economic alliances. McNary was a Salem lawyer, a genial, intelligent leader, who was the state's only figure of national reputation. As cosponsor of the McNary-Haugen plan for agriculture price relief, his name was attached to one of the two or three most prominent political issues of the day. Sensitive to the issues of his constituents, but with a national vision, he was one of the best senators of his time.

By contrast the Democrats had less unity and no figures of national prominence. The party did have able leaders of statewide importance. The two best known were Oswald West and Walter Pierce. When the decade opened, West had the prestige of accomplishment. He had been a progressive governor. He supported prohibition ardently, had seen much social legislation through the legislature, and gained enormous publicity for his vice crusades in Baker and in Portland. But, like many citizens, he seemed to become more conservative with the postwar years. He was hired by a private utility and came to be seen as one who had "sold out" to the hated vested interests.

His principal rival in the party was Walter Pierce. A farmer and rancher from the La Grande area, Pierce was also an old progressive. He supported prohibition and economic reform and criticized Asian immigration. What made him an outstanding politician was his ability to articulate his views, especially as a passionate and emotional orator. (His frequent tears led to his enemies' labeling him "Weeping Walter.") In addition to the division between progressive Democrats, there was a "regular" group that was conservative on the issues. Its members had little interest in politics beyond obtaining office for themselves or their friends and neighbors. Frequently the Republicans gave them political jobs in return for their votes—a conservative alliance.

THE ISSUES

A major issue of state politics in Oregon, as in Washington, was the cost of government and the exact method of paying for it. Government had grown during the war and had not declined afterwards. The traditional tax was the property tax. It bore most heavily upon ranchers and farmers. For years these groups had sought ways to make banks, utilities, industries, and other urban interests share the tax burden. The income tax was their remedy. Pierce, then a state senator, took the leadership of the income tax forces. He pushed for the measure in the legislative sessions of 1919, 1920, and 1921. By the last year there was considerable agreement in the legislature and among lobbying groups that there should be an income tax. A graduated income tax amendment, initiated by the Grange, was a major issue in the gubernatorial election of 1922. Walter Pierce, the Democratic candidate, favored the measure. Ben Olcott, the Republican governor, running for reelection, opposed it. Although Pierce was elected, the tax measure was defeated.

Pierce and the graduated income tax won in the 1923 legislature when the governor's leadership pushed it through. The tax survived a referendum vote in the fall of 1923 but was repealed in an initiative one year later. The chief argument against the income tax was business groups' assertion that it would discourage new industries from coming to the state. The tax was finally passed again in 1930.

Other political issues included highway construction. Pierce and the farmers favored it to facilitate the marketing of farm crops. But they wanted them built from general tax revenues and from automobile license fees. Businessmen favored special bonds for highway construction. No real solution was reached until the legislature in 1925 passed Oregon's first law taxing buses and trucks for use of the state's highways. Coupled with the nation's first gasoline tax, enacted in 1919, this law made it possible to have a modern highway system without bonded indebtedness.

Tax issues continued into the 1926 gubernatorial election. Pierce campaigned for reelection. The main issue was the income tax. Pierce continued to favor it. He also supported irrigation districts, farm cooperatives, and prohibition. It was a rural program and a progressive one. His Republican opponent, Isaac L. "Ike" Patterson, stood for limited government and opposed the income tax. In the fall election Patterson won, profiting from the usual Democratic split between the West-Pierce forces, prosperity, and the historic Republican majority.

Another major issue of the twenties was increasing intolerance. In Oregon, more so than in Washington, bigots, racists, and other varieties of the fearful, took vengeance upon minority groups as scapegoats for modern life. The immediate postwar period was disillusioning. The Great War had not brought peace and stability. Bolshevik revolution progressed in Russia. A short-lived Communist revolution broke out in Germany. The United States rejected membership in the League of Nations. At home, thousands died in a great influenza outbreak. The government moved against radicals as subversives. Race riots occurred in Chicago and East St. Louis. The economy turned downward. Old moral standards seemed in decline as the nation relaxed after the war effort. Contempt for law was marked, especially in violation of the new prohibition amendment, no sooner passed than evaded. The automobile spread the new "immorality" from city to countryside.

Frustrated by these larger forces, many Oregonians turned against minorities. The great issue arose in 1921 and 1922 in the form of an educational measure proposed by a variety of groups within the state. This was the compulsory school bill. What this initiative proposed was that parents be required to send their school-aged children to public schools. The parochial and private schools would in effect be abolished.

There were several arguments advanced in favor of the compulsory school bill. Bigots attacked parochial schools as perpetuating the control of an alien institution over the hearts and minds of American school children. Roman Catholic schools, they said, quite simply made American children the lackeys of Rome ("The Scarlet Harlot of the Seven Hills"). Others attacked the private and parochial schools as institutions for the rich that perpetuated un-American class divisions. Some claimed that public education should be required for all children, because they felt a nation of diverse peoples should have one unifying exposure to the principles and traditions of their country. There was also the argument that private schools were substandard, as many of their teachers were not certified by the state.

The most spectacular organization that supported the school bill was the Ku Klux Klan. The Klan had entered Oregon early in 1921, making its first inroads in the southern part of the state but quickly gaining adherents in all the major towns and cities of western Oregon. It preached a return to traditional American values, which it often equated with

Meeting of the KKK, prob. Portland, Oregon. Oregon Historical Society

hatred of Catholics, Jews, and blacks. The school bill fit the Klan's anti-Catholicism as it did the anti-Catholic sentiment of certain groups within the Masonic Order. The school bill initiative was a part of the exciting election campaigns of 1922. Governor Olcott opposed the bill as a Klan measure. Walter Pierce supported it, although he neither rejected nor accepted Klan support on his own behalf. The bill passed and Pierce was elected. The compulsory school law was challenged in court where its constitutionality was ultimately settled by the decision of the United States Supreme Court in 1925 in the case of *Pierce* v. *Society of Sisters.* The high court held unanimously that the law was unconstitutional as a violation of the property rights of the school proprietors and of the rights of parents to educate their children.

The Klan itself died at about the same time as the Supreme Court decision was rendered. It had not only represented a revolt against modernism, but also provided a colorful social activity and a sense of solidarity for white Anglo-Saxon Protestants, particularly in the small towns. In its heyday it was of considerable—although difficult to measure—influence. Politicians courted its support. The Klan rallied in communities in its regalia of white hoods—thousands marched at Tillamook on Memorial Day in 1924. Its cross burnings were dramatic; at one time the Klansmen suspended a 60-foot burning cross from an airplane, although the plane crashed in the coastal fog. Yet these theatrical events were not enough to make the Klan endure. Its leadership divided. Charges of internal corruption became rife. As the country returned to prosperity, some of the social concerns that produced the Klan dissipated.

More enduring was anti-Japanese hostility. In 1923 Oregon followed Washington in passing an alien land law. The same argument that Japanese were monopolizing the state's farm lands was used as in Washington, although in fact Japanese people owned less than one-half of 1 percent of Oregon's farm lands. As in Washington, Japanese who wished to hold these lands deeded them to their citizen children.

Oregon also contributed to national racist legislation. Chinese had been (with a few exceptions) excluded from immigration to the United States since 1882. In the twentieth century, people who feared Japanese began proposing a similar "remedy" for Japanese migration. After the close of the world war, one of the chapters of the new American Legion was founded in Hood River, Oregon, in the heart of the orchard country where there were many Japanese residents. Japanese exclusion was popular in Hood River. The local Legion chapter raised and supported the issue at the national convention where the Legionnaires overwhelmingly endorsed it. The Legion then presented the plan to Congress in conjunction with appeals from other Pacific Coast chapters and from labor organizations. Congress was amenable, and in the Immigration Act of 1924 Japanese were excluded from the United States.

FEDERAL ELECTIONS IN OREGON

Senator Charles McNary dominated Oregon's congressional delegation. He was a man of style and substance, enormously popular with the state's voters. In 1924 he faced his first postwar test, easily defeating his Democratic opponent, Milton A. Miller of Albany, a state senator. In 1926 Senator Robert N. Stanfield came up for reelection. A drunken playboy, and a flagrant absentee from the Senate, Stanfield was an easy target in the Republican primary, where he was defeated by Frederick Steiwer, a staunch prohibitionist. Stanfield refused to accept the verdict and ran as an independent in the fall. The Democrats nominated Bert Haney. Steiwer easily defeated Stanfield and Haney in the fall. Prosperity was the winning issue. In the House of Representative races, the Democrats prevailed only once in the decade. Elton Watkins won in 1922, the first Democrat elected to Congress since 1879. He defeated Clifton N. McArthur for the Third District seat but was not reelected in 1924.

The Democrats had no success whatsoever in the presidential races of the decade. In none of the three contests did the party carry a single county in the state. Prosperity and the Democratic divisions made Republican victories crushing. In 1920 Harding defeated James Cox by a

Senator Charles L. McNary. Oregon Historical Society

plurality of 48,662 votes. The 1924 election promised to be more interesting. Many of the old progressives had no confidence in either Calvin Coolidge or his Democratic rival, John W. Davis, both of whom were too conservative for their tastes. They supported Robert M. La Follette, the independent candidate, but Coolidge won handily. La Follette, however, finished ahead of the conservative Davis. In 1928 Democrat Al Smith had no chance at all in Oregon. Herbert Hoover overwhelmed him.

The Economy of the 1920s

Agriculture after the war underwent a brief downturn as foreign markets were reduced from the wartime demand. United States government price supports were also eliminated. Farmers lost their farms or reduced their productive acreage. In Washington, for example, by 1924 nearly 750,000 acres had been taken out of wheat cultivation since the end of the war. Some farmers called for increased government aid; the McNary-Haugen plan was pushed hard by farmers throughout the decade. Another response was to turn to specialty crops more profitable than the old staple of wheat. Apples continued to be a lucrative crop; production increased in the decade through better techniques, improved fertilizers, and the development of new varieties. Some of the orchards were irrigated. The number of irrigated farms also rose in the decade, although the total of irrigated acreage declined. By middecade, farm income increased as national markets expanded.

In the lumber industry, too, there was a recovery from the postwar depression. In 1929 lumber production was at an all-time high. It made up one-half the value of regional exports. The decade was prosperous, but also worrisome for lumbermen. Their concerns did lead to some constructive action. One concern was the introduction of building materials that rivaled or replaced lumber: rubber, plasterboard, plastics, cement, steel, and above all, wood by-products. Lumbermen worried too as architects began to experiment with designs for houses with fewer rooms and lower ceilings than those of the past. The lumber market suffered accordingly.

A more apparent worry for most lumbermen in the 1920s was not demand, but supply. Wartime cutting had proceeded at a rapid, indeed furious pace. It could not be maintained. Conservation, which had been anathema to most lumbermen before the war, now received serious attention, although more to hold up prices than to conserve forests for future generations. Most of it took the form of an interest in federal action. Government was responsive, but divided. The old foresters, like Gifford Pinchot, wished for strong federal controls over all forests: national, state, and private. Younger men in the Forest Service stood for a much larger degree of cooperation among the three types of timber owners. Private interests also moved tentatively toward cooperation with the Forest Service.

Suspicions and hostilities rather quickly dissipated after the war and in 1924 the first result of accommodation emerged from a long series of conferences among forest people. This was the Clarke-McNary Act named for John D. Clarke, a representative from New York, and Charles McNary, Oregon's senior senator. It provided for several cooperative measures, including the expansion of national forests; providing funds to the states to add to their forests; giving states nursery stock; and encouraging the states to adopt tax policies that would favor a conservative lumber policy. The main ingredient in Clarke-McNary was fire protection. It provided for cooperative efforts in preventing and fighting fires in national, state, and private forests. The law was important not only in forestry, but as an illustration of cooperative federalism.

In 1928 Congress passed the McSweeney-McNary Act (John Mc-Sweeney was a representative from Ohio). This statute was based upon the precedent of agricultural experiment stations. It authorized the creation of fourteen forestry experiment stations at a cost of $1,000,000 annually. The late twenties was also notable in forest conservation through the work of David T. Mason, a consulting forester, who began to talk of the possibilities of sustained yield during the decade.

In the fisheries business there was also some government action. As the salmon and halibut industries prospered, the fishermen and canners took more and more of their stock. A serious supply crisis was evident in the decade that called forth conservation efforts. In 1918 Oregon and Washington had made an interstate agreement to regulate jointly the fisheries of the Columbia River. Each state was to carry out its regulatory measures independently. Nothing was done, however, until Oregon abolished the deadly efficient fish wheels in 1927. But fishermen, because of the market, caught as many fish with their old gear as they had before. At the international level a Canadian-American treaty in 1922 called for a three-month closed season on halibut and established a study commission on the life cycle of the fish and how to preserve them.

Transportation and Tourism

In the 1920s several changes occurred in the transportation industry. Maritime shipping continued to grow because of the Panama Canal. Railroads fought back by attempting to cut costs and by consolidation, but rate reductions were not very successful in recapturing business, and a 1927 proposal to unite the Great Northern and the Northern Pacific systems was not attempted because of its anticipated cost. The railroads lost passengers to the automobile and bus as did most of the electric interurban lines. The railroads, in order to get permission to abandon unprofitable lines, began to acquire bus lines; as early as 1924 the Spokane, Portland and Seattle company established bus service between Portland and Rainier, Oregon, fifty-three miles west of Portland.

The internal combustion engine produced the most momentous transportation development. It created a demand for modern highways, the "Good Roads Movement," which aided farmers and industrialists and virtually created the profitable tourist business. The first prominent figure to support good roads was the eccentric millionaire, Samuel C.

Hill (son-in-law of the transportation magnate, James J. Hill), not to be confused with the congressman of the same name. Hill conceived the idea of a highway down the north bank of the Columbia River, but the state of Washington would not finance it. Oregon, however, responded to Hill's vision in the creation of a state highway department in 1913. This department hired Samuel C. Lancaster to build the Columbia River Highway, which was completed in 1922. It was designed to add to the commercial possibilities of the area, but also to foster tourism as a business. As Hill put it, "We will cash in, year after year, on our crop of scenic beauty, without depleting it in any way." Lancaster began to advertise the tourist potential of Oregon on an eastern trip in 1916 and 1917.

As tourist attractions the state parks soon followed the state highways. The Oregon Highway Commission in 1919 began the state park system at the suggestion of Commissioner Robert W. Sawyer as a series of roadside parks not only to increase the "livability" of the state, but also to attract tourists. In 1922 the commission received the first donation of land for a park, Sarah Helmick's gift of 5½ acres near Salem. The twenties also saw the rise of another transportation development, aircraft, with the Boeing Company in Seattle. Founded in 1916, the company had begun modestly with defense contracts after American entry into the war. In the twenties the company continued to secure occasional contracts from the government, but what caught the public's eye was Boeing's production of the world's first all-metal plane.

Labor

The men and women whose work produced the economic gains of the 1920s seemed reasonably content with their lot. At least they eschewed unionization as a means to improve it. Unions, after all, were tainted with radicalism, and real wages were higher by the end of the decade than before the war. The Loyal Legion, a company union, continued in the lumber industry. Conditions remained bad, especially for the single men of camps and mills, whose work was long and dangerous and who came home to bunkhouses or to frame rooming houses like one in Grays Harbor: "These dens had an aura of filth, spit tinged with tobacco juice, sawdust around the heating stove to spit in, an odor of stale sweat and stale wine, and an air of homosexuality."[3]

In the next decade people were happy to find work at all. Industries were pleased to find any market. Farmers and fishermen were overjoyed to obtain any buyers. The Great Depression had come.

NOTES

1. Norman H. Clark, *Washington: A Bicentennial History* (1976), p. 141.

2. Robert E. Ficken, *Lumber and Politics: The Career of Mark Reed* (1979), p. 105.

3. Egbert S. Oliver, "Sawmilling on Grays Harbor in the Twenties: A Personal Reminiscence," *Pacific Northwest Quarterly,* 69 (January 1979): 3.

SUGGESTIONS FOR READING

Robert E. Ficken, *Lumber and Politics: The Career of Mark E. Reed* (1979) is especially good on Washington politics in the 1920s. See also Norman H. Clark, *Washington: A Bicentennial History* (1976); Robert L. Cole, "The Democratic Party in Washington State, 1919–1933: Barometer of Social Change." Ph.D. diss., University of Washington, 1972; and Richard Frisch, "A History of the Democratic Party in the State of Washington, 1854–1956." Ph.D. diss., University of Oregon, 1975. For Oregon, see Robert E. Burton, *Democrats of Oregon: The Pattern of Minority Politics, 1900–1956* (1970) and Arthur H. Bone, ed., *Oregon Cattleman/Governor/Congressman: Memoirs and Times of Walter M. Pierce* (1981). On economic life, see Ralph W. Hidy, Frank E. Hill, and Allan Nevins, *Timber and Men: The Weyerhaeuser Story* (1963) and Murray C. Morgan, *Puget's Sound: A Narrative of Early Tacoma and the Southern Sound* (1979). On state parks, see S. H. Boardman, "Oregon State Park System: A Brief History," *Oregon Historical Quarterly,* 55 (1954).

The Thirties

The depression years in the Pacific Northwest were doubly difficult. The economic realities of falling farm prices, industrial unemployment, foreclosed mortgages, all adding up to pervasive despair, were bad enough. What made them worse was that they followed on the heels of the most prosperous decade in regional history. But it did not take long for despair to yield to anger, then anger to determination. In speaking to the unprecedented problems, the two states of the Northwest answered with somewhat different voices. Both Oregonians and Washingtonians, however, in responding to the Great Depression, modified traditional beliefs rather than accepting the radical panaceas advocated by a small minority of communists and socialists.

The Time of Economic Anguish

Misery in the 1930s was nowhere more prevalent than in the Pacific Northwest's major industry. A loss of markets, caused by the worst depression in American history, spelled disaster for the lumbermen. After the crash in 1929 there were virtually no markets, at home or abroad. By 1932, 80 percent of the mills were closed. Layoffs made the men lose confidence in themselves. Some lost faith in the American system. Others began to flirt with communism, but most waited for the New Deal to have its chance. Stockholders were shaken, management at wit's end.

Recovery, however, did come, although slowly. Some hope arose because of an early New Deal law, the National Industrial Recovery Act (to be described later). But progress in adapting wood to new by-products was made without government aid. The Weyerhaeuser Timber Company, for example, opened its first pulp mill in 1931 at Longview, Washington. Operations proved to be so successful that a second such mill was opened at Everett in 1936. Other by-products that were developed in the 1930s included ceiling tile and insulation. Plywood, invented earlier, was improved in the decade as machinery and glues became better. Pres-to-Logs made from wood shavings and chips also came on the market at this time. By the late thirties, even traditional lumber products were showing considerable sales as the nation worked its way out of the Great Depression.

The other major regional industry, agriculture, was also in the doldrums with the collapse of the world economy, although farming remained an important source of employment in the 1930s. The farm population of Oregon was 24 percent in 1940, that of Washington, 20 percent. Wheat, hay, and oats were the principal products, as they had been for decades, with fruits and nuts also important. But in several respects, farm life was different in the 1930s from earlier times. Income was down, which meant that many farmers were forced to sell out to more fortunate neighbors. Tenancy increased, although the percentage of farm ownership in Oregon and Washington remained higher than the national average. The most serious long-term problem for owners or tenants was disastrous soil erosion. By 1940 one-quarter of the crop

Seattle depression shacks (1930s). Photograph by James Lee, Special Collections Division, University of Washington Libraries

land of the Northwest was badly damaged by erosion. In the cattle industry vegetation and soil were similarly injured by overgrazing. The
number of farms shrank as the depression eliminated markets, but those
who hung on increased the size of their holdings.

The depression also took its toll of the fishing industry. Collapsing
markets drove the boats into harbor and their crews to the relief lines.
The industry, which had been declining for several decades, never really
recovered. Tourism also fell off as the depression deepened. Although
railroads and bus lines cut the price of tickets to attract tourists, there
were few persons, within or outside the region, who could buy at any
price. The hotel and tourist court operator, the restaurant owner, and
the service station attendant were in the doldrums.

Oregon Politics

The decade opened with the Republicans bearing the crushing burden
of office during the great national collapse. The cause of their frustration
created a golden opportunity for the Democrats, whose chance first came
in the local and congressional elections of 1930. The state election turned
on the old progressive hope of obtaining public power. In many areas
of the state, especially the rural regions, private utilities had never provided adequate service. The companies had always been deeply involved
in politics and were among the most potent lobbyists in Salem. For most
citizens, their rule had been bearable during prosperity. Now, in depression, their opponents had their chance.

The Oregon State Grange placed an initiative measure on the ballot
permitting the creation of public utility districts. It had the support not
only of farmers, but also of many urban citizens who had long protested
high utility rates. The measure was fought bitterly by the utilities, who,
fearing a precedent, poured in money from all over the nation. The
proposal also became enmeshed in gubernatorial politics.

The Republican nominee was George W. Joseph. A lawyer, and an
old progressive, Joseph backed the Grange initiative. His Democratic
opponent, Edward F. Bailey, equivocated. Joseph seemed to take an early
lead, but died in the midst of the campaign. Circumstances prohibited the
Progressives from replacing him so late in the campaign. The only solution for the public power advocates was to nominate an independent
candidate. The man they selected was Julius Meier. He conducted a
vigorous campaign, making public power the central issue, and won the
election overwhelmingly. Democrats were also pleased by the election of
Charles H. Martin to Congress from the Portland district. This colorful

figure was a career man in the United States Army who had retired to Oregon with the rank of major general in 1927. Martin had entered politics and won an unexpected victory against Representative Franklin F. Korell in 1930. The Grange public power measure also carried handily, yet the irony of the utility district victory was that in the depression there was no capital for local utility districts. So the advocates of public power turned elsewhere.

Franklin Roosevelt had visited the Northwest as candidate for vice-president in 1920. Riding on a train through The Dalles, he had become enamored with the power potential of the Columbia and never forgot it. In a speech at Portland during the 1932 campaign he called for federal power production. After he became president, he continued to advocate giant multipurpose dams at Grand Coulee and Bonneville. He saw them as public works measures, as irrigation opportunities, and as sources of electrical power. But as the dams rose, so did controversy about them in Oregon and Washington.

One group of Northwesterners favored a new governmental agency for the region. This was to be a Columbia Valley Authority based upon the precedent of the New Deal's Tennessee Valley Authority. The Authority would be governed by a board of governors to supervise a valleywide agency for manufacturing and distributing power produced at the dams. The governors would be largely independent from the control of Congress because their revenues would come from the sale of power, not from congressional appropriations. The first discussion of a CVA took place in 1934; the first bill to create it was introduced into Congress by Washington's Representative Knute Hill in the following year. Oregon's principal advocate for CVA was Walter Pierce.

CVA sharply divided public opinion in the region. Those who favored it included farm groups like the state Granges, organized labor, and progressives in general. Opponents were businessmen, conservative opponents of federal government expansion, private utilities, and the city of Portland. Portlanders believed that they could obtain lower rates from Bonneville Dam alone than if they were linked with Grand Coulee in a CVA. Some groups wanted federal power to be produced by familiar government agencies, like the Corps of Engineers or the Bureau of Reclamation, rather than by a CVA.

A second divisive issue of Columbia River federal power was over who would be the main beneficiary of it. Cooperatives and public utility districts wanted to be the preferred customers. Business and private utilities wanted the preference also. The solution to both controversies was the passage of the Bonneville Power Administration Act in 1937. It permitted the Department of the Interior to market the power through a new agency (but not a multipurpose one), the Bonneville Power Administration. Preference was awarded to cooperatives and public bodies.

Federal policies also ignited another hot issue in Oregon. One of the most important features of the New Deal was its role in the organization of labor. Always before, the national government had been on the side of capital, or neutral at best, in conflicts between labor and management. Now, as part of the National Industrial Recovery Act, Congress guaranteed industrial workers the right to organize and to choose their own unions. The existing labor organizations in the United States were almost all under the umbrella of the American Federation of Labor.

In the state, as nationally, the AFL moved under the National Industrial Recovery Act to organize skilled workers. When the NIRA was declared unconstitutional in 1935, Congress retained its labor clauses in the new National Labor Relations Act (the Wagner Act). Within the ranks of the AFL there were officers who urged the union to move quickly to organize a whole new pool of laboring people, the unskilled workers. These dissenters, under the leadership of John L. Lewis, broke away to found the Committee on Industrial Organization, later called the Congress of Industrial Organizations. The AFL and the CIO also became bitter rivals in politics. Candidates supported by the AFL lost CIO support and the reverse. Since most labor-supported candidates were Democrats, labor's internal strife made it difficult for the party to garner the unified forces of this theoretically powerful group. The most famous illustration of this conflict involved Nan Wood Honeyman, Oregon's first woman member of the United States House of Representatives. She was elected to Congress in 1936 from the Portland district. When she came up for reelection in 1938 she received CIO support, thus incurred AFL opposition, and lost the election to Republican Homer Angell.

Another set of issues in Oregon politics revolved about how the state should respond to the New Deal. Even though President Roosevelt was enormously popular in Oregon, with many Republicans as well as Democrats voting for him, the state's citizens were not always willing to implement his programs, especially if they required tax support. Oddly, the chief spokesman of this view was Democratic Governor Charles Martin, chosen in 1934 after two terms in the House of Representatives. Martin attacked many New Deal measures. He opposed Social Security. He opposed federal relief as tending to create a "nation of softies." On the issues relating to Bonneville power, Martin favored the old line agencies and not a CVA. He advocated preference for businesses and utilities rather than for cooperatives and public utility districts. Martin hated the labor policies of the Roosevelt Administration. He opposed the National Labor Relations Act, and the Fair Labor Standards Act, which established

Representative Nan Wood Honeyman. Oregon Historical Society

a national minimum wage. Martin was not the only prominent Democrat who opposed the New Deal. He had allies in Oswald West and Joseph K. Carson, Jr., the mayor of Portland, and other prominent Democrats.

Civil liberties issues were more popular in the thirties than in the twenties. As the depression deepened, a few disaffected citizens were taken by the lure of Marxism. In 1932 twelve Communists were indicted under the state criminal syndicalism law, and one was convicted. In 1937 the syndicalism law was challenged in the United States Supreme Court by Dirk DeJonge, who had been sentenced to seven years in prison in 1934 for speaking at a Communist meeting in Portland and for urging those in attendance to buy Communist literature. The Supreme Court declared the syndicalism statute unconstitutional as a violation of the citizen's right to freedom of speech. The legislature repealed the law in 1939. Among the leaders in fighting the syndicalism law were many progressives who came to form the Oregon Commonwealth Federation in 1937.

The moving spirit of the OCF was Monroe Sweetland, son of a middle class family, whose father was the football coach of Willamette

University in Salem. Sweetland became a convert to socialism while attending Cornell University. He had been an electoral college candidate in Oregon for Norman Thomas, the Socialist presidential candidate in 1936. But the OCF was not a Socialist organization, let alone a Communist one. It included men and women of all parties who were disaffected with the two major parties. OCF members condemned Governor Martin for his opposition to the New Deal. They pushed hard for low rates on Bonneville power for public agencies. More radically, but hardly seriously, the OCF called for state ownership of natural resources, banks, utilities, and monopolies (the last undefined).

Practically, the OCF threw its strength into the 1938 Democratic gubernatorial primary. It supported Henry Hess, a progressive state senator, against Martin. Hess had many allies, including both wings of organized labor, the Grange, and Walter Pierce and Nan Wood Honeyman. Secretary of the Interior Harold Ickes also endorsed Hess, an indirect blessing from President Roosevelt. Hess defeated Martin, but Republican Charles Sprague, a Salem publisher of liberal stripe, easily won over him in the fall elections. Sprague undercut Hess on public power—the leading issue in the campaign—by supporting the New Deal power program at Bonneville. Sprague's victory was not unique for the Republicans also controlled both houses of the state legislature in the depression years and won most of the county offices as well.

At the level of national politics, Oregonians voted for Franklin Roosevelt in 1932, 1936, and 1940. But they elected only Republicans as United States senators. Frederick Steiwer was reelected in 1932 and carried the general election. He resigned in 1938 and was succeeded by Rufus C. Holman who was victorious as a strong public power supporter. Charles McNary was reelected senator in 1930 and 1936 and remained the most influential Oregon politician nationally. As minority leader of a small band of Republicans in the Senate, he tried to keep the party reasonably conservative—occasionally progressive—rather than allow it to be saddled with reactionary programs. On specific matters McNary, even though minority leader, voted for the early New Deal measures most of the time in 1933 and 1934. By mid-1934, however, he began to believe that the New Deal should slow down so that the nation could judge the effect of its first measures before moving on to additional innovations.

By late 1937 McNary had decided that the time had come to push for a Republican renaissance. He decided to oppose the New Deal when he felt principle, partisanship, and practical politics were in tune. In 1937 and 1938 he fought the president's efforts to reorganize the executive branch, fearing its centralizing effect in general and its proposal to transfer the Forest Service to the Department of the Interior in particular.

When the recession of 1937–1938 struck, the president urged Congress to authorize the spending of $3 billion to combat it. McNary was opposed to this pump-priming effort, but it passed the Senate with ease. In 1939 McNary worked carefully with his Republican colleagues and conservative Democrats to attempt to trim relief spending. Their move was partially successful. All in all McNary continued to be a major national figure in the decade. He was one of the few important congressional leaders who had an effect in braking the New Deal, although not in derailing it. In 1940 McNary was Republican vice-presidential candidate with Wendell Willkie.

The only other Northwestern representative to have much influence was Walter Pierce. Pierce served in the eastern Oregon district for ten years, from 1933 to 1943. He was the only member of the Oregon congressional delegation to vote for the extension of selective service in 1941, a measure that passed by a single vote. He was helpful in persuading President Roosevelt to appoint William O. Douglas to the Supreme Court, by gaining the support of the influential Senator George W. Norris of Nebraska. Pierce also played a role in drawing up the Agricultural Adjustment Act of 1938.

Washington Politics

In Washington the Democratic Party, progressive wing, seized its opportunity during the depression. The party did have divisions, but they were not catastrophic as in Oregon. Indeed, the progressives captured the party twenty years before they were able to do so in Oregon. The first step was the selection of Scott Bullitt as national committeeman in 1930. Bullitt and Senator Dill realized that the nation and the state were ready to adopt drastic changes to pull their citizens out of the depression. They corresponded with Governor Franklin D. Roosevelt of New York, who was attempting to lead the Democratic party in progressive directions. Roosevelt also had his eye on the presidential nomination in 1932.

In Washington the liberalizing issue was public power. It had gone into temporary hibernation with the defeat of the Bone Bill in 1924, but the Washington State Grange revived it in 1928. Rural people were continually complaining about the lack of electricity on the farms, but the private utilities asserted the rural business would be unprofitable. The private utilities were in bad odor nationally, however, and with the depression it became popular to expose the evils of big business. One of the revelations made by the Federal Trade Commission in the late 1920s was that Puget Sound Power and Light had contributed thousands of dollars secretly to defeat the Bone Bill initiative in 1924.

What the Grange proposed was an initiative measure in the 1930 election that permitted the formation of public utility districts. It seemed to be a splendid progressive cause, but it had one weakness: it ran into opposition from supporters of the Seattle and Tacoma municipal electric systems which hoped (as under the Bone Bill) to run their lines into the surrounding countryside. However, Bone himself, aided by Senator Dill, led the fight for the Grange initiative, which did pass in the November elections. In the next ten years public utility districts sprouted until by 1940 twenty-three of thirty-nine counties in the state had them.

As the depression deepened, relief, unemployment compensation, and old age pensions joined power as major issues of state politics. Franklin Roosevelt carried every county in the state in 1932; the Democrats captured the state legislature. Democrat Clarence Martin was chosen governor. Homer Bone was elected to the United States Senate. Democrats went to work in the next session and passed many measures modeled on the New Deal but were unwilling to provide money for unemployment insurance. By 1935 there were increasing legislative troubles for progressives, however. Many of them came from Governor Martin. Martin, like his Oregon namesake, became less progressive as his term developed. He balked at raising old age pensions to the level thought desirable by many progressives. He increasingly attacked the New Deal as spendthrift. And Martin's policies and attitudes helped raise up a potent progressive opposition.

One of the fruits of the Great Depression was a scheme devised in California by Upton Sinclair called End Poverty in California (EPIC). This was a program of large-scale government intervention in the economy, designed primarily to aid the unemployed and the elderly. It spread around the country and had a Washington offshoot founded in 1934 called Commonwealth Builders, Inc. This in turn merged in 1935 into the Washington Commonwealth Federation.

The WCF was a force in Washington politics until 1944. Its strengths were its energy and its appeal for change. Its weaknesses were its diversity of beliefs and its radical components. For the WCF welcomed all apostles of change ranging from public power advocates to old age pensioners to communists. Progressive discontent with Governor Martin led to a revolt against him at the 1936 Democratic convention headed by WCF partisans. The WCF had a majority of the delegates and pushed through a radical plank calling for state ownership of basic industries and other progressive measures.

Still, the WCF and other progressives were unable to deny Governor Martin renomination and reelection. Ironically, his victory was enhanced by a strategem earlier favored by one of his opponents. In 1935 the state Grange had successfully pushed through an amendment to the constitution that was a genuine innovation. It permitted voters to vote for each office in any party primary they wished. The Grange had wanted this blanket primary to assure that there would be propublic power candidates nominated by all parties. But in 1936 conservative Republicans supported Martin in the Democratic primary. In the fall election Martin was pleasing enough to conservatives of any stripe to win against former Governor Roland Hartley, who was attempting a comeback on the Republican ticket. The Democrats again controlled both houses of the state legislature by healthy majorities.

Governor Martin regarded his victory as a mandate to move state policies to the right. When the legislature met in 1937, he recommended two proposals that antagonized progressives. One was an increase in old age pensions smaller than what the organizations of the elderly desired. It passed with ease. The other was a bill that would have severely restricted the recently won rights of labor. It placed limitations on picketing and required compulsory arbitration in labor disputes. This bill was too conservative for passage, however. The legislature also had enough progressive spirit to repeal the repressive criminal syndicalism law. Progressives, in their bitter disappointment about Martin's pension bill, determined to found a lobbying organization. Howard Costigan—a secret Communist—formed the Washington Old Age Pension Union as an auxiliary to the WCF.

Struggles between left and right continued as the state was caught in the recession of 1937–1938. This development led to one of the great comic opera affairs of regional history. The basis for it was one constructive response to the tragedy of the depression: humor. Victor Aloysius Meyers was a popular entertainer and wit in Seattle. He had run for local office on zany planks such as having a stewardess on every streetcar. In 1932 he ran for the ceremonial post of lieutenant governor, asserting it was the only office for which he could afford the filing fee. To the amazement of all, name familiarity carried him to victory.

When 1938 opened, amidst deepening recession, Governor Martin eliminated all state contributions for work relief. This withdrawal made the counties solely responsible for it, an impossible burden. The Old Age Pension Union, organized labor, and thousands of unorganized citizens pushed for a special session of the state legislature to have the state resume its obligation. Martin refused to call one. But he made the mistake of leaving the state on a trip to Washington, D.C. Meyers, the acting governor with Martin away, was also out of town, on a fishing trip in California. Pension advocates hit upon the stratagem of summoning Meyers home and having him call a special session. While they searched for the lieutenant governor somewhere on his boat, the governor's aides urged him to return to the state. A race ensued after the respective partisans had made contact with their men. Martin won it, his special plane touching down near Spokane just a few minutes before Meyers arrived at the capitol in Olympia.

The fall elections of 1938 continued the attempts by conservatives to roll back New Deal type legislation. Business groups pushed an initiative measure that would have limited labor's right to strike. Opposed by all progressive groups, it was defeated. Democrats also won their, by now, customary majorities in the state legislature. When the legislators met in the session of 1939 Martin awaited them with a plan for a reduced budget for social security. He did not get it. Progressives, however, did make it possible to fund social security at existing levels by agreeing to a sales tax on food. The decade faded away in Olympia with conservatives and progressives still at each other's throats.

National Politics

Washington voters remained staunchly loyal to the Democratic party throughout the decade. Franklin Roosevelt won the state every time he ran. At the senatorial level, Homer Bone was one who carried the progressive hopes. In the 1932 general election, he defeated the veteran Republican incumbent, Wesley Jones, with a 60 percent majority. Six years later he again won with ease. In 1934 Clarence Dill shocked the voters by anouncing that he would not run again for office. Lewis Schwellenbach was the Democratic candidate for his seat, Reno Odlin the Republican. A strong supporter of public power for many years, and an advocate of all New Deal measures, Schwellenbach won easily.

Democrats also won most of the elections for the House of Representatives in the decade, sweeping all seats in 1936. None of these members gained a national reputation for political accomplishment, but one became famous for antics and for tragedy. Marion Zioncheck was a representative from Seattle. He had fought hard, at times brilliantly, for progressive causes as far back as his days at the University of Washington. After his first term in Washington he became known as a comedian, marrying after a twenty-four-hour courtship and enhancing his reputation as a prankster by a series of ludicrous escapades. But Zioncheck's later life reflected pathology, not comedy; growing dementia drove him to suicide in 1936.

Washington's politics were progressive, even radical, in rhetoric during the 1930s. In results it was a combination of progressivism, conservatism, and reaction. Some progressive measures that cost the taxpayers nothing, such as the repeal of the syndicalism law, passed. But the voters were unwilling or unable to pay for many social measures. The tax rate in Washington, for example, remained low. Voters lowered the property tax and defeated an income tax amendment in 1934 (after passing it two years earlier). However, the legislature did adopt and expand the most regressive tax—that on sales. The result was that while most states doubled their tax revenues in the 1930s, Washington held even. What cushioned the state from the worst blows of the depression was the United States government.

The New Deal in the Pacific Northwest

Franklin Roosevelt and Congress cooperated to bring about the greatest government intervention in the economy in American history. The nation demanded action—almost any action—against the depression. Roosevelt provided action, but kept it carefully channeled in democratic and capitalist lines. His aim was to preserve the system, not to replace it. The keystone of the New Deal's early industrial program was the National Industrial Recovery Act (NIRA) administered by the National Recovery Administration (NRA). The Act permitted corporations in each industry to establish production quotas. It set a floor under wages and limited hours of work. NRA was originally hailed with a good deal of enthusiasm. There were parades supporting it and public opinion was mobilized to persuade people to join. Consumers hurried to sign cards pledging them to patronize only NRA stores. Military analogies were frequent and the symbol of the NRA, the Blue Eagle, took the place of the flag as a rallying point in advertisements, parades, and public meetings.

The actual effect of the NRA was not what citizens anticipated. It was a glaring failure in the region's largest industry, lumber. The lumbermen wrote their codes which had the force of law. They were allowed to set prices and to regulate production cooperatively as the antitrust laws were set aside. There was some difficulty in getting the codes established, but this task was simple compared to seeing them observed. The lumbermen had always been fiercely individualistic. They had rarely cooperated. Now they produced what they wished regardless of the code. And the code was never enforced as law. Finally the entire NRA was declared unconstitutional by the United States Supreme Court in 1935. Few in industry mourned.

Almost none in management regretted one section of the NIRA. This was Section 7(a), which guaranteed workers the right to organize and to bargain collectively. Under this statute, a host of organizing activity occurred in the Pacific Northwest. It began against a rather narrow background, for the IWW and the AFL had almost entirely disappeared from the lumber industry in the period of reaction after the First World

War. Even the Loyal Legion of Loggers and Lumbermen (4-L), the company union, was in decline as workers regarded it as ineffective and the employers had stopped funding it.

Now organizers seemed everywhere. The 4-L took on renewed life. This resurrection was palatable to the employers, but not to many of the workers of woods and mills. The AFL saw Section 7(a) as catering to its aspirations. Its union, the Sawmill and Timber Workers, had shown a revival of militancy when it had struck in support of the Longshoremen and other maritime workers in 1934 (to be described later). In 1935 it was ready to move on its own behalf.

But it did not move smoothly. The national officers of the AFL placed the STW in that year under the jurisdiction of the United Brotherhood of Carpenters and Joiners of America. This body had little experience in forest products. Its organizers knew neither the industry nor the region of the Pacific Northwest. It didn't really want woods workers as regular members. In the spring of 1935 the STW presented its demands to the employers for union recognition, a thirty-hour week, a minimum wage of seventy cents per hour, and paid vacations. The response was uneven. Some lumbermen refused to negotiate; others did so. Some workers awaited the results of negotiations; others walked off the job before time for effective bargaining had elapsed. By May 1935, most of the lumber industry of the Pacific Northwest was shut down.

State government intervened at the behest of the industry. Governor Charles Martin of Oregon had little use for unions; he suggested that local law enforcement officials adopt the following policy for strikers: "Beat hell out of 'em . . . and crack their damn heads! These fellows are there for nothing but trouble—give it to them." [1] Governor Clarence Martin of Washington also called out the national guard to protect strikebreakers. The strike finally ended inconclusively with a gain of union recognition for some workers (but without the closed shop), but they nowhere gained the other goals they sought.

During the year of the strike, Congress adopted the Wagner Act. It succeeded Section 7(a) of the now defunct NIRA. It unleashed a wave of union organizing and a rash of internal conflict within labor. The STW became increasingly restive against the national carpenters union. More important, many mill and woods workers fell in behind the CIO. In 1937 the STW joined the CIO, adopting the new name of the International Woodworkers of America. A minority of the old union remained loyal to the AFL in a union known as the Federation of Woodworkers. The two unions, one CIO one AFL, vied to sign up workers. By the close of the decade the industry was organized, but by two unions, although the CIO union was strongest.

The second major theater of union activity in the Pacific Northwest was in the maritime unions of those who worked aboard ship and those who loaded and unshipped cargo. The longshoremen had always suffered from unsafe working conditions: long hours and split shifts magnified their dangerous occupation of handling heavy cargo. They had no organizational machinery to deal with grievances. Worst of all they had no fair chance to secure what jobs were available. For the employers hired those who were willing to pay bribes or were relatives or favorites. Most definitely they did not hire those who favored unions.

As it had in lumber, Section 7(a) encouraged the growth of the maritime unions. The International Longshoremen's Association, an affiliate of the AFL, took a new lease on life. In March 1934 the ILA made its demands, the most important of which were a single contract for the entire Pacific Coast and for hiring halls controlled by the union where jobs are allocated by seniority to union members alone. The International Seamen's Union made demands for those afloat. The longshoremen, after the failure of mediation, went on strike in May 1934 in the major parts of the Pacific Coast. Their leader was Harry Bridges, an Australian, a left-winger, and a charismatic leader. The employers were adamant, determined to break the strike and the union. Violence flared all along the coast as employers—aided by police and national guard officers— tried to force strikebreakers through picket lines. Mayor Joseph K. Carson of Portland called out 500 special police to patrol the waterfront, and the county sheriff had his deputies present. Governor Julius L. Meier ordered the national guard to assist strikebreakers.

President Roosevelt appointed a panel to end the strike. Its members suggested arbitration, and both parties agreed. In October the award was made granting most of what the longshoremen desired. The victory boosted the leadership of Bridges, but certainly did not deter the employers from a counterattack.

The waterfront employers tried to undercut the 1934 arbitration award by arguing that the unions had violated it. They attempted to regain joint control of hiring which the union—despite the agreement— had refused to grant in practice. As contracts were to run out in September 1936, both sides prepared for a showdown. To make a new contract, the employers demanded arbitration, the union held fast for negotiation. No resolution was achieved and a strike, which lasted ninety-eight days, began on October 29. This time it was peaceful. Although the union won little of moment in terms of specific demands, it was successful in forcing the employers to recognize that unions were there to stay.

Militancy also marked the rise of the Teamsters Union. Dave Beck was a laundry truck driver in his native city of Seattle. He was scarred and scared by the left-wing ideology and the failure of the general strike

Dave Beck. Special Collections Division, University of Washington
Libraries

in 1919. He determined thereafter to work within the framework of
capitalism. His methods of so doing were not always scrupulous. As Beck
rose in the ranks of the union, he became more convinced that both
employers and union would benefit by the closed shop. The union's
gains were obvious, but employers too would profit. With the right union,
the Teamsters, they could be assured of honored contracts. They could
charge higher prices. All would benefit. Employers who did not sign
union contracts saw their business die as truck drivers refused to deliver
to them. Against those who somehow survived the boycott, Beck employed strongarm methods.

Beck's Teamsters not only fought against the bosses. They easily
disposed of the communist influence within their union. They organized

many businesses that had little to do with trucking. They fought a spectacular, often bloody, struggle with the Longshoremen. By the end of the decade the Teamsters had won the warehouse workers. And Beck was en route to becoming one of the most powerful men in America. Through the efforts of the Teamsters, the Longshoremen, and the timber unions, and lesser unions, the Pacific Northwest was one of the most highly unionized regions of the nation by 1940. The role of the federal government through the NIRA and the Wagner Act was decisive in creating this condition of labor prosperity.

Of even more general importance was the federal government's intervention in the realm of natural resources. The most spectacular effect was the construction of two huge multipurpose projects on the Columbia River. The oldest of these—in conception—was the plan of using the waters of the Columbia at Grand Coulee in the state of Washington to irrigate the drylands and make the desert bloom with farms. It was an ancient dream in a new setting. In the 1920s Rufus Woods, editor of the *Wenatchee World,* was the leading spokesman for the Coulee Dam idea. He advocated it tirelessly, and interested leading journalists, politicians, including U.S. Senators Clarence Dill and Wesley Jones, and the Corps of Engineers. This agency produced a report demonstrating the feasibility of an irrigation project at Grand Coulee, but also noting that other uses would follow from building a dam there. While politicians debated, the Puget Sound Power and Light Company built the first dam on the Columbia, at Rock Island near Wenatchee, but this was a single-purpose (for power production only) project.

Finally, in the first year of his administration, President Roosevelt persuaded Congress to adopt a giant public works agency, the Public Works Administration. It was PWA that began the Grand Coulee Project. Roosevelt conceived the dam first as a work relief project. He saw its major long-term contribution as bringing a new chance for farmers who had lost their lands in the Middle West or the Great Plains because of depression, drought, or other natural disaster. Power production, although not a complete afterthought (it had been foreshadowed in Roosevelt's 1932 Portland speech), was a lesser consideration in the president's mind. As the dam arose, the government had to worry about the potential farmers. Qualifications were set so that only experienced farmers with sufficient capital would be permitted to buy land on the project. To prevent speculative windfalls, Congress adopted the Columbia Basin Antispeculation Act in 1937 that limited the amount of land that any one person could own. As the decade wore on, the Coulee Dam progressed. When it was finished in 1941, it was the largest structure ever built. Completed three years earlier was Bonneville Dam located

Bonneville dam under construction. Bonneville Power Administration

lower on the Columbia River, thirty miles east of Portland. Both dams became nuclei for enormous power production grids and the construction of several other dams on the Columbia in later times.

The New Deal also aided Northwestern farmers by other means than irrigation. Central to its agricultural program was the Agricultural Adjustment Act of 1933. This measure was designed to raise farm prices by cutting production. It paid farmers for reducing acreage in the hopes that diminished supplies would give the farmer higher market prices. The AAA was enthusiastically hailed by wheat farmers, many of whom stayed in business solely because of government support. When the AAA was declared unconstitutional in 1936, a second statute of the same name but with even more benefits was enacted in 1938.

Another means of aid to farmers came when Congress passed the Soil Conservation Act in 1935 and established the Soil Conservation Service to give farmers advice on how to protect their land from erosion. The government paid local soil conservation districts established by local farmers for the construction of flood control dams, terraces, revegetation projects, and diversion ditches. Local unemployed people did most of this work. The SCS also provided instruction in farming techniques designed to prevent the loss of irreplaceable topsoil. To implement the federal programs, Washington and Oregon passed laws in 1939 that authorized soil conservation districts to be set up upon majority vote of the landowners in any given area.

Other citizens were aided by the multitude of New Deal programs. These included the Public Works Administration, the Works Progress Administration, the National Youth Administration, and the Civilian Conservation Corps. The programs put many thousands of people to work, providing them not only employment, but hope against a better day. Most popular of all the New Deal programs was social security. It touched practically every family and individual in the region.

Given the terrible state of the economy, it is surprising that there was not more rancor in the depression decade. The period was peaceful, although there was ferment and some sporadic labor strife. The region absorbed thousands of migrants. Radical ideas were widespread. A few demagogues arose. Washington acquired the reputation of a left-wing state around the country, once described by a prominent politician as "the Soviet of Washington."

What actually happened was much less radical. Capitalism survived. Democracy continued. Civil liberties were strengthened. The two-party system persisted. The system survived because it was flexible. The New Deal and the state antidepression legislation were not perfect. But the people accepted enough government intervention in the economy to see it move forward. This intervention furnished them sufficient hope to survive until the better days ahead.

NOTES

1. Richard L. Neuberger, *Our Promised Land* (1938), p. 315.

SUGGESTIONS FOR READING

The politics of the era is dealt with in Robert E. Burton, *Democrats of Oregon: The Pattern of Minority Politics, 1900–1956* (1970); Arthur H. Bone, ed., *Oregon Cattleman/Governor/Congressman: Memoirs and Times of Walter M. Pierce* (1981); Herman C. Voeltz, "Genesis and Development of a Regional Power Agency in the Pacific Northwest, 1933–43," *Pacific Northwest Quarterly*, 53 (1962); Norman H. Clark, *Washington: A Bicentennial History* (1976); Murray C. Morgan, *Skid Road: An Informal History of Seattle* (1960). See also the dissertations by Frisch and Cole in the bibliography of the preceding chapter and G. Thomas Edwards and Carlos A. Schwantes, *Experiences in a Promised Land: Essays in Pacific Northwest History* (1986). For the unions see Jerry Lembcke and William N. Tattem, *One Union in Wood: A Political History of the International Woodworkers of America* (1984) and Walter Galenson, *The United Brotherhood of Carpenters: The First Hundred Years* (1983).

Cultural and Social Life, 1920–1945

In contrast to the fluctuations of economics and politics in the 1920s and 1930s, there was steady progress in social and cultural life in these two decades. The nonwhite minorities gradually became, after great trials, and with one notable exception, more accepted by the majority. In formal cultural affairs, both institutions and individuals acquired greater stature and became more aware of larger national and international developments.

The Ethnic Scene

The first Americans' terrible plight gradually became evident to people in political authority. The failure of the Dawes Act experiment in severalty led to calls for replacement of the policy of individualism that underlay it. In 1928 the Rockefeller Foundation published a report of a study directed by Lewis Merriam. It described appalling conditions of Indian life, especially in health and education. Congress soon made its own investigations, as did the executive branch under President Herbert C. Hoover. The result of these inquiries was momentous, although it did not appear until Franklin Roosevelt's New Deal.

The Indian Reorganization Act of 1934 (the Wheeler-Howard Act) was based upon the assumption that Indian traditions were as much communal as individual. Under this important law Indians who wished to organize into tribes could obtain a charter from the federal government. The charter gave them limited powers of self-government through tribal councils and entitled them to a variety of health and economic benefits from the national government. It would not be applied to any group without its consent. In the United States, by 1938, 189 tribes accepted the opportunities of the Indian Reorganization Act, 77 rejected them. This differing national response was reflected in the Pacific Northwest.

The Umatillas and the Yakimas rejected the new act. On these reservations opposition was based upon a tradition of distrust of the federal government, a feeling that the heritage of broken promises poisoned any federal effort to improve the lot of the Indians. Many Indians hated the federal Bureau of Indian Affairs and wanted to abolish it, not allow it to administer new programs. The Yakimas had also formed already their own governing council. The Klamath, too, refused the Indian Reorganization Act. For them a major argument (which had been a minor theme at Umatilla) was that the act was a species of communism. Although advanced mainly by whites, the theory did have some Indian adherents. The Colvilles, Nez Percé, and Spokanes rejected the act as well. Many Indians who voted negatively believed that a chartered tribe would have fewer rights than a treaty tribe if the federal government could ever be persuaded to live up to its original treaty obligations. In any case the result of rejection was that land continued to slip away from the Indians into the hands of white owners.

This fate did not overtake another of the Oregon Indian communities, however. On the Warm Springs reservation, the three tribes did reorganize under the new statute in 1938. They received their federal charter and created an eleven-man tribal council composed of eight elected members and the hereditary chiefs of the three tribes. This body was able to obtain some federal assistance during the next few years, but the real benefits would not come until the 1950s. Several other Northwest tribes also organized in the 1930s. Some Indians from the region gained from general New Deal programs, and there was a special Indian unit in the Civilian Conservation Corps, but the depression years, at best, were a period of hope for a limited number of Indians.

The Japanese and the Japanese Americans were on a psychological roller coaster in the years from 1920 to 1940. First came the Alien Land Laws early in the 1920s. This blow was in part parried by the economic prosperity of the decade. The Japanese raised fruits and vegetables not only for the regional cities, especially Seattle, Tacoma, and Portland, but also for the urban areas of the East Coast. The Japanese farms also helped support urban life in the ghettos. In Seattle in 1935, for instance, the five most important occupations of Japanese and Japanese Americans were hotels, grocery stores, dry cleaning shops, public market stands, and wholesale produce houses. Communal life flourished around these and other economic pursuits, a part of, but also apart from, the larger regional life patterns.

Institutional life developed in customary ways with the addition of new churches, newspapers, and cultural associations as the population grew in numbers and expanded geographically. In 1928, as a reflection both of the decline of the old culture and a desire to maintain it in some form, James Y. Sakamoto founded the Seattle *Japanese-American Courier,* a weekly printed in the English language. Sakamoto was also a moving spirit in founding the Japanese American Citizens League, an organization composed mainly of the second generation. Takeya (Clarence) Arci had organized a Seattle Progressive Citizens' League in 1922 that was reorganized in 1928. It became a chapter of the national Japanese American Citizens League, founded in 1929, which held its first national convention in 1930 in Seattle. Tacoma had a JACL branch in 1934. In 1936 Sakamoto was elected national president of JACL.

Steady progress in cultural matters was shadowed by the economic dislocation of the 1930s. Fear of privation became pervasive as farm markets shrank. Psychological pressures mounted as tension developed between the United States and Japan. Caucasians began to look upon people of Japanese descent as potential traitors, spies, or saboteurs. To the old stereotypes of clannishness and acquisitiveness was added that of mortal enemy.

In spite of the heritage of discrimination against them, the Chinese of the region made some gains in these years. At least the younger generation did so, although many of their parents begrudged the children's rather rapid turning from ancestral ways. The children rebelled against Chinese language schools on weekends and daily after public school; they acquired greater freedom to date; and some even married Caucasian spouses. They also broke away from the Chinatown ghettos and by the end of the 1930s were distributed throughout the residential areas of the major municipalities. They also moved upward in the professions and in business through the traditional Chinese work ethic which remained undiluted in later generations of Chinese Americans. Although Chinese long fell under the barrier of the Alien Land Laws, this last obstacle collapsed in 1943 when Congress admitted first generation Chinese immigrants to American citizenship because China was an ally of the United States in the war against Japan.

Black citizens of the Northwest continued to walk a difficult path. The terrible pressures of discrimination that they had known everywhere were exacerbated by the Great Depression. But the black experience was, as always, one of fulfillment as well as discrimination. Transportation remained the chief means of livelihood of the black worker. In Portland,

La Grande, and Roseburg the railroad was the principal employer of the black Oregonian. In Seattle, water transportation supplemented that of land as blacks worked as seamen and longshoremen as well as for the Great Northern and Northern Pacific railroads. Black workers were not always docile, although in the 1921 maritime strike they acted as strikebreakers organized into a company union, the Colored Maritime Employees Benevolent Association of the Pacific. In 1934 blacks took a far more different and militant role during the waterfront strike. The seamen joined the free trade union, the Marine Cooks and Stewards Association. When this union joined the CIO in 1938, it benefitted from the CIO's constitutional prohibition against discrimination on the basis of race, creed, or color. The black longshoremen also gained in the 1934 strike as they were admitted to the union at this time.

Urban blacks worked as musicians, maintenance workers, and in business and the professions as well as transportation. But even material success had heartbreaks attached to it. Norval Unthank, a physician, came to Portland in 1931 from Kansas City to be, he later declared, "a little adventurous." Bigotry of his white neighbors forced him to move on several occasions, but he was not without defenders. One couple was fined for vandalizing his property. In 1936 when the state medical association met in Medford, Unthank was denied admission to the convention hotel. The association threatened to cancel the convention, but finally Dr. Unthank's accommodations were provided.

Blacks dominated the Pullman sleeping car porter jobs. Conditions of labor were abominable, for example, overtime pay was granted only if porters worked 11,000 miles or 400 hours a month. To overcome these conditions, A. Phillip Randolph organized the Brotherhood of Sleeping Car Porters in 1925. Not until 1935 was it recognized and only in 1937 did it gain an increase in pay and a reduction in hours.

Off the job, discrimination continued, but not without resistance. The leader in opposition in Oregon was the Portland chapter of the National Association for the Advancement of Colored People, the oldest continuously chartered chapter west of the Mississippi River. Beatrice Canaday was its major force, using the power of her newspaper, *The Advocate,* to advance her causes. She helped organize branch chapters in the logging communities of Vernonia, Oregon and Longview, Washington. The NAACP pushed unsuccessfully for the passage of a public accommodations bill in the state legislature that prohibited racial discrimination in hotels, theaters, and restaurants. Money was raised to defend black people accused of crime elsewhere in the nation.

At the city level the Seattle NAACP continued its work and was joined by a chapter of the Urban League in 1930. Portland blacks also did what they could to combat discrimination. Sometimes they insisted

Dr. Norval Unthank. Oregon Historical Society

on seats at movie theaters. On one occasion they drew up a petition to the city council protesting the canceling of a cabaret license when its owner had permitted interracial dancing. Blacks fought against—sometimes by threat of boycotts—restaurants that posted Jim Crow signs. As in the prewar years Portland blacks objected to the movie, *Birth of a Nation,* for its racist theme. They had the movie banned in Portland in 1926 and again in 1931. Resolute black persons also combated discrimination in the educational system. Beatrice Canaday single-handedly obtained the admission of black children to the Vernonia public schools. Her newspaper campaigned successfully in the late 1920s to permit black children to attend the parochial schools of Portland and Vancouver, Washington.

Realtors, banks, and citizens combined to constrict most black people into racially segregated neighborhoods. If a black person acquired a house in a previously white neighborhood, he would be forced out. The dormitories of the University of Oregon were closed to black students. The NAACP and the *Advocate* fought to overcome prejudice in this realm but had little success in the interwar years. Nor was much gained, in spite of struggles, to allow blacks into unions: they were not permitted to join the Laundry Workers Union or the Teamsters among others.

In politics there were some victories. Although a mere formality, the exclusion clause of the state constitution rankled. In 1926 the people of Oregon voted overwhelmingly by referendum to repeal the exclusion clause. The original constitution had also prohibited black persons from voting. In 1927 the voters through the referendum removed the offensive ban. But in spite of all attempts the legislature never repealed the law forbidding interracial marriage.

In a broader area, the first public accommodations bill came before the state legislature in 1919. It was defeated in the House of Representatives in a close vote. A similar bill reappeared in 1933 at the behest of the Multnomah County NAACP, but it too was voted down, as were public accommodations measures that came up in 1937 and 1939. It was opposed the last time by spokesmen for the Oregon Hotel Association and the Oregon Apartment House Owners Association. These political frustrations at the local level were compounded by the failure of Congress to pass the major civil rights bill of the era, the Dyer Antilynching bill. Lynching and murder were not mere southern phenomena. A black man was lynched in Marshfield, Oregon in 1902. No one was punished. Another black man was murdered in the same community—although not by a lynch mob—in 1924. His assailants were not discovered.

The Northwest became a place of disillusion for another group. One of the victims of the Great Depression was the farmer of the northern and southern Great Plains. Hard times compounded a heritage of attempting to work land that might better have been left in grass. Depression, drought, and dust storms victimized the farmers. Their proposed solution to their problems was the journey westward. The depression migrants came from the states of the Northern Plains, especially Nebraska, North Dakota, Montana, South Dakota, and Kansas. One-half were farmers, one-half from the towns and cities of the region. They endured the depression for as long as possible in their old homes. Finally, they had to give up and in the three years 1935 to 1937, the great majority of them came to the Pacific Northwest. The migrants were not drifters or adventurers; like earlier generations they were purposeful in seeking new economic opportunities in the Northwest. Indeed almost all remained in the same county where they settled upon arrival.

Unlike the first pioneers, however, they found poverty rather than abundance in their new homes. Most were denied the agricultural opportunities they sought; those who found farmland had to take it in the cut-over regions first abandoned by lumbermen, then by their successors, the farmers of the turn-of-the-century years. They struggled with poor soil and uncertain markets. Others tried the lumber camps and mills, or whatever the cities could offer. Many went on relief; many became migrant agricultural workers. For the last, the national government stepped in. Congress created the Farm Security Administration in 1937. Among other duties, this agency created sanitary mobile and permanent camps for migrant workers. The workers contributed their only rent as two hours of labor per week on camp projects. They also had a self-governing (subject to the veto of the camp manager) camp council which levied a twenty-five cent weekly contribution on each family for camp projects. The government provided nurseries and kindergartens for preschool children. The migrants who found no government camps were forced to the shelters provided by the growers: usually filthy camps without running water.

Regardless of their condition, the migrants were almost all united in one respect. They were the first group of white Anglo-Saxon American citizens who were not welcomed to the Pacific Northwest. The old residents were afraid that they would steal a job; that they would require higher taxes to pay for relief measures; that, at worst, they would become riotous or radical. Given these fears it is not surprising that the older residents denied the migrants work relief, old age assistance, and medical services on the grounds that they were nonresidents. The ultimate relief for the great bulk of the white immigrants came with the outbreak of the Second World War which gave them employment either in the military or in the defense industries.

Between the wars the Northwest's Jews flourished. Their material prosperity enabled many of Oregon's German Jews to move from northwest Portland to the West Hills. The East Europeans departed south Portland in large numbers for new subdivisions eastward across the Willamette River. Their children moved rapidly into the professions. Even in the 1930s there was little unemployment among Portland's Jews. As always, there were some problems of latent or overt anti-Semitism. Jews, however capable, were not admitted to prestigious gentile law firms. They could not join the exclusive male or female social clubs. They could not belong to high school or college fraternities.

Similar events occurred in Washington. Both Ashkenazim and Sephardim became more prosperous. Each developed new cultural institutions, for example, an Ashkenazic newspaper, the *Jewish Transcript*, was founded in 1924 and the Sephardic Brotherhood cultural society in 1935.

Seattle Conservative Jews formed their first congregation in 1935. Yet the solidity of the Jewish community was never complete because no one was able to bridge effectively the gulf between the Ashkenazim and Sephardim, a gulf that lingered into the post–Second World War years.

The difficulties Jews worried about most were thousands of miles away. As the Nazis began their campaigns against the Jews, Pacific Northwest Jews helped those who escaped from them. The Portland Committee on Emigres, organized and chaired by Max S. Hirsch, took leadership in the resettlement efforts. Founded in 1936, the committee extended financial, employment, housing, and social contact opportunities to the new arrivals. In Seattle comparable work was carried on by the Washington Emigre Bureau. Sephardic Jews were particularly active in raising money for Jewish victims of Italian fascism.

In conclusion then, the ethnic and racial composition changed somewhat in the interwar period, but the region remained relatively homogeneous in population. In the realms of formal culture, however, there was greater variety.

Architecture

The architecture of the Pacific Northwest went through some important changes between the two world wars. Oregon was much more innovative than Washington (the exact reverse of the situation in landscape painting) in architecture, but the changes did not occur in all types of buildings nor at a steady pace.

The buildings where people worked changed in composition. Before the First World War brick was the principal building material. During the war hollow clay tile came into use. It was lighter than brick and almost as fire resistant. The last was important since cities began—at the behest of insurance companies—to pass fire codes. Their requirements were better met by a material other than brick or tile—galvanized corrugated sheetmetal. It was widely used in the Pacific Northwest after 1920 for safety and as a substitute for lumber. Also important as a new building material was ready-mixed concrete which came into widespread use in the 1920s. Concrete was made even more useful when the steel industry began producing steel bars that could be used to reinforce concrete walls. It made it cheaper to construct manufacturing buildings and more efficient to use them in its flexible floor plans.

Ordinary people lived in homes of imported design. Perhaps because the 1920s and the 1930s were decades of rapid change, people nostalgically based their architecture upon historic styles. Many selected Spanish mission style or ranch houses or Cape Cod cottages. But the favored mode was the bungalow. This was an import from California where it had become popular during the decade of the 1910s. The bungalow was designed to be comfortable, efficient, and secure. On the outside the bungalow was characterized by horizontality; natural, textured materials, for example, in chimneys; and prominent porches to give an illusion of outdoor living. Indoors the bungalow also differed from older styles. As family life grew not only more efficient, but more informal, walls between dining room and living room disappeared. Built-in cabinets and book-cases became the rule as did natural woodwork. Fireplaces and chimneys of rock or natural colored tiles were customary as were exposed ceiling beams. Kitchens were smaller and more efficient with built-in cabinets and drawers. Bathrooms also had these features and also were apt to be floored with tiles.

The depression of the 1930s brought almost a complete halt to much of the building trades, both industrial and residential. But this decade was of enormous importance architecturally. It revealed for the first time the genius of Pietro Belluschi and John Yeon, the creators of the northwest style of architecture.

Belluschi was born in Ancona, Italy in 1899. He became an architect in his native country and then took a degree in civil engineering at Cornell University in 1924. In the following year he arrived in Portland and was hired by the celebrated architectural firm of A. E. Doyle. He executed a few commissions in the late 1920s and then acquired national acclaim in 1930 when he designed a new building, completed in 1932, for the

Jennings Sutor House by Pietro Belluschi. Oregon Historical Society

Portland Art Museum. The design was a partial break from tradition. It was related to other buildings in its setting. Its lines were low and horizontal. In 1936 Belluschi designed a wing to the building that was fully integrated with the original, although even more modern in its functional use of space. This building, with the new wing completed in 1939, and a Portland mortuary built in 1937, were voted among the 100 best designs of the era, 1920 to 1940, by the American Institute of Architects.

Belluschi also did residential architecture. Here, as in all his work, he was a modern architect. That is, he believed with Frank Lloyd Wright, the Bauhaus school in Germany, and others that "form follows function," that a building should look like what it was supposed to be rather than copying some earlier design. A building should also blend into its natural environment and that of surrounding structures. But Belluschi was not simply an apostle of modern, international styles. His great contribution was as a regionalist.

In 1936 Belluschi designed his own house in Portland; it was a city dwelling with rural forms. As he described it: "clean and simple but not modernistic—above all that it be in harmony with the hills and Oregon firs." Belluschi's first famous house was built for Jennings Sutor in 1938. He followed with other residences in Portland, Seattle, and on the Oregon Coast and with the St. Thomas More chapel in Portland. By the outbreak of the Second World War he had defined his concept of regionalism in buildings and in words: "It goes back to nature, if the owner's life is one of response to it. Therefore, we may deduce that a region with similar natural and human attributes may have an architecture harmonious to them. The people are neighbors, their interests are alike, they respond the same way to life, they have the same materials at hand, they have a similar landscape, the same climate." [1]

John Yeon also contributed mightily to the new developments in Oregon architecture. Yeon was another of those influenced by A. E. Doyle, and he and Belluschi influenced one another. Yeon's great reputation began in 1937 when he completed the house of Aubrey Watzek, a Portland businessman. This project was remarkable in two respects at least. Watzek entrusted Yeon with making a design that would be innovative; he also gave the architect the responsibility for designing the house furnishings and planning the garden. The components of the house flowed together. There were few interior walls; the house melded into the garden; from the house and garden the eye went to distant Mt. Hood in the Cascade Range. The interior panels and exterior walls were of native woods and stone.

Two years later Yeon designed a home for Victor Jorgenson that is also a classic of the northwestern style: house and garden blend superbly with the regional environment. Yeon also worked in a somewhat different direction when the Portland builder Burt Smith asked him to design nine houses. What was unusual about Yeon's buildings was that they used exterior fir plywood that had become important only in 1935 when the Harbor Plywood Company in Gray's Harbor, Washington, invented a waterproof glue that made exterior plywood feasible. There were many other innovations in these nine small houses that would be influential in later years: modular construction, the separation of the lighting and ventilation systems, and the use of color as an integral rather than simply a decorative portion of the house. The northwest style of the 1930s was popular for about twenty years until the 1960s saw the triumph of the international style. But it was clearly a regional triumph, this architecture marked in Belluschi's words by "concern for the setting and integration of landscaping, the open functional plan, the broad sheltering pitched roof, and the use of naturally finished woods." [2]

There were other distinguished architects in the region, also, although they were not at this time practitioners of the Northwest Style. These included, in Portland, Herman Brookman, who did the Temple Beth Israel, the Lloyd Frank estate (now Lewis and Clark College), and Julius Meier's estate—Menucha—on the Columbia River; Van Evera Bailey who did mainly residences; and Harold Doty. These architects worked in a variety of styles. In Seattle the most influential architect was Lionel H. Pries, a professor at the University of Washington, who trained a body of famous American architects, including Pete Wimberly, A. Quincy Jones, and Minoru Yamasaki.

On the face of the region something new besides the buildings of the northwest style also appeared. This was the result of New Deal housing legislation that created for the first time federal housing projects. These included housing projects for wartime workers and for the poor. The most famous of the low-income projects was the Yesler Terrace project in Seattle. It combined architectural grace with the human dimension to an unusual degree.

For millions of people the most influential building of these years in Oregon was also a product of the federal government. This was Timberline Lodge, a ski resort on the slopes of Mount Hood, finished in 1937. Like the Watzek house, the building and all its furnishing were designed as an entity. Like the Watzek house it was built of native materials. The great resort was financed by the Arts Project of the New Deal. All the interior furnishings—rugs, weavings, furniture, ironwork, paintings, and murals—were regionally authentic and generally of high craftsmanship. The building was situated so that it provided a capacious view of the Cascade Range of mountains. All in all it became an exemplar of New Deal art: American yet regional, democratic in audience, and enduring.

The World of Painting

The art community of the Pacific Northwest saw several institutional changes and new talents after the First World War. The State of Oregon, for example, was blessed with the addition of an art museum at the university at Eugene. The museum building derived from the generous gift of a remarkable woman, Gertrude Bass Warner, who in 1931 gave a collection of Asian art to the university. President Prince Lucien Campbell then projected a plan for a museum building. Under the leadership of Irene Gerlinger a popular subscription drive succeeded and the building was opened to the public in 1932. It was the largest art museum building at any state university, and remains an ornament to a state small in population and resources.

The older Portland Art Association grew slowly but steadily. Its Art School under Harry Wentz furnished the principal instruction in the state. It continued to flourish when William Givler, one of its own graduates, a landscape painter and printmaker, came in 1931 to teach. Anna Belle Crocker continued to provide devoted service as curator. She set high standards, knew the art of the world (including the most recent) and opened the galleries to it, and let Wentz influence the art community.

Within this community the outstanding artist, in national recognition, was Clayton S. ("C.S.") Price, who moved to Portland in 1928. Price was born in Montana and was self-taught. In Portland he provided—along with Wentz and Crocker—the leadership of the art community. This leadership was furnished in part through his engaging personality, but also through his own willingness to grow in his work—to change his styles with growing maturity.

In the interwar years Price continued the earlier Oregon tradition of painting landscapes. The earlier artists of this genre (all born in the 1890s) were the twin brothers, Arthur and Albert Runquist, Amanda Snyder, and Charles Heany. Although their work was rather different, all were based upon representations of the world of nature.

Younger Oregon artists were also heavily influenced by the landscape. David McCosh moved to Oregon from the Middle West in 1934 to teach at the University of Oregon. In 1941 Carl and Hilda Morris arrived in Portland. McCosh and Charles Voorhies, who came to Portland in 1939, were landscape artists. After studying at the Art Students League in New York, Louis Bunce returned to Oregon in 1935.

SEATTLE PAINTERS

Although they originated later, the art institutions in Seattle were more numerous than in Portland or any other city in the region. The Seattle

Fine Arts Society, founded in 1908, began with its series of annual exhibitions in 1916. The Seattle Camera Club after 1925 began showing paintings. Horace C. Henry, a collector of European and American landscape paintings, opened his paintings to the public in 1927.

The Cornish School continued through these years to provide instruction in painting as well as the other arts. Although Nellie Cornish resigned from the school in 1939, it continued her tradition of serious educational work. The Seattle Music and Art Foundation was founded to provide a range of cultural activities including scholarships for individual students, grants to the Cornish School, and funds for art exhibitions throughout the city.

The most influential institution, however, was the Seattle Art Museum. It was the child of Richard E. Fuller. Fuller was a collector, which was not unusual for a wealthy businessman of cultural sensitivity. What was unusual was Fuller's interest in Asian art. Fuller raised the money for a city museum building erected in 1933, donated his collection to it, and served as director for many years. His collections broadened from Asian art to a wider range that in time encompassed a small but representative collection of world art.

These institutions, the accident of birth, and an intriguing natural environment brought forth a remarkable collection of painters in Seattle. The oldest was Mark Tobey. Born in Seattle, Tobey had begun as a commercial artist in Chicago and had then struck out for New York to paint to please himself. He worked in a variety of modes, leaving himself open to the themes of European modernism, but also, although it did not yet appear obviously in his painting, to Asian thought. In the twenties and thirties he made trips to Europe, Asia, and the Near East. In 1938 he came back to Seattle.

Guy Anderson was one of those he met at this time. Anderson was also born in Washington—in Edmonds. He had studied on the East Coast and had then returned to Seattle and its environs. When Tobey met him he had formed an intellectual partnership with Morris Graves who was also from northwestern Washington. Graves moved to Edmonds in 1936 and began their long friendship at that time. The fourth of what came to be an influential group was Kenneth Callahan. He traveled the world like Tobey and in his studies became especially influenced in the 1920s by the social realism of the famous Mexican mural painters and by abstract art. In the 1930s Callahan was doing mainly realistic paintings of working people.

In the early 1940s these four men, along with the lesser known Margaret Tomkins and William Cumming, came together to form what later became known as the Northwest school of art. The influences that created it are not fully clear. What seemed to influence them was Asian thought and Asian art, the natural environment and living creatures of the Northwest, and partially abstract forms. They talked together and they suffered together. Their great anguish was, of course, the war. Three fellow artists of Japanese background departed. Kenjiro Nomura and Kamekichi Takita were sent to the relocation camps. George Tsutakawa served in the army. Morris Graves was inducted and served eleven months in spite of his pacifist beliefs. Although not called into service, Tobey and Anderson were also pacifists, stricken not only by war but by the enormity of the world conflict. Their paintings spoke of the war in abstractions. But they also dealt with other subjects that were influenced by the regional environment but were not fully regional painting. That is, their paintings dealt with universal themes, but the Northwest was an important ingredient in form and in color.

One other important development is the role of the New Deal's Public Works of Art Project. It became a branch of the Works Progress Administration (created in 1935) with a new title, the Federal Arts Project, and it endured until 1943. In Oregon, Louis Bunce, the painter, was assistant director for the WPA Art Center in Salem, Oregon; William Givler and David McCosh did easel paintings and murals, respectively, for the WPA arts projects. The most famous of these works—rendered by many artists—was the mural painting in federal buildings. The murals depicted loggers, fishermen, and other workers in the regional economy, always rendered in heroic poses. McCosh had the honor of doing a mural in the Department of the Interior Building in Washington, D. C. The Arts Project employed artists as administrators and teachers, commissioned painters, and also paid them to produce works of art at their own pace.

In Washington the federal programs were also beneficial. In Spokane, Guy Anderson, Hilda Deutsch, and Carl Morris (who was the director) were at the federal Art Center. In Seattle William Cumming, Paul Horiuchi, Mark Tobey, and Morris Graves received federal subsidy. Graves's paintings were represented in the Museum of Modern Art in New York when it held an exhibition of WPA work in 1939.

Literature

Like the painters, the best writers struggled to escape the tyranny of local themes and to realize the universal. Their writing is at its best— and regionally the strongest—when they incorporate the local environment into their quest for the universal, rather than using it as a backdrop. Literature in the interwar period, however, was still in the clutches—for the most part—of the nineteenth century.

Harold L. (H. L.) Davis. Douglas Co. Museum, Quentin Davis
Collection, Oregon Historical Society

This literature was characterized by romanticism and parochialism.
The poetry and fiction were essentially descriptive. The characters in
literature were heroic men and women, people without flaws. Most of
the plots were set in the pioneer years, safely removed from the conflicts
and controversies of the present. Any critical note about the region was
absent. It was not surprising that this literature had developed, but it
was discouraging for many twentieth century writers that it lasted so
long.

One representative of the old school was a new poetry magazine.
In 1923 Ernest Hofer, a rural printer by occupation, founded a poetry
magazine in Salem called the *Lariat*. He operated it for five years at
considerable financial loss before selling it. The editor's acceptance policy
was uncritical: he published anything that was presented, so long as it

was, in Hofer's words, "clean literature." In Seattle the story was the same. There was little to admire if one were a follower of the realism and naturalism that undergirded a great movement forward in American literature. The writers wrote as romantics did in Britain or Europe or America in the nineteenth century. For some reason there was no attempt for most writers to draw upon their own rather than an imported tradition.

A reaction against this transplanted culture came. It came in violent form. In 1927 H. L. Davis and James Stevens published privately a literary manifesto called *Status Rerum*. It raised the question about the regional environment and its writers: "Is there some occult influence, which catches them young, and shapes them to be instruments out of which tripe, and nothing but tripe, must issue?"[3] The two young authors said that the poetry magazines, the teachers of creative writing in the universities, and the regional publishers encouraged formula writing for money, such as western short stories, or mediocre imitations of an outdated genteel tradition. The response to this indictment was immediate, furious, and productive.

Challenged to do better than those he had criticized, Davis responded with a long novel, *Honey in the Horn* (1935), which won the Pulitzer Prize in the next year. Davis was a native Oregonian, born in Yoncalla, who already had reached national acclaim as a poet. *Honey in the Horn* is the story of a variety of Oregon occupations from 1906 to 1908. It is an honest and critical book that depicts the descendents of the pioneers as failures rather than successes. It excels in its description of life in the small towns, the beauty of the natural environment, and the heartbreaks of those who continued to believe in the American dream of owning one's own farm after the good land was all gone. Although Davis later published several novels, short stories, and popular articles (he became fonder of Oregon after he moved away from the state in 1928), his more complimentary work lacks the power of *Honey in the Horn*.

In poetry there were circles in Portland and Seattle of serious artists. Some received national attention. The Portland poets were the most famous. They included Davis, Albert Wetjen, Howard McKinley Corning, Borghild Lee, Ada H. Hedges, Mary C. Davies, and Charles O. Olsen. Yet they were regional only in place of residence, not in subject matter. Their poems in periodicals such as *Poetry, Nation, New Republic,* and *American Mercury* were unusual in that they were the only cultural products of northwestern intellectuals to reach a national audience. To do so they had, significantly, to abandon their region. The price was worth it to them, but their sacrifice was not appreciated by their fellow citizens who cared little about cultural distinction of any type.

NOTES

1. Thomas Vaughan and Virginia Guest Ferriday, eds., *Space, Style and Structure: Building in Northwest America,* 2 vols. (1974), II: 479.
2. Ibid., p. 476.
3. Quoted in *Pacific Northwest Quarterly,* 61 (1970): 27.

SUGGESTIONS FOR READING

Indians are the subject of James B. Kennedy, "The Umatilla Indian Reservation, 1855–1975: Factors Contributing to A Diminished Resource Base," Ph.D. diss., Oregon State University, 1977 and Theodore Stern, *The Klamath Tribe: A People and Their Reservation* (1965). An excellent account is Kazuo Ito, *Issei: A History of Japanese Immigrants in North America* (1973). On the Japanese, see also Roger Sale, *Seattle: Past to Present* (1976) and Marvin G. Pursinger, "Oregon's Japanese in World War II," Ph.D. diss., University of Southern California, 1961. Blacks are the theme of Elizabeth McLagan, *A Peculiar Paradise: A History of Blacks in Oregon, 1788–1840* (1980). Cultural matters are dealt with in Thomas Vaughan and Virginia G. Ferriday, *Space, Style, and Structure: Buildings in Northwest America* (1974); Rosalind Clark, *Architecture: Oregon Style* (1983); Sally B. Woodridge and Roger Montgomery, *A Guide to Architecture in Washington State* (1980); National Collection of Fine Arts, *Art of the Pacific Northwest: From the 1930s to the Present* (1974); Martha Kingsbury, *Art of the Thirties: The Pacific Northwest* (1972); Sale, *Seattle: Past to Present;* and Howard McKinley Corning, "All the Words on the Pages, I: H. L. Davis," *Oregon Historical Quarterly,* 73 (1972); "Charles Alexander: Youth of the Oregon Mood;" "A. R. Wetjen: British Seamen in the Western Sunrise;" "The Prose and Poetry of It," all in *Oregon Historical Quarterly,* 74 (1973).

The Second World War, 1939–1945

The Second World War rescued the economy of the Pacific Northwest. It brought further diversification to the population as it increased the numbers of nonwhite residents. It continued the tradition of discrimination against the Japanese and Japanese American. The war boosted the power of organized labor. The years of conflict accelerated urbanization with the creation of instant cities. Most of all, the war disrupted the lives of thousands of Oregonians and Washingtonians who served in the military forces or whose friends and relatives did so. A total of 148,039 Oregonians were in service and 224,083 Washingtonians. Of this number, Oregon suffered 5,314 wounded and 2,826 dead. There were 6,967 Washington wounded and 4,147 deaths.

The Wartime Economy

The United States government continued to dominate the regional economy. But its role as "colonial master" was even greater than during the New Deal era. In Oregon the principal war industry was shipbuilding. Washington produced aircraft as well as ships.

Federal contracts were not new for Boeing. The company had developed a connection with the federal government during the late 1930s when it had built some bombing aircraft including the B-17, the Flying Fortress. After Pearl Harbor the United States purchased hundreds of planes from Boeing. The technical knowledge gained from the production of the B-17 led to the development of the B-29, the Super Fortress, which became the principal long-range bomber of the last years of the war against Germany and Japan.

The significance of the Boeing enterprise was momentous. Thousands of people came to Seattle. They taxed the housing facilities of the city and forced the government to create hundreds of units of new housing. In 1939 Boeing employed 4,000 people; in 1944 there were 50,000 workers on the company's payroll. Outside of Seattle the major Boeing plants were in Renton, Bellingham, Chehalis, Everett, and Aberdeen.

The other major wartime industry was the building of ships. The story of Portland shipbuilding pivots about a single economic genius, a great Northwesterner, Henry J. Kaiser. Born in New York State in 1882, Kaiser moved to Spokane in 1905. He entered the construction business, made a fortune, and then, in the 1930s became internationally famous. He gained his reputation because of the Boulder Canyon project on the Colorado River, the first multipurpose project in the world. The core of the project was an immense dam at a place called Boulder Canyon. No one had ever designed and built a dam of this magnitude. Because of his reputation for honesty, efficiency, and meeting cost and time requirements, Henry Kaiser became a part of the construction syndicate, which also included several Portland contractors. Kaiser's work at Boulder Can-

Boeing B-17. Special Collections Division, University of Washington Libraries

yon gained him an even larger job. This plum was a part of the Grand Coulee project in central Washington, for years the largest dam in the world. Success bred success and Kaiser became the primary contractor on the second New Deal multipurpose project in the Northwest, Bonneville.

Kaiser's reputation, his contacts made with federal officials and other leaders of the construction business, and his willingness to take risks led him into shipbuilding in the Northwest and to steelmaking in California. In January 1941 Kaiser began building ships, although it was for the British rather than for the United States government. In time Kaiser had two shipyards in Portland. His Oregon shipbuilding corporation built Liberty ships, the famous 441-foot long freighters that kept the Allied cause alive with food, arms, and supplies. His first Liberty ship was christened *Star of Oregon* at launching on May 19, 1941. In time, techniques were refined and construction speed accelerated. The record for a Liberty ship was ten days. Kaiser also built escort aircraft carriers ("baby flattops"), tankers, Victory merchant ships, and other vessels. Kaiser yards received many awards from the United States Maritime Commission and Henry Kaiser came to be known as Sir Launchalot. In addition to Kaiser's ships, Willamette Iron and Steel Company built ships in Portland. Indeed this firm turned out the first vessels of the war, two amphibious loading ships for the United States Navy.

In Washington ships were built at Seattle, Tacoma, Bremerton, and Vancouver. The story of shipbuilding in Seattle is somewhat repetitive of the First World War experience. Todd Shipyards Corporation was the major builder, but twenty-nine shipyards worked in the city during the war employing more than 40,000 persons. Seattle produced destroyers and smaller vessels. In Tacoma the Todd interests founded a new corporation, the Seattle-Tacoma Shipbuilding Corporation. It built a new yard for cargo ships and for escort aircraft carriers, which were antisubmarine vessels that were used in both the Atlantic and Pacific theaters.

At the Bremerton Navy Yard about 30,000 workers were employed. The yard did both repair work and new construction in facilities that were the largest and most modern on the Pacific Coast. It was at the Bremerton Yard that the naval vessels sunk by the Japanese at Pearl Harbor were repaired. In Vancouver Henry Kaiser constructed a shipbuilding yard that eventually included twelve ways. In this yard the company built Liberty ships—the first was named *George Vancouver;* landing ship tanks (LST's); and small aircraft carriers. As in Portland, Kaiser contributed many innovations to ship construction, the most important of which was the preassembly of ship parts. The various sections of the ships were built in separate buildings and then brought together on the ways.

The war also brought a new industry to the region, aluminum. It was a wartime industry because of the abundant supply of low-cost power produced at Bonneville and Grand Coulee dams and because it was necessary to produce aluminum close to the aircraft plants. The Aluminum Company of America built and operated plants at Troutdale, Oregon and Vancouver, Washington. The Reynolds Metal Company constructed an aluminum plant at Longview, Washington.

Many older firms also benefited from the war economy. They numbered literally hundreds of contractors and subcontractors dependent on the major enterprises. Employment of course was not confined to manufacturing plants. The service industries grew: department stores, restaurants, and other places of public accommodation. These enterprises flourished with the arrival of war workers in the major communities. Local businesses also benefited from the many military installations in the region, some new, some old. The largest was Fort Lewis near Tacoma. Military personnel from Fort Lewis flocked into Tacoma for rest and recreation as did servicemen from other posts into Walla Walla, Yakima, Bremerton, Corvallis, and other communities.

The War Workers

Wartime prosperity was based upon the labor of men and women who migrated to the region. There were simply not enough local people to do the job. Defense employment included not only those who worked in private yards and plants, but also civilian employees of the federal government in bases and shipyards. The recruitment effort was originally the concern of private employers. After 1942 it fell to two federal agencies, the War Manpower Commission and the Civil Service Commission.

THE BLACK WORKERS

A large number of war workers who came to the region were blacks, whose experience was one both of frustration and achievement. The black population of Seattle grew from 5,789 in 1940 to 6,330 in 1945; blacks in Portland increased from 2,565 in 1940 to 25,000 in 1944. On the positive side the war provided a much higher material standard of living for the black migrants, most of whom came from the poor states of the South or the border regions. Housing was their principal negative experience. Obviously the black migrants, indeed newcomers of any race, had to have a place to live. Private enterprise was unwilling or unable to provide homes for black war workers. Thus local housing authorities, federally financed, had to construct their dwellings. When the war broke out the Yesler Terrace project in Seattle was the only federal one in the city. It had been racially integrated from the beginning. But the white population objected strenuously both to new housing projects and to blacks residing in them when they were built at Duwamish Bend Homes and in the West Seattle, Sand Point, Holly Park, and Rainier Vista areas.

In Portland the problem of housing the war workers was enormous. It resulted in an especially heartrending set of subproblems for black workers. Little private housing was available; the Federal Housing Authority, through its local affiliate, the Housing Authority of Portland, provided temporary housing projects. Portland had no experience whatsoever in public housing before the war. It was therefore remarkable that the Housing Authority of Portland did build twenty-five projects. The greatest wartime project, Vanport, was begun by Henry Kaiser and later taken over by the Housing Authority of Portland. Vanport, a totally planned community lying on the Oregon side of the Columbia River between Portland and Vancouver, is an interesting story for many reasons, among them, its racial policies. Vanport and two smaller housing projects in Portland had racially segregated housing. That is, blacks were assigned certain residential areas in these housing projects. The projects' stores, churches, and other facilities, however, were open to people of all races. The responsibility for residential segregation at Vanport was

Yesler Terrace Housing Project, Seattle. Special Collections Division, University of Washington Libraries

denied by the Housing Authority of Portland, but it clearly had established this policy.

Blacks also suffered for a time in employment because of the prejudice of the unions. In the Boeing plants the black workers had a great deal of trouble. The principal union at Boeing was the International Association of Machinists, whose affiliate, Local 751 of the Aero Mechanics Union, was the bargaining agent at the plants. The local voted to accept blacks in July 1940 and to recommend that the international union abandon its policy of racial discrimination. The local reversed itself in October when a new executive board was appointed by the international.

The Seattle-Puget Sound situation was not unique. Outraged blacks across the nation expressed their desire for equal opportunities in industrial hiring and in union membership. Their pressure worked when in June 1941 President Roosevelt created a Fair Employment Practices Committee to regulate labor in the defense industries. Seattle blacks complained to this new agency, which obtained a partial success at Boeing. The FEPC required Local 751 to issue work permits to blacks; this gave them jobs, but it did not give them all the benefits of union membership. Black workers also had to pay for their work permits.

The picture was brighter for blacks who worked in the shipyards of Puget Sound. There were two major unions of shipyard workers. The International Union of Marine and Shipbuilding Workers of America was racially integrated. The larger International Brotherhood of Boilermakers left race relations to its local affiliates. The Washington boilermakers' locals did admit black workers to full membership.

This was not the case in Portland. At the various shipyards there, discrimination was rife. About all the Boilermakers Union was willing to do was to establish segregated locals. In Portland this was called Auxiliary Local 32. Many blacks joined it out of necessity. Lee Anderson did not. Anderson sued the Boilermakers and Kaiser's shipbuilding company for admission to the regular boilermakers union. The union struck back. It forced the Kaiser firm to fire all black workers who refused to join the segregated union. Black leaders went to the nation's capital to complain to the FEPC. Finally in March 1945, the FEPC ordered the union to abandon its segregated local, but by the end of the war it had not yet obeyed the government's mandate.

Other unions were also recalcitrant. Like the machinists the Longshoreman's International Union did not officially discriminate, but its local workers did with a vengeance. As in the case of the Boeing workers, the union consented to temporary black employment, but not to full union membership. In Portland, Harry Mills, one of these second-class longshoremen, applied for union membership, but was denied. Service unions also discriminated, for example, the Portland laundry workers. Indeed the freeing of blacks from union, corporate, and citizen prejudice had to await the postwar years.

Citizen prejudice was hardest to eradicate. It popped up in both subtle and overt forms. Most difficult to accept was prejudice at the hands of other black people, prejudice that appeared in both Portland and Seattle. Black newcomers were condescended to as rural, backward, and southern. One black editor said that racial harmony could not survive the "public discourtesy, boorishness, uncleanliness, obscene language, garish display, and drunkenness of a small minority of Negroes." White racial prejudice was evident not only in labor relations, but in Jim Crow practices. Seattle's municipal swimming pools were closed to blacks until 1944. Almost all of Walla Walla's restaurants refused to serve blacks. In Portland the black population could not use city recreational facilities outside the ghetto, except on a once-a-week basis. One officer of a Portland business group declared: "If it is necessary to bring in large numbers of Negro workers, locate them on the edge of the city. . . . It would be much better for all concerned." [1]

The response of both the newer and older black residents to those indignities varied. So too did that of white persons. Indeed the war years saw a strengthening of integrated defense groups. The Portland chapter of the Urban League was founded in 1944. Citizens also formed a Committee on Interracial Practices and Policies in that city.

In Seattle race relations were taken more seriously by municipal officials than in Portland. Seattle's mayor, William F. Devin, in February 1944, created the Civic Unity Committee. The mayor was important in the history of race relations by not only creating the committee, but in taking its work seriously. The CUC was composed of prominent community leaders, most of whom were white businessmen. It needed all the prestige that its leaders could give it, because it had no powers of enforcement and only one employee, a part-time secretary. Almost all that it accomplished was through the work of volunteers from within and without the committee.

One effort of the CUC was to get the Seattle bus company to hire black drivers. The effort began in March 1944. It involved negotiations with the company, the union, and the Urban League. It took over a year to gather a pool of applicants, overcome resistance, and conduct the tests. The first driver was finally hired in April 1945. The CUC was able also to force the city to abandon racial discrimination at one of the municipal swimming pools.

The black experience of the war years was one in which a definite black consciousness developed. Blacks became more militant in defending their rights. They also for the first time became really visible to white

Northwesterners who gained some knowledge of the virtues of a heterogeneous community.

THE HISPANICS

The Second World War also contributed a considerable number of Hispanic citizens to the Pacific Northwest for the first time. Beginning in the 1850s a small number of Hispanics had worked as muleteers and cowboys. Skill, courage, and responsibility brought some of them important positions such as foreman. But these jobs disappeared by the turn of the century as large-scale wheat farming caused the disintegration of the big ranches. In the 1920s and 1930s United States citizens of Mexican descent began a new pursuit in the Northwest—migratory agricultural labor. These workers were mainly single men, residents of Texas, Arizona, and New Mexico, who followed the crops north to California, Oregon, and Washington in the track of the ripening fruits and vegetables. They worked especially in the Willamette Valley of Oregon and in the Yakima Valley of Washington. Little is known about them, but their working conditions and social lives could hardly have been very good.

The Second World War altered the Hispanic composition of Oregon and Washington. Most American citizens, regardless of race or culture, went into the armed forces or the defense plants. This created a grave vacuum in the supply of agricultural labor. It was a national problem, critical to the war effort, and one addressed by the federal government, which made two arrangements with the government of Mexico. The first was an executive agreement made in 1942, the second was a treaty agreed to in 1943. Together these agreements authorized the bringing of temporary contract workers (called *braceros*) to the United States to labor for specific employers. The government agency responsible for placing the workers was first the Farm Security Administration, later the Extension Service and the War Food Administration. These agencies were supposed to protect the workers as well as gain them employment. They also provided the labor camps in which they lived.

The reception of the *braceros* in the Northwest was enthusiastic. They were regarded as playing an important role in the war effort against the Axis powers. They were hardworking and docile laborers whose low pay (by United States standards) was quite acceptable to them. They made no complaints about their poor working, dietary, and housing conditions. Whites emphasized the colorful features of the Mexicans' culture—food, dancing, clothing—and stereotyped them as a quaint people. But they discriminated against them in places of public accommodation. Since most of the *braceros* were single males, they developed as few institutions in the United States as the typical migrant farm laborer. The Hispanic was an exotic, a man who whites felt was temporary—here a few months of the year, to be gone permanently at war's end. Their status as temporaries would change, however, after the war.

Concentration Camps for Americans

When the two nations went to war following the Japanese attack on Pearl Harbor on December 7, 1941, the Japanese residents of the Pacific Northwest became victims of the greatest mass violation of civil liberties in American history after slavery. On February 19, 1942, President Roosevelt issued an order relocating Japanese and Japanese Americans from their homes west of the Cascades to interior camps in California and Idaho. The justification for the order was military. All persons of Japanese ancestry were regarded automatically as potentially dangerous to the war effort, as allies of Imperial Japan. People who lived in the "war zone" were ordered to register, placed under a curfew, and told to report to evacuation centers by May 1, 1942. Oregonians were sent to Portland and Washingtonians to Puyallup. There they spent several demeaning weeks before being sent to the camps. Most Washington Japanese were sent to a camp in Idaho, Oregonians for the most part to Idaho and California.

There were many ironies in this terrible dislocation, one of which was that the order applied not only to citizens of Japan living in America (enemy aliens), but also to American citizens of Japanese ancestry. People descended from the nation's other enemies, Germany and Italy, were not placed in camps. As it turned out, during the course of the war there were no instances of sabotage committed by Japanese people, while there were some by German Americans and Italian Americans.

Reactions to the relocation order varied. A few white Americans challenged it, but most went along, including prominent defenders of civil liberties. The Japanese American Citizens League, with reluctance, counseled its members out of necessity to submit to the demands of the government. No Oregon or Washington group protested the evacuation order. No church, newspaper, or politician. Not the American Civil Liberties Union; not liberal Governor Sprague; not the Longshoremen; not the Communists; not the Oregon or Washington Commonwealth Federations. But some Japanese Americans did not consent to the abridgement of their liberties as American citizens. One young man from each state stood out in this principled resistance.

Minoru Yasui was a native Oregonian, a graduate of the University of Oregon, and of its law school. Yasui was also a reserve army officer,

Japanese Assembly Center, Japanese evacuees, August 30, 1942, at Pacific International Livestock Exposition Building (Portland). Oregon Journal Photograph, Oregon Historical Society

having been commissioned through the Reserve Officers Training Corps and his university. Yasui intentionally violated the curfew order, alleging it could not be constitutionally applied to an American citizen. He was sentenced to a $5,000 fine and to a year of forced labor. Upon appeal the United States Supreme Court upheld the constitutionality of the curfew.

Gordon Hirabayashi was a Quaker, a citizen, and a conscientious objector to military service. He refused to register and he did not obey the curfew. He was sentenced to three months in prison; he appealed his conviction, but the Supreme Court upheld it as a valid exercise of the Congressional power to wage war. After serving his jail sentence, Hirabayashi also spent another twelve months in prison for refusing to forswear allegiance and loyalty to the Emperor of Japan. Hirabayashi had no loyalty to Japan, but his Quaker conscience prohibited him from taking oaths of any type.

Those who went to the camps suffered not only the shame and impotence that experience required. They were thrown into contact with people they did not know, people more or less willing to resist imprisonment, more or less sympathetic to Japan. Incarceration bred group conflict, individual malaise, fighting, and suicide. Family member turned against family member. What unity there was was in the pervasive condemnation of injustice.

There were ways out. Several Japanese were allowed to leave the camps to work in Idaho as well as the beet fields of Nyssa, Oregon. Others could be released to attend school or colleges, but not in the war zone. The government permitted Japanese Americans to enlist in the armed forces. One unit, the 442d Regimental Combat Team fought in the European theater; it was one of the most heavily decorated units. Yet its distinguished record did not wipe out the Japanese Americans' racial stigma in the minds of some of their neighbors. In December 1944, the Hood River post of the American Legion removed from its roll of honor the names of the Japanese Americans from that community in military service.

The reaction to this decision indicated that many white Americans, including some from Oregon, rose above at least this manifestation of bigotry. The news was spread across the country and resulted in pressure from the national commander of the American Legion and President Truman to put the names back on the plaque. In Hood River itself, a Methodist clergyman, Sherman Burgoyne, was the chief opponent of the Legion's action, but other citizens joined him in organizing the Hood River League for Liberty and Justice. Finally the names of all but one (whose military record was not deemed honorable) were restored. But while this was going on the Hermiston post of the Disabled American Veterans voted "never to allow a Japanese or Negro veteran" to become a member of the post.

Organized Labor During the War

The war afforded an opportunity for organized labor. The shortage of workers and the necessity of high defense productivity for national survival meant that the lot of workers should improve. On the other hand, strikes were suspect and the national government, through its War Labor Board, had absolute authority over wages and working conditions.

On the waterfront the war years were quite tranquil. In November 1940 the industry reached a contract covering the entire Pacific Coast waterfront. Members of the union agreed that wage increases would be tied to efficiency, based upon data gathered after 1935. The employers granted a wage increase in February 1941, but turned down another in August 1941. The dispute was taken to arbitration and the federal arbitrator, Wayne L. Morse, dean of the law school of the University of Oregon, ruled in favor of the longshoremen.

After June 1941 peaceful labor relations were fostered because Germany invaded the Soviet Union. Unions with leadership sympathetic to communism, like the Longshoremen, now urged their members to redouble their efforts in order to beat the Nazis. There were no strikes on the waterfront for the duration of the war, although there was a vigorous dispute during 1944. The employers wanted to reduce wages because of declining productivity. They also asserted that the union job dispatchers were inefficient. The War Labor Board took jurisdiction of the dispute and granted a wage increase.

Labor in Lumber

The lumber industry scoured the nation for workers during the war years. The labor shortage in this industry was met not by Hispanics or blacks, but by a range of Caucasians who had not worked in industry before. One historian wrote: "The Weyerhaeuser logging operations and sawmills recruited as labor women, old men, teen-agers, interned Italian seamen, physically disabled men, malaria convalescents, and even two college professors. Women made the greatest contribution." [2]

The federal government also helped. The War Manpower Commission prohibited the rehiring of workers who quit jobs in the lumber industry unless they obtained a certificate from the United States Employment Agency. The War Production Board required the companies to work a forty-eight hour week. The Selective Service Board gave occupational deferments from the military draft to employees in the forest products industry.

The war years were generally peaceful ones in labor relations. There were strikes in April and May of 1941 for traditional goals: improved wages and benefits. A left-wing faction among the leaders of the CIO International Woodworkers of America was sympathetic to the Soviet Union. But when Germany made its surprise attack upon Russia in June 1941, the Woodworkers wheeled in behind the war effort.

Wartime Politics

The war years did not seem spectacular in terms of issues or personalities. Beneath the surface, however, the war had an effect on political life that would become more evident at the end of hostilities. In the first place, the war workers who migrated to the Pacific Northwest were largely Democrats. This infusion bolstered the strength of the party in Washington, where it already dominated politics, and it was a hopeful sign for the Oregon Democrats, although they did not capitalize on the fact until after the war. Second, the war created a much larger industrial base in the region than heretofore. This meant that politicians had to grapple with urban-labor-racial issues more frequently. Finally, the war accustomed people to reliance upon the federal government as supplier of capital and regulator of economic life.

In terms of electoral results, the war changed little. The state legislature in Washington remained Democratic, that in Oregon, Republican. There were two gubernatorial elections in Washington. Arthur Langlie won a Republican victory in 1940 as a moderate and as beneficiary of the internal strife among Democrats of liberals, conservatives, and radical Commonwealth Federation members. In 1944, however, United States Senator Mon Wallgren defeated Langlie. In Oregon the lone gubernatorial race was in 1942 when Republican Earl Snell defeated his opponent, Lew Wallace, a conservative Democrat, almost by a four-to-one margin.

In federal elections, Franklin Roosevelt carried both Oregon and Washington in 1940 and 1944 with healthy margins of victory. The voters buried New Deal antagonism to support the architect of wartime victory. The United States Senatorial elections were also productive of progressive victories. In 1942 Charles McNary won as usual but died two years later. Guy Cordon was elected to succeed him in 1944. There was another senatorial election in that year, in Oregon, an election that the Republicans won with a liberal member of their party.

Their candidate was one of the most colorful and controversial politicians ever to appear in the Pacific Northwest. Wayne L. Morse was born in Wisconsin, took two law degrees at Columbia University, and then became successively law professor and dean of the University of Oregon Law School. While dean, Morse was selected in 1936 as one of the attorneys who compiled a five-volume report on prison release procedures for the Attorney General. Two years later he was appointed a federal arbitrator in the Pacific Coast maritime industry.

His work here gave him his first national attention. The industry had long been wracked by bitter disputes between labor and management and between the maritime unions themselves. There was death and bloodshed in the strike of 1934 and more strikes in later years. Neither side had love or respect for the other. In forty consecutive cases, however, Morse's decisions were accepted by both the longshoreman's union, headed by the radical Harry Bridges, and the employers. In the forty-first case, Bridges rejected Morse's decision. Morse made a public statement, "The Union must answer to public opinion." Bridges gave in and accepted the award.

As the nation girded for war, President Roosevelt made Morse chairman of an emergency board to head off a threatened railroad strike.

Morse secured an agreement on the eve of the scheduled strike, December 7, 1941, after strenuous negotiations. In early 1942 Roosevelt recognized Morse's talents by appointing him to the War Labor Board which had authority over all labor-management relations affecting the war industries. Morse was one of the four public interest members of the twelve-person board. In 1943 Morse again came to national attention as a fearless man of principle. There was a strike in the coal mines led by John L. Lewis, the head of both the United Mine Workers and the CIO. The War Labor Board gave this powerful leader's union a wage settlement that he desired. Morse alone dissented from this decision. He said that it violated the board's policy of refusing to give pay increases to employees who were on strike.

Morse's reputation as an opponent of Bridges and Lewis stamped him as a man of principle appealing to conservatives. But organized labor also liked him because many of his arbitration awards were favorable to it. Oregon Republicans were impressed with his progressive, but not radical stances. They fit well with the times and with the state's political history. And they contrasted vividly with the philosophy of Republican Senator Rufus Holman. Holman was an ineffective senator, isolationist in foreign affairs, conservative, indeed reactionary, in domestic politics. Morse defeated Holman easily in the primary election. In the fall he defeated Edgar W. Smith of Pendleton, a conservative Democrat. Morse won every county in the state. To do so he made some thrusts at the New Deal, refused money and support from the CIO, and established himself clearly as a man of the center.

In Washington the senatorial results confirmed the state's support of the New Deal. In 1940 Lewis Schwellenbech, an ardent New Dealer, was appointed to the United States district court and Mon Wallgren was elected in his place. In 1944 Warren Magnuson, another liberal, began what became a long and influential career in the Senate, after Senator Bone was appointed to the United States Circuit Court. The war continued in both states, in summary, the political patterns of the 1930s. But it also began developments that would affect political life for many years after the war.

The New Cities

The war produced a new phenomenon in the region, the instant city. These were Vanport in Oregon and Hanford in Washington. Vanport was the largest and, in terms of its significance in pointing to postwar domestic problems, the most important. The city was begun by the Kaiser Corporation; designed by the architectural firm of Wolff and Phillips;

and was run by the Federal Housing Authority of Portland (HAP). It was completed in September 1943.

Vanport's history was brief and unhappy. Before it died in the flooding waters swirling through a broken railroad dike in May 1948 (which killed fifteen or sixteen persons), Vanport's residents had encountered a myriad of problems, including the racial issues that we have already discussed.

People of all races met unusual circumstances at Vanport. Their political situation was very different from that to which they had been accustomed. There was no representative government whatsoever. The HAP officials ran the community in most respects. The Portland School District provided educational facilities. Multnomah County furnished police protection.

The residents' work patterns were also different from their familiar ones. The shipyards ran three shifts, twenty-four hours a day. Women contributed mightily to shipyard employment. Thus families often did not see each other during the week. For many small children, light was turned into dark, night into day. Day-care centers and schools ran long hours to take care of children of employed parents.

Housing at Vanport was not adequate. The project construction was a rush job, just as was everything else connected with the war effort. Materials available to the builders was not of the highest quality, for the best supplies were used in higher priority enterprises. It is not surprising then that a congressional investigating committee faulted the quality of construction and of public services. Others attacked the entire planning of the city.

Finally, Vanport became known, without evidence, as a city ridden

Vanport, Oregon. Photograph by Delano Studios, Oregon Historical Society

with crime. While police data did not indicate that this was true, non-Vanport residents, given their general prejudice against the war workers, were convinced that the rate of crime in Vanport was much higher than in the rest of the metropolitan area. Doubtless this perception was also shared by the Vanport residents themselves whose lives were disoriented in so many other ways.

Uncertainty about crime symbolized the life in Vanport. Obviously the Vanport years were not a very happy experience for anyone who lived there. What is remarkable is not that the massive job (and Vanport was the largest wartime project in the nation) of providing new wartime housing was done poorly; what is remarkable is that it was done at all.

Hanford's experience was similar, although on a smaller scale. As the year 1943 opened, Hanford was a community of 250 persons slumbering in southcentral Washington. In that year, because of its isolation, small population to be displaced, and electricity and power facilities from the Columbia River, it was chosen to produce plutonium for the atomic bomb. The Du Pont Company was the principal contractor for the project. By a year later, 45,000 workers were employed and at the end of 1944 plutonium was in production. Ironically, only a handful of all these workers knew the purpose of their work, which was not revealed until the war was over. At nearby Richland—a village of the same size—twenty-five miles down the Columbia, the federal officials located the headquarters of the project. To build the plutonium plant and to house its workers in this isolated region was in some ways more of a challenge than to establish industry in the metropolitan areas of Portland and Puget Sound. But the task was accomplished and the nuclear power industry, established at Hanford during the war, remained as one of the war's legacies to the region along with greater racial heterogeneity, enormous population increase, and vast powers accorded to the federal government.

NOTES

1. Elizabeth McLagan, *A Peculiar Paradise: A History of Blacks in Oregon, 1788–1940* (1980), p. 176.
2. Ralph W. Hidy, Frank Ernest Hill, Allan Nevins. *Timber and Men: The Weyerhaeuser Story* (1963), p. 462.

SUGGESTIONS FOR READING

The wartime economy is dealt with in Roger Sale, *Seattle: Past to Present* (1976); Norman H. Clark, *Washington: A Bicentennial History* (1976); and E. Kimbark MacColl, *The Growth of a City: Portland, 1915–1950* (1979). Social conditions are described in the above works and Elizabeth McLagen, *A Peculiar Paradise: A History of Blacks in Oregon, 1788–1940* (1980). For the unions, see Ralph W. Hidy, Frank E. Hill, and Allan Nevins, *Timber and Men: The Weyerhaeuser Story* (1963); Charles P. Larrowe, *Harry Bridges: The Rise and Fall of Radical Labor in the United States* (1962); and Donald Garnel, *The Rise of Teamster Power in the West* (1972). Richard Slatta deals with the Hispanics in "Chicanos in the Pacific Northwest: A Demographic and Socioeconomic Portrait," *Pacific Northwest Quarterly,* 70 (1979), as does Erasmo Gamboa, "Mexican Labor in the Pacific Northwest, 1943–1947: A Photographic Essay," *Pacific Northwest Quarterly,* 73 (1982) and "Mexican Migration into Washington State: A History, 1940–1950," *Pacific Northwest Quarterly,* 72 (1981). On shipbuilding, see Frederic C. Lane, *Ships for Victory: A History of Shipbuilding under the U. S. Maritime Commission in World War II* (1951). For politics, see A. Robert Smith, *Tiger in the Senate: A Biography of Wayne Morse* (1962) and Robert E. Burton, *Democrats of Oregon: The Pattern of Minority Politics, 1900–1956* (1970). Vanport is described in MacColl, *Growth of A City* and Manly Maben, *Vanport, Oregon: The Life and Death of An Instant City* (1986). See also Paul John Deutschmann, "Federal City: A Study of the Administration of Richland, Washington, Atomic Energy Community," Ph.D. diss., University of Oregon, 1952.

Post–World War II People, 1945–1985

After the close of the Second World War the population of the Pacific Northwest became more diversified than ever before. Yet by the census year 1980 Oregon (94.5 percent) and Washington (91 percent) remained heavily Caucasian. Most who lived here, regardless of racial or cultural background, also came to enjoy a more prosperous, freer, and varied life than their parents or grandparents had known.

The Oldest Inhabitants

The Indians of the Pacific Northwest experienced great changes in the almost forty years since the end of the war. Some of these changes they initiated, while some were in response to fluctuating policies and programs of the federal government. Yet not all Indian groups were affected in the same way by these changes.

The first alteration in federal policy, and a disastrous one, was called termination. Termination was a reaction to the Indian Reorganization Act (the Wheeler-Howard Act) which was based upon the principle of the tribes' limited control of their affairs through government-chartered corporations. Of those who accepted the terms of the Indian Reorganization Act, not all saw striking changes in their daily lives. Some, however, made progress in educational and health benefits and in an improved standard of living.

These gains, however, did not save the Indian Reorganization Act from destruction. After the war's close, a conservative spirit arose in the United States. Some of those embracing this ideology easily identified the communalism of the Indian Reorganization Act with Marxian communism. The postwar years were also ones in which citizens called for reducing government expenditures. The Indian Reorganization Act prescribed special aid for the Indian people that did cost the taxpayers money. Their resentment was magnified because earlier federal laws had exempted Indians living on reservations from federal, state, and local taxes. Other people simply felt that the Indians would be better off if they were not given any special benefits.

Out of this welter of feelings that began to crystallize in the late forties came a congressional resolution adopted early in the Dwight D. Eisenhower presidency in 1953. One of its main supporters was Oregonian Douglas McKay, Eisenhower's secretary of the interior. It stated as government policy that Indians should have no more or no fewer privileges and responsibilities than other citizens. Reservations would be broken up. Special programs for the benefit of Indians would be terminated. This last provision led to the popular name for the new policy, *termination.* As the termination policy was enunciated, developed, and applied, it was denounced by most Indians and their non-Indian allies. At the same time as termination was enacted into law, Congress permitted states to extend their civil and criminal legislation to the reservation. Not until 1969 was the law modified to require the consent of the Indians before state laws were extended to any specific reservation.

Termination had a disastrous effect in the Pacific Northwest. In 1954 Congress passed two termination laws; one was for the Klamath and the other for all remaining western Oregon Indians. The tribe that received most publicity was the Klamath. It had a large and valuable stand of ponderosa pine forest desired by private lumber interests. Its contest with the termination policy went on for a long time. And the tragic results of the policy for the Klamaths helped bring it to an end nationally.

Termination for the Klamaths proceeded under the guise of the consent of the Indians. Under their law the lands of the reservation were to be sold and the proceeds of the sale and the tribal trust funds were to be apportioned among the individual members of the tribe. The Indians were to be consulted only in one sense. They could accept either their individual shares of the land sales and the trust funds or they could agree with other like-minded tribal members to have their shares managed under a trust administered by a private corporation. In either case, the specific federal programs for the Indians would cease.

When the Klamath people voted, most took their share of the tribal assets, which would be their per capita portion of the money chiefly gained from the sale of the great pine forest. This sum amounted to some $60,000 per person. A smaller percentage decided to exchange their federal trusteeship for one ultimately established for them by the United States National Bank of Oregon.

The vast majority of the tribal members who elected to take their proportionate share of the tribal wealth lost their money almost immediately. And the fate of the Klamath was only more spectacular than that of other tribes in Oregon as well as elsewhere in the nation. No tribes were actually terminated in Washington, although the Colvilles and the Makahs suffered the agonies of being at one time scheduled for termination. The disastrous condition of the Klamath became well known and in the administration of President Richard M. Nixon in 1970 termination was abandoned. In this sense a large northwestern tribe, in its harsh fate, was decisive in its influence upon national Indian policy.

The remaining Klamaths—those under the trust—ultimately fared better. In 1969 a majority of the tribe decided to divide the trust. A fair price for the trust assets was insured when the federal government bought the remaining 135,000 acres of Klamath land and incorporated them into the Winema National Forest. The roughly 600 Indians entitled to payment from the government received on the average about $120,000 per person.

Almost the reverse of the Klamath story occurred some 200 miles to the northeast. The Warm Springs Indians had organized a tribal government under federal charter in 1938. This decision enabled the tribe to gain some experience in self-government, practice that became valuable and evident after the war. In 1958 the federal government made a $4 million settlement with the tribe for the loss of its historic fishing grounds. They had been flooded forever when the Corps of Engineers constructed its huge multipurpose dam at The Dalles. There was a brisk debate among the tribal members about what to do with the money. Some favored a per capita division, but the elected tribal council voted to invest most of the money for the benefit of the entire tribe.

The first step was the construction of a tourist village and restaurant, named Kah-Nee-Ta, on the banks of the Warm Springs River in 1964. It became popular immediately and led to the construction of an additional 145-room luxury resort three miles from the original village. This enterprise, aimed at both the tourist and convention trades, was soon inadequate and plans for future expansion have been laid. Most of the tribal payroll came from the forest products industry, however. In 1967 this business began with the acquisition of a sawmill that had been operated by white persons on the reservation. It expanded to include a plywood plant, stud mill, and veneer factory. In 1968 the tribe began an electronics subassembly plant that has been used by a variety of firms. Other enterprises that produce community benefits as well as employ-

Kah-Nee-Ta Resort, Warm Springs Indian Reservation. Rockey/Marsh Public Relations, Inc.

ment opportunities are the federal fish hatchery on the Warm Springs River, a new water system for the reservation, and a hydroelectric power plant on the Deschutes River.

In the 1980s the tribal net income ranged between $5 and $8 million for the benefit of the 2,100 Indians living on the reservation. Money not dispersed in individual dividends is spent in scholarships, home building loans, rental housing, social security programs, health, and education. Although income is not yet at the state average, and unemployment in 1984 was 39 percent (compared to 51 percent on reservations nationally), the Warm Springs Reservation is a relative success story.

Other tribes improved their material condition. The Yakima Nation owned in 1983 36 percent of the stock of the American Indian National Bank, a bank located in Washington, D. C., the shares of which are held exclusively by American Indian tribes, tribal enterprises, or individuals. But for many Indians the economy was still in the hands of others. In 1975, for example, only 5 percent of the cropland on the Umatilla Reservation in Oregon was operated by Indians.

Northwestern Indians have also enjoyed successes in the legal realm in the postwar years. The first of these came in 1946 when Congress created the Indian Claims Commission. Tribes were allowed to sue the United States government for land taken without proper compensation.

The Cowlitz and Yakima tribes of Washington were among those who benefited from successful suits. Indians have also won important court victories over the interpretation of the original treaties with the federal government. The most dramatic have involved fishing rights on the Columbia River and on Puget Sound. The original treaties of the 1850s and 1860s reserved to the Indians the right to take fish at "their usual and accustomed places" even if these were off the reservation boundaries. As industrialization of the region developed, and as population increased by leaps and bounds, dams, pollution, and overfishing took heavy toll of both the fishery resource and the Indians' "usual and accustomed places" for their off-reservation fishery. The states of Oregon and Washington regulated the fisheries for conservation purposes. They insisted that the Indians, even at their "usual and accustomed places," must obey the state fishing seasons and catch limits. The Indians, although maintaining that their fishing practices were conservative, asserted that the states had no right to interfere with their off-reservation fisheries. In the 1960s all of these economic, social, and legal forces came to a head.

The form it came in was the fish-in. The name came from the sit-ins practiced by black southerners in protest against the segregationist laws of their states. Militant Indians believed that their only remedy was to court arrest to dramatize their cause and to seek a judicial decision of their fishing rights under the old treaties. The fish-ins (all of which occurred in the state of Washington) received a good deal of publicity in the region. They antagonized most of the white population who condemned the Indians as wanton publicity seekers or as greedy persons desiring to take fish away from non-Indian commercial or sports fishermen.

The fish-ins typically involved a few Indians—observed by a varying number of their supporters and representatives of the mass media—fishing at their usual places out of season. They would be arrested by agents of the state police or the fish or game commission. The trials would be held later, sometimes years later. They finally were decided in the federal courts. One of the novel features of these cases was that the United States government intervened on the side of the Indians. In 1968 the United States Supreme Court ruled in the case of *Puyallup Tribe* v. *the Department of Game* that the State of Washington could regulate the offreservation fishery of the Indians even under the treaty. But this right was accompanied by three specific restrictions: the regulations must be necessary to conserve fish; they must not discriminate against the Indians; and they must meet appropriate standards.

In 1969 federal district judge Robert Belloni decided the important case of *Sohappy* v. *Smith* The specific economic issue in the case was whether or not the state of Oregon could close the salmon fishery above the Bonneville Dam on the Columbia River to all fishermen including Indians. The Warm Springs and other Indian tribes of the Columbia and the United States government said that the Indian treaties required that the Indians obtain some fish at their usual places (even above the dam) and that the treaties under the federal constitution were supreme over state law, including conservation regulations. Judge Belloni declared that the state must protect the salmon run by, if necessary, reducing the non-Indian quota in order to insure that the native Americans have some of the fish at their usual places. At this time he did not specify what that amount might be.

Specificity came in February 1974 when George Boldt, a federal judge in Washington State, decided the case of *U. S.* v. *State of Washington*. He followed the line of reasoning laid down in the *Sohappy* decision about the supremacy of federal treaties guaranteeing the Indian's right to take fish at the usual places in common with the citizens of the territory. What was most controversial about the decision was Judge Boldt's ruling that the phrase "in common with" meant that the treaty Indians had the right to take 50 percent of each species of fish passing the usual places after a certain amount had been set aside for conservation purposes. In May 1974 Judge Belloni also ruled that Indian treaty fishermen were entitled to take 50 percent of the harvestable fish. In 1975 and 1976 the Ninth Circuit Court of Appeals upheld the Boldt decision and the second Belloni decision. In 1976 the Supreme Court refused to review the Circuit Court decisions in the *U. S.* v. *Washington* case. But in 1977 the Washington State Supreme Court ruled that Judge Boldt had misinterpreted the treaties. Finally, in 1979, the United States Supreme Court settled the matter by upholding the essence of the Boldt decision.

Other Indian victories were won in Congress. Some of the terminated tribes were able to recover their status as federally recognized tribes. Three in Oregon were the Siletz, Grande Ronde, and Confederated Tribes of Coos, Lower Umpqua, and Siuslaw Indians who obtained federal recognition in 1977, 1983, and 1985, respectively. Some Washington tribes, although they had not been terminated, sought recognition also. Among those that gained this status are the Upper Skagit, the Sauk Suiattle, the Stillaguamish, and the Nooksack. Federal recognition was important, for it meant special Indian aid programs in education, health, and economic development would again be available.

All of these gains were part cause and part reflection of cultural advances. As the Indians took greater pride in their culture, they became more assertive in politics and economic matters. Legal and material gains in turn enabled them to institutionalize their cultural heritage. For example, Oregon Indians created a Chicano-Indian study center at Camp

Makah Museum in Neah Bay, Washington. Makah Museum

Adair and a museum and cultural center at Coos Bay. In Washington the Quileutes reconstructed their tribal language and tribal history. At Neah Bay, a modern archaeological museum, owned and operated by the Makah people, opened in 1979. The Suquamish maintain a tribal cultural center at the town of Suquamish. Urban Indians (58 percent of the Indian population of Oregon in 1980, 59 percent in Washington) also developed their own institutions. One of the earliest was the Portland Urban Indian Council (1971), a multiservice human resource organization.

The Hispanics

After the Second World War ended, the *bracero* program for agricultural migratory labor continued but was finally terminated in 1964 when the opposition of organized labor across the United States forced Congress to kill it. It was a blow to farmers, but not one that removed the Hispanic influence. The great movement of American Hispanics to the northwest began after the Second World War. Labor continued to be badly needed in the fields and Washington and Oregon farmers advertised widely in the Rocky Mountain area and the Southwest for migratory workers. The Hispanics were family members, not single men, and the family remained their main reliance, along with the Roman Catholic church, in shielding them against the problems of their new homes, problems that were numerous and serious.

Hispanics may have been successful in improving their material lot, but their life was not very attractive when measured against that of non-Hispanic residents. Pay was low, hours long (when work was available), housing conditions poor. Mobility meant little or no education for the children during the long harvest season. It meant that the migrants had no interest in or influence over the communities in which they resided.

Recognition of these facts by non-Hispanics began in the Northwest in Oregon in 1955. In that year the Oregon Council of Churches created a Research Committee on Migrant Labor. The Council of Churches investigation revealed the shameful conditions of life of the migrant workers. The report stimulated public concern that was reflected in the Oregon State Legislature. In 1959, under the leadership of representative Don S. Willner, the legislature passed laws making it a criminal offense for growers to exploit their workers.

By the 1960s laws were but one way that the lives of Hispanics were changing. Employment conditions were different. More and more Hispanics were settling down, abandoning migrant labor to become permanent citizens of the Northwest or remaining in their homes in California and the Southwest. The principal reasons for this change were government programs aiding the migrants—to be described below—and the introduction of mechanization in some crops. When machines were used for some crops, the migrant's annual pattern of employment was broken. They found it unprofitable to harvest one crop, then wait weeks until another was ready for hand picking. It was better to try and seek settled employment. Many Hispanics decided that their permanent homes should be in the Pacific Northwest. Once this decision was made they could develop institutions like those of other cultural groups. They also participated in organizations for those who continued as migrant workers.

One of the most important of these was an offshoot of the War on Poverty declared by President Lyndon B. Johnson, the Office of Economic Opportunity. The Oregon Council of Churches, as in the case of employment legislation, took the lead in taking advantage of OEO funds. In 1965 the council obtained a grant from OEO to form the Valley Migrant League which set up centers in six Oregon communities by the end of that year. In these opportunity centers the VML provided a range of social services.

Although the VML had several successes, it also had both internal and external problems. Over the years Hispanics objected to Anglos holding staff positions; they demanded these positions for people of their own culture. The external problem was the uncertainty of federal funding. OEO grants were on an annual basis; they rose and fell with the federal budget and as the 1960s wore on, the trend was downward as more money was spent on the Vietnam war.

While these events transpired within VML, migrant workers attempted to improve their economic conditions. Their inspiration was Cesar Chavez's United Farm Workers Organizing Committee founded in Delano, California, in 1965. UFWOC became the first successful agricultural union in the United States. By 1968 UFWOC was organized in Oregon. It attempted both political and economic action. The union tried to get the state Democratic and Republican parties to endorse legislation to aid farm organization; to modify state labor law to allow farm workers to organize; to improve health standards for farm labor camps; and to require these standards to be enforced by state rather than county health departments. It also tried to organize strikes during the harvest season. But neither political nor economic action was successful.

Besides publicity and public education, Hispanics turned to the courts to alleviate their problems. In a historic action, a group of Washington County migrant workers sued a berry farm employer in federal court for breach of contract. This litigation, the first class-action suit in the nation involving farm workers, resulted in Judge Alfred T. Goodwin upholding the workers and granting them damages in August 1970. Hispanics have also made administrative complaints against corporations, school districts, local governments, and the Bonneville Power Administration for alleged discriminatory practices. Assertiveness comes not only from the favorable climate for social justice that arose in the early 1960s, but from the important fact that more and more Hispanics have settled down, abandoning migrant labor for roots in a single community. The year-round presence of Hispanics in formerly all-Anglo communities has also resulted in the development of numerous cultural institutions.

The earliest of these institutions that marked the rooting of the Hispanic migrants was Centro Chicano Cultural (the Chicano Cultural Center) founded in Woodburn in 1969 in Oregon's Willamette Valley. Money for the building and the land was contributed by the Roman Catholic church. There was a good deal of opposition to the institution from local residents who feared people of a different culture. But the programs began and soon became popular. They included arts and crafts classes, a newspaper, a television program, and a class in police-community relations. A similar center, Washington County Centro Cultural, began in Cornelius in 1972. In Washington the first Spanish-language radio program was presented in 1950. In the next decade the first Spanish-speaking priest came to the Yakima Valley.

The Roman Catholic church is deeply involved in the lives of Hispanic people. One of its social action agencies, Stella Maris House, was one of the first institutions to assist migrant workers. It was a participant in establishing the Valley Migrant League, and the church in many other ways has been sensitive to the needs of its Hispanic parishioners.

Hispanics, both migrants and settlers, have participated in new educational developments. As early as 1961 the state of Oregon established

Centro Cultural of Washington County. Eric Stewart and
Washington County Museum

special summer programs for Spanish-speaking migrant children. In
1965 the national government stepped in with programs designed to
help Hispanic children, whether or not they were migrants. Most children
in the 1970s got special aid for five years after their parents left migrant
status. The nature of this assistance was a matter of controversy in one
notable respect, however. Indeed, a running battle has been fought for
over a decade over the teaching of a second language. Attendance is
another point of contention between the two cultures. Hispanic children
are often more loyal to the family than to the school. To help out economically a child may be kept home from school.

Controversy also marked the short history of Colegio Cesar Chavez.
Founded in 1973 on the former Mount Angel College campus at Mt.

Angel, Oregon, the college was intended to be the first Hispanic center of higher education in the United States. The college's troubles were largely financial. It had great difficulty in paying loans due to the United States government. It also had difficulties in retaining students, almost all of whom came from low-income families. These problems in turn led to loss of accreditation in 1981 and to closure of the institution in 1983.

But in spite of these problems the Hispanics have become the largest minority group in the Pacific Northwest, the largest in Oregon, the second largest in Washington. More and more they have shed their rural heritage. In 1980 only 33 percent lived in rural regions in Oregon, 28 percent in Washington. Urbanized, youthful, increasingly educated, their presence is being felt across the region.

The Blacks of Oregon

Since the close of the Second World War, the blacks have gained in legal rights, economic opportunities, community respect, and cultural consciousness. Their life has hardly been without difficulties, but their gains over the years have been significant. One old problem was magnified dramatically in Oregon on Memorial Day, 1948.

On that day a dike on the Columbia River broke and the city of Vanport was washed away. Blacks made up a significant percentage of the residents of the stricken city. These homeless people had a great deal of trouble locating new places to live in the Portland area. On the surface Portland was integrated, for at least a few blacks lived in almost every section of the city. But almost all resided in the Albina ghetto in north Portland. In Seattle, too, there was a dispersion almost everywhere, but concentration in the Central District. In Eugene the small number of blacks clustered originally in three areas. One of these communities was dislocated in 1948 when a new highway was constructed. Again, in 1965, urban renewal destroyed many black homes for a bridge and highway through another of the ghetto areas. In Portland as the interstate freeway was built on the east bank of the Willamette River in the 1950s, and as urban renewal destroyed buildings in South Portland, housing difficulties magnified.

One of the difficulties was the real estate business. In Oregon each real estate broker was sworn to uphold a sentence in the state manual for brokers that declared: "A realtor should not be instrumental in introducing into a neighborhood a character of property or use which will clearly be detrimental to property values in that neighborhood."[1] This policy meant in effect that blacks should be confined largely to areas where they already lived. To address the problem in Portland was one of the major concerns of citizen groups. The NAACP, the Urban League, and individuals were all involved. A major effort was the Coordinating Committee for Minority Housing made up of the above two organizations and several other groups. Organized in 1953 the CCMH took a variety of actions to alleviate housing conditions. In 1957 another interracial group, the Albina Neighborhood Council, requested the *Oregon Journal* to study the Portland minority housing situation. But the principal reason the real estate business became less prejudicial was the passage of the Oregon Fair Housing Act in 1957. In 1960 the Urban League, the Albina Neighborhood Council, and the City Commission on Intergroup Relations held a housing conference that led to the formation of the Albina Neighborhood Improvement Project. The committee was designed to work with the city's urban renewal agency which had the responsibility for clearing houses for the interstate highway. By the late 1960s there were results from all of these activities and from the liberal national and local social climates of the era.

In the area of employment northwestern blacks and their white allies worked hard to break down barriers. Initial efforts were designed to persuade businesses to hire black people other than in their traditional menial positions. In Portland the first groups to become active were the Committee on Interracial Principles and Practices, the Urban League, and the National Association for the Advancement of Colored People. In the department stores, for example, the only jobs open to blacks had been elevator operators and maids. Their organizations entered into laborious negotiations with store managements in an attempt to open up sales and telephone operator positions. It took a long time, many hours of volunteer labor, and the threat of action under the state's new Fair Employment Act passed in 1949, before successes were gained in the private sector. By the middle forties the first Portland blacks were working as nurses and teachers and employees of city and county government.

Black parents were concerned as always about the quality of their children's education. Until the 1960s this concern had been expressed in a desire for integrated education following the United States Supreme Court's decision in *Brown* v. *Board of Education* (1954). It followed the national argument that segregated education, however competent or useful otherwise, was inherently inferior. It was best expressed nationally and locally by the NAACP. In 1964, for example, when the Portland School Board established its model schools program within the ghetto area, the local NAACP took a strong position in opposition: "The establishing of the model school facility to segregate citizens of color and class is no advantage and offers no present or future improvements . . . . The model school program as proposed is in essence a negation of all the past and current convictions and efforts of the NAACP to obtain integrated education for Negro children."[2]

Throughout the 1960s and 1970s controversy raged about whether black children should be educated in neighborhood schools even if *de facto* segregated. Some black parents who had originally favored integration changed their minds. The issue became caught up in those of the declining tax base for urban schools, busing to accomplish racial balance in schools, and black consciousness.

The most militant advocate of black pride as expressed through black separateness was the Black Muslim organization. Its philosophical appeal originally was not only based upon separation but upon hatred for the white race. Its most charismatic leader, Malcolm X, spread the Muslim message throughout black America to the horror of most white people. His appeal to black northwesterners had mixed success. In Portland, the Black Muslims began organizing in 1961 and gained a few adherents throughout the decade. The local Urban League in a memorandum of 1961 to "selected Organizations and Churches" suggested that these groups deny the Muslims a forum. The initial response of the local NAACP was expressed by its vice-president and office manager: "They wanted to have a meeting at our place, . . . we kicked them out, and told them we wanted no part of it. . . . We don't participate in activities of any crackpot group, white or black."[2]

Far more effective was another local affiliate of a national organization, the Black United Front, organized in Portland in 1977. The Front, composed only of black persons, attempted to instill racial pride in the worthiness of the black experience. Its specific actions have been directed to ensuring that school board policies do not scatter black children throughout predominately white schools; that black studies be included in the public school curriculum; and that academic standards and the quality of teachers be raised throughout the school system.

Beyond the realm of education, blacks moved in their historic pattern. They supported their traditional organizations, dug their personal and cultural roots deeper, sought better economic opportunities, and participated in political life. In this last respect they passed certain milestones. Since 1964 in Portland the first blacks have taken their places as school principals, city council members, county commissioners, school board members, and superintendents of schools. Oregon was one of the first states to pass a fair employment practices act (1949) and a public accommodations act (1953). The Oregon legislature passed a fair housing law in 1957 and ratified the Fifteenth Amendment in 1959. The law against interracial marriage was repealed. Barriers to admission to the National Guard collapsed.

Old and new social and cultural organizations added to the cultural pattern. Illustrations include the Prince Hall Masons and their Eastern Star Auxiliary which created benevolent and community service programs. Black women have the Delta Sigma Theta sorority and The Links, Inc., which have a wide range of activities designed to foster their members' participation in civic affairs. The churches remain powerful institutions. New black newspapers appeared.

Washington Blacks

In Washington the black communities underwent many of the same experiences as their neighbors across the Columbia. As in Oregon, what was mainly different about the postwar years was the role of government in assisting the black population. In 1947 the legislature created the Washington State Board against Discrimination. It was charged with dealing with complaints under old and new civil rights laws. In the fall of 1957 it established four advisory councils around the state at Olympia, Pasco, Spokane, and Tacoma.

The WSBD began with public accommodations. In 1958 it held the first civil rights hearing in the state. After taking evidence, the board ordered a tavern owner in Tacoma to serve people of all races without discrimination. Housing also occupied a great deal of the board's attention. In 1957 the legislature made it illegal for owners of "publicly assisted" housing (that covered by Veteran's Administration or Federal Housing Authority financing) to discriminate in the sale or rental of housing. The legislature defeated a comprehensive open housing law in 1959, but did pass a law making it unlawful for financial institutions to ask for race, creed, color, or national origin on credit applications. The most important housing case was the O'Meara case. In 1961 the Washington Supreme Court declared the housing section of the 1957 law unconstitutional because it applied only to people with federally insured mortgages. Finally the housing laws were revised and decreed constitutional in 1967. Meanwhile some small victories were gained. The public housing projects in Pasco and Kennewick dropped racial designations on their housing application forms in 1959.

The year 1959 also marked a breakthrough in the area of employment. The first black usher was hired in a Seattle downtown movie theater. The first black telephone operator was hired in Yakima, the first black taxicab driver in Seattle, and the first black fireman in the state, also in Seattle. After a complaint and an investigation by the WSBD, the first black service station attendant outside the Central District of Seattle was hired.

In the 1960s new federal antipoverty agencies were of some benefit to black persons. The Office of Economic Opportunity, created in 1964, worked mainly through Community Action Agencies (CAA) governed by boards of trustees composed of government officials, community leaders, and elected representatives of poor people. These agencies planned programs appropriate to local conditions. In the black ghetto of Tacoma, for example, the local CAA provided such things as day care, medical and legal referrals, free transportation to social and health agencies, and a youth center.

In the realm of education, Seattle, like Portland, originally pursued the strategy of integration. The Urban League, civil rights leaders, black and white clergymen, and the school board worked out a voluntary transfer policy that the board adopted in 1963. Five years later the board created racially integrated middle schools that went into effect in 1972. In 1977 the school board, supported by the Urban League, the Chamber of Commerce, the Municipal League, and other establishment groups and politicians, and under the threat of litigation in the federal courts, adopted a plan requiring reassignment of pupils to accomplish integration through mandatory busing. Yet prejudice died hard. In 1978 Washington voters passed an initiative measure prohibiting pupil assignments for the purpose of racial desegregation. However, the United States Supreme Court in 1982 declared the initiative measure unconstitutional.

There were black pride and black power movements in Seattle also. The most militant organizations were the Black Student Union and the Black Panthers, respectively. Although their tactics of confrontation, sit-ins, and hostage taking were appalling to almost all whites and to the older established black leadership, they reflected the aggressive spirit of the deprived as well as the continuing frustrations peculiar to blacks. Black pride led to the creation of several institutions in the 1960s: the Garvey Book Store and the New Group Theater among them. Some of these institutions endured, others failed; some, like the Black Panthers, became less militant. Some blacks' rage could not be contained by institutions or nonviolent protest. In July and August 1968 serious racial disorders broke out in Seattle. The trigger was a Seattle police department search of the headquarters of the Black Panther Party. Two Black Panther leaders were arrested. For two days in the ghetto there was sporadic rock throwing, arson, and one instance of shooting at a police car. Several blacks were arrested, although none were brought to trial.

In the 1970s the black community of Washington became quieter. It had never been as tense in Tacoma or Spokane as in Seattle, but in all cities the quiet was not reflective of contentment. Although the 1980s saw the end of all formal discrimination, full respect for blacks by whites remained distant.

Japanese and Japanese Americans

After the war was over the Japanese and Japanese Americans who chose to do so made a relatively easy readjustment to life in the Pacific Northwest. There are two major exceptions to this generalization. One is that a substantial number of the detained people did not return to the region. They had no desire to come back to a heritage of bigotry. The other exception is more comprehensive. Everyone, returnee or not, suffered a financial loss for their property that they had to abandon.

For most white citizens the postwar consequence of concentration was shame. When a few zealots in Hood River and Multnomah counties in Oregon demanded either mass deportation or strict enforcement of the old Alien Land Laws, they had little support. When some Gresham, Oregon, citizens after the war formed an Oregon Property Owners Protective Association, Governor Charles Sprague, banker E.B. Mac-Naughton, and prominent Democrat Monroe Sweetland went to Gresham to speak publicly against the association. In a relatively short time, the resistance collapsed. In Seattle the mayor's Civic Unity Committee worked with many civic groups to smooth the ways of the returning Japanese over the objection of individuals who wished to deport them or at least prevent their return, such as the Japanese Exclusion League, Remember Pearl Harbor, and the State Federation of Labor.

Remorse for the evacuation appeared in other ways. The Oregon Supreme Court declared the Alien Land Law unconstitutional in the case of *Namba* v. *McCourt* in 1949 as a violation of the due process and equal protection clauses of the Fourteenth Amendment to the United States Constitution. The Washington legislature repealed that state's Alien Land Law in 1967. In 1948 Congress passed a statute permitting the evacuees to sue in federal court for monetary compensation for the losses of personal and real property sustained by them. Over the years the cases were decided. Those who sued (many did not) received as a national average about ten cents on the dollar. Another step that reflected this sense of shame was taken in 1952 when Congress passed a comprehensive immigration law. It abandoned race as a qualification for immigration to the United States. It also barred race as a criteria for citizenship. Congress in a single stroke thus destroyed the nineteenth century bars against Asians becoming citizens and the 1924 statute prohibiting Asian immigration.

The Japanese of the Northwest are convinced that the wartime experiences should not be forgotten. They wish them commemorated as an important if horrible part of national history. Some also want additional monetary compensation beyond that given to some for property losses. This payment would be reparation for every Japanese and Japanese American who had been incarcerated during the war. On February 17, 1979, Portland Japanese-American community groups held a Day of Remembrance ceremony commemorating the evacuation. They unveiled a plaque on this occasion furnished by the Multnomah County Historical Sites Project, at the Multnomah County Exposition Center, the detention center for Oregon Japanese and Japanese Americans before they were sent to the camps.

In 1980 Congress, pushed hard by the Japanese American Citizens League, opened the questions of internment and reparations when it created an independent Commission on Wartime Relocation and Internment. One of several hearings held on the West Coast was in Seattle. The commission reported unanimously that "a grave injustice was done" to Japanese Americans. It recommended, with one dissenting vote, that Congress pay $20,000 to each of the approximately 60,000 Japanese Americans who had been in the camps. It also proposed creation of a foundation to study the internment experience.

In the affairs of ordinary life the Japanese experience in the postwar years has been an outstanding success. All formal barriers to prejudice seem to have dropped away. In education, Japanese Americans have exceeded other ethnic groups in the population in the percentage of enrollment in colleges and universities and in acquiring advanced degrees. Many are successful in business and the professions, no longer confined to farming, construction labor, and Japanese groceries. Some, such as Ray T. Yasui, who was appointed to the Oregon State Board of Higher Education, have taken on public roles. In the arts, Northwestern Japanese have become prominent nationally and internationally. One of the distinguished architects of our time is Minoru Yamasaki. In painting Kenjro Nomura, Paul Horiuchi, and George Tsutakawa, among others, are names to be reckoned with. Tsutakawa also became a powerful sculptor. In literature Monica J. Sone's autobiography, *Nisei Daughter* (1953) and John Okada's novel, *No-No Boy: A Novel* (1957) are excellent accounts of growing up Asian in Seattle and the searing experience of the concentration camps and the immediate postwar years. Although the Japanese seem accepted and successful, the bitter communal memory of earlier persecution continues as does the dilemma for each person of the degree of assimilation to pursue.

The Chinese moved ahead, too. They had the free choice of the degree of assimilation that they wished to adopt. Many became successful in the regional economic and educational life. One proof of this success was the ease with which the ethnic heritage, once scorned or evaded by the second generation, was now prized. In Seattle, for example, the Wing

Luke Museum was dedicated in 1967. Its focus is upon the Chinese and Japanese heritage in the arts and serves as a memorial to the first Chinese city councilman in Seattle.

The Jews

Just as the German Jews had become a welcomed part of regional life by 1900, so too had the East European Jews by 1950. The economic path upward from lowly jobs continued. Sam Schnitzer, for example, arrived in Portland in 1905. He became a tobacconist's clerk, then a junk dealer in Astoria and Portland. He wrote of the early days: "I had no money to buy a horse or wagon, so I started in the junk business, and I was my own horse and wagon. I bought old sacks, brass and copper, old iron and bottles, and carried them on my back till I got as much as I could carry."[4] Today his descendants control a worldwide empire of real estate and construction. The Schnitzers are only the wealthiest of scores of Jews in the business world. Success has come in education, the professions, and the arts, too. Neil Goldschmidt became mayor of Portland (1973– 1979) and later a member of President Jimmy Carter's cabinet, only the third Oregonian to attain cabinet rank. Richard Neuberger was United States senator (1955–1960). But accomplishments were not won without the pain of prejudice. Not until the 1960s did Jews gain admission to prestigious town and country clubs and to membership on regional boards of directors and partnerships in major law firms. Even to the present, vestiges of anti-Semitism remain in civic and private life, another reminder of one of the heritages of a homogeneous society, suspicion of difference.

In Washington most Jews continued to reside in Seattle. From 1946 to 1978 this community grew very rapidly from a population of 10,300 to one numbering 19,300 men and women. In these years the Jews expanded from their urban base to suburbia. Geographic mobility accompanied the rise to the professions and success in business proprietorships and management, until, by 1978, 70 percent of the heads of Seattle's Jewish households were in those categories. Yet the community as a whole is somewhat unusual compared to most in the United States. One distinguishing feature is the large Sephardic component. Another is the large percentage (26 percent in 1978) unaffiliated with the formal institutions of the Jewish community. Finally, the Jews who are committed to their faith have had difficulty coalescing, perhaps because of the long-standing Ashkenazim-Sephardim split. Not until 1955, for example, did Seattle Jews form a Jewish Community Center, the last of the intermediate-sized Jewish communities in the country to create one.

Senator Richard Neuberger. Oregon Historical Society

The Refugees of War

The Pacific Northwest has always been a place of refuge, no more so than after the Second World War when displaced persons arrived here. The Jews who escaped the Holocaust death camps were among these. Through luck or courage or the divine will they escaped the gas chambers. With indescribable heroism they kept living in the new world. Their story is the great exception to the experiences of northwestern people whose lives have generally fallen in pleasant places.

Some Jews escaped the Holocaust, returned to their East European homes, then fled again in the late 1940s when the communists seized their countries, revived anti-Semitism, and forced official atheism upon the people. Others who fled communism were Russians. They came from three directions. The largest group were escaping Chinese communism. Originally these people had gone to China after the Bolshevik Revolution in 1917. When the civil war came to China they left interior cities to move to Shanghai. After all of mainland China fell to communism the

Russian exiles came to the Philippines, then to San Francisco, finally to Portland and Seattle. Contrary to what one might expect, their adjustment to the United States was not as difficult as that of many groups, for they had learned English in Shanghai or in the Philippines and their ambition and skills soon led to jobs in their new homes.

Another strand of Russian displaced persons were those fleeing Germany and Austria. Their principal places of residence in the Northwest were Portland and Longview, Washington. A few Estonians also came in these years. A third Russian group were not Orthodox Christians. They were either schismatics from Orthodoxy (the Old Believers) who had broken away beginning in the Seventeenth Century or were founders of new, dissenting groups (the Sectarians). Most were Old Believers who came to Oregon in the 1960s to settle about the Willamette Valley community of Woodburn. Their place of origin was Turkey, Chinese Turkestan, and Manchuria. In Oregon they worked in industry in Portland or in agriculture. Most became successful economically; they had some social difficulties, however, when their belief that public education should end at the seventh grade clashed with state law.

The newest migrants are the refugees from Southeast Asia. Unlike any other northwestern immigrant group, almost all of them are the immediate victims of war. After the long military struggle beginning in the Second World War, the French rulers were forced out of Laos, Cambodia, and Vietnam by a nationalist and communist revolution of the colonial peoples. Beginning at the same time the United States gradually intervened against the communist forces in Vietnam. The conflict escalated and spilled over from Vietnam into Cambodia and Laos. In the appalling destruction of war and in the aftermath of the communists' conquest of Vietnam, Cambodia, and Laos in 1975 and the Vietnamese invasion of Cambodia in 1978, thousands fled to neighboring countries (many of whom were subsequently admitted to the United States) or were evacuated directly to the United States. A large portion of these refugees became resident of the Pacific Northwest. In 1981 the Southeast Asian population of Washington (25,476) was the third largest in the nation, while that of Oregon (16,077) took ninth place.

Their problems of adjustment were staggering. Not only were the refugees of different nations, but they were divided in other ways. They included not only Vietnamese, but also Chinese (the overseas Chinese) whose private property was confiscated by the communist governments of Vietnam and Cambodia; Laotians who fled the leftist Pathet Lao who took over the nation in 1975, refugees themselves divided into lowland Lao, Hmong, and Mien groups; and Cambodians escaping the inhumanity of the Pol Pot government that seized the nation in 1975. Some Southeast Asians are Buddhists (a faith itself divided), some Roman Catholics, some animists. Their backgrounds include several languages, farms and cities, highland and lowlands.

Much in America added to the refugees' difficulties. Practically everything in the new social and natural environment from language to climate differed sharply from their old homelands. Nevertheless, through their own tenacity, federal and state assistance, and church and secular benevolence, they made a new life. Some gained dramatic success in school, in business, and in the professions. Most got along, a few gave up. As always the young adapted better than did the old, but people of all ages faced the traditional problem of immigrants: how much of their new culture to accept, repudiate, or integrate with the old. However painful these decisions were for the refugees, for the region as a whole, the most recent newcomers have already made their contribution to social diversity and to cultural and economic progress.

NOTES

1. Elizabeth McLagan, *A Peculiar Paradise: A History of Blacks in Oregon* (1980), p. 142.

2. Portland NAACP, "Statement of NAACP on the Race and Education Report of October, 1964."

3. *Oregon Journal,* August 31, 1961, p. 1.

4. (Portland) *Sunday Oregonian Northwest Magazine,* January 25, 1976, p. 6.

SUGGESTIONS FOR READING

In addition to the works cited in Chapters 7, 12, 13, 14, and 15, see articles by Richard W. Slatta, "Chicanos in the Pacific Northwest: A Demographic and Socioeconomic Portrait," *Pacific Northwest Quarterly,* 70 (1979) and "Chicanos in the Pacific Northwest: An Historical Overview of Oregon's Chicanos," *Aztlan* (vol. 6, no. 3, 1975) and Frederick Dennis Garrity, "The Civic Unity Committee of Seattle, 1944–1964," M.A. thesis, University of Washington, 1971. For the Japanese and Japanese Americans, see Commission on Wartime Relocation and Internment of Civilians, *Personal Justice Denied* (1983). The metropolitan newspapers and magazines are major sources for information about the social history of recent years, as are Tricia Knoll, *Becoming Americans: Asian Sojourners, Immigrants, and Refugees in the Western United States* (1982); Doris H. Pieroth, "With All Deliberate Caution: School Integration in Seattle, 1954–1968," *Pacific Northwest Quarterly,* 73 (1982); and James McCann, *A Study of the Jewish Community in the Greater Seattle Area* (1979).

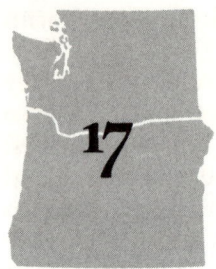

Cultural and Social Life, 1945–1985

The World of Art

The art world in the Pacific Northwest after the war reflected many of the developments in American art. The artist in both region and nation came to confront a variety of styles and a variety of themes. Dominant was abstract expressionism, centering in New York City, but prominent throughout the Western World. It seemed to be the complete opposite of regional, social, representational art. In turn abstract expressionism gave way to pop art and minimalism and other manifestations of the newer artists' reaction to pop.

The rise of abstract art in the last half of the 1940s and the first half of the 1950s coincided with enormous publicity for the Puget Sound artists who were known nationally as the Northwest school. Indeed, two of them, Morris Graves and Mark Tobey, gained international acclaim. In 1947 the term *Northwest school* was being used to describe certain regional painters in a traveling exhibit shown in five museums in the East. The term became nationally famous in 1953 when *Life* published a six-page color article of the work of Tobey, Kenneth Callahan, Graves, and Guy Anderson. These artists, the article stated, were primarily mystics whose sources of creative inspiration were the oceans, rainfall, mountains, and forests of the Pacific Northwest. There was some truth in this interpretation, as well as in *Life's* explanation of the artists' sources as including the art of Asia. But the success of these men, and others, at this time and later, was more complex than regional environment and Asian influences.

Nature as well as the specific Northwest environment was a force for inspiration and celebration. Sometimes it appeared in landscapes like Guy Anderson's *Dry Country* (1955), sometimes in symbolic, quasi-representational art as in Kenneth Callahan's *Rocks and People* (1945–1946) or *Insect* (1966) or Morris Graves' *Ceremonial Bronze Taking the Form of a Bird* (1947) and many other of his bird paintings. The artists of the Northwest school were not only familiar with the environment of the Pacific Northwest but they knew their region and took it with them. Graves said he carried it along when he went to Ireland. Callahan in 1947 summed up this concern with both nature and specific locale: "Nature is almost without exception the source of all my work. Forms in nature from microcosm to macrocosm constitute an unending source of fascination for me. I try to build living from these. . . . This is a rugged country—the mountains tower; great jagged cliffs, tortured and distorted, pile one on another; innumerable waterfalls twist and scatter out of clouds of mist and fog which swirl and alternately blanket then disclose the peaks . . . "[1]

Preoccupation with nature was one of the ways that the Northwest school reflected an old tradition: romanticism. The members of the school were also romantic in their belief that human beings could transcend the material world to come into contact with spiritual as well as material reality. Their paintings reflected this quest. It was a reason why so many were interested in the art and philosophy of Asia, which makes this search central. In their paintings they used heavenly bodies, light, the technique of white writing, and the vertical organization of their paintings to illustrate their search for transcendence.

Finally, the Northwest school was influenced somewhat by the mainstream of modern, nonrepresentational art. As Mark Tobey put it once: "Some critics have criticized me for being what they called an Orientalist and for using Oriental models for my work. But they were wrong. Because when I was struggling in Japan and China . . . I became aware that I would never be anything other than the Westerner that I am."[2] Tobey indeed was contemptuous of those Westerners who had claimed to master the complexities of Asian philosophy—he never did so himself. Instead, the school knew the work of all the modern masters from Kandinsky to Klee to Picasso.

The Northwest school reached its apex in the 1950s. After that time, many vigorous painters, printmakers, and sculptors continued to work. But their paintings cannot be classified into any school. It is not surprising, this personal variety, for one can now become easily familiar with all the currents of international art. The world art community and its works are available by means unknown before the war: cheap and reliable air travel; art reproductions made available by the great museums through the mails; video activity; traveling exhibits to museums and galleries (the Portland Center for the Visual Arts founded in 1972 was a pioneer in this respect). Above all the increasing interest by the public in works of art in the postwar years caused a boom in art journals, in museum attendance, and in political pressure that resulted in Congress creating the National Endowment for the Arts and the National Endowment for the Humanities, both in 1965. These organizations have given financial aid of immeasurable importance to the art community. Private fortunes remained important, too. For example, a bequest of Charles Frye made possible the building of the Frye Museum in Seattle in 1952.

Public interest in the arts has also caused a rise in the number of galleries. In 1949 there was not one commercial art gallery in the Pacific Northwest. It was a daring move thus when Louis and Eda Bunce created the Kharoula Gallery in Portland in that year. Seattle's first gallery was opened in 1951 by Zoe Dusanne, a cosmopolitan woman who knew the art world of New York and Paris. Two years later Otto Seligman opened a gallery that soon became prestigious. In the 1970s and the 1980s interest justified the opening of several galleries not only in the metropolitan areas, but in small towns and resort areas also.

The taxpayers were also willing to support the arts in the colleges and universities. Departments of art and architecture arose. Artists-in-residence programs developed. All of these institutional developments contributed to the experimentation and creativity that followed the apex of the Northwest school and that of abstract expressionism, both of which culminated about 1960.

The most dramatic of the new developments was to break down the barriers among the arts. Paul Horiuchi of Seattle is a fine example. Originally an oil painter, Horiuchi became dissatisfied with the medium, and turned to collages made from rice paper prepared with color. Lee Kelly of Oregon began to paint his welded sculptures in the abstract-expressionist manner. Others were versatile in several media. George Tsutakawa began as a painter in ink and oil, then turned to metal sculpture. Portlander George Johanson is a painter and printmaker. James Hibbard, also an Oregonian, does drawings and paintings and also is a printmaker. James W. Washington of Seattle began as a painter, but turned to stone sculpture of natural forms and then to relief works.

Among those who have concentrated upon sculpture in the state of Washington, Robert Maki, Jonn Geise, Lawrence Beck, James Fitzgerald, and Ted Johnson stand out. Several Oregonians have gained ranking in this medium. One was a European refugee, Manuel Izquierdo, who fled the Civil War in Spain. Working in metal (and also occasionally making prints), he emphasizes the monumental and the permanent in his sculptures. Frederick Littman was also of European birth, a Hungarian who lived in Portland after 1941.

As abstract expressionism faded, new styles of painting developed. One reaction was pop art, based on the premise that the abstract expressionists had gotten away from the reality of ordinary life. Minimal art, also a reaction to abstract expressionism tried to depict reality by presenting forms, stark and essential, that derived from logic and control. All of these schools had followers in the Pacific Northwest, but the best painters of the post–Northwest school, young and old, were individualists, learning from all movements. In this creative journey, a Northwestern influence in terms of any discernible influence of regional, social, or natural environment seemed to disappear.

For example, the abstract expressionist William Ivey proclaimed a loose identity between nature and form. Leo Kenney and Charles Stokes did impressive abstractions. Of the older Washington painters, Guy Anderson and Ambrose Patterson continued to experiment. In Oregon various forms of modern movements were and are also reflected. Louis Bunce continued to paint his powerful works. Clayton S. Price, whose first one-man exhibition was in 1925, developed an abstract style in the last few years before his death in 1950. Jack McClarth's somber philosophy of existence is apparent to the astute observer beneath his many-hued paintings of the scenes of daily life. Milton Wilson is an abstract painter, while George Johanson emphasizes the human figure in his etchings as does Jay Backstrand in most of his paintings.

Literature

Don Berry is the most versatile cultural figure in modern Northwestern history. Berry became interested in Oregon history as a source for fiction after a long apprenticeship as a writer of science fiction. The first result of this new interest was *Trask*, published in 1960. In the novel, Trask, the protagonist, goes down the Oregon coast from the mouth of the Columbia to Tillamook Bay in the company of two Indians, Wakila, a young man caught between the values of the whites and those of the Indians, and Charley Kehwa, a medicine man. Trask's purpose on the journey is to look over the Tillamook region as potential farmland. But he also develops a genuine interest in the Indians whose view of nature is radically different from that of the whites. The culmination of the book sees Trask participate in the Indian spirit quest.

The successor to *Trask* is *Moontrap* (1962). Again, Berry returns to the theme of the contrast between the primitive and the civilized. In this book the primitive is represented by an old trapper, Webb, who is visiting his friend, Johnson Monday, who has settled down with his Indian wife to farm near Oregon City. Monday is halfhearted about farming, while

Webb despises it. Their lack of allegiance to material progress and other aspects of the building of civilization in the Willamette Valley embroils them with their Oregon City neighbors. The sequel is *To Build A Ship* (1963), a fictional account of the efforts of Tillamook Bay settlers to construct a vessel to take their produce to the outside world. Their triumph is to build the ship with the aid of only one skilled shipwright. Their tragedy is the human loss in completing the task successfully. Berry's last book is a careful and interesting account of the American fur traders based in St. Louis in the years 1822–1834. *A Majority of Scoundrels: An Informal History of the Rocky Mountain Fur Company* was published in 1961. Since writing his novels and his history, Berry has pursued other interests. His creativity had led him since the 1960s into a concern with mathematics and computer science, into African and electronic music, and into bronze sculpture.

Ken Kesey is another major regional novelist of the Pacific Northwest. A native Oregonian, Kesey attended Springfield, Oregon High School and the University of Oregon from which he graduated in 1957. He reached national acclaim with the publication of a novel, *One Flew Over the Cuckoo's Nest*, in 1962, which was highly praised by critics. The story involves the adventures of a young man adjudged insane who is placed in the Oregon state asylum. Kesey tries to reveal that there is a thin line between actual madness and that which society judges insane. This somber topic is enlightened by Kesey's humor, his splendid characterization, and his effective use of the Oregon setting.

Oregon's environment and culture was of much greater importance in his second novel, *Sometimes a Great Notion,* published in 1964. The story, later made into a movie (as *Cuckoo's Nest* had been), recounted the encounter of three generations of the Stamper family with the Oregon coast. The grandfather, baffled by nature, returns to Kansas, but the son (Old Henry) and grandson Hank establish an independent logging business on a coastal river. The action of the novel occurs during a strike of lumber workers against the giant Wakonda Pacific Lumber Company. The Stampers are supplying logs to the company in defiance of the union. While this is going on, Hank's college-educated half-brother, Lee, is called back to work in the family business. A triangle develops among Lee, Hank, and Hank's wife, Viv. The mounting tension in both the logging strike and the domestic conflict makes the novel enthralling, but so does Kesey's description of the setting. Like H. L. Davis he knows the people of Oregon, their small town life, and the intricacies of the changing seasons. Although his style is somewhat difficult, Kesey is a memorable writer, although not of the first rank.

The most accomplished Northwestern novelist is Ursula K. Le Guin. She has become a master of two literary genres: science fiction and

Ivan Doig aboard a Puget Sound ferry during the writing of Winter Brothers. Photograph by Wayne D. Sourbeer, Courtesy Ivan Doig

fantasy. Since the publication of her first novel, *Roncannon's World* in 1966, Le Guin has won many literary awards and distinctions. Erudite, imaginative, skillful in her craft, Le Guin's passions for nature, freedom, love, and mystery have produced a marvelous corpus of work that includes novels, short stories, and literary criticism. Her Earthsea trilogy, *A Wizard of Earthsea* (1969), *The Tombs of Atuan* (1972), and *The Farthest Shore* (1972), is a fantasy series for older children. The last of the three books won the National Book Award for Children's Literature in 1973. Her distinguished novels of science fiction are *The Left Hand of Darkness* (1969); *The Lathe of Heaven* (1971)—set in Portland; *The Word for World Is Forest* (1972); *The Dispossessed: An Ambiguous Utopia* (1974); *The Eye of the Heron* (1978); and *The Beginning Place* (1980). Whether these works—

and her short stories—set in the country of the mind and the imagination depend directly upon the author's residence in the Pacific Northwest is conjectural. Le Guin is certainly not a regional writer, but it is the region's good fortune that she resides here.

Another of the versatile writers of the Pacific Northwest is Seattleite Ivan Doig who has produced three excellent works of different styles. Born in Montana, Doig's memoirs, *This House of Sky* (1978), focuses on the author's youth in his native state. It is an authentic account of a boy's growth to maturity, with the support of his father and grandmother, in the ranches and small towns of the region. Doig followed *This House of Sky* with a change of locale and a change of genre. In *Winter Brothers: A Season at the Edge of America* (1980), Doig reviews the life of James G. Swan, Indian agent among the Makahs at Neah Bay and inveterate diarist, who recorded life in the Northwest from 1862 to 1890. He follows Swan's footsteps around the region for ninety days and eloquently records his responses to the area that Swan had written about. The juxta-position of prose of discerning writers—sometimes separated by more than a century—is original and rewarding. Doig's first novel, *The Sea Runners* (1982), relates the escape of four Scandinavian indentured servants in 1853 from the Russian-American settlement at New Archangel. The men steal a canoe and try to make the twelve-hundred-mile journey to Astoria in the United States. The exciting story is based upon Doig's journey along the route and upon archival research.

POETRY

In the world of poetry the Pacific Northwest became home to two giants in these years. William E. Stafford, born in Hutchinson, Kansas, in 1914, and raised in the small towns of that state, came to Oregon in 1948. His work combines a simplicity of style with a profundity of insight. Stafford's poems are eloquent, but direct, and occasionally slip by the reader through their seeming artlessness. Like most creative artists, Stafford's concerns and themes are universal and he denies correctly that he is a regional poet: "A regional poet is somebody who lives someplace not recognized as the center of things."[3] But many of his poems are enhanced by their regional setting. Stafford has won many honors including the National Book Award in 1963 for *Travelling Through the Dark*.

Theodore Roethke came to the Pacific Northwest a year earlier than did Stafford. Roethke was born in Saginaw, Michigan, in 1902, the son of a commercial florist. In 1947 he came to the University of Washington where he taught until his death in 1963.

Roethke was already a mature poet when he came to Seattle. There he completed his experimental poems, "The Lost Son" and "The Shape

Theodore Roethke. Special Collections Division, University of Washington Libraries

of the Five." He then began to break new ground in a cascade of brilliant poetry which addresses such themes as the contrary loves of nature and women, the symbolic landscape, and human longing. He later turned in the North American sequence poems to his old concerns from his younger days: the comforts to be secured in the quest for God, in the continuity of past and present, and in memories of childhood. He approached these matters in other sequences, published posthumously in *The Far Field* (1964). This last work continued to show his development as one of the major poets of the twentieth century. Roethke, who considered himself at base as "a poet of love, a poet of praise," won the Pulitzer Prize, the National Book Award, and the Bollinger Prize. His influence upon the poets of the Northwest was enormous. Among American poets his reputation is in the forefront.

Although Stafford and Roethke were the most famous Northwestern poets of modern times, other distinguished ones appeared in the region. Among these are numbered Kenneth O. Hanson, Richard Hugo, Carolyn Kizer, and David Wagoner. Hugo, perhaps more than the other three, wove the physical environment of the Northwest into his work. All have drawn upon diverse cultures and regions of the world for their poetic content and technique.

Architectural Forms

After the war architecture lost much of the unity provided by the Northwest style. The growth of population, the instant communication with the rest of the nation, and the sprawl of suburbia made the region more like the nation. This homogeneity was reflected in architecture. Although some beautiful new buildings arose, particularly on college and university campuses, ugliness and pomposity prevailed. The International style, based on functionalism, and sparing of ornamentation, came to dominate. In this vein Pietro Belluschi himself built an innovative skyscraper, the Equitable Building in Portland, in 1948. It was his use of glass and aluminum sheathing that made the building innovative.

The tract houses of suburbia, the dominant form of domestic architecture, were imitations of the California ranch houses. They were functional, but largely tasteless, even in planned communities. Banks and office buildings testified to the increasing power of outside corporate might in the region. Tall, massive, disconnected from the life of the streets, buildings of the 1960s, 1970s, and 1980s symbolized the upward thrust of material growth. By and large the new factories, highways, and bridges were also disappointing. Exceptions to these trends were Portland's Georgia Pacific Building, the tallest reinforced concrete structure in the nation when erected; the Weyerhaeuser Building in Federal Way, Washington; the Pope and Talbot mill at Oakridge, Oregon; the Fremont Bridge across the Willamette River at Portland; and a series of U.S. National Bank branch buildings in Oregon. Government buildings were unimpressive, the most offensive being Michael Graves's Portland Building, a testimony to ossified bureaucracy.

Of the campuses, one of the most attractive in the nation is in Bend, Oregon. The Eugene firm, WEGROUP, designed the Central Oregon Community College campus from furniture to buildings to landscaping. It is magnificently integrated with the natural setting. Alva Aalto did the superb library at Mt. Angel Seminary in Oregon, a beautiful building that also revealed natural views. Other notable achievements were the Faculty Center at the University of Washington and the brilliant landscaping at Pacific Lutheran University and Western Washington University which links rather disparate buildings into a unified community.

The newest architectural challenges in the Northwest have been in the area of planned resort communities. The first of these was Salishan, on the Oregon Coast. Developed by John Gray after 1961, the designer was John Storrs. Salishan encompasses a hotel, golf course, restaurant, apartments, condominiums, and private homes. The last must be built in conformity to the standards laid down by the developer including the use of indigenous Northwestern materials. Gray followed Salishan with another resort, but in a vastly different environment. Sunriver is located along the Deschutes River in central Oregon. It has a similar variety of accommodations as at Salishan with the addition of bicycle trails, horseback riding, and fishing. Black Butte, owned by California and Portland developers, is a similar development in central Oregon where the Warm Springs Indians also have their Kah-Nee-Ta Resort.

Although the International style dominated postwar architecture, it did not entirely displace regionalism. The new resort complexes depended upon the use of local materials and tried to display the Northwestern scenery to its best advantage. Their low roofs and significant landscaping also connected the work of Belluschi and Yeon with the new era. Both of these men continued to be influential after the war. Yeon's Portland Chamber of Commerce Visitor Information Building was voted one of the ten most significant designs in Oregon's history. Belluschi built another building for Equitable in 1960, a modern skyscraper, and has executed scores of commissions and won many awards. In 1982 his first Equitable Building received the American Institute of Architects Twenty-Five Year Award; the awards jury declaring that "its advanced technology pointed the way for a generation of successors." The houses of Oregon architect C. Gilman Davis and those of John Storrs as well as his Salishan resort continue the Northwest style. But there is no dominant trend at the present as architects grope for satisfying forms among the uncertainties of the 1980s.

Beyond the formal arts, the Northwest's cultural life remains undistinguished. The great population boom after the Second World War produced many new schools and several new colleges and universities; especially numerous at the level of higher education were the community colleges. Television joined the press as purveyor of news and popular culture. Historical agencies developed. Yet the fundamental fact of the Northwest's cultural life, formal or popular, is that the citizens of Oregon and Washington have not generally expected, demanded, or paid for institutions that go beyond the merely competent. Almost none are of the highest national standard.

The Advance of the Suburb

Population growth in the Pacific Northwest was extremely rapid after the war. Washington's population grew 20 percent from 1950 to 1960; 19 percent from 1960 to 1970; and 21 percent from 1970 to 1980. Oregon's growth was 16 percent from 1950 to 1960; 18 percent from 1960 to 1970; and 26 percent from 1970 to 1980. Most of this growth was in the suburbs, growth that had a range of side effects: demand for housing, transportation changes, styles of merchandising, and the attraction of industry from central cities.

In Seattle the boom in the aerospace industry made for a megalopolis from the Kent River valley south of the city north to Everett. Population leaped across Lake Washington to the east into the communities of Bellevue and Kirkland. Around Tacoma there was expansion northward to Kent and south to Parkland and Spanaway. To the east, the city advanced to the Federal Way region, site of the new international headquarters of the Weyerhaeuser Corporation. Spokane expanded, although not at nearly the rate of the Puget Sound communities. Growth of suburbs came to the smaller towns as well. Yakima moved to the west. Vancouver has grown eastward along the Columbia River and to the north. In Oregon, Portland has spawned suburban growth. Westward, new developments have surrounded old towns like Beaverton and stretch almost to Hillsboro. To the east and south the farmlands have given way to housing developments. In Salem and Eugene tract housing has proliferated with the growth of state government and the university, respectively. In southern Oregon in the Rogue River valley the population has increased with migration of industry and the development of retirement and second homes.

To facilitate the movement of people from their suburban homes to their places of work, new highways, given the name of freeway, have been constructed. Ostensibly designed to connect separate cities across the nation, their real purpose was to benefit the commuter. Funding came in the Federal Highway Act of 1956 which allocated 92 percent of the funds for the interstate highway system to the federal government. In the Pacific Northwest, sections of three interstate highways were built. Highway I-5 ran from the California line to Canada, passing through Roseburg, Eugene, Salem, Portland, Olympia, Tacoma, Seattle, Everett, and Bellingham. Interstate 80-N (now 84) followed the Columbia River east of Portland through The Dalles, then on to Pendleton, and Boise in Idaho. In northern Washington, Interstate 90 crossed from Seattle to Spokane and on to Idaho. These routes facilitated intercity communication. They did some damage to the railroads' business, but their principal destructive force was in urban areas. In Portland I-5 sliced through the black community of Albina and North Portland's white working class sections. It destroyed the ethnic neighborhoods south of the city. In Seattle, quite simply, the city was cut in two and many neighborhoods leveled. Similar damage was wreaked by interstates in other communities.

The pull of suburbia was damaging to older business as well as residential districts. People left the central city not only to live, but to shop. Their mercantile desires were met by the development of the shopping center (or shopping mall). This was a national phenomenon, not confined to the Northwest. The first major modern shopping center in the world was Northgate, constructed in 1950 in Seattle. The most famous early center, proudly proclaimed as the world's largest when completed in 1960, was the Lloyd Center built on the east side of Portland. Its major distinguishing feature was that almost all of its parking spaces were covered. By 1985 practically every town and city, however small, had some kind of shopping center, more or less carefully planned, more or less attractive in architecture and landscaping. The main attractions of shopping centers were simple: plenty of parking and proximity to the suburban tracts. The major centers were all placed on the freeways, another indication that the purpose of these highways was to serve the suburbanite. Industry went to the suburbs also. The Boeing Company expanded south from Seattle into the Kent River Valley. Oregon's Tektronix firm was based in the bedroom community of Beaverton. Office campuses as well as industrial parks proliferated. For a time it seemed as though the only reasons for existence for a central city in the future would be to draw people to the records of government and business centered in city halls and courthouses. By the beginning of the 1960s suburbia seemed the wave of the future.

The Recovery of the Cities

The city, in spite of the appeal of the suburb, had its defenders and saviors. Urban renewal was the first attempt to reshape and revitalize the cities. Beginning in the 1950s, fueled by federal money, city governments allied with developers to level old neighborhoods and to build anew. The results of this crusade were very mixed indeed. The human cost was high. Many old people were displaced from their ancestral homes. The poor among them were driven to decaying hotels in the central district or to welfare; the better off found refuge in nursing homes or in the suburbs. The losses were not only personal, but civic, as colorful ethnic neighborhoods, attractive buildings, and historic associations— variety in other words—were swept away. The process did, however, contribute much of social value.

In Portland the City Council chartered the Portland Development Commission (PDC) in 1958. Its director was Ira Keller. Wielding its power of eminent domain ruthlessly, the PDC condemned scores of city blocks. Its principal achievements were the creation of the Lovejoy Fountain, the closing of streets in the South Park blocks near Portland State University to make an improved park, Pettygrove Park, and the Auditorium Forecourt park and fountain in front of the refurbished Civic Auditorium. Three massive apartment buildings, the Portland Center Complex, arose in the southcentral part of town.

In Seattle and Spokane, this type of urban renewal clearing of housing for office buildings and apartments was supplemented by civic fairs. These were occasions, familiar to the world, of promoting a city through social, cultural, and economic exhibits and entertainment. Seattle's Century 21 Exposition was held in 1962. Its grounds included an opera house remodeled from the old civic auditorium and the striking new structures of the Space Needle with revolving restaurant in the tower; Playhouse—a drama center; Exhibition Hall; and Pacific Science Center. The fair appealed to tourists—it lost no money—and left a cultural legacy for Seattle.

Spokane's turn came in 1974. The site of the fair was the banks of the Spokane River and an island in the center near the falls of the river. After the fair was over the city retained the beautifully landscaped River Front Park and the valuable Riverpark Center contained therein. The last included the opera house, an auditorium, and convention center. The blending of manicured and natural grounds in the park was successful; the marriage of the new Center building with the existing structures less so.

Another rescue effort to save the city was the downtown shopping mall. Portland closed some streets to automobiles, provided bus lanes, and did a small amount of landscaping to form its transit mall. The first pedestrian malls (streets which prohibited vehicles) were in Coos Bay and Eugene in Oregon and in Camas, Washington. Eugene did an elaborate program of street closing, bicycle routes, fountains, and beaches. There were requirements for signs and the landscaping was varied.

Cities became more attractive as they became more culturally sophisticated. In the Seattle area the city and King County both had public arts commissions which provided funds—if matched by private donations—to a variety of the arts. By 1981 Seattle had the largest per capita public support for the arts of any city in the United States. Individual businesses and the Corporate Council for the Arts had given money to arts organizations and to artists. In 1984 Seattle had an art museum, ballet, opera, orchestra, and five equity theaters among its cultural treas-

Space Needle, Seattle. Special Collections Division, University of Washington Libraries

ures, most developed in the last two decades. Although Portland has made some progress in these years, its cultural institutions still lag far behind Seattle. The city, however, has great hopes for its Center for the Performing Arts. It will include a concert hall and two theaters. Eugene opened its Hult Center for the Performing Arts in 1982. But the small city of Ashland is home to Oregon's most famous cultural institution. In 1935 Angus Bowmer founded the Oregon Shakespearean Festival. Bowmer constructed the first Elizabethan stage in North America and he and his successors built a small summer theater program into a major attraction for Oregonians and visitors to the state.

In the late 1960s and early 1970s businessmen, politicians, and ordinary citizens made new, more constructive approaches to city planning than urban renewal. Basic was the rise of neighborhood associations determined to protect the residential quality of their neighborhoods rather than see them turned over to industry and to be a participant in, rather than a recipient of, municipal agencies' decisions. Their organization and determination made them influential in city halls. One way that the urban dwellers came to preserve their homes was to participate in the historic preservation movement. Congress in 1966 passed the National Historic Preservation Act. This statute expanded the National Register of Historic Places to include state and local properties of architectural or historical significance. For this purpose the federal government provided funds to State Historic Preservation offices (SHPO). In Washington the Office of Archaeology and Historic Preservation was created in 1967 and placed in the State Parks and Recreation Commission. In Oregon the responsibilities of the State Historic Preservation Office were first given to the State Highway Engineer in 1967. The SHPOs receive nominations for the National Register. After approval of their advisory committees, the state agencies forward the nominations to Washington, D.C. Several benefits come to the owners of historic properties. Their property is protected from the impact of federal projects. In both Oregon and Washington the state gives tax incentives to the owners of National Register properties. For commercial buildings, federal law permits costs of improvement to be amortized over five years or to be depreciated at an accelerated rate. Preservation programs in the Pacific Northwest have moved ahead vigorously since 1967. Many properties have been placed on the National Register and others have received protection through local ordinances. Several cities have founded agencies to protect historical and architectural landmarks. Seattle's Landmarks Board (1973) was the first in Washington. In Oregon, Portland's Landmarks Commission, founded in 1975, was the first in the state.

The most famous of these preservation efforts is linked with another response to the pressure of suburbia, the movement to rehabilitate the central area of the cities. In Portland developers William and Samuel Naito took the lead in reshaping much of the Skid Road area into shops and restaurants. This Old Town region is proof of the economy of restoring old buildings to draw people back to the central city. The Skidmore-Old Town area and the Yamhill area are both districts on the National Register. In Seattle the old farmers' market, the Pike Place Market, was under pressure from urban renewal after the Second World War. Seattle's Pike Place Market Historic District was created in 1970, the first district listed on the National Register. Its defenders were able to save the market from demolition for apartments, a hotel, and a parking garage by the passage of a city initiative measure in 1971. A dedicated preservationist group was also able to save the original center of Seattle through the creation of the Pioneer Square Historic District. Both of these districts have been profitable in bringing tourists and residents to the central city. In 1985 there were forty-four Washington historic districts listed on the National Register; there were twenty-one in Oregon.

Innovations in regional government also helped save the cities. Both Seattle (1958) and Portland (1970) developed metropolitan-wide service districts to handle matters such as sewage, zoos, and waste disposal that were beyond the effective power of existing metropolitan agencies. Portland's was the first in the nation to have directly elected officials, a proposal principally developed by a Portland State University professor, Ronald C. Cease, and was the first to include several counties within its area. Seattle's Metro took over the bus lines. In Oregon the legislature created in 1969 a Tri-County Metropolitan Transportation District (Tri-Met) to run Portland's buses. It absorbed the city's suburban lines in the following year.

NOTES

1. University of Oregon Museum of Art, *A University Collects: Oregon Pacific Northwest Heritage* (1966), p. 10.
2. Ibid., p. 45.
3. Portland, *Willamette Week*, June 25, 1979, p. 9.

SUGGESTIONS FOR READING

The best sources for recent cultural developments are the metropolitan newspapers. *Seattle Magazine* (1964–1969) is helpful in this area. On architecture, the best surveys are Thomas Vaughan and Virginia G. Ferriday, *Space, Style, and Structure: Building in Northwest America* (1974); Sally B. Woodbridge and Roger Montgomery, *A Guide to Architecture in Washington State* (1980); and Rosalind Clark, *Architecture: Oregon Style* (1983). For art, see National Collection of Fine Arts, *Art of the Pacific Northwest from the 1930s to the Present* (1974); Martha Kingsbury, *Northwest Tradition* (1978); University of Oregon Museum of Art, *A University Collects: Oregon's Pacific Northwest Heritage* (1966); Seattle Art Museum, *Northwest Traditions* (1978); Michael R. Johnson, ed., *Kenneth Callahan: Universal Voyage* (1973); Federick S. Wight et al., *Morris Graves* (1956); Foster White Collection of Fine Arts, *Mark Tobey* (1974); National Collection of Fine Arts, *Mark Tobey* (1974). On urban renewal see Carl Abbott, *Portland: Planning, Politics, and Growth in a Twentieth Century City* (1983). Two anthologies dealing with cultural matters are Edwin R. Bingham and Glenn A. Love, eds., *Northwest Perspectives: Essays on the Culture of the Pacific Northwest* (1979) and William G. Robbins et al., *Regionalism and the Pacific Northwest* (1983).

Politics and Economics after the Second World War, 1945–1985

The postwar years were exciting ones that saw many superficial changes take place in political and economic life. Below the surface, however, the Pacific Northwest remained fundamentally conservative politically and continued to be a dependent region economically. No more than in the cultural realm was a homogeneous, self-satisfied citizenry eager to launch into new directions. Paradoxically, even the innovations were designed to preserve the best of the past.

The Politics of Interest and Party

The American political system has always included interest groups which have organized politically to advance their causes. In these years in the Northwest old interest groups did not fade away, but new ones did spring up as society became more complex. Farmers were far fewer than in the days of the pioneers and less progressive than before the Second World War. Their old organization, the Grange, became more conservative.

Business itself, like agriculture, did not present a united front politically. Timber companies, for example, could be divided into those with their own stands of timber and those without. The former favored government policies permitting log exports, the latter opposed them. In a general way business supported the existing tax system (sales and property taxes in Washington, income and property taxes in Oregon), favored efficient government, opposed government regulations such as those controlling pesticides, and resisted certain types of labor legislation such as state monopoly of workmen's compensation.

Labor—the AFL State Labor Councils, the Teamsters, and the Long-shoremen—was active in politics, but it was very difficult for a labor organization to deliver the votes of its members. In general, labor was more effective on labor issues, far less so in supporting causes or candidates not strictly identified with improving wages, hours, or working conditions. Labor's influence has fallen with declining membership; for example, the Oregon AFL-CIO lost about one-third of its membership (106,000 to 70,535) from 1974 to 1984. Schoolteachers, senior citizens, and environmentalists have had a good deal of influence within their limited spheres. The state employees represent a formidable group, almost always opposed to government reorganization or reduced programs. They unite with senior citizen groups in the pursuit of improved pensions.

The fortunes of political parties rose and fell in no particular pattern after the war. They remained weak, with internal rivalries occupying them as much as struggle against their rivals. In Oregon, the Democratic party became more liberal as leaders such as Howard Morgan, Monroe Sweetland, Edith Green, Richard Neuberger, and Don S. Willner shaped the party's policies. In general, the liberals represented urban interests which desired a greater role for government in education and welfare matters. Their supporters were the standard Democratic coalition of labor, teachers, intellectuals, and members of ethnic groups. In the 1950s they won control of their party and several elections, restoring Oregon to the ranks of two-party states that it had lost at the turn of the century.

In 1954 Edith Green was elected to the national House of Representatives from the Portland metropolitan district and Richard Neuberger to the United States Senate (the first Democrat to hold that position since George Chamberlain who left office in 1921, except for Alfred E. Reames, who served nine months by appointment in 1938). In 1956 Robert Holmes was elected governor to fill out the unexpired term of Paul Patterson (who had died in office), ending a Democratic drought since 1939 in that position. In 1958 the Democrats won three of four national House seats, and both houses of the state legislature for the first time since 1878. However, the liberal Democrats were neither without problems nor without conservative Democratic rivals. The major liberal difficulties began when Wayne Morse initiated a feud with Neuberger, based mainly on personality conflicts, and forced Democrats to choose sides. The conservative group was a carryover from the 1930s reinforced by conservative elements among the migrating war workers of the 1940s. Their influence was considerable, for at times they joined with the minority Republican party to control the state senate and to block several progressive measures in that house.

In Washington the Democrats continued their prewar dominance of the state legislature after a brief setback in 1946 when the Republicans elected one United States senator, five of six representatives, and won both houses of the state legislature. But the party continued its progressive-conservative split. Progressives won control of the party and most of the elections since 1956 when the Democrats captured both houses of the state legislature; Albert Rosellini was elected governor in 1956 and 1960. By the 1960s there came to be three factions in Washington's Democratic party. The liberals, composed of the same elements as their Oregon counterparts, who had backed United States senators Henry M. Jackson and Warren G. Magnuson, now divided as many opposed Jackson's support of the Vietnam War. The conservative Democrats, heirs of the Bourbons of the 1930s, were the third element. One of their own, Dixy Lee Ray, the state's first woman governor, was elected in 1976, although her conservatism became more evident after her election than before it.

The Democrats gained power in the federal House of Representatives. In 1964 they turned a six to one Republican advantage into a five to two Democratic margin, the first Democratic delegation from the state since 1945. The delegation has remained Democratic since that time. But the demise of the old New Deal Democratic coalition was vividly marked by the defeat of Senator Magnuson in 1980 whose vigorous opponent as well as whose own age, poor health, big-government advocacy, and loyalty to the unpopular President Jimmy Carter cost him the election. In 1983 the party sustained a further loss with the death of Senator Jackson and the subsequent appointment and election of former governor Daniel Evans, a Republican, in his place.

In spite of Democratic gains since the 1940s, the Northwest remains very much a two-party region. In Oregon, the Republican party was placed on the defensive by the Democratic gains of the 1940s and 1950s and by the tragic death in 1947 in an airplane crash of Governor Earl W. Snell, Secretary of State Robert S. Farrell, Jr., and Senate President Marshall E. Cornett. After liberal Republican Mark O. Hatfield, Jr., was elected governor in 1958, his policies contributed to intraparty divisions by alienating Republican conservatives. But the party recouped its fortunes in the mid-1960s by fielding many able candidates (who played down partisanship) from its progressive wing. Although the Republicans have not retaken control of the Oregon legislature, they have won back both United States Senate seats, in 1966 and 1968, respectively, and have prevailed in most of the statewide elective offices. In winning these contests, the backbone of the party has been business, professional people, and the ever-growing number of suburbanites.

Similarly in Washington the Republicans have become more electable since their troubles in the 1950s. The party nadir was in 1958 when the Republicans were divided badly over a right-to-work initiative which contributed to its minority status. Hard work, attractive candidates, and competition for party control between moderates and right-wingers led to a Republican resurgence in the 1960s.

Governor Daniel Evans (1955–1977) was the Republican leader. He was the youngest person ever elected governor of Washington and the only one ever elected to three consecutive terms. Another young progressive Republican, A. Ludlow Kramer, was elected secretary of state in 1964. In 1980 Republicans John Spellman and Slade Gorton were elected governor and United States senator, respectively. In 1983 Evans replaced Henry Jackson in the Senate, joining his political ally to form a Republican team to replace the Jackson-Magnuson tandem. But the Republican party has been by no means united. It was moderately conservative under the leadership of Governor Arthur Langlie throughout the 1950s. In the 1960s and early 1970s progressive Governor Evans assisted by his attorney general Slade Gorton kept the party out of the hands of the right-wing John Birch element—centered in Yakima and Spokane, although there were many in Seattle, too—for most of his three terms in office. Then in the mid-1970s Republican conservatives, enraged by the liberal accomplishments of the Evans' wing captured control of the formal party apparatus by diligent organizational work. Although conservatives have won control of the Republican party, their causes— opposition to abortion, prayer in public schools, for example—have not found favor with the electorate. Since 1940, indeed, most Republican victors have belonged to the progressive wing of the party. Republicans, mostly very conservative ones, won control of the legislature in 1980 for the first time since 1956, but lost it in 1982.

Regardless of their components Pacific Northwest political parties are very weak. There are several reasons for this condition including direct legislation; the Washington blanket primary; the presence of a presidential primary in Oregon which means that state and presidential nominating delegates are not chosen by party conventions; the tradition of political independence; the habit of switching parties; and the practice of splitting tickets. Above all the social and economic homogeneity of the region means that political parties are not needed to help particular groups achieve something from government against the wishes of another. Until the retrenchment of the 1970s there has seemed to be enough for all, especially since everybody wanted the same thing. As a result, historically, voters have felt free to vote for candidates on the basis of their personalities or their stand on the issues, not the party label.

The Issues

Some of the issues attacked by the interests and parties were short-term (e.g., civil rights and government reorganization) while others endured, for example, taxation and environmental use. After the war blacks gained as the two states were among the first to pass a full range of civil rights laws. Oregon adopted a public accommodations law in 1953, Washington in 1971. Fair employment legislation came to Oregon and Washington in 1949. The national guard was integrated. Blacks moved into the political process as candidates and officeholders. Democrat William McCoy was the first black person elected to the Oregon legislature (1973); the first black legislator in Washington in the twentieth century was Republican Charles M. Stokes, chosen in 1950. In 1969 Stokes became the first black chosen as a justice court judge in the state's history. Voters elected the first black to the city council in Portland in 1976, and in Seattle in 1967. James E. Chase was elected mayor of Spokane in 1981, one of the few black mayors of large cities west of the Mississippi River. School systems in the major cities, although not legally segregated, moved toward greater integration, although not all blacks approved the particular methods or the aim of integration in their communities.

Although (or perhaps because) they are not very numerous, other nonwhite groups have also had a good deal of political success. Indians obtained favorable federal judicial and legislative actions, although they lost in federal court in 1982 their struggle to keep the state from collecting liquor and cigarette sales taxes on the reservation. In Washington and in Oregon there were gubernatorial commissions established for blacks, Hispanics, Indians, and Asians (the last in Washington only). These gains were not controversial for most of the white electorate (except for the commercial fishermen and sportsmen enraged by the Indians' fishing rights, and those who contested Indian water rights) never felt itself in danger of being swamped by people of different races.

As befitting a region that has emphasized governmental efficiency, government reorganization has been a recurring issue in the past few decades. The region has also reflected a national interest in governmental reorganization, a concern over the growth of all levels of government. There has been a lot of interest in this issue by good government groups and by businesses hopeful of reducing taxes for state services. Some of the federal programs of the 1960s required the states to make their budgetary procedures more efficient. As the executive branch became more professional, the state legislatures in turn sought to acquire budgetary, fiscal, and research offices to match the informational resources (hence power) of the governors.

In Washington, Governor Dan Evans proposed several legislative measures to modernize the state government. He wanted, above all, to create a department of transportation from several existing agencies, but the legislature, responding to pressures from bureaucratic, highway, and port interests, repeatedly defeated or sidetracked this measure. Evans was successful, however, in getting approval in 1970 for consolidation of several agencies into two new departments: the Department of Ecology and the Department of Social and Health Services. After Evans left office, the legislature did create a Department of Transportation, but not in the form he had desired. In Oregon relatively little was accomplished. In 1961 Governor Hatfield tried to reshape the 141 agencies which reported to the governor. The purpose of Hatfield's reorganization plan was to give the governor, who was responsible in the eyes of the voters, more authority over the executive branch. He wanted a series of larger departments whose heads would serve as the governor's cabinet. But the forces of inertia and self-interest, represented by the state bureaucracy and the economic groups it depended upon, were brought to bear upon the legislature which defeated comprehensive reorganization. The legislature, however, accepted a Department of Commerce in 1967.

Governor Thomas L. McCall tried again in the late 1960s. The legislature did adopt some of McCall's recommendations. In 1969 it created the Department of Transportation from the former Highway Commission, Board of Aeronautics, Department of Motor Vehicles, and the Marine Board. It also created a formal executive department that included responsibility for finance, local government relations, personnel, and economic development. Another major change was the establishment of the Department of Human Resources (1971) to be responsible for the state's welfare, correctional, and healing institutions. Most controversial of all was the merger of the formerly separate fish and game commissions into the Department of Fish and Wildlife in 1975. All of these changes affected bureaucratic and special interests, and all were achieved in the face of their fierce opposition. In 1981 the legislature reorganized the court system by giving the chief justice administrative authority over the appellate, circuit, district, and tax courts. Defense of governmental reorganization as a measure to save taxes was what probably convinced the voters whenever they supported it.

The citizens' fear of change that could not or was not presented in taxsaving terms was evident in the defeat of a new constitution in Oregon. In 1961, the Oregon legislature established a Constitutional Revision Commission but its efforts were defeated in the state legislature in 1965. In Washington, also, attempts to revise significantly the state constitution or to call a convention to form a new one were proposed in 1965, 1967, and 1978. All resulted in failure.

The legislatures did succeed in improving their efficiency. Oregon was one of the first two states to have a legislative fiscal office. Washington legislators expanded their office space; those in Oregon built two new wings on the capitol building for this purpose. After 1972 the Washington legislature moved to a system of year-round committees with permanent staffs. In 1979, the voters approved a constitutional amendment providing for regular annual sessions. By 1981, Oregon and Washington were two of ten states in the nation with sophisticated legislative information systems.

Reapportionment of the state legislature was accomplished in these years in Washington state, but only through the prodding of the federal government. The rural counties of the region were overrepresented in the legislatures and legislators refused to reapportion themselves equitably. The legislature of Oregon had not reapportioned itself since 1911, of Washington, not since 1901, although the Washington legislature was reapportioned by initiative in 1930. This reluctance was not so much due to the rural voter's fear of democracy, but the desires of politicians and agribusiness interests to keep the status quo.

In 1952 the Oregon voters approved an initiative measure to reapportion the state legislature equitably. It was the first state to do so voluntarily. Four years later, Washington voters approved an initiative measure to reapportion their legislature, but it was amended to uselessness by the legislators in 1957. Finally, the United States Supreme Court decisions in the cases of *Baker* v. *Carr* (1962), *Reynolds* v. *Sims* (1964), and *Wesberry* v. *Sanders* (1964) required that both state legislatures and congressional districts be fairly apportioned according to the principle of "one man, one vote."

In 1961 the Oregon Supreme Court ordered the secretary of state to reapportion the state legislature. Four years later the state legislature reapportioned the state's congressional districts in a special session. It did so again in 1981 after the state gained a fifth congressional following the 1980 census. The Washington legislature both reapportioned itself, and the state's congressional districts, in 1965. In 1972 the courts appointed a special master to reapportion the legislature after the legislature had failed to reapportion itself in 1971 and 1972. The legislators reapportioned the congressional seats again in 1981 when Washington gained a ninth seat after the 1980 census. The congressional reapportionment held for the 1982 elections and then was rejected by the judiciary. Finally in 1983 Washington voters overwhelmingly passed a constitutional amendment requiring a bipartisan commission to redistrict every ten years.

Taxation remained the most persistent, most emotional, and most intractable governmental problem of the entire postwar years. As the period opened, both states depended heavily upon the property tax for local expenditures, Oregon more so than Washington. State revenues derived mainly from the sales tax in Washington and the income tax in Oregon. Even though the system was inequitable in many respects (although primarily beneficial to business in both states), fear of the consequences of changing it has prevented the development of a fair and efficient tax system.

What many voters craved was a reduction in property taxes, indeed a reduction of their total tax burden. In Oregon this desire took the form of recurrent attempts to amend the constitution to place a limitation on the property tax. In 1968 the voters defeated a property tax limitation as they did again in 1978 and 1982.

Pressure for property tax reduction required some other form of revenue raising unless state and local services were to be drastically curtailed. One candidate in Oregon was the sales tax. Although it had been defeated in earlier years, it was brought up again in 1969 and submitted to the voters. It was defeated by a margin of eight to one. In 1971 Governor McCall drafted the most imaginative tax plan of the era. His proposal was that the state should increase its support of public schools by raising income taxes on personal and business income over $15,000 and by equalizing state school funds among rich and poor school districts. Although most of the citizens of the state would have had lower tax bills, wealthy people and business assailed the measure. It was defeated in a campaign of mudslinging and misrepresentation. But no one in Oregon has developed a convincing program to afford property tax relief while raising sufficient money to run a modern government. In recent years the burgeoning high technology industry of Oregon has become the militant vanguard of a pro sales tax, anti–increased property and income tax movement. In 1984 a state lottery was instituted, but a sales tax was again defeated in 1985.

In Washington the tax reformers wished to introduce an income tax as a supplement to the state sales tax and as a means to reduce the property tax. Property taxes were limited or reduced in 1932, 1934, 1972, 1975, 1977, and 1979. They became even less important after a ruling by Thurston County Superior Court Judge Robert Doran (a decision upheld by the Washington Supreme Court in 1979) that the state constitution required that adequate state funds be spent to provide a basic education for each pupil in the state. This decision had the effect of substantial equalization of state expenditures in every school district in the state. Both before and after the Doran decision, the need for state revenue led to renewed efforts by educationists, some labor unions, and the good government forces to obtain an income tax or other source of revenue. However, voters overwhelmingly defeated some form of the income tax in 1967, 1970, 1973, and 1975. Sales taxes on food were on a roller coaster. They were part of the original tax in 1935, removed in 1978, restored in 1982, removed in 1983. As a desperation measure, the voters adopted the regressive state lottery in 1981 as an allegedly painless and exciting source of revenue. Indeed, four years earlier, the *Wall Street Journal* called Washington's tax system "the most regressive in the nation." The core of all this maneuvering over taxes is that, as Oregonians, Washingtonians have been unwilling to tax themselves beyond support for a bare competence of state services. They have exercised much ingenuity in attempting to evade the fiscal obligations of modern life.

Environmental Protection

One contribution that did not cost money to individual taxpayers directly, but was progressive, indeed of national importance, was environmental legislation. Pioneered in Oregon, it also received support in Washington. The origin of it was the postwar baby boom in Oregon, the huge population movement into the state, and the rising national affluence that made it possible for vast numbers of Americans to become tourists. These new phenomena seemed to threaten the traditional Oregon appreciation for nature as economic provider and as aesthetic and spiritual inspiration. Out of these developments came forth enormous pressure on the natural environment from residential subdivisions, airports, condominiums, coastal and desert resorts, and shopping centers. Farmland, beaches, and deserts seemed on the path to rapid disappearance. Sewage and industrial pollution fouled lakes and rivers. Air became laden with smog.

The Willamette River was Oregon's longest river and one with numerous historical associations. It was also by 1961 unsafe for bathing and deadly to fish. Its condition caused the first public attention to Tom McCall as an environmentalist. While a television broadcaster in Portland, McCall was principally responsible for preparing, in 1961, a program, entitled "Pollution in Paradise," that emphasized the fouling of the Willamette. The program reached a wide audience and spurred the State Sanitary Authority to action. The Authority earlier had set water quality standards, but it lacked power to prosecute violators of these standards. After McCall became governor in 1967 he obtained a new law—over the opposition of municipalities and paper companies—that required permits for discharging polluting materials. The results were spectacular. People could now swim in the Willamette and fish could live in it.

The same success in rolling back this particular industrial evil occurred in Seattle. The water jewel of the city, Lake Washington, was beslimed and besmirched by municipal sewage. The environmental nerve that had been touched in Oregon responded. A group called Forward Thrust assumed leadership in Seattle. The voters turned to and created the Metropolitan Municipality of Seattle ("Metro") with authority to clean up the lake. The task was completed in the years from 1958 to 1970.

In the 1960s land was as much a matter of concern to the region's citizens as water. Again, Oregon led, Washington followed. Again, in Oregon, the Willamette River was the first concern. For many years Karl W. Onthank, dean of students at the University of Oregon, had been advocating some means to preserve the still largely unspoiled banks of the Willamette River. He wanted to preserve the river principally as a site for recreation for the growing urban population of the Willamette Valley.

The chance to do so came in the 1966 gubernatorial campaign. Both candidates, first Robert Straub, then Tom McCall, endorsed the idea. When McCall won he persuaded the legislature in 1967 to pass the Willamette River Park System Act over the opposition of farmers who feared that the new parks adjacent to their property would lead to vandalism or to the building of trails across their lands to connect the parks. The state also purchased some lands along the river banks that was not up to park quality to protect them from development.

In 1973 the legislature adopted the Willamette River Greenway Act. It required the Department of Transportation to develop a plan for the various components within a "greenway" along the river. The 1973 law also provided for state acquisitions of scenic easements, for five major parks, and for a commitment to maintain farming as a legitimate Greenway use. All in all, some progress was made during McCall's administration in realizing the Greenway concept, but it was modest.

After Robert Straub was inaugurated as governor in 1975, the Land Conservation and Development Commission (described below) obtained the authority to oversee the Greenway plan. This change brought down upon the Greenway many of the progrowth enemies of LCDC: gravel pit operators, lumbermen, land developers, and industrialists. By 1985 the Greenway included 510 miles of bank land that belonged to the state and local governments. (The entire length of the river is 270 miles.) In a way the Greenway was an exercise in nostalgia; it was an attempt by urban people to preserve wild nature and historical uses of nature. Although flawed and criticized, the Greenway was testimony to the willingness of Oregonians to use government rationally for the public interest.

A truly progressive measure—one that was the first in the nation—was the statute establishing statewide land use planning administered by a Land Conservation and Development Commission in Oregon. Its general causes were the historic Oregon dependence on the land and the

Governor Tom McCall. Thompson photograph, Oregon Historical Society

population pressures of the 1950s and 1960s. The specific beginning was the passage of a law in 1969 that required each town and county to begin land classification, to assign specific uses for all land according to a list of ten goals. If the local units failed to adopt these goals, then the statute empowered the governor to do so. The law was epochal, and infuriating to land use speculators, developers, real estate interests and farmers hoping to sell land for subdivisions; believers in absolute private ownership of land; and all those who feared defense of the public welfare would crimp their personal schemes to make money. They placed, by the initiative process, a measure to repeal the planning law on the ballot in the 1970 general election. The repeal measure was soundly defeated, but the law did have one major weakness. It provided no financial support to the local governments to meet the goals.

Governor McCall took the leadership in framing a revised planning statute. In an address to the legislature in 1973 he declared: "The interests of Oregon for today and in the future must be protected from grasping wastrels of the land. We must respect another truism. Unlimited and unregulated growth leads inexorably to a lowered quality of life."[1]

McCall and Senators Ted Hallock, Hector Macpherson, and L. B. Day were the moving forces in reshaping the law. The enforcement agency was no longer the governor, but a newly created Land Conservation and Development Commission, although the goals remained and the initiating body was still local government. Each county and city was required by 1976—although many extensions were subsequently given—to draw up a comprehensive land use plan. The plan would be approved by LCDC when it met all ten of the goals. It then had the force of law. However, the plan could be modified at a later time if conditions changed. In other words, the plan was flexible, not fossilized. A person objecting to part of the plan could appeal it to the special Court of Land Use Appeals. The court would then rule if a component of the plan met the goals or not; if not, then the plan would have to be changed. The process was holistic and continuing until the LCDC ruled that the plan met all the goals. This bill, passed later in 1973, was influential far beyond the borders of Oregon.

It led to an attempt by Senator Jackson of Washington in alliance with Representative Morris K. Udall of Arizona to get federal land use legislation passed. After President Richard M. Nixon called for land use planning in 1970, Jackson got a land use bill through the Senate twice in the 1970s. His bill would have given money to the several states to develop land use plans for resource use of "more than local concern." The Jackson-Udall measure was defeated in the House of Representatives in 1974 after the Nixon administration, catering to the wishes of business groups, withdrew its support.

LCDC also faced sporadic opposition from interest groups and far-right ideologists within Oregon. In 1976, 1980, and 1982 they placed repeal measures on the ballot, but the electorate defeated them. Besides the citizens, a special defender of LCDC was a unique pressure group, the 1000 Friends of Oregon, founded in 1975 by Tom McCall, Glenn Jackson, powerful chairman of the state highway commission, and other defenders of the environment. Its sole purpose was to monitor, by legal challenges if necessary, the local plans submitted to LCDC. The Friends have forced many changes in local plans through timely litigation that have preserved the state's landed heritage.

A related measure was the bottle deposit law. Oregonians and Washingtonians were not immune from the national disease of littering, an unseemly by-product of the "throwaway" society. Again, Tom McCall was the political leader in Oregon to attack this problem; his principal civic ally was businessman John Piacentini. They hit upon a simple, practical device, as novel as the Greenway and LCDC. This was the bottle bill enacted in 1971. It required that all beer and soft drink containers be returnable, that is, that a deposit fee be charged on each beverage container, to be refunded when the container was returned to the store. This was an imaginative action that required no state enforcement whatsoever, the collection agency being beverage purchasers and citizens, both old and young, who would scour the countryside and urban trash barrels in an endless quest for cans and bottles.

The original bill faced one source of major opposition—certain labor unions who feared (erroneously, as it turned out) that the replacement of the throwaway container would cost them their jobs. Their fight was joined by brewers and soft drink bottlers who argued that the deposit fee would price their product out of the market. Opponents were not able to prevent passage of the bill in the legislature. Undaunted, they challenged the law in court, but it was upheld at every level. It also became a matter of national interest. Many states considered similar laws, and by 1983, nine had adopted them. By this date, also, a national Beverage Container Reuse and Recycling Bill was before Congress. One state which did not follow Oregon's example was neighboring Washington. Both in 1970 and in 1982 the voters turned down a bottle bill convincingly, accepting the extremely well-financed arguments of the unions and the beverage corporations.

Washingtonians expressed a similar disdain for the protection of nature in their lack of concern for the scenic gorge of the Columbia River. This 480-square-mile area, extending from the city of The Dalles to Portland, was hallowed by Indian and pioneer history, and, surprisingly, was reasonably well preserved, especially on the Oregon side where most of the land was in federal hands. By the late 1970s, however, the pressures of civilization began to bear heavily upon the gorge. It was not hard to predict their results in destruction of the environment. Between 1980 and 1982 a voluntary association, the Friends of the Columbia Gorge, composed mainly of Oregonians, gathered support and had introduced a bill into Congress to create a national scenic area in the gorge. The fate of the measure is in doubt, because of the opposition of speculators, developers, and antigovernment forces.

Other areas in which Oregon has been in the environmental forefront include preservation of wild rivers, the ban on aerosol spray cans, and air pollution control. In 1970 the Oregon legislature declared certain portions of six rivers, the Deschutes, Illinois, John Day, Minam, Owyhee and Rogue (Sandy and Clackamas were added in 1973 and 1975 and the north fork of the middle fork of the Willamette River and Waldo Lake, both in 1983) to be protected from dams or impoundment. In 1975 the Oregon legislature passed a law banning the use of fluorocarbons in aerosol spray cans because of their potential destructiveness of the earth's ozone layer.

There was nothing potential about another danger. In the 1960s hundreds of residents of Oregon's Willamette Valley suffered severe attacks of air pollution from smoke. They suffered from the fumes produced when farmers who raised grass seed burned their fields in the late summer and fall to kill destructive rodents and insects. When the grass seed industry refused to cooperate voluntarily, McCall used his executive powers in 1969 to prohibit field burning temporarily. Subsequently, the state worked out an accommodation that limited field burning to a few weeks in the year. In the 1970s the widespread use in both Oregon and Washington of wood-burning stoves for heat—begun in part as a conservation measure—created another source of smoke pollution.

Washington's Environmental Concerns

Washingtonians were also active in environmental causes. They participated in environmental groups including branches of local organizations such as the Sierra Club, local groups, and the Washington Environmental Council, an "umbrella" group. Environmentalists obtained the North Cascades National Park in 1968. They forced the municipal utility, Seattle City Light, to abandon plans for nuclear plants. Also, City Light had to give up its plan to raise the height of two dams because thousands of acres of North Cascades wilderness would have been flooded in return for only a moderate amount of new electric power. They prevented the Northern Tier pipeline (a plan to move Alaskan oil from Puget Sound to the Middle West).

Among their victories were a State Environmental Policy Act (1971) requiring a formalized environmental impact statement on actions with a substantial impact on the environment and the Shorelines Management Act (1972) requiring a complete inventory of the state's shorelines and specific land use plans for them at the local level. For several years the state government had attempted to stem the loss of farm, open space, and timberland by using appraisals for tax purposes based on current use rather than the highest potential use. Washington tried to ban the transportation of high-level radioactive waste through the state, but the federal courts overturned this statute. Environmentalists were not always successful, but they remained persistent and showed signs of remaining a powerful interest group.

Labor Issues

Labor issues were not as spectacular in the postwar years as in the New Deal era. The principal innovation was the adoption in both Oregon and Washington of laws permitting collective bargaining by state government employees. They were pushed by the public school teachers unions, the Washington Education Association and the Oregon Education Association, and the civil service unions. Washington civil service laws in 1960 and 1967 authorized collective bargaining for classified employees as did an Oregon statute in 1963. In 1965 both states passed statutes that permitted negotiations between school boards and certified employees. Washington's legislature in 1967 passed the Public Employees Collective Bargaining Act, the state's first comprehensive law authorizing nonstate public employees to organize for collective bargaining. The effect of these laws is difficult to measure, for organization has come at a time of severe retrenchment in state expenditures. Labor has been successful in both states in obtaining some of the most generous workers compensation benefits in the nation. In 1947 Washington established a public employees retirement system which incorporated city employees in a statute of 1971. In 1945 the Oregon legislature established a public employees' retirement system.

The National Scene

The Pacific Northwest's contribution to national politics has been limited to a few politicians and issues. Of these individuals, Wayne Morse was one of the most famous. Although without prior experience in elective office, he had been elected in 1944 to the United States Senate. In the Senate Morse was a member of the liberal, internationalist wing of the Republican party. He supported the efforts to contain Soviet and Chinese expansion: the Marshall Plan, the North Atlantic Treaty Organization, and the Korean War. He championed the rights of labor—opposing the Taft-Hartley law of 1947—and resisted efforts to dismantle the New Deal. He became a prominent member of the armed services and the foreign relations committees. Although progressive in his views on domestic matters, Morse was not a big spender; he opposed a bill to establish a Columbia Valley Administration; and he made a national reputation in insisting that surplus federal property be disposed of at a fair price to the government.

Always known as an independent within the state of Oregon, Morse gained national attention during the Korean War when he publically defended President Truman's decision to dismiss General Douglas

Senator Wayne Morse. Oregon Historical Society

MacArthur in 1951 as constitutionally proper and strategically sound. But Morse's independence and identification with natural resource issues also made him famous. President Eisenhower and his secretary of the interior, Douglas McKay, a former governor of Oregon, began to push in 1955 what they called their power partnership policy. Although never fully defined, it presumably meant that private enterprise would build power dams that they could afford and that the federal government would not construct them in competition with private industry. It also meant that the federal government would construct multipurpose dams with private groups installing the electricity generating features. This policy became more than a theory in relationship to Hells Canyon on the Snake River. This was the last site in the Northwest suitable for a high multipurpose federal dam. Eisenhower and McKay wanted the

Federal Power Commission (FPC) to license the Idaho Power Company to build three low dams on the Snake River that would provide power, but not navigation, flood control, and recreational benefits. Morse wanted a high dam at Hells Canyon. The FPC approved the power company proposal. Morse was joined in his opposition by most residents of the Northwest, regardless of party affiliation.

Eisenhower's natural resource views was the principal reason for Morse's sensational abandonment of the Republican party in 1952. He remained an independent for three years and then joined the Democratic party in 1955. This switch plus the election of Richard Neuberger in 1954 gave the Democrats control of the United States Senate and made Lyndon B. Johnson majority leader. The showdown between Morse and his old party, and a regional referendum on Eisenhower's resource policy, came in 1956 when Morse overwhelmingly defeated McKay who had resigned his cabinet post to run against him for the Senate.

Morse's final influence on national politics came in the Vietnam conflict. He opposed United States participation from the beginning because he believed the war to be illegal since it had not been declared by Congress and was not sanctioned by the United Nations. "In Vietnam," he declared, "we have totally flouted the rule of law, and we have flouted the United Nations Charter."[2] When in 1964 the administration obtained a resolution from the Senate authorizing the United States to retaliate against North Vietnam for its allegedly unprovoked attack upon two American destroyers in the Gulf of Tonkin, Morse and Senator Ernest Gruening of Alaska were the only two senators voting against it. Eventually the Morse position against American involvement in Vietnam became the national consensus, but at the time it contributed to his defeat in the 1968 election at the hands of Republican Robert Packwood.

For a time Morse was joined in the United States Senate by another Democrat, Richard Neuberger, elected in 1954. Neuberger was a nationally known journalist who fought alongside Morse against the exploitation or disposal of federal resources. He pressed for other liberal measures in the conservative 1950s until his death in 1960. His wife, Maurine, also a former journalist and state legislator, won election (with Morse's support) in 1960, but did not choose to run again in 1966. At that time Mark Hatfield was elected for the first time to the Senate seat that he still holds.

The only member of the House of Representatives from Oregon that has been identified with important national legislation in the postwar years is Edith Green. A former schoolteacher who was first elected to Congress in 1954, Green was the moving spirit in writing the National Defense Education Act of 1958. Passed as a reaction to the Russian technological success of Sputnik, this measure furnished large sums of

Senator Henry M. Jackson. Special Collections Division,
University of Washington Libraries

money for grants and loans for college and university undergraduate
and graduate students across America. It also provided millions of dollars
for new buildings at universities and colleges. It was the largest monetary
commitment of the federal government to education in history. Green
was also instrumental in seeing that the moneys flowing to the states
under the federal government's War on Poverty programs of the late
1960s were controlled by state and local politicians rather than by federal
officials. Disillusioned by the pressures of office and the turbulence of
the national political scene, and because of her own growing conservatism
that seemed out of touch with the times, Edith Green retired from office
in 1973.

   Washington's most influential senators in the era were Warren Magnuson and Henry Jackson. They represented longevity in public office
made possible by faithful attention to the needs of their constituents.
First chosen to the Senate in 1944, Magnuson served until defeated in

1981. Jackson, first elected in 1952, remained in the Senate until his death in 1983. Their long years in office gave them the powerful committee appointments that enabled them to channel millions of federal dollars into the state of Washington. This money ingratiated them still further with the voters. They voted for defense appropriations and took a militant position in foreign affairs (Magnuson less than Jackson), all of which helped secure defense contracts for the Boeing Company, the manufacturing backbone of the state. Trusted by both labor and business for their proeconomic development stances, Magnuson and Jackson were efficient and faithful servants of their constituents.

The issue other than defense that Jackson influenced was natural resources, where he was important in bringing about the Wilderness Act (1964), the Redwoods National Park Act (1968), the Environmental Policy Act (1969), and the North Cascades National Park Act (1968). Jackson also was successful, with Magnuson's help, in preventing Congress from diverting Columbia River water to the American Southwest.

Jackson became as well known nationally as Morse had been. John F. Kennedy considered him carefully for the vice-presidency in 1960. Jackson also aspired to the presidency and made serious efforts to win the office in 1972 and 1976. His name was often mentioned in the 1970s as a possibility for the position of secretary of defense and occasionally for the post of secretary of state. Jackson also opposed Wisconsin's Senator Joseph R. McCarthy's red-baiting tactics; he was a member of the special committee of the United States Senate that censured McCarthy in 1954. Magnuson played a major role in securing consumer protection and public broadcasting legislation. He was also decisive in gaining federal health legislation.

Women and Radicals

Two interesting developments in regional politics in the postwar period were the rising participation of women in governmental affairs and the spasmodic growth of radical movements. The openness of parties and the high level of education of the region's citizens doubtless were general explanations of the phenomenon of women's increasing power in politics. More specific causes were the abilities of the particular women politicians and the need of the weakening Republican party of the state of Washington to get able candidates in the 1970s to enhance its chances at the polls. Edith Green was not the only powerful woman in Oregon's public life. Helen Frye in 1980 became the first woman appointed to the federal bench from Oregon. Betty Roberts was the first woman appointed to the state appeals (1977) and supreme courts (1982). Norma Paulus was elected secretary of state in 1976, the first woman to hold elected state-wide office.

In the same period, the number of women in Washington public life rose. In 1958 Catherine May of Yakima became the state's first woman federal representative. In 1976 Democrat Dixy Lee Ray, former member of the federal Atomic Energy Commission, was elected the Northwest's first woman governor. In 1980 the percentages of women in the Washington (23.8 percent) and Oregon (22.2 percent) legislatures was the second and sixth highest in the nation.

Legislation affecting women in Washington included two statutes passed in 1971. An abortion law ratified via referendum was among the most liberal in the nation. It required no specific reason for abortions, but left the decision to a woman and her doctor. The second statute made gender a part of the state's antidiscrimination statutes, a measure included in Oregon law two years earlier. An advisory Woman's Council also was established in 1971 by Governor Evans. It obtained statutory authority in 1977 through pressure from women's groups, but was abolished by referendum in a backlash against feminism in 1978. Washington is one of the nine states in the Union with a community property law. Oregon also has a liberal abortion law, a state advisory commission for women, and a state prison apprenticeship program for nontraditional job training for women inmates. In 1975 Oregon adopted affirmative action laws declaring that state government should lead in providing fair and equal employment opportunity and creating the position of director of affirmative action within the governor's office. Both states have laws prohibiting credit discrimination on the basis of sex or marital status. Oregon and Washington both ratified the Equal Rights Amendment to the federal constitution, and Washington added one to its own constitution in 1972.

Radicalism in the era appeared first in rightist form. It took the garb of enthusiastic support of McCarthyism in Washington, but gained little support in Oregon. After the war right-wing radicalism appeared as a crusade against domestic "Reds" led by Senator McCarthy. For much of the 1950s, especially the years 1950–1954, the country was preoccupied with McCarthy's (and his imitators') outlandish charges of communist penetration of all aspects of national life.

In Oregon, McCarthyism took the form of a proposed statute to require loyalty oaths from teachers. The bill passed the Senate 25 to 5, with the small band of opponents (containing both liberals and conservatives) including Robert Holmes, later governor, and Richard Neuberger, later United States senator. Although the bill passed the Senate, it was never voted on in the House. Former governor Charles Sprague and William Tugman, editor of the Eugene *Register-Guard,* led the fight against the oath. The state American Legion also opposed it. Oregon remained one of the few states in the Union without a teacher's oath law. The Oregon House also killed at this time a bill passed by the Senate requiring an anticommunist oath for all candidates for public office. Perhaps the impotence of left-wing radicalism prevented more successful conservative attacks upon it.

The fight against communists or perceived communists proceeded more vigorously in Washington. It began earlier than the sensational career of Senator McCarthy. One explanation for Washington's anticommunism is that, historically, the state had been both more radical and more reactionary than Oregon as each side fed upon the misperception of the other. In any case, in 1947 the Washington legislature created the Joint Legislative Fact Finding Committee on Unamerican Activities. Its activities were aimed mainly at radicals on the faculty of the University of Washington. Its chairman was a representative from Spokane, Albert F. Canwell. In 1951 the legislature passed the Washington State Subversive Activities Act. The law penalized membership in "subversive" organizations and required suspected subversives to take a loyalty oath that they were not subversive. In 1955, the Communist party was made illegal in the state. In the same year state employees were also required to sign a loyalty oath.

Anticommunism also became a factor in political campaigns. Opponents tried to pin the charge of communism on Warren Magnuson in his 1950 campaign. Representative Canwell made unsuccessful races for Congress in 1952, 1954, 1962, and 1964 on his antisubversive record. In 1954 the Democratic State Central Committee refused to give party funds to a legislative candidate because he had once been a communist. In 1962 John Goldmark, a legislator from Okanogan, was defeated in the Democratic primary campaign amidst charges by Canwell, organizers for the reactionary John Birch Society, and the *Tonasket Tribune* that he was a communist. Goldmark later sued his detractors for libel, won a $40,000 award, but was not able to collect it because the United States Supreme Court had recently ruled (in *New York Times* v. *Sullivan,* 1964) that public officials could not gain damages unless the untrue statements had been made with actual malice. The judge ruled that this had not occurred in the Goldmark case.

By this time McCarthyism had pretty well run its course. In June 1964 the United States Supreme Court declared the Washington loyalty oath for state employees to be unconstitutional. Governor Evans by 1966 had broken the grip of the John Birch Society on the state Republican party. In Oregon the Republican party had some John Birch members, but the party as a whole never came close to embracing its programs.

Radicalism of the left was also of minor importance after the war.

The communists were discredited by the late 1940s through the horrors of Stalinism and the Russian seizure of Eastern Europe. Some Washington communists and Democrats were convicted in the federal courts of violating the Smith Act of 1940 which prohibited conspiring to overthrow the government. The labor unions abandoned their social militance, confining their efforts to improving wages, hours, and working conditions. The largest group of people who talked of radicalism (although it was not clear what they meant by the term) was the minority of young people—some students, some not—who became enraged by the Vietnam War. From 1966 to 1972 they protested American participation in the war, especially the draft. Others tried to take advantage of the political and cultural malaise of the late sixties and early seventies to replace, peacefully or violently, democracy and capitalism with socialism, communism, or a refurbished version of the cooperative commonwealth. Their favorite targets were not federal officials nor federal installations,

Campus destruction, University of Washington. Special Collections Division, University of Washington Libraries

but rather college and university buildings and administrators. Although most protests took the traditional forms of speeches, letters, meetings, and marches, there were denials of the free speech rights of the majority through sit-ins, classroom disruptions, and campus closures. Even more ominous, university buildings were bombed at the University of Washington and the University of Oregon. Fortunately no one was killed or injured. But the goal of most seemed to be more anti-Americanism than support of any ideology. When the draft was suspended in 1973 the protests largely stopped, and the basic conservatism of the region reigned again.

The Postwar Economy

The postwar years as a whole, although marked by the cycles of a dependent economy, were the most prosperous in the region's history. The war left Washington with the dominance of Boeing in the state's economy; with a population growth from war workers and service personnel; and with labor and capital free for the first time to expand in industries not dependent on natural resources. Oregon, too, gained from these last two developments. The economy still rested upon natural resources, but the manufacturing sector became more varied and the service industries grew mightily. Government continued to play a significant role in regional development. Most important of all the region has become much more closely integrated into the national economy as distance is no longer the great limiting factor that it was in the past. Jet aircraft have drastically reduced travel time and the center of national population has moved westward.

AGRICULTURE

After the Second World War, farming became almost unbelievably complicated as farmers were caught up in enormous changes. The profits of the war years enabled many to take advantage of new developments, but others became victims of the rapidity of change. Agriculture became unprecedentedly productive in these years, but not all shared in its benefits.

One cause of productivity was technological and scientific change. Massive—and expensive—self-propelled combines, circular sprinkling systems, and specialized trucks were developed. Chemical pesticides and insecticides became widespread as did chemical fertilizers. Agricultural scientists developed new strains of wheat that could efficiently use the new fertilizers and resist disease. Farmers raised their land's productivity by becoming more efficient businessmen: cost accountants, calculators, and computers became as common as once were horses, cowboys, and plows. Farmers worked with soil experts and other scientists from the region's agricultural colleges to control erosion and solve other problems. They had to remain aware of price support, crop restriction, marketing, and other agricultural programs of the federal government.

Many farmers lacked the capital, adaptability, or enthusiasm to keep up with change. As a result there were fewer farmers and larger farms with each passing year. The number of farms in Oregon declined from 63,125 in 1945 to 36,000 in 1982; the decrease in Washington in these years was from 79,887 to 39,000 farms. In this same period average farm acreage rose in Oregon from 312.9 acres to 502 acres, in Washington from 209.3 acres to 418 acres. Some of the larger farms were corporate owned. Many of the corporation farms became involved in irrigated agriculture and most of them were capitalized from outside the region or abroad. The first water from the Grand Coulee project flowed on the land in 1952. After 1965 the desert lowlands of the Columbia Plateau opened to the irrigator. But the business was risky and many corporate farms failed with falling markets for potatoes and sugar beets.

Both large and small farmers had to become more knowledgeable about foreign markets. As domestic markets became saturated and as citizens of foreign nations became more affluent, Pacific Northwest farmers looked abroad. Wheat led the way as the principal export. Japan, Korea, the Republic of China (Taiwan), India, and the People's Republic of China were the chief wheat markets. Fruits, alfalfa, specialty crops, and processed foods were also sent abroad.

In spite of all these changes, the agricultural commodities remained the same as in prewar years. In both Oregon and Washington the most valuable agricultural commodities in 1982 were beef cattle, wheat, milk, and hay. Cattle in the postwar years no longer were raised on the open range or went over the long drive. They were raised to sell to feed lot operators who prepared them for the slaughterhouse. The finished meat was sold in the Northwest and in California. The sheep business changed too. Dietary changes, synthetic fibers, and the difficulty of securing competent labor for the tedious business of tending sheep all made the enterprise ever more discouraging. Most who still engaged in the sheep business were farmers who ran a herd of sheep auxiliary to their principal activities. The great continuity between past and present, however, was not the farmers' commodities. It was two other conditions: the need to produce for a commercial market and the vagaries of the weather. Pacific Northwest farmers never had much control over them from the time of the first pioneers. They continued to be at their mercy far too often.

THE FISHERIES

Many changes have occurred since 1895 when the Columbia River was the largest salmon producer in the world. By the 1970s Oregon and Washington each had but 2 percent of the United States canned salmon pack. And in 1979 the last Oregon salmon cannery closed down. The federal and state salmon hatcheries could not maintain adequate commercial fish runs against the pressures of dams, irrigation, and chemical and thermal pollution. Those remaining in the fish processing business, although still concentrating on salmon, turned to other fish and shellfish and to frozen fish processing rather than canning. Other major developments since the war include increased foreign competition from factory ships that catch and process fish at sea. To strike back at foreign nationals, Congress passed the Fisheries Conservation and Management Act in 1976. This law extended the United States jurisdiction in offshore marine fishing waters from 12 to 200 miles. In spite of these actions, depletion of the salmon and other fisheries continued. Federal court decisions guaranteeing Indian fishing rights have also affected the industry. There have been some efforts by the Weyerhaeuser Company in Oregon and the Lummi Tribe in Washington, among others, to farm fish commercially.

FOREST PRODUCTS

The forest products industry remains important in the Pacific Northwest, but it has not stood still. The post–World War Two housing boom enabled the industry to continue its wartime prosperity for several years, although periods of tight money made the industry cyclical. There were downturns in the years when the federal government tried to control inflation. Another great change was technological. The invention of the whole-log barker, for example, made it possible to use an entire tree to make lumber, pulpwood fiber, and chips. In turn this technological advance had a business dimension. The old rivals, lumber and paper, disappeared into a single corporate structure. Companies could now produce the full range of forest products rather than confine themselves to single lines such as lumber, plywood, or pulp.

Other new developments in forest products included the invention of the Kraft process of making pulp from nonwhite-wood trees, like the ponderosa pine. This discovery opened up the area east of the Cascades for the pulp maker, for the ponderosa is the dominant tree in that region. Since pulp uses sawmill wastes—especially for Kraft paper—pulp plants could be built on sawmill sites.

Besides the growth of the pulp industry, plywood and hardboard have become significant. Although plywood was invented in 1904, it became widely used after the war because of the necessity of harvesting old growth trees before their quality declined. By the 1960s, however, southern plywood producers challenged the Northwest as the region's old growth timber was harvested. Hardboard was invented in the 1930s. This wood aggregate became valuable when the quantity of high-grade logs for lumber declined and when cost efficiencies demanded a ruthless crusade against waste of any wood product. More recent particle boards were waferboard and orient-strand board. In the realm of conservation the tree farm idea, begun in Washington in 1941, spread to Oregon after the World War. Private companies and state and national governments expanded their research expenditures and stressed fire protection measures such as public education with slogans and symbols such as "Keep Oregon (or Washington) Green" and Smokey the Bear. In the 1970s the industry began to develop faster growing varieties of Douglas fir and to use even faster growing hemlock rather than Douglas fir for pulpwood. Red alder has become the basis for the western hardwood industry for furniture making.

The forest products industry has changed and survived, but its future is not assured for there are a whole range of volatile factors that affect it. One is that the industry remains remarkably fragmented, made up of many variegated and competitive units. More important the national and world housing market is capricious: forest products corporations must take into account rates of population growth, interest rates, changing agricultural styles, competing building materials, and fluctuating foreign demand.

Yet more and more the productive units became larger. Weyerhaeuser, based in Tacoma, was the sixty-sixth largest American corporation in 1984. The company grew in part by adopting new technology such as computers and lasers in its sawing and measuring operations and the thermo-mechanical pulp process for making newsprint and other papers. By 1982 it had acquired 2,714,000 acres of forest lands in the Pacific Northwest, sufficient to make it the only major American forest products company to have enough trees to supply its own plants and mills. Weyerhaeuser is the largest producer and seller of lumber in the world and also disposes of a variety of other forest products through its own sales organization. The company also has tree farms and a real estate subsidiary, explores for minerals, and sells nursery, chemical, and food products.

By contrast the smaller operators have suffered. They own very little timber themselves and have to purchase it from private owners, state forests, and the federal Bureau of Land Management and the Forest

Service. In the late 1970s many bid up the price of federal timber. When their contracts came due, the collapse of the housing market in the depression of the early 1980s made it impossible for them to meet their commitments. New competition for plywood has hurt the smaller manufacturers of that product and new technology has been too expensive for them to acquire.

AEROSPACE INDUSTRY

The great manufacturing industry of Washington, the Boeing Company, reached its position of eminence only during and after the Second World War. Its wartime contracts made the company successful and allowed it to assemble a skilled production force, outstanding engineers, and a magnificent plant. But the postwar depression almost ruined the company as federal orders fell off. It was saved under the leadership of Howard Allen, who became president in 1945. Boeing developed a series of products for both the national government and the civilian aircraft industry. The Cold War provided orders for B-47 and B-52 bombers and Titan and Minuteman missiles. Then came the decision to produce the world's first civilian jet airplane, the 707, which went into commercial use in 1958. Another Boeing jet, the 727, has sold better than any other. Also popular was the 737 short-range jet and the long-range 747. One product that failed was the Supersonic Transport (SST). The Boeing Company invested heavily in the project and also relied upon a federal subsidy. The airplane was pushed hard by the Washington congressional delegation, Boeing, and the aerospace unions. Yet the technological wonder of the SST could not overcome the times. Environmentalists who feared energy waste and air and noise pollution, and taxpayers who wished to limit deficits raised a formidable opposition. Congress voted on the SST twice, in the fall of 1970 and the spring of 1971, and defeated it on both occasions.

This heavy blow, coupled with a relative decline in demand for passenger airlines, ushered in the Boeing recession of 1970–1971. The government also abandoned temporarily the B-1 bomber in 1971 for which Boeing was a subcontractor. As in the postwar recession of 1945–1946, many people wrote off the company, but, after the doldrums of the 1970s, Boeing projects a recovery in the 1980s based upon its new, small, and fuel-efficient jets, the 737-300, the 757, and the 767. In the military realm it undertook production of Advanced Warning Aircraft Control Systems and Air Force Air Launched Cruise Missiles. Boeing also produced many space craft including the Lunar Rover Vehicle. The company in 1984 was the largest industrial corporation in the Pacific

Northwest (and the twenty-ninth largest in the nation), the largest commercial jet aircraft manufacturer in the world, and one of the top five military contractors in the United States.

ALUMINUM

The aluminum industry has undergone a changing course since the Second World War. Cheap electric power brought it to the region in 1938; indeed it was cajoled by politicians, businessmen, and newspapers to come to the Pacific Northwest to justify the construction of the Bonneville and Grand Coulee projects. The industry became indispensable for aircraft production in the Second World War. The aluminum companies signed long-term contracts for interruptible power from the Bonneville Power Administration. The last of these, signed in 1963, was for twenty years. The industry became a major employer. By 1975 the Pacific Northwest produced more aluminum than any country in the world, and 30 percent of that in the United States. By this date it had taken 30 percent of the power produced by BPA and employed about 12,000 workers.

Soon thereafter a combination of circumstances placed the industry in a precarious position. BPA determined to raise power costs for customers taking interruptible power. This charge would take effect for aluminum in 1983. The higher costs revealed another problem. The industry had done little to modernize its operations. Cheap power had made it possible to avoid modernization and still remain competitive. By the 1980s this neglect was no longer possible, and competition from other regions of the United States and from Australia made the industry's future uncertain.

FOREIGN TRADE

By the 1980s the Pacific Northwest was coming closer to realizing the old dreams of "limitless foreign markets," especially those of Asia. Oregon alone exported one billion dollars of wheat annually. Tektronix made 41 percent of its sales outside the United States. In the 1880s 90 percent of Oregon's food production was consumed in Oregon; in 1979, only 15 percent was.

Export markets, especially in Asia, have arisen because of a worldwide desire, made possible by growing income, for regional products. This desire can be gratified because northwestern ports are a day closer to Asia than those of California. Especially gratifying to northwesterners was the reopening of diplomatic relations between the United States and China in 1977. Regardless of distance, both Seattle and Portland handle their cargoes through modern port authorities that furnish exporters and importers with subsidized warehouses and extensive container handling capacity. All of this had resulted by 1983 in the Northwest leading the nation in share of employment derived from foreign trade. It is also the only region in the United States than ran a trade surplus with Japan. Trade rose spectacularly in the decade, 1970 to 1980. Exports from the Oregon Customs District (which also includes the ports of Camas, Longview, and Vancouver, Washington) rose from $786,000,000 in 1970 to $3,763,000,000 in 1980; imports increased from $382,000,000 to $2,658,000,000 in the same period. Comparable figures for the Seattle district (which includes the rest of Washington) are, for exports, $1,904,000,000 to $12,006,000,000 and for imports, $1,269,000,000 to $9,177,000,000.

RECREATION AND TOURISM

The recreation enterprise has expanded. After the war the Pacific Northwest, for the first time, drew large numbers of people from around the nation. This increase in visitors led to the construction or reconstruction of private resorts (such as the addition to Timberline Lodge in 1981), the creation of a new national park, North Cascades in Washington in 1968, and the formation of new state parks. Cities and states poured money into tourist promotion and local governments raised money from hotel and motel room taxes.

Tourism more and more was directed at a different target. Although nature continued to appeal, tourists also came to urban areas. Seattle and Tacoma built domed stadia and convention centers. They and other urban areas constructed new convention hotels. Cultural inducements were revealed to prospective visitors, such as the Seattle (1962) and Spokane (1974) world fairs. In fact the urban dimension of tourism can perhaps be dated to the Seattle fair which was credited with an increase in out-of-state visitor spending of 40 percent in the year of the fair from the previous year. The growth of cultural institutions in Seattle and Portland also was attractive.

The visitors provided revenue, but placed minimal demands upon the environment. But some Oregonians saw a danger in the visitor—he might become a resident. Especially when the visitors arrived with favorable predispositions to the region, an attitude fostered by outside assessments in the 1970s. For example, in 1975, the Environmental Protection Agency rated Portland as the metropolitan area (of more than 500,000 population) with the highest quality of life in the country; Eugene scored the highest in the 200,000 to 500,000 population category. Governor McCall became famous for his shocking invitation to conventioneers first delivered in 1971: "Come again and again. But, for Heaven's sake, don't move here to live."³ But most citizens assented to the demand of the recreation industry that government promote the region as a tourist's paradise.

THE HIGH-TECHNOLOGY INDUSTRY

The greatest change in the economy of the Pacific Northwest was the coming or development of the footloose industries. These enterprises, especially high technology (electrical machinery, computers, and measuring and controlling instruments), are not dependent on natural resources or local markets. They require a hardworking, trainable labor force, with a substantial number of educated workers and administrators. Where the product of footloose industries is manufactured is not important. They are not, in other words, the traditional natural resource based economic business of the region.

The first major high-technology industry in the Northwest was Tektronix. It was the product of a scientist, Howard Vollum, and a businessman, Jack Murdock. Vollum, born and raised in Portland, was a graduate of Reed College where he studied physics. At Reed he displayed an interest in oscilloscopes, devices for measuring electrical impulses and displaying them on a cathode ray tube. During the war Vollum served in the Signal Corps, concentrating on the relationship of radar to oscilloscopes. After the war he renewed an acquaintance with Murdock, and the two men became the principal partners in incorporating Tektronix in 1946 in southeast Portland. In 1951 the plant was moved to a suburban area west of Portland and has expanded enormously since that time. In 1984, Tektronix became the 252d largest corporation in America, with plants in Oregon, Washington, California, the Channel Islands, the Netherlands, England, and Japan. The company expanded from its oscilloscope base to the manufacture of several test and measurement and information display products that are used in the electronics, computer, medical, and communication businesses.

In Washington, as early as the 1940s, the state's electrical assembly firms began to serve the prime military contractors like Boeing. In 1958 Tektronix and Hewlett-Packard opened plants in Vancouver. High technology spread to the Puget Sound area throughout the 1960s and 1970s, with a particular concentration in the Bellevue, Kirkland, and Redmond areas on the east side of Lake Washington. Bellevue has become a major center of software production. There were several major reasons for this development: military contracts, research facilities (especially those of the University of Washington and the Battelle Institute), the social and environmental amenities of the region, an advanced work force, and a

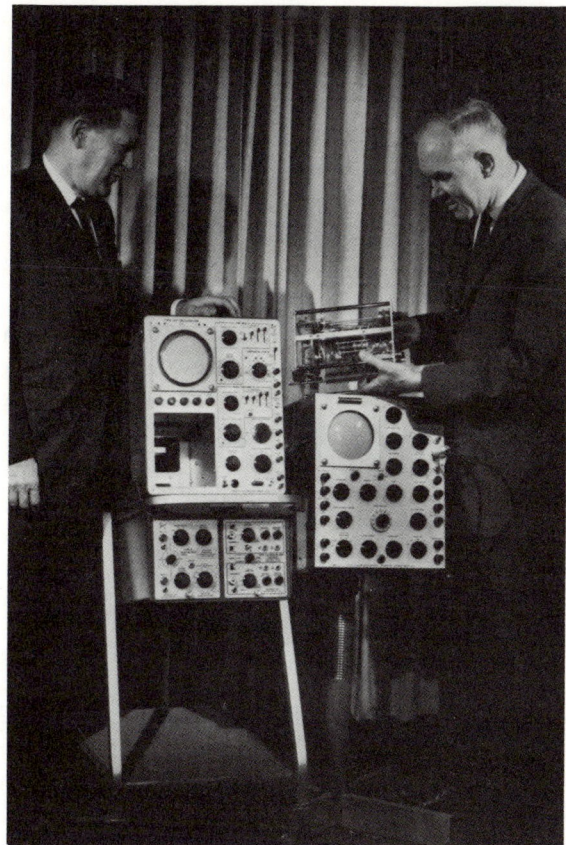

Jack Murdock (left), Howard Vollum (right), co-founders of Tektronix with original oscilloscope. Tektronix, Inc.

competitive tax and energy structure compared to other parts of the nation.

ENERGY

Since the building of the New Deal dams at Bonneville and Grand Coulee, the Pacific Northwest had been blessed with abundant supplies of cheap hydroelectric energy. It seemed destined to remain abundant forever. But in the late 1950s and early 1960s population growth and economic development threatened to require new sources of power. Cheap energy thereafter remained a central public issue, the most controversial of all these years. It was an issue involving federal, local, and private utilities.

The United States government placed in service more multipurpose dams on the Columbia in Oregon and Washington: McNary (1953), Chief Joseph (1955), The Dalles (1957), and John Day (1968) and some on the Willamette and its tributaries. It made a treaty with Canada in 1964 that authorized four new dams in Montana and British Columbia and it authorized a power intertie with California. The purpose of these complex arrangements was to sell surplus Pacific Northwest power in California at a price it was uneconomical for the Northwest to pay and to market Columbia River power made available under favorable water conditions.

Many in the Northwest became convinced in these expansive years that there would not be sufficient hydroelectric power to meet its needs. For some of them nuclear power was the answer. In 1966, the nation's largest nuclear power plant was placed in operation at Hanford, Washington. At Rainier, in Oregon, Portland General Electric placed a nuclear plant in commercial operation in 1976, a plant owned by it, Pacific Power and Light, and the Eugene Water and Electric Board. Although frequently attacked as overheating the water of the Columbia River, as polluting the atmosphere, and as threatening dangerous radioactivity, the plant has survived.

In Washington nuclear power produced high drama and terrible fiasco. Its history resulted—in part—from the old progressive dream of combining material progress, engineering efficiency, and public control of natural resources. Several publicly owned utility districts in Washington had banded together to form the Washington Public Power Supply System (nicknamed "Whoops") in 1957. The nineteen public utility districts and four municipal utilities that composed the System undertook an ambitious program in the early 1970s to finance and manage the construction of five nuclear power plants. At that time electricity demand was projected to rise 7 percent a year indefinitely. The Bonneville Power Administration stated that the Pacific Northwest would need 10 nuclear plants by the year 2000. Urged on by BPA and banks within and without the region, the System borrowed $8 billion to construct the plants, making it the largest single issuer of tax-exempt bonds in the United States. Three plants were backed by revenue from the Bonneville Power Administration, while the remaining two were backed by eighty-eight private and public utilities and electric cooperatives.

By July 1983, WPPSS had become the greatest engineering and financial failure in regional history and the largest municipal default in the history of the United States. The miscalculations of its promoters were myriad. The Pacific Northwest joined the nation in recession. Electricity consumption figures were revised to a 2 percent growth figure annually. Construction estimates ballooned horrendously from $4.1 billion to $23 billion. Management practices were questionable. The public turned against nuclear power on grounds of safety. In 1980, for example, Oregon rejected any new nuclear plants pending acceptable methods to dispose of nuclear waste. By mid-summer, 1983, two WPPSS plants had been canceled; construction had been halted on two others; only one (the Hanford plant) was on the verge of completion. After the default, attempts to escape their obligations by the utilities who had lent to WPPSS were widespread and assiduous. In desperation they challenged their obligations in court. After default, the utilities had little to show for their foolish participation except the grim alternative of slipping credit or raising their customers' rates to pay their obligations.

Federal energy participation in the Pacific Northwest took another form. As power shortages were projected in the 1970s, BPA told private utilities they would no longer have excess power (that beyond the needs of the preferred public utility and cooperative customers) after 1973. In 1976 the direct service customers (mainly aluminum companies) were told their contracts for excess power would not be renewed in 1983. After years of wrangling among BPA's customers over who would get firm commitments, Congress passed the Pacific Northwest Power Planning and Conservation Act in 1980. The statute guaranteed power to private utilities and called for conservation efforts. If conservation is inadequate to meet regional electricity needs, the BPA is for the first time given the responsibility to acquire additional power from various sources. Congress earlier had authorized additional generating capacity at Grand Coulee (completed in 1980) and Bonneville (completed in 1983).

TWO CONSTANTS: DEPENDENCE AND NATURE

In spite of the increased diversification of the regional economy, it remained in at least two ways similar to that of the days of Cook and Gray and Hezeta and the other white discoverers and explorers. The nature of dependence changed, but it remained. Wall Street, California, in recent years Canada, are all major sources of private investment. The federal government remains an enduring source of capital. It provided in 1983 about 5 percent of the region's wages and salaries (about one-fourth larger than the country as a whole) for workers on federal dams, forests, public lands, and the BPA and for those working in the numerous federal installations. There were air bases near Tacoma and Spokane and substantial naval activity at the Puget Sound Naval Shipyard and at the Bangor submarine base. The United States in 1980 possessed 54 percent of the land area of Oregon, 29 percent of Washington. The government provided the great multipurpose projects, contracts with Boeing for aerospace projects, labor and civil rights laws, and timber from the national forests.

The federal government also provided a great variety of aid to the states, most coming since the close of the Second World War. It gave grants-in-aid for highways and public assistance. Since 1972, the federal government has had a revenue sharing plan for general purposes for state and local governments. It also provided block grants, monies for broad program or policy uses. It also gave localities part of revenue payments for federal operations such as national forests. It furnished loans, for example, for urban renewal plans. The national government sent money to state and local governments where they act as agents of federal government, for example, unemployment compensation for federal employees. It was the source of research and training grants to private and public agencies from the National Science Foundation to the Atomic Energy Commission. Uncle Sam disposed of his surplus federal property at cost to state and local governments. But the government can also take as well as give. It canceled the SST and, for a time, the B-1 bomber. Its fiscal and budgetary policies are life and death for the housing industry. Protectionist tariffs could stifle trade. BPA's energy policies can thwart as well as advance industries and the economy. The Jones Act, which closes the coastal trade to foreign vessels, helps American shipping, but reduces the coastal trade.

State government also plays a role undreamed of by the pioneers. It attempts to foster economic development. Its fiscal policies are bones of contention. In 1970, Washington established a Governor's Economic Advisory Committee to prepare economic reports and give the governor advice on drawing industry to the state. Oregon has an Economic Development Department (1973) designed to aid business, local governments, and the general public with economic development services. Its purpose is to advertise the state's potential for economic growth; its success has been limited.

The region, in spite of the new footloose industries, remains close to nature, the second great economic constant. The sea, the soil, and the forest are principal means of livelihood. So too is tourism, still largely dependent upon nature's beauty. The great waterways remain an indispensable ingredient to economic success, although the tug and barge have replaced the *voyageurs'* canoe, and hydroelectric power rather than Indian commerce is their chief economic return. But if outside capital can control as well as contribute, so can Nature destroy as well as create. Never was this paradox more evident in modern times than on May 18, 1980 when Washington's Mount St. Helens volcano exploded. The top 1,313 feet of the mountain was torn off. Smoke and ash spread over vast areas. Huge mudslides caused appalling destruction. Thirty-six people were killed; twenty-one remain missing; many more lost homes and possessions. The property damage and restoration costs were calculated at over $2 billion. Yet within a few weeks the first plant life appeared on the mountainsides; a proof of the resilience of nature, a symbol of renewal for mankind.

NOTES

1. Tom McCall, *Tom McCall: Maverick* (1977), p. 200.
2. *Congressional Record*, September 23, 1965, p. 24902.
3. McCall, *Tom McCall: Maverick*, p. 190.

SUGGESTIONS FOR READING

Recent political life is most thoroughly covered in the metropolitan press. The *Western Political Quarterly* has articles on the biennial elections, 1948–1970. The Council of State Governments, *The Book of the States* (1935–1985), is a mine of information. Journalistic accounts are Neil R. Pierce and Jerry Hagstrom, *The Book of America: Inside 50 States Today* (1983) and John Gunther, *Inside USA* (1947). Scholarly works are Eleanore Bushnell, ed., *Impact of Reapportionment on the Thirteen Western States* (1970); Frank H. Jonas, ed., *Politics in the American West* (1969); Robert E. Burton, *Democrats of Oregon: The Pattern of Minority Politics, 1900–1956* (1970); W. Frank Mullen, et al., *The Government and Politics of Washington State* (1978); and Hugh A. Bone, et al., *Public Policymaking, Washington Style* (1980). A useful biography is A. Robert Smith, *The Tiger in the Senate: A Biography of Wayne Morse* (1962). *The Oregon Blue Book* (1911–1985) contains much detail on politics and economics. Federal resource policy is the subject of Elmo Richardson, *Dams, Parks, and Politics: Resource Development and Preservation in the Truman-Eisenhower Era* (1973). For right-wing radicalism see William L. Dwyer, *The Goldmark Case: An American Libel Trial* (1985) and Jane Sanders, *Cold War on the Campus: Academic Freedom and the University of Washington, 1946–1964* (1979).

Economic sources are more fugitive. The general and business press are helpful. So too are the annual reports of industrial corporations and of banks. The publications of the U.S. Bureau of the Census and of state agencies are mines of information. The *Oregon Blue Book* (1911–1985) contains basic data. There are two good corporate histories, Ralph W. Hidy, Frank E. Hill, and Allan Nevins, *Timber and Men: The Weyerhaeuser Story* (1963) and Edwin T. Coman and Helen M. Gibbs, *Time, Tide, and Timber: A Century of Pope and Talbot* (1949). Hydroelectric energy is the concern of U.S. Bonneville Power Administration, *Columbia River Power for the People: A History of the Policies of the Bonneville Power Administration* (1981). See also G. Thomas Edwards and Carlos A. Schwantes, eds., *Experiences in a Promised Land* (1986).

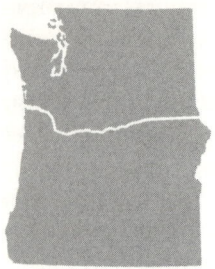

Epilogue

Over the years, it has been easy to be an Oregonian or a Washingtonian, especially if one were a Caucasian. Nature has been generous economically and aesthetically. Job opportunities have been plentiful. Few residents have ever had to meet the challenge of living with people of different color, creed, or ethnicity. There has been room enough for almost all the white men or white women who have migrated here.

The ease of making a life in the Pacific Northwest—the absence of severe class or cultural or economic or environmental conflict—has made for a pleasant, undemanding life for most residents. It has made possible a civilized, independent political life within the confines of colonialism. It has created an adequate cultural life. It has permitted a reasonable degree of careful civic and economic experimentation. Ease has meant, with but few exceptions, decent conservatism. Northwesterners have been able to indulge themselves in a world with few tensions, a world that has satisfied most of them. Northwesterners maintain that they have attained the golden mean. Outsiders, and many who have left the region, say what they have reached is contented mediocrity.

The price of this easeful condition is two-fold. One is that the region has continued, as have all American frontiers, to attract people like those who are already residents. Quiet, competence, moderation have perpetuated themselves generation after generation. The old residents change little; the migrants resemble them in fear of both change and distinction. The second price is that a life of ease may be no longer adequate. As population grows, as pressure on the environment and on social services increases, as the world economy diversifies, as the region is pressured by homogenizing national cultural, economic, and political forces, Oregonians and Washingtonians will have to become more imaginative, to bear greater public burdens, and to be less self-indulgent than in the past.

There has not been much tragedy for white people in the history of the Pacific Northwest. It has been a place where people could start over by escaping from their constraints to carry on the old ways better in a new environment. It is perhaps most typically American in this characteristic of providing a chance to start over. One of the region's best writers said of his native state (and he could have said it of Washington too): "It was Oregon all right: the place where stories begin that end somewhere else. It has no history of its own, only endings of histories from other places; it has no complete lives, only beginnings. There are worse things."[1]

Yet the tragedy of this lack of tragedy is that the lives of Pacific Northwesterners have historically been too successful. They have mastered their few difficulties with relative ease. Yet their undemanding past may have left them unprepared for the adversities that lie ahead. Indeed, if they do foresee difficulties, their history may lead them to overemphasize their abilities to solve them. There are better things.

NOTES

1. H. L. Davis, *Kettle of Fire* (1959), p. 48.

Index

Gordon B. Dodds is professor of history at Portland State University, where he has taught since 1966. He is the author of *Oregon: A Bicentennial History; The Salmon King of Oregon; Hiram Martin Chittenden: His Public Career;* and editor of *Autobiography of a Pygmy Monopolist.* In addition, he is the author of numerous articles on the fur trade for journals and collected works.

The American Northwest: A History of Oregon and Washington was copyedited by Joyce Goldenstern. Production editing was carried out by B. W. Barrett; cover design was rendered by Roger Eggers. Elizabeth Rubenstein and Carolee Lipsey proofread the text. Maps were drawn by James A. Bier. Text typesetting and page makeup were performed by Page Types; display type was set by J&L Graphics, Inc. The book was printed and bound by McNaughton & Gunn, Inc.